National Visual Arts Standards for Grades 5–8
Developed by the National Art Education Association

Content Standard	Achievement Standard	Chapters in This Text
1. Understanding and applying media, techniques, and processes	Students a) select media, techniques, and processes; analyze what makes them effective or not effective in communicating ideas; and reflect upon the effectiveness of their choices b) intentionally take advantage of the qualities and characteristics of art media, techniques, and processes to enhance communication of their experiences and ideas	Chs. 18–19, Chs. 23–32
2. Using knowledge of structures and functions	Students a) generalize about the effects of visual structures and functions and reflect upon these effects in their own work b) employ organizational structures and analyze what makes them effective or not effective in the communication of ideas c) select and use the qualities of structures and functions of art to improve communication of their ideas	Ch. 2, Chs. 18–19, Chs. 22–32
3. Choosing and evaluating a range of subject matter, symbols, and ideas	Students a) integrate visual, spatial, and temporal concepts with content to communicate intended meaning in their artworks b) use subjects, themes, and symbols that demonstrate knowledge of contexts, values, and aesthetics that communicate intended meaning in artworks	Ch. 2, Chs. 6–11, Ch. 14, Chs. 18–22
4. Understanding the visual arts in relation to history and cultures	Students a) know and compare the characteristics of artworks in various eras and cultures b) describe and place a variety of art objects in historical and cultural contexts c) analyze, describe, and demonstrate how factors of time and place (such as climate, resources, ideas, and technology) influence visual characteristics that give meaning and value to a work of art	Ch. 1, Ch. 9, Chs. 18–22, Inside back cover timeline
5. Reflecting upon and assessing the characteristics and merits of their work and the work of others	Students a) compare multiple purposes for creating works of art b) analyze contemporary and historic meanings in specific artworks through cultural and aesthetic inquiry c) describe and compare a variety of individual responses to their own artworks and to artworks from various eras and cultures	Chs. 12–13, Chs. 18–19, Chs. 20–22
6. Making connections between visual arts and other disciplines	Students a) compare the characteristics of works in two or more art forms that share similar subject matter, historical periods, or cultural context b) describe ways in which the principles and subject matter of other disciplines taught in the school are interrelated with the visual arts	Chs. 6–13, Chs. 18–19

Emphasis Art

Emphasis Art

A Qualitative Art Program for Elementary and Middle Schools

EIGHTH EDITION

Frank Wachowiak
Late of University of Georgia

Robert D. Clements
University of Georgia

Boston   New York   San Francisco   Mexico City
Montreal   Toronto   London   Madrid   Munich   Paris
Hong Kong   Singapore   Tokyo   Cape Town   Sydney

Series Editor: Traci Mueller
Senior Development Editor: Virginia L. Blanford
Series Editorial Assistant: Janice Hackenberg
Senior Editorial-Production Administrator: Beth Houston
Editorial-Production Service, Text Design, and Electronic Composition:
    Elm Street Publishing Services, Inc.
Senior Marketing Manager: Krista Groshong
Composition and Prepress Buyer: Linda Cox
Manufacturing Buyer: Andrew Turso
Cover Administrator: Linda Knowles

Between the time Website information is gathered and then published, it is
not unusual for some sites to have closed. Also, the transcription of URLs
can result in typographical errors. The publisher would appreciate
notification where these errors occur so that they may be corrected in
subsequent editions.

Library of Congress Cataloging-in-Publication Data
Wachowiak, Frank.
    Emphasis Art : a qualitative art program for elementary and middle
schools / Frank Wachowiak, Robert D. Clements.—8th ed.
        p. cm.
    Includes bibliographical references and index.
    ISBN 0-205-43962-4 (alk. paper)
        1. Art—Study and teaching (Elementary) 2. Art—Study and
teaching (Middle school) I. Clements, Robert D. II. Title.

N350.W26 2006
372.5'044—dc22   2004061958

Printed in the United States of America
10 9 8 7 6 5 4 3 2   09 08 07 06

Brief Contents

Detailed Contents

Part 2

Teachers and Teaching   21

Chapter 3

The Teacher's Role: Strategies and Management   23

Chapter 4

Motivating Learning   34

Chapter 5

Creating Objectives and Evaluation Criteria   43

Chapter 22

Teaching Art Criticism and Aesthetics   234

Part 6

Teaching Art Production   247

Chapter 23

Drawing   249

Chapter 24

Crayon and Oil Pastels   271

Preface

The Eighth Edition of *Emphasis Art* has its origin in the approach to teaching art to children developed by Frank Wachowiak (1913–1998). For fifty years, he taught and studied children's art all over the world, especially at the University of Iowa Lab School and the University of Georgia Children's Art Classes. His inspiring words, the beautiful examples of children's art, and his clear technical directions continue in this new edition. As in the last three editions, on all of which I have worked, Frank Wachowiak's belief in the intrinsic worth of the art-studio experience remains central. I have added considerably more material on current approaches to art education, but the emphasis remains on art—art as an adventure, a flowering, a celebration, and a discipline with its own singular demands, unique core of learning, and incomparable rewards. One hundred and fifty new child artworks have been added to this edition, and the book now contains over 900 illustrations. Readers familiar with the Seventh Edition of the book will note the following changes in this Eighth Edition.

1. **A focus on integrated curriculum.** *Emphasis Art* has always included information on integrating art with other subject areas. But this kind of integration has become more important in recent years, and this edition of *Emphasis Art* expands its focus on integrating art in the general classroom. You will find a new, separate chapter on integrating art with mathematics, an expanded chapter on integrating art with language arts and reading, and revised chapters on integrating art with science, social studies, and the performing arts. General classroom teachers will find strategies for each of the major content areas. In addition, this entire section on curricular integration has been moved forward in the book.

2. **In the Classroom and In the Community features.** Although *Emphasis Art* has always included a multitude of activities—in fact, to

try to identify activities as such would mean labeling virtually every paragraph in the book!—we have in this edition highlighted certain activities that are particularly useful for general classroom teachers. These activities also underline the usefulness of art in teaching other content areas.

3. **Expanded emphasis on social and cultural issues.** In previous decades, art and art education centered on *art* issues, such as abstraction, modernism, and formalism. In recent years, both art and art education have turned increasingly to an examination of social, cultural, historical, and political issues. While this direction appears throughout the book, it is mainly discussed in Chapter 9, Art and Social Studies, and in Part 5, Appreciating Art: Art History, Criticism, and Aesthetics. Of course, in truth, these two approaches—art as art and art in context—really do interconnect. One cannot stand without the other.

4. **Technology.** Chapter 28 on Visual Technology has been substantially revised and updated to include more material on digital photography, as well as enhanced coverage of the melding together of various technologies including computer art and publishing, video and film, and photography.

5. **Websites and additional readings.** Material that once appeared at the back of the book is now placed at the end of chapters, to make it more accessible. The Website references for each chapter have been expanded.

6. **The National Visual Arts Standards for Grades K–8** are included on the inside front cover pages, along with chapter references indicating where related material is covered in this book. This quick guide to standards of art learning will help prospective teachers understand what is expected from students at all levels.

7. **A timeline of artists, art movements, and world events** is printed on the inside back cover. This timeline is intended to provide a quick, general snapshot of artists and the world around them; it is by no means a comprehensive historical document. Web searches on any of the names or terms in the timeline will offer a wealth of information.

Over the years, the response of educators at all levels to *Emphasis Art* has been gratifyingly positive. The book's clarity, structure, and wealth of colorful illustrations have found enthusiastic endorsement. The art teaching strategies, motivations, techniques, and evaluative procedures described in the text are based on actual experiences and observations of outstanding elementary- and middle-school art practices both in this country and abroad. This new edition again concerns itself with the adventures, joys, responsibilities, problems, and rewards of teaching art to children; with the strategic, guiding role of the teacher; and with the ongoing evaluation of lesson objectives in design and composition, art history, art criticism, and aesthetics.

Emphasis Art is designed first and foremost for elementary- and middle-school teachers of art who want to augment and enrich their art programs, but this edition makes it even more useful for prospective and practicing classroom teachers in search of high-quality elementary- and middle-school art practices. It offers a lucid description of a proven, dynamic program for those teachers who seek continuing challenges, new techniques, and art projects for their instructional repertoire.

ACKNOWLEDGMENTS

The following teachers have helped in this Eighth Edition. Continuing contributors Barbara Thomas, Toccoa, GA, and Mary Lazzari and Beverly Mallon of the Clarke County Schools, Athens, GA, have contributed new works for this edition. New contributor Pat Kerner, Trinity School, Atlanta, GA; Brian Baugh, Leonard Piha, and Reuben Williams, Athens, GA; and continuing contributors Joyce Vroon, Trinity School, Atlanta, GA, and Baiba Kuntz, Glencoe, IL, have been very helpful.

I wish to acknowledge the contributions of two professors who co-authored earlier editions. Without the shared efforts of these authors and Frank Wachowiak, the earlier book(s) would not have come into being. David W. Hodge, Emeritus Professor of Art, University of Wisconsin, Oshkosh, who was coauthor of *Art in Depth,* has contributed 46 new artworks for this Eighth Edition. Thanks also to Theodore K. Ramsay, Professor of Art, University of Michigan, Ann Arbor, coauthor of the first and second editions of *Emphasis Art.* For assistance with 21 child art pictures, thanks to Dr. Barry Moore, Curator of the International Collection of Child Art, Milner Library, and Professor of Art Emeritus, at Illinois State University in Normal, Illinois. These slides are credited to ICCA in the credits.

For editing chapter drafts, thanks to Dr. Richard Siegesmund (Chapter 5) and Dr. Carol Fisher (Chapter 7), both of the University of Georgia, and to Steve Kassay (Chapter 8) of Athens, Georgia.

For continuing permission to use illustrations, I am grateful to Jenni Horne, Flat Rock Middle School, Tyrone, GA; Katrina Bonds, Austell, GA; and LaVonne McPherson, Gwenda Malnati, and Eric Hamilton of the Athens Montessori School. Many thanks go to Dr. Melody Milbrandt, West Georgia State University, Carrollton, GA; Jackie Ellett, Rockbridge Elementary School, Gwinnett County Schools, GA; Debby Lackey, Fulton County Schools, Atlanta, GA; Donna Cummins, Rockview Elementary School, Atlanta, GA; Carol Case, Cobb County Schools, GA; Alisa Hyde, Savannah, GA; Julie Phlegar, East St. Tammany Parish School District, Slidell, LA; and Sharon Burns-Knutson, Iowa City Schools, IA. Thanks to ongoing contributions from Fay Brassie, Nancy Elliott, David Harvell—all from the Athens, GA, schools. Also, my appreciation goes to the Crayola® Dream-Makers® program. Thanks to those who taught with Frank Wachowiak in his University of Georgia children's art classes and who have continued to give permission to use artworks: Dr. Mary Hammond, Athens, GA; and Dr. Patrick Taylor, Kennesaw, GA. Other teachers throughout the nation have works reproduced: Shirley Lucas, Oshkosh, WI; Alice Ballard Munn, Anchorage, AK; Ted Oliver, Marietta, GA; Carolyn Shapiro, Brookline, MA; Mary E. Swanson, Nashua, NH; and Dr. Lawrence Stueck, Watkinsville, GA. The USSEA Art Collection of Dr. Anne Gregory, Los Angeles Public Schools, is represented by works of students of Barbara Bluhm, Maine, and Susan Whipple, Oregon Christian School. My colleagues at the University of Georgia who are involved in art education also have helped: Dr. Richard Siegesmund, Dr. W. Robert Nix, Dr. Carole Henry, and Dr. Diane Rives. My wife, Dr. Claire Clements, has contributed student artworks, as well as constant encouragement.

The beauty of this book has also been made possible through the contributions of art teachers from around the world: Chen Huei-Tung, Tainan, Taiwan; Jean Grant, coordinator, arts and humanities, Department of Defense Dependents' Schools (DODDS), Atlantic Region; Eric Ma Presado, Manila, Philippines; James McGrath, coordinator, arts and humanities, DODDS, Pacific Region; George Mitchell, Atlanta, GA; Federico Moroni, Santarcangelo, Italy; Michihisa Kosugi, Saga, Japan; Norihisa Nakase, art education liaison, Tokyo, Japan; Michael F. O'Brien, American High School, Seoul, Korea; and Linda Riddle, Heidelberg, Germany. For permission to use published material, thanks to Masachi Shimono, editor, Nihon Bunkyo Suppan, Osaka, Japan; and Professor Osamu Muro, Executive Director, *Art Education Magazine,* Tokyo, Japan. Nostell Priory, Yorkshire, England; the Boston Museum of Fine Art; the Norman Rockwell Museum at Stockbridge, MA; the National Gallery of Art and the Hirshhorn Museum in Washington DC; Yad Vashem Holocaust Museum, Jerusalem, Israel, among others, have given permission to reproduce artworks in their collections.

For the cover, Allyn & Bacon has selected the lion's head collage drawing by Joseph Meuller, Grade 2, of Littleton, Colorado.

I would also like to thank the following reviewers for their comments and suggestions during the revision process: Victoria Fergus, West Virginia University; Lon Nuell, Middle Tennessee State; Barbara Rhoades, Elon University/University North Carolina; and Linda Ross, Penn State University, Harrisburg. To the members of the editorial and production staffs at Allyn & Bacon and Elm Street Publishing Services, my grateful acknowledgment for their contributions—especially those of Acquisitions Editor Traci Mueller and her tireless assistant, Janice Hackenberg; Developmental Editor Ginny Blanford; Production Editor Beth Houston; and Project Editor Eric Arima.

Robert D. Clements
Rclements1@charter.net

Part 1

Introduction to Art

*B*oth art and schools mirror society—including society's conflicts. Norman Rockwell depicted the school integration conflict in this painting for a magazine cover in fall, 1960, following the Supreme Court's Brown v. Board of Education decision. Here Rockwell shows us first-grader Ruby Bridges entering William Francz Elementary School in New Orleans under the protection of Federal marshals.

Norman Rockwell, "The Problem We All Live With." Collection of the Norman Rockwell Museum at Stockbridge, Massachusetts. Reproduced by permission of the Norman Rockwell Family Agency, Inc.

*W*hy should children study art? How can anyone go about making art that is pleasing or beautiful or good? The first two chapters of this book about teaching art to children explore these important questions.

Children might say they should study art just because it is fun: fun to make things, fun to draw things, fun to use art materials, fun to talk about pictures—a welcome relief from other subjects. But there is more than that. In Chapter One, we will explore the value of art in education and for society.

In Chapter Two, we will think about what makes a picture beautiful—or what makes art, art. We probably agree on some answers: care, thoughtfulness, attention to detail, practice, assuredness. But here we will learn a new vocabulary, the language of art, its formal elements and principles, and also introduce the idea of contextualism—that is, what art is about.

Chapter 1

Art in Society and the Schools

Why is art education important? Now more than ever? As we move into the twenty-first century, art education is struggling for its life in the public schools. Budget cuts and a curricular emphasis on "back to basics" have hurt or even eliminated art programs in many schools. Yet learning about—and producing—art is a critical part of what our children need to be doing as they develop their awareness of the world around them and their own abilities to function effectively in that world. Indeed, understanding visual symbols, cultural differences, and individual expression may be more important now than ever before.

Here are some reasons—there are many more.

- **Cultural understanding.** Art is an international language, universally accessible even to those who know little about how art was used in a culture. It communicates meaning without words—but because it does come from a specific culture, art is relative to the time, place, and circumstances of its creation. For the members of a cultural group, art provides a mirror, reflecting the group's unique sense of cultural identity. Indeed, art is one way in which cultural identity is transmitted, maintained, and analyzed.

  Culture is more than a simple heritage of creations and behaviors. It is the shared values, attitudes, belief systems, and cognitive styles; culture gives meaning to life. Art is both intentionally and unintentionally a carrier of cultural value and meaning, encoded in a sensuous medium.

Although art communicates some of its meaning across eras and cultures, its creation is relative to its culture. It helps to create a sense of cultural community and identity. ***Top:*** Dropped Bowl with Scattered Slices and Peels, 1989, Claes Oldenburg and Coosje van Bruggen, Art in Public Places Program, Miami, FL. ***Middle:*** Native-American kachina. ***Bottom:*** Mola (reverse appliqué) by San Blas Native Peoples.

3

Courtesy of Alice Ballard Munn and Diane Rives.

Second-graders acquire an appreciation of Native-American culture by studying the myths and art of the northwest and southwest Native-American cultures. Each second-grade class selected its own power animal. ***Top left:*** Wolf kachina with exciting patterns. ***Bottom left:*** Blue bird kachina based on southwest Native-American stories. ***Top middle:*** Boy with symbolic collar and headpiece. ***Top right:*** Black-and-white-striped doll based on Hopi clown kachina. ***Bottom right:*** A girl in white costume enacts the northwest Native-American myth of how the loon lost her voice.

Art education helps students understand the connection between what is depicted in art and how it is depicted, and the culture and time in which that connection of content and form was created. Art helps students see culture as an interpretive social schema that people project upon existence in order to create their own identity.

- **National needs.** Art education helps create the citizens this country needs—citizens who can think for themselves, communicate effectively, and appreciate our nation's diversity. As our culture becomes more and more visual, citizens capable of responding intelligently are increasingly important.

- **Celebrating ordinary experiences.** More Americans go to museums than to sporting events. Over one million Americans call themselves artists. Communities and cultures make art because art makes everything special. When art celebrates ordinary experiences, these experiences take on new significance. By making events and things stand out from the commonplace, art transforms and reorganizes our concept of the world.

- **Personal communication and expression.** At the heart of arts learning is the process of giving form to and making meaning from personal experience. The idea that a person can make an individual

Courtesy of Melody Milbrandt.

Pride is evident as third- and fourth-graders show off their class-painted mural about fun activities in their community: playing ball, jumping rope, flying kites, and skating together. Notice how the space was suggested by overlapping and diminishing sizes of figures and objects in the foreground, middle ground, and background.

Courtesy of David W. Hodge.

A personal expression of family togetherness.

Left: *Courtesy of Beverly Barksdale Mallon.* Right: *Courtesy of Joyce Vroon.*

Left: An integration of art, ecological awareness, writing, lettering, and advertising occurred when this fifth-grader won first place in the state of Georgia for her conservation poster. The art teacher emphasized the design principle KISS ("keep it simple, silly"). Students role-played that they were graphic designers at an advertising agency charged with creating an ad for an ecological cause. **Right:** Sports advertising is one of our nation's largest businesses and fourth-grader Ross Baird's memory drawing testifies to its power.

statement through art—one that brings meaning and pleasure to self and others—is powerful. This rationale is all the more poignant in a technologically advanced society where so much of what we use is made by unseen others in remote parts of the world.

- **Creativity.** Art education promotes higher thought processes, such as a willingness to imagine possibilities, a desire to explore ambiguity, and an ability to recognize multiple perspectives.

- **Vocations.** Art in schools can breed interest in many careers involving visual creativity, from film-making and photography to architecture and landscape design, from computer graphics to fashion.
- **Aesthetic awareness.** Art education heightens our awareness of nature, art, and life. Spider webs, cloud formations, Van Gogh's sunflowers, and beautiful moments in daily life are experienced more vividly if we have been sensitized to them in art classes.
- **Visual literacy and integrated learning.** Education should develop a young child's literacy in all symbol systems, all modes of thought, and all means of inquiry. This goal is especially applicable in early childhood, when perception more than logic governs views of reality. Children relate to the arts as media for expression and communication and develop an ability to interpret visual symbols that may later coalesce into sophisticated reasoning and problem solving.

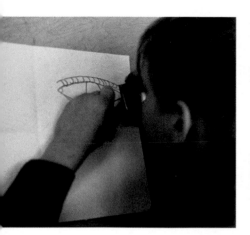

Courtesy of David W. Hodge.

Art is a welcome way of learning—here, using our eyes to think.

Second-grade children learned about poisonous and nonpoisonous snakes through creating this stitchery mural.

The arts are great partners in academic learning. Integrating art into other disciplines—social studies, math, science, reading, and so on—adds richness, meaning, and excitement. In a curriculum crowded with academic subjects, art is a welcome means of learning about self and word. The language of art uses a different symbol system—one that fuses into a single entity the cognitive, affective, and psychomotor aspects of learning. Art gives students a unique opportunity to communicate in a language that is neither verbal nor mathematical.

A QUALITATIVE APPROACH TO TEACHING ART

What some observers call *art* in a child's drawing very often is not art at all, but simply a visual report that relates to factual writing. Art is more akin to poetry, which, like all fine arts, distills the essence of an experience through highly expressive and discriminative choices. That is how the qualitative method of teaching art differs from other methods. As the quality of verse depends on choosing the expressive word and employing the tools of language exquisitely, so the most evocative children's art employs art principles to create unity and rich design very different from more ordinary work.

Frank Wachowiak, whose approach to teaching art is represented in this book, stressed that children learn to see more, sense more, and recall more—they become more aware of their changing and expanding environment, and they realize that art is not something special done by special

people—when they are enriched and stimulated in art classes by a teacher's varied and challenging motivations. Anyone can put an imprint on a piece of paper. What a child does may indeed be that child's visual statement, but it is not necessarily a quality work of art. Only children who express their ideas, responses, and reactions with honesty, sensitivity, and perceptiveness from within a framework of compositional principles and design actually create art.

Qualitative teaching requires teachers to move beyond initial stimulation and to invest more time and more thought into the teaching process. From preliminary drawing to finished product, the teacher must guide the process. This means encouraging students to evaluate their work in terms of the lesson's objectives, since without critical evaluation, we cannot assume that students will develop either aesthetic awareness or artistic potential. Without a teacher's help, the average art production by a child, often created in a limited time period, is apt to be cursory and sterile. With it, the kind of art that you see reproduced in this book can be standard.

How long does it take for a child to create a work of quality art? Longer, certainly, than a single session. Motivation and preliminary drawing alone often take one 45-minute art period, and a completed project may take three, four, or five such periods. The time needed can be reduced a little by strategies like using smaller paper (9 × 12 inches, rather than 12 × 18 inches, for example), but children need real, substantial time devoted to art every week. When art plays a subordinate role to every other subject, or is relegated to creating stereotypical holiday decorations, it cannot perform a vital role in children's creative growth.

Courtesy of Frank Wachowiak and Mary Sayer Hammond.

A qualitative artwork, such as this "pet in a garden" oil pastel, takes time to create. On 12- × 18-inch violet-colored construction paper, it took three 50-minute class periods. The preliminary drawing was made in school chalk, then gone over with a large-sized, black felt-nib pen. Color then was applied up to, but not covering, the black lines. Instructional objectives for color: to use color imaginatively and to repeat colors for unity. The pet was drawn first; the garden environment added afterward.

A print by a Japanese youngster. Observe the care with which the block is cut and the attractive background texture.

For Frank Wachowiak, helping children make beautiful art was almost a religious quest.

A child in Italy did this beautiful painting of a posed standing girl wearing a wonderful big fringed hat, holding a pitcher, and accompanied by spectacular roosters.

Art has unquestioned merit as a unique avenue to cognitive, social, and individual growth. Qualitative art instruction nurtures better citizens who are more culturally aware and understanding, as well as simply more joyful and confident individuals. Artistic creativity should be recognized and embraced, and every lesson should be designed to augment both basic

When art is taught both purposefully and qualitatively and the instructional objectives to be mastered are made clear, beautiful work results. A St. Petersburg, Russia, first-grader's scene of children skiing in the snow fills the page with many figures.

learning of the "language" of art—the body of skills and knowledge that it comprises—and every child's ability to perceive, read, analyze, and build a vocabulary in every aspect of education.

FOR FURTHER READING

Blandy, Doug, and Kristin Congdon. 1990. *Culture and Democracy.* New York: Teacher's College Press.

Chapman, Laura H. 1982. *Instant Art, Instant Culture: The Unspoken Policy for American Schools.* New York: Teacher's College Press.

Dissanayake, Ellen. 1988. *What Is Art For?* Seattle: University of Washington Press.

Feldman, Edmund. 1996. *Philosophy of Art Education.* Upper Saddle River, NJ: Prentice Hall.

Gagné, Robert. 1975. *Essentials of Learning.* New York: Dryden.

Gardner, Howard. 1973. *The Arts and Human Development.* New York: Wiley.

Goodlad, John. 1984. *A Place Called School: Promise for the Future.* New York: McGraw-Hill.

National Commission on Excellence in Education. 1983. *A Nation at Risk.* Washington, DC: GPO.

Perkins, David. 1994. *The Intelligent Eye: Learning to Think by Looking at Art.* Champaign: University of Illinois Press.

Read, Herbert. 1955. *Icon and Idea: The Function of Art in the Development of Human Consciousness.* Cambridge: Harvard University Press.

Read, Herbert. 1973. *Education Through Art,* 3d. ed. New York: Pantheon.

Smith, Ralph, and W. Levi. 1991. *Art Education: A Critical Necessity.* Urbana, IL: University of Illinois Press.

Wygant, Foster. 1993. *School Art in American Culture.* Cincinnati: Interwood Press.

Zimmerman, Enid. 1990. "Questions About My Culture and Art Education or 'I'll Never Forget the Day M'Blawi Stumbled on the Work of the Post-Impressionists.'" *Art Education* 43(6): 8–24.

WEB RESOURCES

For a fine overview of web art education:

http://www.getty.edu/artsednet/resources

http://www.getty.edu/artsednet/advocacy

http://www.princetonol.com/groups/iad/lessons/middle/arted.htm

http://artsedge.kennedy-center.org/teach/wlk.cfm

http://www.howard.k12.md.us/connections/arthome.html

For an overview of advocacy for all the arts:

http://aep-arts.org/tfadvocacy/tfadvocacy.html

For the official National Art Education website for teachers:

www.howard.k12.md.us/connections/arthome.html

Tip: If a web address will not work, try truncating the term back to just the first part (the first slash), and then look for a menu guiding you to the term you want. Websites change over time, so, if one does not work, try another.

Chapter 2

Art as Art:
The Design Fundamentals

$\mathcal{A}$rt is made for many reasons. Usually its creators want to express something. In children's art, for example, young artists may want to say something about their friends, or their pets, or something about their lives or the world around them. They may simply want to say something about decoration and design, or they may make art to meet some real, immediate need, as in creating a poster for a play. Their feelings come out as they make the art.

As they strive to express their feelings and ideas, however, children—like all artists—must either instinctively or consciously wrestle with the *elements* and *principles* of art: elements such as line, shape or form, value, color, space, and texture and pattern, and principles such as balance and symmetry, variety, emphasis, and domination-subordination.

We teach this language of art as if elements and principles have clear distinctions. Design elements and principles are not written in stone, however; rather, they merge and blend together. And, obviously, not every element and principle is applicable to every work. An Impressionistic painting may have little to do with line; a Navajo rug may have little to do with asymmetry.

ELEMENTS OF ART

Line *Line* in art is a human invention—a unique method of perceiving and documenting the visible world. Expressive, sensitively drawn lines vary in weight, width, and emphasis. They may be made delicately or boldly; they may be made with freedom and spontaneity or with deliberate action. In their manner, they may flow or jerk. In their direction, they may converge, radiate, run parallel, meander, twist, skip, and crisscross to create confusion, rhythm, order, or chaos.

In width, lines can be thin and light or thick and heavy. Their movement can be wavy, fish-scale, jagged, or zigzag. They may suggest a per-

Courtesy of Frank Wachowiak.

Lines depict a variety of types of fish. The seaweed lines create varied interlocking shapes that tie the design together.

sonality that is bold, careful, or tentative. Lines of differing weights and characteristics can create outlines, inner edges, paths of motion, and sheer decorative delight in patterns. While much Western art relies on outlines, this is not true of some other cultures. Teachers and students should turn to nature and select products of human activity for limitless sources of line variety: frost, roots, spider webs, water ripples, lightning, veins in leaves, feathers, seashells, grain in wood, insect wings, shopping carts, birdcages, wicker furniture, and tree bark and branches.

The curvilinear shapes of fish and crescents spiral and radiate in this upper-elementary-grade class mural.

The dark-and-light values contrast boldly in this scratchboard.

Shape Any study of pictorial design—of composition in painting, prints, and posters—eventually centers on the *shape* of things. The shapes created by lines merging, touching, and intersecting one another take many forms. They may be square, rectangular, round, elliptical, oval, triangular, or amorphous; they may emerge as nonobjective, figurative, or free-form. Often, shapes may be flat and two-dimensional, like squares, or they may suggest volume and three-dimensions, like rectangular solids, cubes, cones, and pyramids. Often teachers use the term *form* rather than *shape* in describing three-dimensional volumetric objects.

With shape as with line, nature is by far the richest source of our inspiration. Indeed, many artists turn to aging, dilapidated buildings, where nature has been at work, for their inspiration instead of the coldly geometric shapes of much contemporary architecture. Often, teachers rely too much on formulas and rules of perspective in teaching students to draw tabletops, doors, windows, fences, roofs, sidewalks, and other geometric shapes. Instead, encourage your students to give vitality to static imagery through meaningful distortion, omission, exaggeration, and free-form interpretation.

The shapes of objects or figures in a composition, such as trees, houses, people, animals, furniture, and vehicles, generally are called *positive shapes*. The empty area around them is referred to as *negative space,* even though this space may include ground, water, and sky. Many artists pay as much attention to the negative shapes as to the positive shapes in order to achieve a strong figure/ground relationship. When the positive shapes are varied in size and shape, the negative spaces or shapes often will consequently be just as varied and interesting.

Value Simply stated, *value* refers to a composition's light and dark elements. Every shade (dark value) and tint (light value) of every color or hue can be thought of as having a place on a value scale. An attractive disposition of values in a picture is even more important than color. When repeated throughout a painting or design, values create movement in the artwork, leading the viewer from one part of the composition to another. Value analyses of master paintings and prints can help students to understand and appreciate the principles employed in achieving successful light-and-dark orchestration. Compositions with sharply contrasting values generally are more dramatic and dynamic in their visual impact.

When American artist Georgia O'Keeffe was studying to be an art teacher, her professor at Teacher's College of Columbia University, Arthur Wesley Dow, stressed the importance of value. In both his lectures and his writing, he emphasized how interesting the pattern created by different

Courtesy of Fay Brassie.

To see an issue in black and white means to see its essential structure. Here, seventh-graders' display of celebrities.

values could be. Perhaps as a result of his teaching, value patterns are often acknowledged as one of the strongest features in O'Keeffe's paintings.

Color Can you imagine a world without color? How dull it would be. *Color* has three properties or components: *hue,* the name of the color; *value,* the lightness or darkness of the color; and *intensity* (saturation), the brightness or dullness of the color. Unfortunately, its most amazing property—its magic—often is ignored.

Limiting the color palette can help young artists master the orchestration of color. You may want your students to use only black, white, and

Courtesy of Baiba Kuntz.

Limiting colors to greys and tans gives a unifying sense of serenity to this fifth-grade student's collage of an imaginary house.

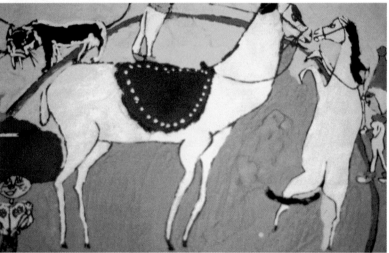

Courtesy of Shirley Lucas.

Limit the colors. One color dominates each of these paintings and provides unity. Notice the mixtures of blue and violet and blue and green in the top painting and the mixed yellow-brown color in the bottom painting. Many tints and shades were blended. Small areas of other colors provide brilliant contrast. Theme: "If I ran the circus" by fourth-graders.

one color in all of its various tints and shades, a system that is very effective. Or you might have them use analogous or related colors—those adjacent to one another on the color wheel, such as blue, blue-green, green, and yellow-green. Two or three colors are usually enough; five are too many. Ideally, one color should dominate and set the tone for the whole color scheme.

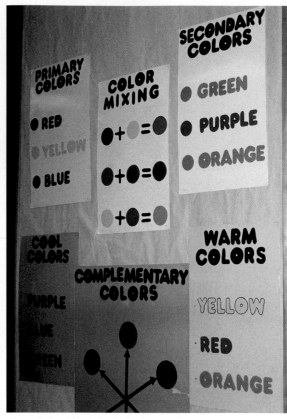

Left: The teacher's strength in teaching about color is evident here. The peacock is crayoned mainly in green and its variations, along with strong, pure accents of blue, red, and yellow. White crayon is especially effective with the dark grey crayon resist. **Middle:** The color spectrum forms the surreal background, the nose, and the spiraling eyes for this eighth-grader's black, heart-shaped abstract face done in acrylics. Note the color spectrum around the eyes. **Right:** A primary-school display teaches about primary, secondary, complementary, warm, and cool colors.

To avoid pitfalls of clashing color or strident chromatic relationships, you can guide your students to minimize the intensity (or brightness) of colors in a composition. This process, sometimes referred to as *neutralization* or *dulling* of a color, involves mixing or combining a color with its complementary hue, which can be found opposite to it on the color wheel. Red and green are complementary colors, as are blue and orange. Many colors now available in crayon, oil pastel, and tempera already are neutralized—for example, sienna, brown, umber, ochre, and chrome green.

A little bit of bright, intense color will easily hold its own against a more generous employment of neutralized colors. Surrounded by duller colors, brighter colors in the middle of the picture give it a sense of glowing light. Colors can be repeated to create movement and unity, but remind students to vary the size and shape of the repeated color. Dark, cool colors generally recede; bright, warm colors usually advance. Complementary colors such as red and green in their fullest intensities create vibrant contrasts when juxtaposed. Black, grey, and white can be combined with any color scheme without creating harmonic conflicts. Often, as in the case of black outlining, the dark linear accent gives a contrasting sharpness and sparkle to the composition. The character, identity, and impact of a color depend a great deal on the colors that are adjacent to or surrounding it. For example, a green shape on a turquoise background may be relatively unnoticed, but intense orange against an intense blue (a complementary relationship) will vibrate and arrest the eye.

Ironically, to make colors beautiful, we must consider first not hue but value, because it is the main pattern of values or shades that gives a picture its overall effect and strength. Varying shades is more important than varying hues. Contrasts of light and dark colors will make a picture bold.

The painters of the Postimpressionist era, including Franz Marc, Marc Chagall, and Odilon Redon, as well as contemporary colorists such as Karel Appel, Helen Frankenthaler, Richard Anuskiewicz, and Victor Vasarely, have provided the art world with eye-opening creations in color, with surprises such as blue horses and multihued people. Teachers and students also should turn for inspiration in color usage to the luminous stained-glass windows of Gothic cathedrals, the jewel-like miniatures of India and Persia, the shimmering mosaics of Byzantium, and the fascinating *ukiyo-e* color woodcuts of Japan.

Space Space is an element in both pictorial composition and abstract design that often confuses the student. In two-dimensional art expression, *space* sometimes is designated as the negative area between positive objects. This kind of space often is referred to as *decorative* or *surface space*. Another category of space to be considered is space-in-depth, which is often studied as if comprised of three sections: foreground, middle ground, and background. Common pictorial devices for achieving the illusion of space-in-depth on a two-dimensional plane, as in a painting, include:

- Using vertical placement to suggest depth
- Diminishing sizes of objects as they recede in the distance

Courtesy of ICCA, Milner Library, Illinois State University.

Depth created by overlapping and diminishing the sizes of the dancers' heads. Note the effect of hundreds of dancers in the community folk-dance celebration. Eleven-year-old from Kastamonu, Turkey.

Courtesy of ICCA, Milner Library, Illinois State University.

Creating depth by vertical placement. Although the shoppers' heights remain constant, this market scene from Turkey shows depth through more distant figures being placed higher in the picture.

Courtesy of Barbara Thomas.

Depth created by diminishing sizes of farther objects. In the fifth-grader's Antarctic scene, the biggest penguin is four times as large as the distant penguin. Also, penguins are at different levels.

- Drawing sharp, clear details in the foreground and blurred, indistinct elements in the background
- Overlapping shapes or forms
- Drawing objects that are farther away from the observer higher on the picture plane
- Using bright, intense colors in the foreground and dulled colors in the background
- Employing perspective-creating techniques such as converging lines and horizon lines

Applying the rules of perspective doesn't guarantee the success of a composition, however. Rules of perspective should not be imposed on children unless they indicate a need for them. Most children must be guided in mastering the intricacies of space-in-depth, which include perspective and foreshortening.

Similarly, young artists need to learn to understand *point of view.* Is the art depicted from above (a bird's eye view) or below (an ant's eye view)? Are we seeing the art close-up, as if through a microscope, or in the distance, as if through a telescope?

Texture and Pattern
Texture and pattern usually are considered secondary, or adorning, elements that add richness and variety. They can, however, also become the main feature of a design—in the design of floor tiles, for example, or in the repetitions of windows and columns in a work of architecture. Names for textures include rough and smooth, actual and implied, bumpy and jagged. Artists such as Rembrandt, Rubens, and Velasquez were virtuosos in painting the textures of hair, silk, velvet, and fur.

Patterns can be regular, irregular, stripes (bands), zigzag (chevron), scallop (fish scale), plaid (crossband), notched (crenellated), or checkerboard (counterchange). Patterns can be created by setting up a series of parallel lines or lines that crisscross, often at right angles. These lines can be straight, curved, wavy, or jagged.

Patterns in nature usually have a mathematical basis. For example, the arrangement of seeds in the head of a sunflower and the bumpy divisions on a pineapple are two of the many natural occurrences of the mathematical series called a *Fibonacci series.* Such seemingly random patterns as those formed by cloud formations, tree branches, or a coastline's indentations are in fact governed by the same geometric phenomenon, *fractal geometry.*

Both pattern and texture can be created by the repetition of individual elements—for example, lines to make grass or circles to make apples on a tree. Patterns usually are made up of the repetition of one or more clearly discernible shapes. In textures, however, individual elements are merged into the whole and are difficult to distinguish. Making a distinction between pattern and texture is not always easy. Seen from a distance,

Courtesy of Frank Wachowiak and Mary Sayer Hammond.

Pattern: Inventive patterns of circles, checkerboards, stripes, and diamonds grace this upper-elementary child's oil pastel on pink paper. It was drawn with white chalk and inspired by a stuffed bird and photos of birds.

Courtesy of Baiba Kuntz.

Patterns and textures: A feast of carefully planned patterns and textures enrich fifth-grader Kay Soloman's detailed colored marker drawing of a still-life arrangement.

Courtesy of ICCA, Milner Library, Illinois State University.

A textural gradient, shown in this Cuban sixth-grader's painting in the way the water's waves appear different from front to back, is an effective way to show depth.

Courtesy of David W. Hodge.

Textures: Clay is the supreme material for creating textures. Buttons, wire mesh, bottle caps, and kitchen tools are used.

Courtesy of Dahria McClelland.

This fifth-grader's tempera painting of jitterbuggers shows a riot of pattern, along with variety, repetition, and asymmetrical balance.

apples on a tree may create a texture, but seen from up close, the same apples may create a pattern. Microscopes and telescopes can further determine whether something—for example, a view of the galaxy—is perceived as a texture, a pattern, or a shape.

Both pattern and texture can be used overall to create a rich, busy effect, but they may take on even more importance when they are used judiciously and separated by empty, plain areas of a solid, unvaried color. When a texture changes progressively, as from distinct in the foreground to blended in the distance, it is called a *textural gradient*. This phenomenon can be seen in views of ocean waves, clouds, and fields of trees and crops.

PRINCIPLES OF ART

Balance and Symmetry Your students need to become familiar with the two types of compositional balance: symmetrical or formal balance, and asymmetrical or informal balance. Although formal balance has gone

Patterns and textures abound in nature. Help your students to see the patterns and shapes in nature's leaves and seeds. These exquisite sunflower oil pastels on black paper fill the page. Each seed, petal, leaf, and leaf vein are carefully drawn. Arranged alternately on the stem, the leaves run off the edges of the picture creating exciting black background shapes. **Left:** Here is variety in the leaves. **Middle:** A flower is drawn in side view, and exciting background negative shapes. **Right:** Subtle blending of colors on the leaves and petals contrast with the bold, black-patterned seed heads.

in and out of favor as styles have changed, a symmetrical arrangement in which objects or figures on the right balance similarly weighted components on the left generally makes a more rigid, static composition. *Bilateral symmetry* is an arrangement in which two sides are similar. *Quadrilateral symmetry* has four similar quarters.

A common misconception about art composition is that emphasis can be achieved by drawing something very large at the center of the picture. In fact, size and placement by themselves do not ensure domination. To be noticed, the object must be emphasized through the use of other attributes as well—contrasting value, color, and detail, for example. While there are no hard-and-fast rules, a pictorial creation is often much more interesting and attractive when the principal subject is not placed exactly in the center of the composition.

Variety, Repetition, Emphasis, and Domination-Subordination

Variety may be the most important fundamental principle in composition and design. Analyses of past and present art masterpieces reveal the artists' reliance in their compositions on a variety of shapes and forms in their compositions. Seldom are two shapes alike. Look at a score of multifigure paintings by recognized artists throughout the centuries and you will discover endless variety. No two heads are on the same level; no two figures are in the same position; no two figures stand on the same levels in the foreground.

Nature reflects an abundance of variety—in the wings of a butterfly, the stripes on a zebra, the spots on a leopard, the feathers on a bird, the scales on a fish, the web of a spider, the cracks in an ice floe, and the flakes of frost on a windowpane. No two wings or stripes or spots are alike, just as no two of us are alike. Yet, despite our own uniqueness, we must all be

Variety: The cats' faces of blue, yellow, striped, and banded show much variety in this "animals in the garden" scene.

Variety: Riotous variety in this primary-grade child's wonderful marker-pen harbor scene! No two cabin cruisers are alike. The beach house architecture, the intensely colored empty spaces, and the windswept trees and hairstyles are delightful.

taught to employ variety in every aspect of our graphic imagery. We need to learn to provide variety—in line, shape, value, color, pattern, texture—to give excitement and interest to a work of art.

Variety must be counterbalanced by a *repetition* of those art elements, however, to achieve the desired unity. Just as in living, variety is most effective when combined with structure and organization. Too much variety can result in a hodge-podge. There must be some repetition to give structure and strength, some constancy in a sea of flux. Art needs both differences and similarities.

Emphasis (that one object or motif should stand out above others) and *domination-subordination* (that equality is to be avoided in favor of a dominant object or motif) are concepts related to variety. The following techniques are helpful for varying the placement of objects in a composition:

- Change the size and shape of objects.
- Begin objects on different planes.
- Terminate objects at different heights.
- Touch the edges of the picture plane at different points to introduce lines into the composition.

- Strategically overlap objects to create even more varied shapes and negative spaces.

FORMALIST, CONTEXTUALIST, AND MEDIA APPROACHES TO TEACHING ART

One way to teach art is to revisit, time and again, over the course of many art assignments, the elements and principles introduced in this chapter. These basic elements and principles can provide a practical design foundation on which to build a qualitative art program over the years. This approach to teaching—a *formalist* approach—is used in many art classrooms: Art's job is to be beautiful. Contrasted to the formalist approach to teaching art is the *contextualist* approach, which focuses on what art is about—its content, and especially the context and society in which art is made: Art's job is to make society better. (We will explore contextualism further in later chapters.) A third approach, the *media* approach, means simply the teaching of art by exploring the numerous media by which art can be made. This media approach is addressed in the last third of this

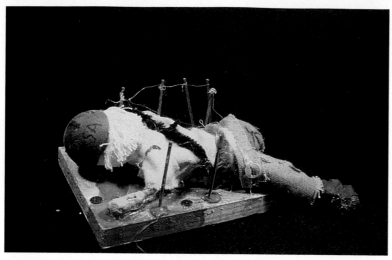

Courtesy of Joyce Vroon.

A contextualist orientation to art is one that focuses more on the story or context shown, rather than on the arrangement of the formal elements. It is shown here in fifth-grader Michael Owens's expressive plaster-of-paris-strip sculpture depicting the horrors of war.

book. But before exploring these approaches, let us first look at teachers, teaching, and *how* children make art.

FOR FURTHER READING

Biren, Faber. 1965. *History of Color in Painting.* New York: Reinhold Publishing Corporation.

Chijiiwa, Hideaki. 1987. *Color Harmony: A Guide to Creative Color Combinations.* Gloucester, MA: Rockport Publishers.

Rogue, Georges. 1996. "Chevreul and Impressionism: A Reappraisal." *The Art Bulletin* (March).

Wong, Wucius. 1993. *Principles of Form and Design.* New York: Van Nostand Reinhold.

WEB RESOURCES

For design elements and principles:

http://daphne.palomar.edu/design/fandg.html

For simple examples of the art elements, for example, texture:

http://www.sanford-artedventures.com/study/g texture.html

For definitions of art terms:

http://www.artlex.com/

For example of aerial perspective:

http://www2.evansville.edu/studiochalkboard/ap-aerial.html

For examples of the color wheel:

http://www2.evansville.edu/studiochalkboard/c-wheel.html

For color and Impressionism:

http://www.blehert.com/lessons/lesson15.html

For correlating color and the discovery of pigments:

http://www.whitebottom.com/philipball/c01 05.asp

For tens of thousands of terms related to art and architecture, such as names and types of patterns:

http://www.getty.edu/vow.AATHierarchy?find=&logic=AND&note=&subjectid=300010108

Part 2
Teachers and Teaching

A former public school art teacher, Tim Rollins has created a student art workshop in a difficult New York City neighborhood. The collaborative artworks that he and his students create grace major museums throughout the world. In this one, a beautiful overall pattern is created by the mysterious abstract forms. They remind one of boxing gloves, trumpets, gears, and windows. They might even remind a teacher of a classroom full of energetic children. What do the forms suggest to you?

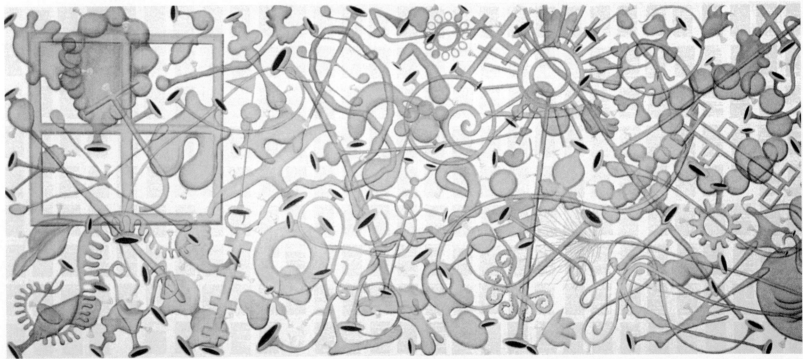

Tim Rollins and K.O.S. (Kids of Survival), Amerika, Land of the Free. Courtesy of Hirshhorn Museum and Sculpture Garden, Smithsonian Institution, Joseph H. Hirshhorn Purchase Fund, 1991. Photograph by Lee Stallworth.

*W*herever there is an art program of quality and promise, there is an enthusiastic, resourceful, knowledgeable, imaginative, and gifted teacher at its center. The teacher of the successful, productive art class invariably is a planner, an organizer, an expediter, a counselor, a dreamer, a goal setter, and most of all, a lover of children, life, and art. The school that boasts a modern physical plant, generous budget, and administration sympathetic to art is fortunate, but if it does not attract teachers who are prepared to teach art confidently, enthusiastically, developmentally, and qualitatively, it has little chance of establishing and implementing an art program of excellence and stature.

The best teachers of art—classroom teachers or specialists—believe wholeheartedly in art's unique spirit-enhancing and rejuvenating power. In every project, they seek to perfect the critically important motivations, the technical intricacies, and the evaluative strategies. They organize materials, tools, space, and time schedules to produce exemplary working conditions. They search for inspirational stimuli to renew children's interest in a project whenever the initial excitement wanes. In their enthusiasm, which they display openly and generously, teachers encourage students to open their eyes to the design, color, form, rhythm, texture, and pattern in the world around them, and they believe in art's power to give students a language with which to communicate and express their feelings. They identify with their students and are elated when one makes a discovery or masters a skill. Conversely, they are genuinely concerned when students encounter difficulties that defy resolution.

A creative, confident, and enthusiastic teacher with a love for children and an understanding of art fundamentals is the catalyst in a productive and qualitative art program. The teacher's own immediate enjoyment of the teaching experience helps students enjoy the intrinsic rewards of learning. The successful teacher must constantly plan, organize, experiment, motivate, evaluate, and build resources, yet the privilege of sharing the contagious, exuberant, magical world of students as they explore, discover, and invent compensates beyond measure for the extra effort that is required.

Chapter 3
The Teacher's Role: Strategies and Management

$\mathcal{M}$ost art teaching is done by elementary classroom teachers. Some of these teachers feel handicapped by their limited backgrounds in art fundamentals. One reason for this feeling of inadequacy is the minimal art experience that these teachers had during their own school years. Another may be the lack of an art education course during their college preparation and in-service work. Nonetheless, three-quarters of these elementary classroom teachers teach either all or part of the art that their students

Mary Lazzari, who contributed many pictures to this book, is proud of her students and her art program.

receive in school. The classroom teacher has flexibility in scheduling and can have small groups of students work on certain phases of art projects while others engage in different subjects. Because only one group of students is involved, storage of materials is not a major problem, and there is little chance that elaborate still-life materials will be upset.

In some schools, art is taught by an itinerant art teacher, who may see 500 to 800 students per week, in twenty different classrooms, in two to five different schools. Supplies—and what passes for an office—are in a closet.

Courtesy of ICCA, Milner Library, Illinois State University.

The St. Petersburg, Russia, teacher of this student was well rewarded for the planning and motivation done when this ten-year-old's story illustration showed such a sophisticated use of analogous colors and spatial divisions.

While the classroom teacher may or may not remain in the room, the art teacher in practice usually is left alone to handle discipline. Unfortunately, the art teacher often has little opportunity to observe how the classroom teacher handles disruptive incidents.

Finally, art may be taught by an art teacher in a school equipped with an art room that provides more elaborate equipment like hot plates, looms, and sinks. A complicated still life can be constructed and remain intact. Most middle schools maintain art rooms and art specialists, but only a fraction of elementary schools do. The middle school teacher typically sees 125 students a day. The elementary art teacher with an art room may see as many as 500 students each week. This teacher has one 45-minute art period in which to motivate the students, distribute supplies, monitor the lesson, clean up, evaluate the lesson, and store artwork if the project is to go on for a second week.

Top row and bottom left and middle: *Courtesy of Baiba Kuntz*. Bottom right: *Courtesy of Frank Wachowiak*.

A teacher's influence goes on forever. Master art teacher Baiba Kuntz, while in college a student of Frank Wachowiak's, had her fifth- and sixth-graders create these carefully observed drawings from a still life of birds. The taxidermic specimen of an owl, pictured top left, was passed on to her by Wachowiak when he retired; note the wonderful use to which the owl continues to be put. Baiba's students' large (19- × 25-inch) colored marker drawings were made with no preliminary pencil drawings. The bottom right is an oil pastel done by a sixth-grade student of Wachowiak.

THE TEACHER'S ROLE: GUIDING STUDENTS TO CREATE AND TO APPRECIATE

To appreciate their students' developmental possibilities and limitations, teachers must have a basic understanding of the kinds of art that children do naturally. The qualitative art program espoused by this book, however, demands more of students than what they do naturally. Some students do perceive, draw, and compose sensitively, but most require guidance and motivation. Because the teacher is the catalyst, it is the teacher's responsibility to establish a positive learning climate in which inquiry, creativity, and individuality thrive. Teachers of art may ask their students to set higher standards of performance for themselves or demand greater effort than the children have been accustomed to making. In most instances, the best art is the result of perseverance—of purposeful, consistent, and time-consuming effort. The results are not accidental, nor is the product one of undemanding, trivial, or thoughtless activity. Indeed, to teach that art is undemanding is to create a false impression. Teachers can maintain an effective, positive, and productive atmosphere in their classes when they can alert the students to an awareness of the project's objectives and the satisfaction to be achieved in a purposeful art endeavor.

In addition to developing an understanding of the kinds of art that children do naturally, experienced teachers avoid assigning a new, untried technique to their classes. The teacher's confidence and effectiveness are heightened immeasurably if he or she has explored ahead of time the materials and tools that are available to the students and has created successfully with those tools.

It is a goal of every effective art teacher to guide his or her students toward a fuller aesthetic awareness of their environment—for example, to see beauty in the commonplace, such as droplets of morning dew glistening in a moisture-laden spider's web. Students are highly impressionable and susceptible to visual influences over which teachers and parents have little control. Television and MTV, movies, computer and video games, musical recordings, makeup, magazine illustrations, recording covers, posters, cars, clothes, and package design clamor for their attention, shape their developing taste, and help to form their cultural values. While students' discriminative choices often differ from those of adults, an effective art teacher can help guide students to consider aesthetic choices. In teaching art criticism, art history, and aesthetics, top-notch teachers of art use as many audiovisual aids as possible. These include original works of art, reproductions, films, photographs, slides, video recordings, magazine articles, colorfully illustrated art books, and examples of student work. Although little or no money may be budgeted for purchasing visual materials such as slides and reproductions, the dedicated teacher purchases them out of pocket and taps the resources of libraries and museums,

spending about 45 minutes a day in planning time. (Chapter 23 discusses still-life arrangements, and Appendix B lists some audiovisual sources.)

The Teacher's Positive Personality, Rapport, and Respect A positive, cheerful, and outgoing personality is a major asset for teachers of art. Teachers must learn in sometimes difficult and trying situations to be patient, calm, and resolute. Children want to believe in their teachers. They need the security of a teacher's abiding confidence in the worth of the subject being taught. Students come to rely on their teachers for help with important choices in resolving perplexing problems, and they become skeptical of those who confuse them with vague generalizations or those who place all the responsibility for decision making in their hands.

Teachers of art should learn to listen to children's descriptions of their experiences, both real and imaginary, with sympathetic interest. They

Courtesy of Bernardo Hopkins and Leonard Piha.

A teacher's success depends on the empathic rapport developed with one's students.

Illustrations from Frank Wachowiak's university classes.

College and university students preparing to teach art should explore varied art materials and techniques. This knowledge will build their confidence as they guide children's art production endeavors. ***Top row:*** Oil pastel, plaster relief, tempera batik. ***Bottom row:*** Oil pastel, yarn collage, crayon engraving.

should avoid a detached, keep-your-distance approach. Instead, their commitment, concern, and excitement for the project must be evident in their actions, words, and facial expressions. Veteran teachers learn to cultivate a ready sense of humor, which can help to alleviate many tension-fraught situations. Teachers who really care about children do not talk down to them; neither do they underestimate their potential to excel.

A teacher's success in the art class often is based on the empathic rapport that can develop between instructor and students. Classroom teachers will obviously know their students well, but for art specialists, getting to know the students is more challenging—and especially important because of the one-to-one relationship demanded in a creative atmosphere. Name tags and a seating chart (with movable tabs to expedite changes) will hasten memorizing the students' names. Once teachers establish a climate of cooperation and mutual understanding, their ability to challenge their charges becomes their teaching strength. Teachers who have a greater sense of their effectiveness produce higher achievement gains in their students. These teachers believe: If I try hard, I can get through to the most difficult, unmotivated students.

A visitor to a classroom in which qualitative art learning is taking place can immediately sense the electric involvement, purposefulness of endeavor, and genuine rapport that exists between students and a teacher. The special quality that distinguishes dedicated teachers of art from average instructors is their ability to respond intelligently, sympathetically, and purposefully to the children's creative efforts. They can communicate with the students both knowledgeably and honestly regarding their progress in art. The best teachers evaluate their students' work seriously and objectively; their critical attention gives the work importance and significance in the students' eyes. These teachers show sincere respect for what the individuals are trying to do as they strive to give form to their ideas. Most important, they take the students seriously as artists.

Courtesy of Baiba Kuntz.

The room teaches. Attractive bulletin-board displays help stimulate students' achievement. The color chart over the board is used to suggest why certain colors go together. It shows the beauty of related colors combined with accents of others. Some of the most sophisticated color usage reproduced in this book was done in view of such a display.

GETTING OFF TO A GOOD START

The first week of school, the first art class, the first art project, and the first motivation are especially important in establishing a qualitative art program. A word about maintaining a productive atmosphere in the art class: Experienced teachers know there is no single solution to the varied behavioral problems with which they must cope. Yet veteran instructors of art generally find it expedient to begin classes with a serious, organized approach, which can be modified later if the situation warrants. This is better than allowing so much uninhibited freedom that it is impossible to later bring the class under control when necessary. If students suspect that the teacher is unconcerned when they waste time with idle chatter or horseplay, they will develop a self-defeating, laissez-faire attitude in art class.

The room's impact on students during the opening day of school is, for all purposes, the teacher's first art lesson. The appearance of the classroom or art room reflects the teacher's art convictions and awareness of design as a vital environmental influence and conditioner. Make the classroom orderly yet inviting, visually stimulating but not chaotic. Children's artwork, attractively mounted, should brighten the walls. Hanging mobiles of fish, shells, birds, or butterflies created by preceding classes add a surprising element of color in motion. The creative teacher relies on a variety of eye-catching resources, including attractive bulletin-board exhibits, found-object displays, living plants, animals or birds, art-book displays,

hobby collections, antiques, and original works of art and craft. These make the room into a perpetually changing world of wonders.

STRATEGIES FOR TEACHING ART

Teach Nonverbally The best teachers do not rely on verbal instructions alone. The teacher's spoken, personal interaction with each student should be reinforced by the written and display materials. For example, teachers of art can enhance their instructional effectiveness by using the white marker board to emphasize their motivational presentation and outline the specific objectives of a project. Students entering class can read the instructions on the board and proceed to their work without wasting time. The board can be used to identify and clarify the various possibilities and steps of the project. Evaluative criteria in the form of questions posted on the board allow students to make their own evaluations of their in-progress work (see Chapter 5). Using the board minimizes students' dependence on their instructor and discourages the refrain of "Am I finished?"

Plan the Distribution, Collection, and Organization of Materials Crucial to an art project's ultimate success is housekeeping. The teacher must organize the classroom or art-room facilities so there

Courtesy of Barbara Thomas.

Well-planned procedures for distributing and collecting supplies will facilitate both the production of artwork and cleanup, as shown by the basket and tray for materials.

Courtesy of David W. Hodge.

The art room was decorated with these colorful figures to stimulate other classes (see page 252). They were drawn from class models on large 24- × 36-inch colored construction paper and colored with oil pastels. Then they were cut out and mounted on construction paper of a complementary color. Two eighth-grade students cooperated on the coloring of each figure.

will be adequate working space, a sufficient supply of materials and tools, varied storage facilities for both projects in progress and those retained for exhibition, a diversity of display spaces, and effective cleanup facilities (see Appendix B).

Plan carefully the distribution of student work in progress, art supplies, and tools before the class begins so that valuable time is not wasted. Expedite the return of artwork by having students put their names on their work at an early stage and having it collected in an organized way, such as table by table. Materials can best be distributed either through a student-monitor system or by having students come up by tables or rows to a central supply area. Because disciplinary problems can arise when supplies run short and students have time on their hands, the teacher must ensure that the supply of materials and tools is adequate for the project at hand.

Begin the Lesson: Get Their Attention Getting the class session off to a good start is a major step in creating a productive studio atmosphere. When students come to an art room at the beginning of the period, meet them at the door. Your positive, cheerful greeting can start off the class in the right mood. If some of the incoming students are boisterous, the problem can be resolved before it gets out of hand. For an art lesson in the general classroom, make sure that students understand that you are starting something new.

Before they provide motivational material or give demonstrations, experienced teachers usually wait until they have everyone's attention. Arouse student attention by starting a class with something novel, different, or unusual. Never start a class the same way day after day. Bring an original painting, perhaps one of your own artworks. Borrow a sculpture or piece of folk art to bring to class. Play a song on a cassette player. Tell the class a special guest is coming today, step out of view, slip on an artist costume, and transform your persona into that of a famous artist. Create situations where structures can be discovered. Teaching does not mean transmitting structures to be assimilated only at the verbal level.

Keep the Motivation Brief In striving to make sure the students understand the project's objectives, sometimes the motivational session is mistakenly too prolonged. Three to five minutes may be ample to arouse interest and show one or two art historical exemplars. Be alert for those unmistakable signs of disinterest: the shuffle of chairs, the tapping of pencils, the whispered conspiracies, and the far-away looks. Learn to stop before students reach their fatigue point. Students need information, but they do not like to feel cheated out of their studio or activity period; they want to get on to their work. Perceptive teachers can detect when students are only half-listening, or more intent on some distracting gadget they possess, than on the teacher's remarks. If you spot wandering prodigals, bring them back with a pointed question, reprimand, or simply a pause and a meaningful look in the offender's direction. When holding a discussion before studio activity, do not distribute the materials and tools until the discussion is over, because students naturally are tempted to explore the materials at hand instead of giving their full attention to the teacher's presentation.

Get the Design Off to a Good Start The first few minutes of creative work are critical. Here, the parameters of a successful work are laid down; the main compositional features are put into place. Just as a push is needed to set objects into physical motion, an extra push is often useful to initiate the working period. The first three minutes immediately following the motivation, when students pick up their art media for the first time, is crucial. While most students will be eager to do art, some may be overcome by uncertainty or fear. Students who are insecure about their own creativity may not be able to self-start. Some may sit perplexed, overcome by waves of confusion, self-doubt, and inadequacy. Some may be absorbed in negative thoughts about their life situations. One way to spur the uncertain and fearful students into creative action is to give them one specific task to do. For example, say to a student who requires direction, "To begin, place a line for the head at the top edge of the paper and a line for the feet at the bottom edge." Guided-drawing techniques at the start get students working—for example, drawing goggles for a subsequent under-

Get the design off to a good start. "Make the clown's hat touch the top of the page and his feet touch the bottom edge." This statement helped the children to create a composition that effectively filled the page and offered sufficient room to show important details. In addition, making the figures large helps to eliminate the problem of filling up empty background space. Crayon encaustic then was used for the paintings.

sea picture or drawing roller-coaster curves and then turning these into an amusement park.

Prevent Bad Starts Left to themselves, some students—perhaps those who daydreamed while instructions were given—will get off to a poor beginning and make mistakes that threaten their ultimate success. For example, some will draw tiny, tiny figures that cannot be painted or cut out. Instead of getting the overall picture put into place, others will use too much time and worry in drawing one small part. They will insist on erasing one small object repeatedly, trying to "get it right." Still others may set an unrealistically high goal. Forestall such problems by giving instructions or materials that will prevent their occurrence. To prevent fussing with and erasing timid pencil lines, have the students draw bold outlines with yellow chalk. Instead of criticizing the negative, focus on the positive. On seeing a problem, hold up as a model a student's artwork that avoids the mistake.

Nurture Creativity During the Working Period During the working period, the teacher should not only keep students focused on the instructional objectives, but also look for examples of creative uniqueness. Model, instruct, reinforce, question, and explain strategies for thinking in new ways. Look for those students' works that show imagination, elaboration, and new variations. Then use these exemplars to stimulate others to arrive at their own individual solutions. Holding up a student's work, call the class's attention to the particular creative inventiveness in evidence. "Look at how this composition fills up the paper. Four dancing figures are repeated, and the arms and skirts of several touch the sides of the paper, here, here, and here, to give the design a feeling of unity. I wonder in what ways other artists are filling their papers and giving their designs unity?" Two words of caution are in order, however. The teacher should be careful not to embarrass any one student by excessively singling out one "star" student. Also, while the class is working seriously, the teacher should not constantly interrupt with calls to "look at this." Even so, when attention flags, you may use students' exemplars, as well as reproductions, to rekindle the fires of motivation.

Foster Perseverance Perseverance, which probably contributes as much as anything to a successful artwork, is central to the qualitative method. In their desire for instant gratification, too many students race through assignments; the resulting lack of sustained effort regrettably brings with it little or no gratification. It is a mistake to equate speed of execution with freedom of expression, because a genuinely spontaneous

Courtesy of Beverly Barksdale Mallon.

One way to ameliorate lagging student interest is to intersperse long and short projects. Many art projects by students of Beverly Mallon of Chase Street Elementary School in Athens, Georgia, take three, four, or more periods. But shown here is a quickie filler project for second-graders—a pastel of a fantasy rooster on black paper, cut out and mounted on white paper decorated with a border. The artworks of animals were auctioned off at an Athens Humane Society fund-raiser event. All were sold, and the students received recognition over the PA system and in the school newsletter. Students learned both the importance of public service and the value others place on their artwork.

Courtesy of William Sapp.

Perseverance contributes much to the quality of an artwork. Students too often stop short, when extra effort could make the difference. Here, in contemporary artist William Sapp's 8- × 10-foot piece entitled Dogpack (1992) are not just a few clay figures but a thousand.

and sparkling quality in a work of art is not achieved easily. Many successful projects even in the primary grades take three, four, or even five class periods, sometimes stretching over a month or two in duration. Teachers can maintain an effective and productive atmosphere in their classes when they continue to make students aware of the project's objectives, which unfold session after session. Then they will have the ultimate satisfaction, being proud of an artwork well done.

Combat Lagging Interest, Stimulate Extra Effort One major problem that an art teacher must face is lagging student interest once the initial excitement of a new project or technique has waned. Almost every class contains students who are satisfied with only a superficial effort, who do not develop a real concern for the subject matter involved, or who find it difficult to persevere. They insist they are finished with their work sooner than the others. They feel that they have exhausted the possibilities of the project while their classmates still are busily involved. Here, the challenge is to find the right balance between what the children may be willing to settle for and what they are capable of if given sensitive teacher guidance.

If teacher and students together develop objectives in both expression and design at the outset of a project, children will be less likely to rush through their work. Perseverance is reinforced when students are involved and internally motivated. That is to say, when students want to express something personally meaningful, they will work for a long time. This is why developing instructional objectives that encourage the expression of feelings is so important. For upper-elementary- and middle-school students, posting the process and evaluative criteria on the board allows the teacher to function effectively as both a classroom manager and a facilitator for individual students. Avoid repeating the criteria ad infinitum to each individual student in a time-consuming procedure. When questions arise, the teacher can clarify and resolve them for the entire class by referring to the posted criteria.

Encourage students to go further, to "weave in" the figures in their pictures, to tuck some objects behind others, to create rhythm. Encourage them to make their pictures swing, to have rhythm through repeating forms. One way to encourage a child to go further is to combine praise with suggestion. For example, a teacher may say, "Now Mandy is starting to put in the children; I wonder how many are in the line at noon?" Mandy likely will respond to the teacher's expressed faith by putting in many figures.

A suggestion offered to one student often will trigger fresh ideas for others who may have reached a creative impasse. Using students' work in progress, call attention to compositional requirements as well as variations in expression. To the child who says "I spoiled mine," reply that "the only way a picture is spoiled is not to do it in your own, personal way." Another method to stimulate extra effort is to have students anticipate a special show of their work. For example, ask the kindergarten teacher if she would let your class come in for a few minutes to show their artworks.

At the upper-elementary- and middle-school levels, the practice of writing brief, constructive remarks on the back of a student's work or on slips of paper attached to that work will promote perseverance. Although time-consuming, this strategy for evaluation can help the conscientious teacher to give individualized instruction. It gives the teacher a chance to evaluate studio performance during a time that is relatively free of distractions and other responsibilities. It strengthens the possibility that every student in class will receive specific, individual help at some point during the project, and provides students with a definite working direction for the ensuing studio period.

Clean Up and Evaluate Cleanup procedures should be planned in advance to ensure that enough time has been allotted and the process will

Courtesy of Frank Wachowiak.

The teacher encouraged these students to go further and add more figures. Then, students were encouraged to break up the empty background space in inventive, beautiful ways. Illustrations on this page are by upper-elementary-grade children. They took turns modeling with sports equipment and musical instruments in the center of the room.

occur in an orderly fashion. Because cleanup comes at the end of the lesson when students are ready to do something else and often requires several students to be out of their seats at once, planning is vital to avoid problems. For example, confusion and possible disruptive behavior at the sink can be prevented by sending only students from one row or table at a time to that facility.

Use the remaining time after cleanup for evaluation, so the period does not end with idle chatter. The after-cleanup period can be used for a summing-up or an evaluation session. This is a time to come full circle and demonstrate how the instructional objectives have taken form in the students' work and produced positive results.

MANAGE THE CLASS BY YOUR PRESENCE

A common complaint of students is that teachers have eyes in the backs of their heads—and it's true. You need to be aware of what is going on in the room and be at strategic stations at critical times. During materials distribution, you should be near the supply area. When lecturing, avoid facing

Courtesy of Melody Milbrandt.

Students work intently, facilitated by the cigar box containers full of crayons that afford students a wide choice in colors as they enrich their watercolor paintings.

Courtesy of David W. Hodge.

The teacher's presence is important in managing the class. Here, in front of the still life, she can point out its features.

the marker board with your back to the class or standing in front of the glaring light of a window. Effective instructors move among the students during a studio activity rather than staying at their own desk. Experienced teachers do not let themselves get beleaguered by demands from a bevy of questioning students when they should be monitoring the class as a whole, especially during the opening minutes of class or at cleanup time. Let the students know that they will be advised one student at a time, and remind them to take turns when conferences are necessary.

Unless children have your permission to move about, they ordinarily should remain in their assigned seats during class. In large classes, students should take turns obtaining and returning materials and tools, either by tables or by rows. The quality of artwork produced generally diminishes as the amount of students' unguided socializing increases. You should make clear that unruly behavior—excessive talking, laughing, whistling, running, throwing things, gum chewing, propping of feet on desks, table hopping, and crowding at sinks—will not be tolerated. Problems of student apathy, disinterest, and errant behavior are heightened by insufficient lesson planning, meager motivational material, too little visual stimulation, insufficient knowledge of the technique, weak rapport between teacher and student, and a lack of conviction by both regarding the worth of the art experience.

Discipline and Redirect Students learn to take advantage of an instructor who makes idle threats and fails to carry them out. Explore all possible avenues of motivation and persuasion, of reasoning and strategic reconciliation, before resorting to chastisement of any sort, whether it involves moving students to other seats or sending them to the principal. As a rule, do not act hastily when disciplining students. Never mete out punishment during the heat of a crisis. Admonish the errant students, and tell them that you will discuss the infraction with them after class. Once you have stipulated a punishment, put it into effect. Keep in mind that some student behavior may reflect deeper problems, as we discuss in Chapter 12 on working with children with special needs.

Students do have a need to communicate. Talking in class can be a common, natural occurrence, especially during studio activities. However, when the talking becomes so loud and disruptive that it prevents concentration on the project, you need to act. Shouting "Quiet!" or "Settle down!" or rapping a desk with a ruler, ringing a bell, or clapping hands may calm the class for a few minutes, but will the calm last? Experienced teachers instead use positive, constructive approaches such as redirection and positive reinforcement. They call the class to attention, emphasizing some aspect of the project that needs amplification. They also might hold up a student's work in process and point out specifically creative solutions that were achieved. Prepare and photocopy in advance some remarks and rewards to clip to students' artworks. By using positive strategy, teachers maintain motivation and order while they avoid being seen as martinets in the eyes of their students.

During art sessions in which you build respect for serious endeavor and minimize boisterous socializing, student performances will be of a consistently higher caliber than those in highly permissive situations. A class is less likely to be bored or cause disturbance when it has been guided to see the many possibilities of the project and has been richly motivated. Motivation is the subject of the next chapter.

FOR FURTHER READING

Feldman, Edmund. 1993. "Best Advice and Counsel to Art Teachers." *Art Education* 46(5): 58–59.

Holmes Group Executive Board. 1986. *Tomorrow's Teachers: A Report of the Holmes Group.* East Lansing, MI.

Courtesy of David Harvell.

In this elementary classroom are posted five rules: (1) Listen. (2) Respect others. (3) Be polite and helpful. (4) Follow directions. (5) Take care of the room and materials. The first offense results in a warning; the second and third offenses result in varying lengths of time-out.

Johnson, Andra. 1992. *Elementary Art Education Anthology.* Reston, VA: NAEA.

Nyman, Andra (ed.) 1996. *Instructional Methods in the Artroom.* Reston, VA: NAEA.

Phillips, Lauren Christine. 2003. "Nurturing Empathy." *Art Education* 56(4): 45–50.

Susi, Frank D. 2000. "Behavior Management: Principles and Guidelines for Art Education." *Art Education* 55(1): 40–45.

Susi, Frank. 2002. *Student Behavior in Art Classrooms: The Dynamics of Discipline.* Reston, VA: National Art Education Association.

Wong, H. K. 2004. *The First Days of School: How to be an Effective Teacher.,* Mountain View, CA: Harrison K. Wong Publications.

WEB RESOURCES

For teaching methods and a glossary:
   http://www.greatschools.net/cgibin/glossary_browse_theme/CA/5

For The National Art Education—helpful links:
   www.howard.k12.md.us/connections/arthome.html

For ideas on beginning and ending class lessons:
   http://www.goshen.edu/facultypubs/Bartel.html

For classroom management:
   http://www.proteacher.com/030001/shtml.

Courtesy of David W. Hodge.

Recalled imagery of riding one's bicycle. The everyday interests of young adolescents can motivate them to create art: sports, bicycling, rock celebrities, TV and movie idols, and electronic games. In the mixed-media collage by a middle-school youngster, the rider fills the space and, brilliantly, the wheel motif is repeated in the analogous color areas of the background to create unity.

Chapter 4
Motivating Learning

*M*ost children need some form of stimulating motivation, either visual or verbal, to achieve high-quality results in their studio-art endeavors. Students must have something to say if they are to give it visual form. An art lesson's introductory phase should kindle the spark that ignites curiosity and piques interest. It is unfair to expect students to be challenged or excited by a teacher saying "Draw what you want today" or "Paint the way you feel." The many successful ways to begin an art project include:

- Guiding a class discussion in recalling a past experience and defining goals for the new project
- Showing visual materials on the theme
- Viewing examples of previous work
- Demonstrating the technical process with student participation
- Calling attention to a bulletin board or marker board presentation prepared for the project
- Having a guest speak, perform, and/or model for the students
- Using poems, stories, chanting, songs, and recorded music as motivation

Inspiration for children's art expression may spring from their experiences at school and at home, from their playground activities, or from their visits to special places. Art interest may come from nature, science, math, social studies, or the other arts. In these academic areas, the regular classroom teacher can make lessons do double duty and reciprocally motivate both fields—that is, well-planned art lessons can motivate both art learning and learning in an academic subject.

USING PERSONAL EXPERIENCE AS MOTIVATION

The most vital and successful art-project motivations usually result from vivid and meaningful personal experiences. Here, your role is to help

Courtesy of ICCA, Milner Library, Illinois State University.

A Philippine child recalls a favorite game, "Jumping over the stick." Two schemas are used: one for profile figures and one for frontal figures. Also foreground figures are larger and background figures smaller.

Recalled memory motivation often gives a charm and intellectual clarity to artworks. Here, in this Greek child's scene of the terraced countryside, we see boats pulled up onto the beach, houses lining the shore, switchback roads, distant islands, and the surprised sun peeking around the mountain.

Courtesy of Marla Mallett.

Children from near Cairo, Egypt, create weavings directly from memory. They use no prior drawings and often weave with the image sideways. Rowhia Ali, considered the most talented of the child weavers, is now 60 years of age and she recently created this 42- × 66-inch "Bedouins Entering the Village at Night."

students graphically clarify the significant aspects of the experience. There are two main types of personal experiences that can be used for art-lesson motivations: recalled experience and direct perception.

Recalled Experience In recalled experiences, children do not actually see the objects before their eyes; rather, they recall them in their minds. Teachers must activate the children's store of knowledge and help them to tap into the power of their memories. Perhaps students have visited some special place, such as an aquarium or a farm, or have seen a carnival, parade, dog or cat show, or sporting event. Perhaps they regularly experience some activity, such as dancing, playing a sport or a musical instrument.

The power and charm of designs that young children create based on their personal experiences is nowhere better illustrated than in Weissa Wassef's project, Weaving by Hands (see top right). Young children in a small Egyptian town (Hourranie, near Cairo) create beautiful designs and transform them into utilitarian and aesthetically satisfying weavings of significant economic value.

Using Who? What? How? Where? When? and Why? to Help Children Recall Experiences Because some children are not able to recall enough specific attributes of an event or an object, they may complain that they do not know how to draw it. You may need to act like a detective, helping

them bring new life to the experience by asking questions. The "what" is the overall experience that the child is being asked to recall—for example, a scary dream. To revive the "what" and "how" in students' minds, ask the children to physically act out the experience, using their bodies to re-create what was frightening in the dream, such as spiders or ghosts.

The purpose of "where" and "when" is to make passive knowledge active. To continue the dream example, ask the child to describe the room and the setting, its location in the house, who uses the adjoining rooms, the time of day or night, what else can be seen in the room, and the feeling the experience gave. The purpose of asking "who" is to give the child an opportunity to express self-identity and relationships with others. For example, a child may say, "I am in bed with my teddy bear in my arms, and Papa has tucked me in."

The "why" question is for the teacher. Teachers should ask themselves why this particular theme is considered to be important enough to warrant being done. In the scary-dream example, the hope is that by representing and sharing the frightening event with the group, the individual will gain a feeling of personal control over its scariness. A theme of playing on the playground may be chosen to promote an individual's feelings of group belongingness. A sociological theme such as equal justice or women's roles

Courtesy of the USSEA art collection of Dr. Anne Gregory.

"Where" can motivate an entire artwork. "My Bedroom" is an excellent topic for recalling significant things in a student's life. Here, student Catie Trezise very thoughtfully shows herself, her three cats, her wall decorations and furniture. Rather than just solid colors, teacher Barbara Bluhm of Maine taught the students to make graduated, blended colors with oil pastel.

can elicit the sharing of personal memories and can ultimately lead to a more fair world. Or a lesson topic might be chosen to stimulate a certain type of artistic representation. For example, depicting "my street" and "ring-around-the-rosy" would stimulate the use of foldover drawings, and depicting "what's inside my body" (or "inside my house") would stimulate the representation of transparency or X-ray images.

Direct Perception While recalled experience uses mostly the mind and memory and is one kind of motivation, another is direct perception, which combines the mind with the eyes. Long before we are cognitive beings, we are aesthetic beings, responding to the world through touch, taste, smell, sound, and sight. One of the teacher's greatest challenges is to turn students into *noticers* and *questioners*—avid and inquisitive observers of color, structure, and design in their environment. You can contribute to enriching students' lives, perhaps forever, by leading them to become aware of nature's patterns, beauty, and diversity. Children who notice and draw, for example, the unique cornice on a door, the intricate shapes on a violin, the forms of an antique sculpture, the moving reflections in water, the hexagonal cracks in dry mud banks, the blue shadow of a tree on the snow, or the partitioning veins in a leaf or dragonfly's wing may never see again in their old stereotyped way. Students can see and think about what is seen, motivated by the teacher's asking, "What else does it remind you of? What else can you show me about its structure?" Direct contact with and immediate observation of an actually perceived object will elicit detailed, richly expressive responses.

Avoid "draw-anything-you-want" assignments and instead emphasize drawing meaningful things that can be perceived directly. Help your students see the unusual in the usual, and you will help them to become inquisitive visual explorers for the rest of their lives. (See also Chapter 23, Drawing.)

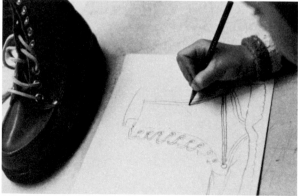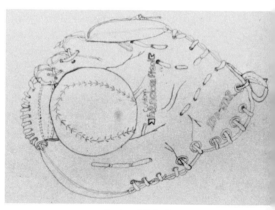

Courtesy of Baiba Kuntz.

Contrasted to recalled memory drawing is the other way to draw: from direct perception. Shown here are favorite everyday objects, jackets, boots, and baseball mitts.

First, draw a still life keenly from direct perception; then, add background objects from memory.

Combining Recalled Experience and Direct Perception A general tendency is to use recalled experiences more often in the primary grades and direct perception from still lifes, nature, and models more often in the later grades; however, both methods effectively supplement each other. Encourage students to add things from their memories or their imaginations or their knowledge to the background of a picture derived from direct perception. Mature artists often blend the two methods. Artists doing a scene from memory may turn to using real objects or photos to acquire supplemental information. And, vice versa: the French painter Marc Chagall did still-life paintings from bouquets of flowers and then, from his memory, added simply drawn human figures to the background.

USING STILL-LIFE MATERIALS AS MOTIVATION

The elementary classroom or the art room can be the child's first, and often most enduring, art lesson. Stimulating, eye-catching, still-life arrangements should be on view for sketching purposes. Students should be encouraged to contribute to the store of found objects and nature's treasures in the classroom. The teacher's organizational ability, however, usually is needed to create a source of beauty and stimulation; what may be a source of exciting motivation to one person may be just a source of clutter to another. Whereas other chapters point out ways that still lifes can be integrated with other school subjects, still lifes can also be arranged solely as sources for artistic, eye-catching motivation to promote students' perceptual skills. Here are some suggestions:

- Drape and pin different kinds of fabric, both plain and patterned, and large, colorful quilts and bedspreads against a cork bulletin board. Pin the material to create bunches of fabric balanced by draped swags.
- Pin up an array of colorful hats against drapery.
- Invite students who are willing to remove their shoes to stack them up for a still-life arrangement—or stack lunchboxes, bookbags, raincoats, or umbrellas.
- In late spring, bring in materials to create a still life about pleasant summer activities: beach balls, floats, thermos, colorful towels, picnic supplies.
- Boots, shoes, shoulder pads, hats, caps, helmets, and gloves can provide appealing organic shapes for drawing, or use thematic arrangements to pique student interest—a Western theme of boots, saddle, and harness.
- Make a still life of colorful desserts, a la Wayne Thibaud.
- Combine sports equipment—skis, skates, bats and balls—with student models dressed to participate in the sport.
- Create a visually interesting understructure for your still lifes by stacking several chairs or stools one atop another, with some sticking out at different angles, and weaving some drapery or beach towels in and out of the openings.

In middle school, students can create a contour drawing of the setup and then suggest that they paint the negative shapes instead of the positive ones. Or have students participate in building a color environment as a motivation for painting in tempera and watercolor. Make it a class "happening," and incorporate colored tissue paper, crepe paper, fabrics, beach towels, ribbons, colored streamers, fans, banners, balloons, posters, party hats, beach balls, and Day-Glo materials. If the arrangement is near a window, incorporate colored cellophane for a stained-glass effect.

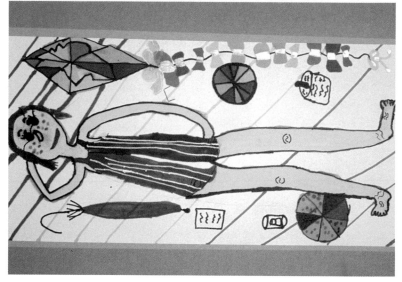

What second-grader in May could resist being motivated by anticipating pleasant summer days, foreshadowed by this beach still life of balls, buckets, shovels, goggles, and Frisbees?

Gather some of the following resources early in the year, since you will find many occasions to use them in still-life arrangements to enrich your art programs:

Fluorescent paint and papers

Fishnetting and glass buoys

Window-display mannequins

Duck decoys

Model cars and airplanes

Plastic-foam wig holders

Wallpaper sample books

Theater costumes and makeup

Tissue paper in assorted colors

Full-length mirror, face mirrors

Sports equipment

Contemporary posters

Old fashioned hats, shoes, and purses

Texture table, felt board

Spotlights for illumination

Bicycles, motorcycles, and helmets

Stained glass

Acetate or acrylic plastic in varied colors

Cowboy boots, hats, jackets, and riding equipment help fourth-grader Jenny Guillaume capture the Wild West.

Watercolor felt-tip markers are richly and beautifully used by student Sarah Dody in this scene of a home set in "purple mountains' majesty."

USING BULLETIN BOARDS AS MOTIVATION

Bulletin boards and displays allow students to appreciate completed projects and whet their interest in future art endeavors. However, they should be changed often, lest they just be taken for granted as if a part of the woodwork. Bulletin boards, videotapes, and reproductions of paintings,

sculpture, prints, and crafts illuminate and intensify the objectives of the lesson. Printed or projected images of art, crafts, and architecture; of design elements in nature and in constructed objects; of creative work by children worldwide; of examples illustrating the technical stages in a project; of people in active work, in sports, and in costume; and of nature's forms and creatures can motivate children. Similarly, books, biographies, and periodicals can lead to a project's richer interpretation. (See Part 3 for an in-depth discussion on incorporating art history, art criticism, and aesthetics.)

Left: An unusual medium: Plaster-of-paris strips over a wire armature will fascinate upper-grade students, eager to depict their interests; shown here, fifth-grader Natalie Bennett's "California Beach or Bust, Surf or Die." **Right:** An unusual medium: Pastels on black paper; here, fourth-grader Rachel Nimmons's autumn still life.

USING ART MEDIA AS MOTIVATION

The materials, tools, and techniques of the various art projects themselves can fire students' efforts. Your demonstration can intrigue and challenge the students. In the primary grades, introduction of new, vibrant colors in oil pastel, tempera paint, watercolor felt-nib markers, crayon, and construction paper elicits enthusiastic response. Colorful tissue paper delights upper-elementary children working in collage when they discover new colors through overlapping. In the upper grades, the teacher can heighten students' interest by introducing them to melted crayon for encaustic painting, discarded tiles for mosaics, waxes and dyes for batiks, plaster for carving sculpture and bas reliefs, glazes for ceramics, and unusual materials for construction projects (see Part 6).

Critics of art-education practices have called attention to the proliferation of media and techniques in school art programs, citing their deleterious effects. Although some of this criticism is justified, it usually is not

Courtesy of Joyce Vroon and Marlee Puskar.

Left: This display of "Stars" paintings by third-graders was made interactive by it being necessary to lift the papers to uncover the celebrity's name.

Right: Putting relevant three-dimensional material—here, egg cartons and straw—in with two-dimensional displays makes an exciting display.

the new materials and techniques *per se* that are to blame. Instead, the fault lies in how the materials are used: *as the sole motivation and purpose of the lesson.* The solution is to teach for qualitative art excellence and incorporate a range of valid lesson objectives. Any teacher can testify that a poorly motivated student, equipped with the newest and most expensive art gimmick, may produce a careless, nonartistic monstrosity, whereas another individual, using only discarded remnants from a scrap pile, may create an object of singular beauty.

TIMING AND PACING MOTIVATION

Timing is of utmost importance. Because most children can absorb and retain only a few ideas at a time, avoid overwhelming them with an avalanche of suggestions. Motivations should be provided in small doses. Rather than swamp the students at one session with a plethora of ideas, introduce, if possible, a new and exciting attention-getter each time the art class meets or when interest flags. Rather than read an entire story for motivation, read just a brief passage or just show the pictures, while talking through the plot. Sense when students have reached a fatigue point. Because students are most receptive at the beginning of a period, this is the best time to introduce new motivations, materials, and techniques; teachers should not interrupt a busily engaged class to point out something that could have been handled at the outset.

USING EXHIBITIONS AS MOTIVATION

Having one's work put on exhibition is motivating! As teachers, we can introduce students to this important aspect of the art world: exhibiting. One principle is that the further away from the classroom, the more selective the exhibit needs to be. In the self-contained classroom, every student's work might be exhibited. Each student might assume ownership of a designated place, identified by the child's large name label. Even high places and very low places can be assigned. In the school hallway, only the most significant works of a child need be exhibited.

At some time during the term, every child should have his or her artwork on exhibit. Some teachers save each student's work in a folder, from which they select pieces for exhibition. Then, they send all of the works home at special times of the year, such as Mother's Day or the winter holiday.

Group Displays A group display can bring together all the artwork of the class's students incorporated into a whole. Two clever ways to show all the students' artwork at one time is to assemble the pieces into a quilt-type design, or to assemble students' individual scenes of a story or history or process into a unified whole. To display group projects, another way is to bring a fairly large, dead tree branch into the classroom. Mount it against a light-colored area of wall or a bulletin board and display on it paper sculpture or papier-mâché birds, butterflies, painted eggs, fish.

Sharing students' artwork with the community and the larger public provides valuable social interaction. Teachers of art can help children to develop such interests, which can provide lifelong leisure satisfaction. Observe the high degree of artistic organization in this elementary-school art bulletin board. It contains paintings of individual sunflowers by Grades 3 and 4 and paintings of sunflower arrangements by Grades 5 and 6.

To avoid displays that look disorganized, align the pieces horizontally and/or vertically. Traditionally, artworks are mounted with a border that is 3- to 4-inches wide on three sides and about $\frac{1}{2}$-inch larger on the bottom. A more elaborate way is to *double-mat* the pieces: first, let a strip of white paper, $\frac{1}{2}$ to 1 inch, show around the artwork's perimeter, and then mount this onto another sheet of colored paper with 3- or 4-inches of colored paper showing.

Permanently installed hanging strips on school hallways have the advantage that any type of fastener can be used in them, yet the disadvantage of permanently establishing the level at which the work is hung, Another solution is permanent display panels of composition board screwed to the hallway walls. Tacks and staples can be freely used in these, although using any flammable boards may violate fire codes. Another alternative, suitable for school open-houses, is a free-standing, lightweight, temporary display, which can be made from a few 4- or 8-foot, foam-core display boards attached together along the edge with duct tape.

Check with school administrators for official policies or preferences before work is to be hung on the walls. Can tape be used, which might pull off the paint during removal, or are tacks or staples preferred, even though they will leave tiny holes? Another consideration is the audience. Hang artwork to favor students' eye level, rather than the eye level of teachers and adult visitors.

Be a good steward of the school's aesthetic order. Avoid disorganized displays. Alternating columns and rows of underwater pictures, origami, and stained-glass pictures make a stunning, varied, and colorful hallway display.

IN THE COMMUNITY

Displaying Student Art

Move out into the community for even greater motivational power. Tell the students that some of their work from a project will be exhibited at a store, branch bank, or a parent's restaurant. Children's art is charming when displayed in the local post office at holiday time. Attention-catching exhibitions can be hung in unusual places, such as in the windows of a vacant store, and murals can be painted on fences or walls.

Although commercial exhibitors usually pay a fee, school art often can be exhibited for free at community events such as fall festivals, county fairs, and arts-and-crafts exhibits. Middle-school students can take part in the local museum's exhibitions by serving as junior docents for children's tours. Hospitals have underwritten the production costs for a full-color calendar of children's artwork advertising the hospital's departments. A newspaper may have an annual design-an-ad contest at Halloween. Exhibiting students' artwork in the community is a way to bring recognition to your school and to your art program's educational effectiveness; most importantly, displays are a way to motivate your students.

Go out into the community for support for your art program. **Left:** Display artwork on each of eight levels of the downtown parking garage stairwell.

Right: Display your students' art in a custom jewelry store; here, the proud owner of Aurum Studio shows her favorite piece.

FOR FURTHER READING

Clements, Robert D. 1978. "Art Teacher Appeals: A Way to Motivate and Discipline." *Art Education* 31: 51–17.

Hamblen, Karen. 1984. "'Don't You Think Some Brighter Colors Would Improve Your Painting?' Or Constructing Questions for Art Dialogues." *Art Education* 37(1): 12–14.

Saunders, Robert J. 1982. "The Lowenfeld Motivation." *Art Education* 11:30.

Zuk, Bill, and Dalton, Robert (eds). *Student Art Exhibitions: New Ideas and Approaches.* Reston, VA: National Art Education Association.

WEB RESOURCES

For a discussion of elementary students' motivation:
  http://www.ericfacility.net/ericdigests/ed370200.html

For motivational techniques:
  http://www.nwrel.org/request/oct00/strategy.html

For helping the unmotivated student:
  http://eric.uoregon.edu/publications/digests/digest092.html
  http://www.proteacher.com/030001.shtml

For theories of motivation:
  http://www.ericdigests.org/1999-1/motivation.html

For articles on motivation:
  http://www.naesp.org/ContentLoad.do?contentID=73

Chapter 5

Creating Objectives and Evaluation Criteria

$\mathcal{L}$earning objectives and assessment are two sides of the same coin: "What do we want the students to learn?" and "Have they learned the concepts or had the experience that we intended?" The assessment of a student's art learning obviously involves much more than just written tests. It may include:

- Examining artworks both in progress and after completion and talking with the student about those assessments

- Ongoing monitoring of the learner's progress, which might include examining a portfolio of the student's projects
- Assessing learning in art criticism, art history, and aesthetics through informal journals, in-class written assignments and tests, and contributions in class discussions
- Engaging students in verbal and written expression concerning the meaning they attribute to their artwork.

Courtesy of Baiba Kuntz.

Students, unaware, were caught by the teacher's camera as they sat and assessed a wall display of their classmates' in-process profile portraits. This kind of spontaneous assessment, peers with peers, is very effective. This photo also shows how important it is, for assessment, that teachers make attractive displays of student work in process.

Courtesy of Joyce Vroon.

In-process evaluation helps students to assess if they have attained their goals. Here, sixth-grader Zibby Stokes deliberates on her next course of action for her Celebrity Collage Sculpture.

THE NEED FOR OPEN OBJECTIVES AND EVALUATION CRITERIA

Today, many school systems require clearly stated, unambiguous, sequential educational objectives along with clearly spelled-out standards for assessment. The National Art Education Association has developed standards for art education (printed on the inside front cover of this book) and certainly these standards set a baseline for establishing objectives for any school art program. As teachers of art—a personal, poetic subject filled with wonder and uncertainty—we also must value that which is open, indeterminant, and imaginative. Art teachers can address the concerns of the school and remain true to the foundations of art by developing educational objectives that value demonstration of poetic interpretation, creative brainstorming, or the ability to adapt to the unexpected.

Much quality art production occurs during what appears to be nondirectional play—"water-gazing," if you will. It appears that the artist is just "fiddling around"—that the objective is unclear even to the creator. A teacher of art must allow for this. Art education has been criticized for trying to force students into a curriculum with predetermined contents and goals. But encouragement in art class can and should be given for the irrational and the quirky. Where else will the mysterious, the subversive, and the unexpected—elements necessary for our society's continuing renewal—be nurtured?

Rich educational play should not be confused with mindlessly repeating stereotypical images appropriated from popular culture. Children often receive considerable praise from their peers (and boosts to their self-esteem) for their ability to draw popular television characters, but the endless repetition of these characters is not creative expression. You should be alert to maintaining play as an open arena of exploration and discovery.

From Robert Clements and Lawrence Stueck, "Earthworks: A Two-Hundred Ton Art Media," *Art Education, July 1983.*

Artistic activity can occur in a state of openness, when the objective is unclear even to the creator. Allow for meditation. A mound of loose clay can provide an exciting medium for the unplanned, the unexpected, and that which is full of wonder.

THE NEED FOR DEFINED OBJECTIVES AND EVALUATION CRITERIA

Although art teachers need to value spontaneous creativity, defined objectives are also important, both to meet standards and to provide clarity for assessing student performance. Educators emphasize the importance of *expectancy*—the need to inform learners in advance about the objectives of any task they are asked to perform. This idea is also referred to as *backward design* of curriculum: If you begin planning a lesson by articulating what students will be able to do at the end, you can ensure that all the steps in the lesson-planning build towards these learning outcomes. Thus, objectives and assessment become part of a single learning and teaching process.

GOALS, OBJECTIVES, AND OUTCOMES

Writing lesson plans in terms of objectives is a skill required in many teacher-education programs and even, in an increasing number of states, to receive teacher certification. Two-thirds of our nation's school districts and their elementary schools have art-curriculum guides that specify instructional goals and student outcomes. Over a third of elementary-level art programs use student textbooks that include instructional objectives.

State or local systems often set broad goals. Increasingly, these are based on national guidelines that have been recommended for *standards-based* art instruction, developed by the Consortium of National Arts Education Associations. Individual teachers must then develop specific

---

IN THE CLASSROOM

Giving Appropriate Feedback

Your feedback can identify and reinforce imagination and poetic interpretation: "Makeela's picture has a sense of mystery in it—the feeling that we can't quite tell what is going to happen when the figures in the picture meet." Children learn about art through continually coming back to main concepts in a holistic, contextually sensitive way. Valuing imagination can provide powerful opportunities for encouraging creativity in other areas. For example, all the children in Makeela's classroom could be invited to imagine what happens next and to write about it—transforming art into language arts.

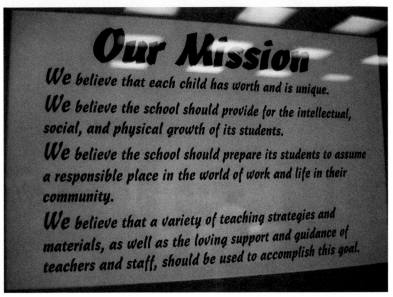

Courtesy of Robert Clements.

The school's objectives are posted in the hallway in a Mission Statement.

Courtesy of Joyce Vroon.

The general goal was to increase perceptual skill and drawing skill. The specific objective was that students depict the forms, folds, and patterns of three-dimensional objects, specifically in the old dolls, as seen in fifth-grader Erica Silverstein's drawing.

Courtesy of Joyce Vroon.

One goal was that the students appreciate the art of modern masters. An objective was that fourth-graders apply Matisse's concepts of shape and pattern to their own art making. Matisse's use of pattern was carried on in Lindsay Garfield's patterned wallpaper, tablecloth, and curtains setting off the distant fishbowl scene.

objectives that will allow students to achieve those goals. (Objectives are always clear, identifiable behaviors that a teacher can observe a student demonstrate.) For example, a system-mandated goal might be: "Students will appreciate the art of diverse cultures." But "to appreciate" is not an observable behavior. A specific objective derived from this goal might be: "Students will be able to differentiate photos of pre-Columbian, Mississippian Native-American, and Greek Cycladic sculptures." (Bloom's *Taxonomy of Educational Objectives* continues to be an excellent guide for defining clear, meaningful objectives.)

Whether you begin from national standards or from school system goals, you must carefully examine each goal and determine the specific outcomes that you will accept as evidence of mastery, based on your own skills, interests, and beliefs.

Some educators believe that art learning has at its core achievements of a subtle, cerebral, inner, intangible, even spiritual nature, and that art learning defies behavioral measurement. Their assessment methods emphasize looking and talking with students about their artworks and portfolios,

Stress only a few objectives each lesson. During the first lesson in this Japanese classroom, line was used to delineate every part of the bicycle. Filling the picture plane also was stressed. Later lessons focused on using color to set off the bicycle from its background.

Courtesy of Barbara Thomas.

As you teach, you will acquire the insight to know what is within reach of each class.

and reading student journals. No matter how quantitative or qualitative the assessment methods, however, educational objectives can always be employed. For example, students may be asked to cite visual evidence in their artwork to justify how they created personal meaning. If a student claims to have created a scary picture, how many visual examples can the student cite in the work that support the claim of *scary*? What is the quality of line? What is the quality of color? What are the expressive features?

The sensitive art teacher can often see evidence of student imagination by observing students working or in their artworks themselves. While this experience is visual and nonlinguistic, students can be invited to write about this experience—sometimes with surprisingly powerful results. As a result, art teachers are sometimes able to engage underachieving students in impressively fluent written expression—and reach students who have been marginalized in other academic coursework.

ART OBJECTIVES AND ASSESSMENT

Just as there are many ways to teach, there are many different ways to evaluate lessons; teachers choose to emphasize objectives that reflect their personal values about art and education, their teaching style, and the ages, ability levels, and learning styles of their students. Teaching students with differing ability levels and learning modes, as well as those with developmental disabilities, will require that you emphasize different objectives. As

Courtesy of Robert Clements.

A student evaluates his and his peers' photographs.

you teach, you will acquire the insight to know what specific skills are within the general grasp of a given class of students, and you can customize the general objectives to address special needs. By using several categories of objectives, you will create powerful motivations that will sustain the learning activity of all your students.

To keep *art* itself the central focus, we will look at five types of art objectives:

- Art production
- Artistic perception
- Art criticism
- Aesthetics
- Art history

Remember that these categories are not totally separate entities. Instead, like ingredients in a well-cooked stew, they blend.

Objectives and Evaluation of Art Production As art teachers, we must teach first about art. In too many instances, we find art teachers apologizing for making suggestions to children, initiating projects, and emphasizing art fundamentals. Let the truth be known! Where promising,

Courtesy of David W. Hodge.

Here, in this work by an intermediate-elementary-grade student, the human figure is interpreted through crayon, collage, and paint.

Courtesy of Beverly Barksdale Mallon.

Too many directions all at one time can confuse students—better to give a few directions in one period. The motivation for this first-grade project, covering four 35-minute periods, was "If I were a king or queen." The first period the students drew in pencil their figures with heads, torsos, arms, and legs, to fill the picture space. The second period they watercolored their figures' clothes and background and foreground objects. The third period they used marker for additional details in the background, figures, and foreground. The fourth period they enriched their pictures, with sequins and glitter for jewels, fireworks, and patterns in clothing. Following this long project, they did an immediate gratification project.

sequential, imaginative, and qualitative elementary- and middle-school art programs exist, the classroom or special art teacher is on the job organizing, coaching, motivating, questioning, demonstrating, evaluating, approving, and advising—in other words, teaching. The importance of actively helping students learn to apply art concepts in their creation of art cannot be overemphasized.

Be Specific Objectives like "Students will draw the still life" or "Students will use colors with good design" are too vague to allow appropriate assessment. More useful objectives would be "Students will draw the

Courtesy of David W. Hodge.

Instructional objectives to break up the space into small areas, to leave the space of the chalk line unpainted between forms, and to imaginatively use colors helped the sixth-grader in this tempera resist painting with India ink to create this "Bouquet with Owl."

Courtesy of David W. Hodge.

Frank Wachowiak urged students to delve deeply into carrying out the lesson's objectives.

Courtesy of Barbara Thomas.

This third-grade boy's gesture appears to indicate that he believes he has met the criteria of dividing the space.

table plane, suggesting depth by overlapping and creating avenues in depth," or "Students will show how at least seven objects and forms overlap," or "Students will compose the design so at least three of the objects go off the edges"—tasks that are readily evaluated.

Stay Focused In carrying out a project, stress only a few art objectives each class period. Do not confuse students with too many directions at once. In a drawing project, for example, emphasize the quality of line and the full use of the picture plane during the first session. During the second session, guide the students in identifying and evaluating the variety of shapes and overlapping planes in their drawing. During the third session, challenge the students to enrich their drawings with detail, texture, and pattern.

Encourage Depth Rather Than Range Encouraging students to delve deeply into art making results in their personal investment in the image they have created. They have put something of themselves into it; they have cared about the creation of this object. Personal expression, connectiveness, and caring are powerful emotions that are not normally associated with the experience of school. Students may not even recognize they are engaged in these dimensions of experience unless you draw attention to it through sensitive assessment.

Objectives and Assessment of Artistic Perception Artistic perception helps students identify elements of beauty and interest in their daily lives. If you can bring children to notice something they have never noticed before, to see with their inner eye, you will have started them on an endless, exciting, and rewarding journey toward a thousand discoveries. Three sources for perceptual objectives are the classroom, the artworks, and the students' daily life experiences.

The Classroom Examples of perceptual objectives based on what can be seen in the classroom are: "The student will identify at least three triangular shapes in the classroom" or "The student will describe analogous color schemes from among the colors seen in classmates' shirts."

Artworks An example of a perceptual objective based on what can be seen in the artworks presented and created is: "From the artwork of a group of classmates, the student will be able to point out instances demon-

strating (1) exaggeration and (2) swinging design." (Note that a perception objective about artworks becomes the same as a type of art criticism objective.)

Daily Life Experiences Outside the Classroom Perceptual objectives also can be based on what the students have seen outside the classroom. ("The students will be able to recall the order of the colors in a rainbow." "The students will be able to describe and depict the design of insects' homes that they have seen." "Students will identify the use of complementary and contrasting colors in sports teams' logos.")

All three sources of observation are rich in potential for developing students' metaphorical skills. The ability to use metaphor in both vision and language is the very essence of thinking. Art learning is replete with opportunities for visual observation and association, and the art lesson often provides more possibilities to teach metaphor than any other kind of learning.

IN THE CLASSROOM

Assessing Artistic Perception

Artistic perception can be evaluated through class discussion, or through individual testing. Here is an interesting questionnaire, with actual student responses, to assess perceptual sophistication:

A Perceptual Exercise

If you were to describe these things to a person without sight, what words would you use?

1. The intricate pattern of a spider's web
   like squares

2. Cracked shapes in mudflats and ice
   like hexagons

3. The blue shadows on fallen snow
   never saw

4. The variety of grain pattern in wood
   like creepy lines

5. The varied textures and patterns of tree bark
   bumpy

6. The shadows of tree branches on building walls
   scary

7. The lines and patterns of bridge girders and cables
   beams

8. The pattern in leaf veins
   lines

9. The pattern in insect wings
   beautiful

10. The pattern of frost on a windowpane
    never saw

11. The changing formations of clouds
    like T. rex dinosaurs

12. The dew on early morning spiderwebs
    like gumdrops

13. The undulation of reflections in water
    zigzag lines

14. The moody, misty colors of a foggy or rainy day
    foggy lines

15. The flashing colors of stoplights, neon signs, and beacons in the rain
    bullets

16. The tracks of animals in the snow
    holes

17. Peeling paint on old wood and metal
    peeling bark

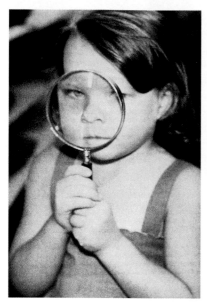

Left: *Courtesy of Athens Montessori School.* Right: *Courtesy of Robert Clements.*

Look closely to see. See and think with the eyes of children.

Objectives and Assessment of Art Criticism We talk about general objectives in art criticism in Chapter 22, but we will look at specific objectives here. One goal in art criticism is to ensure that students use the language of art appropriately. To evaluate an art criticism objective focusing on a single art element—for example, depth—an objective might be: "Using classmates' artworks, describe three ways to indicate that an object appears to go back in space." Students might respond, while looking at the Turkish student's artwork shown on page 15 as an example: "1. The figures

---

IN THE CLASSROOM

Encouraging Critical Skills
Using the sculpture that appears on page 51 you could use the following questions, which can be posed to individual students for written or verbal responses, or to the class as a whole.

Dropped Bowl with Scattered Slices and Peels by Claes Oldenburg and Coosje van Bruggen, 12 × 50 × 50 feet, 1989, Miami, Florida

Describe this artwork: What colors are used? How are shapes used? How do you think it was made? What does it mean? Why do you think it is in Miami?

---

in front are bigger; 2. The figures in front overlap; and 3. The figures in back are up higher on the page."

Assessment of learning can be facilitated by each student taking notes on the points raised, using two sides of a vertically folded sheet of paper, labeled, "FOR" and "AGAINST."

FOR	AGAINST
good	(dumb) ugly
nice	
cute	sTupid
preTTy	makes iT look bad
figurisTic	
makes someThing beTTer	junky

Expertise in art criticism can also be assessed by asking students to identify how art impacts feeling. A sample objective might be "Students will describe how [an artwork] uses artistic devices to show different kinds of feelings." Responses might include that the dark lines around a figure's eyes make him look tough, or that the lighter lines in another picture support a gentler, kinder feeling. Students should always be challenged to identify the visual evidence in the artwork that supports their claim; saying that Jose's work is sad or that Kimberly's work is pretty is not enough. Students need to be able to identify specific visual details, *qualities* of art, that support their emotional response. You may find that students change their minds when they explore a work in detail. Picasso's *Guernica* may seem, on first glance, to be a happy painting, but sensitive discussion in which students are asked to look for visual evidence will bring most viewers to the conclusion that the painting is tragic.

Objectives and Assessment in Aesthetics Aesthetics involves ideas of beauty or the nature of art (see Chapter 22). This book treats aesthetics as distinct from art criticism—as rooted more in ideas and less in art objects. Learning about aesthetics can best be evaluated through class discussion about the nature of art and is difficult to encapsulate in specific objectives. You may, however, want to define behaviors like: "Students will

Dropped Bowl with Scattered Slices and Peels, 1989, Claes Oldenburg and Coosje van Bruggen, Art in Public Places Program, Miami, FL.

This picture in Chapter 1 began this book. Now, in art criticism, students should demonstrate their knowledge of art by describing an artwork.

Debating Art

Encourage students to debate about art. For example, show them a newspaper clipping about a piece of public art sculpture with the headline, "Sculpture Detracts, Says Neighborhood." Ask them for their own reactions, based on a picture of the work, and ask them to explain why others might disagree with them. Ask older students to read about the reaction of French critics to the first display of Impressionism. How might they have reacted? Why? Or ask students to react to the design of a public park or new building, to graffiti on walls, or to the work of environmental artists like Andy Goldsworthy or Christo, whose art has no permanence but exists only temporarily. How might prevailing cultural norms influence our perception of what is "art"?

discuss varying ideas of what makes a good picture," "Students will debate whether art that does not realistically represent objects and figures can be considered good art," "Students will debate whether ugly subject matter can make good art."

While there is often no one right answer to such questions, the teacher can nevertheless assess ability from the quality of the discourse and the sophistication of the language, either in whole-class discussions or in small groups.

Objectives and Assessment of Art History Learning Lower-level art history objectives lend themselves to evaluation by paper-and-pencil tests. You might, for example, hold up a series of reproductions (or show slides) and ask students to identify the artist, the style or historic period, or the historic event represented from a list of choices written on the board. Sample objectives include the following:

- "In class discussion, working in pairs or small groups, or on individual tests, students will identify different art styles." To test for this skill, you might ask: "As I display six pictures, hold up fingers to show me the piece's style: one for medieval, two for Persian, three for Impressionism, four for Realism, and five for twentieth-century abstraction."
- "Students will describe how and why a theme, for example, 'City Life,' has been shown differently throughout several centuries." To test for this skill, you might ask: "Comparing the mysterious Peruvian Nazca lines in Peru to Robert Smithson's Spiral Jetty (1970), how do you think the cultures might differ?"
- "From examples of Persian and medieval art, students will analyze and apply the concept of overlapping to their own artwork." To test for this

Courtesy of Joyce Vroon.

Aesthetics concerns ideas of beauty and the nature of art. Fifty years ago there was much debate about whether splatters, such as those used in Jackson Pollock's paintings, could be considered art. Abstract expressionism espoused the idea that accidental effects enhance an artwork. Here, a student and artwork illustrate a way to make this awareness real. If a brave teacher wishes to do this activity, it requires careful supervision, outside, with water-based paints, and students wearing old clothes.

skill, you might ask: "After studying the Persian and medieval art examples, make a thumbnail sketch below showing how overlapping occurred in those pictures."

Courtesy of Gwenda Malnati.

From a study of Van Gogh's sunflowers, primary student Dalton Tyler drew in pencil and then used sponges to paint these sunflowers.

Students should also be able to locate and use information to write a report. To collect material, the student can use the resources at a learning center in the classroom, in the library, or on the Web. Such research can be a fertile prompt for students' art making. From the nearly inexhaustible library of art images available on the Internet, students can download images of their own favorite artworks, and even manipulate these images on the computer. Printouts can provide images to apply to student collages, and various skills can be assessed by asking for the knowledge of works they have appropriated and their justifications for changing the image.

REPORTING ART PROGRESS TO PARENTS

Most likely your school system will have a standardized report card you are to use. Reporting of students' art progress varies from school to school, from primary and intermediate through upper elementary to the middle school grades. In early grades, students often receive letter evaluations:

S for satisfactory, N for needs improvement, I for improving, or U for unsatisfactory, for example. By middle school, most systems use an A, B, C, D, F letter-grade system. Some schools employ separate evaluations for behavior and subject mastery.

When letter or numerical grades for art are given, teachers often take into account the students' classroom working habits and behavior as a factor in their evaluation. Forewarn students that their seriousness of effort, behavior, and conduct will affect their grades, because in almost every instance, the student's prudent use of class time will result in higher-quality work. For reporting to parents, it is helpful to list the main goals of the program, as on the report below (although your school may mandate a standard reporting form by the art, music, and physical education teachers).

Since an elementary-school art specialist teacher may work with anywhere from three hundred to a thousand students, reporting needs to be streamlined so that it is both fair and an accomplishable task. Art specialists may find it helpful to photocopy a progress report, like the one that follows, that describes the goals and abilities assessed, along with multiple-choice checks (for satisfactory or needs improvement) for evaluating individual achievement and space for individual comments.

The best indication to parents of what their children are accomplishing is to see examples of actual work, ideally with comments from the teacher attached. You may want to send home student artwork throughout the year, or a portfolio of art at the end of the year that shows progress. Also include any writing that was done in art class in connection with the artwork. A teacher-prepared sheet accompanying the return of the work describing the art program and the unit objectives and providing other information about upcoming art units and exhibitions is particularly helpful to parents.

A Very Simple Art Progress Report

Ability	Satisfactory	Needs Improvement
Drawing ability		
Design ability (ability to use repetition and variation of shapes, lines, colors, patterns, and textures)		
Interest and ability in looking at and talking about art and art ideas		
Enjoyment of a positive experience in class		
Seriousness of effort		

A More Elaborate Art Progress Report

Satisfactory	Exceptional	Needs Improvement	
			Discovery (seeing possibilities, finding alternatives)
			Pursuit (taking initiative, staying on task, developing works over time)
			Perception (visualizing, showing attention to details)
			Expressing feelings and communicating though arts media (emotions shown in art and captions, using symbols)
			Self- and social awareness (tapping into personal feelings, sharing discoveries, tolerating frustration, cooperating, negotiating, appreciating others' contributions)
			Skill use (muscle coordination, demonstrating a sense of standards)
			Creativity (responding flexibly to different situations, crossing artistic domains)
			Analysis (describing to others what is seen, imagined or done, showing an interest in using arts vocabulary, giving opinions)
			Critique (talking about their own works and those of peers, accepting and incorporating suggestions, using others' works for inspiration)

IN THE CLASSROOM

A Sample Progress Report

January–May Art Report, Fourth Grade

In April of this year in art, the fourth-graders studied and drew insects, using newly emerged real insects and photos. Notice particularly the variety of pattern and texture used in the details in wings, mandibles, and legs. Thanks, parents, for your contribution of insects and insect collections to draw! The project was done using analogous colors in a crayon resist technique, and the project accompanies this report.

Our study of repetition in pattern and texture was preceded in March with the built-up bas-relief bracelets covered in aluminum foil and antiqued, which were sent home in time for Mother's Day.

In January, in connection with a social studies unit on nineteenth-century America, we did a unit on still-life drawing of Americana agricultural equipment and antiques using markers for direct line observation of interior and outside edges and emphasizing the depictions of overlapping forms to give depth. These pictures have been on display in the school and at the U.S. Department of Agriculture Building on Broad Street. Following up on this, in February we studied cultural history and art history, particularly of the Industrial Revolution.

Next fall we will begin by studying architecture and community planning, so on your travels this summer, keep an eye out for interesting buildings and architectural features. For this project we need boxes, so please save shoe boxes, and cereal boxes, and any other smaller boxes.

Eight pieces of fourth-grade art will be on display at the new El Dorado Restaurant during June. Hope you saw the article on our November dinosaur project in the *Daily News,* January 14, section B, page 12.

If you are interested, the Recreation Department is having Art Camp this summer (call 489–1221). This summer, draw with your child and do fun art activities. Next fall, I'd like to see what you did!

Sue Varanco, art teacher,
West Adams Elementary School
e-mail: varancos@brunswick.k12.TX.US
School assignments phone number 548-0033, box 1444.

Courtesy of Baiba Kuntz.

To achieve a chromatic unity, the color scheme is limited to analogous colors, yellow through green. What concentration the fifth-grade girl displays as she colors her sunflowers! She is using oil pastel on black construction paper. A preliminary sketch was made in silver.

SCHOOL EXHIBITIONS AS ASSESSMENT TOOLS

Besides enlivening the school, exhibitions of student artwork are great opportunities to explain the learning that students have accomplished in the art classroom. With the display, always include an explanation that explains the artistic problem and draws specific attention to the different ways that students solved it. Parents, principals, and other teachers often are surprised to discover the depth of learning that students are engaged in during art instruction. Always use exhibitions in the school, at the board of education, or in public buildings around town as an opportunity to toot your own horn on student learning.

FORMATIVE AND SUMMATIVE EVALUATION

Summative evaluation summarizes both the students' learning and the teacher's effectiveness. It is differentiated from formative assessment used to

Courtesy of Baiba Kuntz.

Top left: Sixth-grade student Ali Schier did this multiperiod marker drawing with no initial pencil drawing, from a posed model; she captured the turning on the hat's every straw strand and the myriad patterned and folded cloth designs. **Top right:** Laura Towbin added a background, envisioning the sophisticated individual a century later sitting on a big-city high-rise balcony. **Bottom:** The teacher laminated the drawings to prevent the marker color from fading. Nine 20- × 40-inch frames were grouped in this four-way hallway intersection to create a wonderful display.

help the student in the process of making the artwork. Summative evaluation is used to diagnose, to revise curricula, and to determine if objectives have been met. Usually it is done at the end of the academic year, or when artwork portfolios are returned. Save the students' work in portfolios, and periodically go over them to determine if your goals are being met. Through photos and video, document three-dimensional work and exciting art events. Older students might keep journals to document what they are learning. Ask the students to help you, either through questionnaires or class discussion, to determine whether the program is leading students to understand art, whether the students are finding satisfaction in the process, and whether the language the students use in discussing aesthetics and writing about art is becoming more advanced.

Evaluating Our Year in Art This questionnaire can be helpful in looking back at the art program for the year. It should be accompanied by a list of projects accomplished.

- Did you learn any new words or art ideas this year? What?
- What was good about art this year?
- What was not so good about it this year?
- If anything did not work out for you, how would you handle it in the future?
- What did you learn this year about how to make art?
- Did we do anything in art that helped you to learn about science or social studies or other subjects? What?
- How is art different from other subjects?
- How could the teacher make art class better and be better to the students?
- What could the other kids do to make art class better?
- When you are older, how will you use anything you did in art this year?
- How would you change what we did this year?
- Do you have any ideas about how we could make art more real and not just like school?
- Do you have any ideas for ways to make art class better?
- How did you like it when the class talked about art and thought together about art?
- Outside of school and on your own, did you do any things that were like art? What? Did you do it by yourself or with someone?
- Outside of school, did you talk with anybody about art ideas? What was the discussion about?
- Did anything good about art happen in the community?
- Why do you think students should study art in school?
- From the following list of what we did in art this year, mark those activities that you really liked, or from which you learned a lot. Write if there was anything about the activity that made it especially good.

Courtesy of Baiba Kuntz. Students Megan Munitz, Joel Savitzsky, Rana Brizgys.

Sixth-grade students enjoyed the novel experience of creating a collage picture out of colored felt. First, students looked at undersea pictures; then, with no drawing ahead of time, they directly cut the fish out of the felt and decorated it, using white glue to attach pieces. They carefully selected a 22- × 24-inch background color, which the teacher glued to a piece of cardboard with rubber cement (a process requiring skill and speed). Then students made and added other elements and unique border designs, gluing them down with white glue.

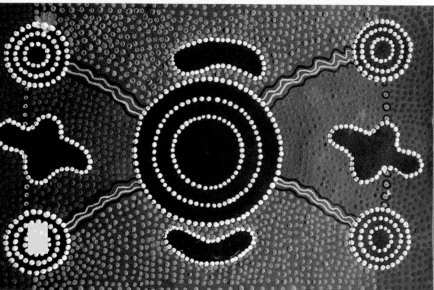

Courtesy of Dahria McClelland.

Fifth-graders' Australian art designs.

SELF-ASSESSMENT

You may also want to reflect on your own skills, strengths, and weaknesses as a teacher. Setting up a video camera in the rear of the classroom to make a recording of your own teaching is effective for achieving a deeper understanding of your personal practice. Such a tape can help you identify and correct habits that diminish your effectiveness and help you build even more upon your positive traits.

FOR FURTHER READING

Armstrong, Carmen. 1994. *Designing Assessment in Art.* Reston, VA: NAEA.

Bloom, Benjamin S. 1984. *Taxonomy of Educational Objectives: The Classification of Educational Goals.* New York: Longman.

Clements, Robert D. 1975. "Instructional Objectives or Objectionable Instructions." *Journal of Aesthetic Education* 10:107–118.

Consortium of National Arts Education Associations. 1994. *National Standards for Arts Education.* Reston, VA: Music Educators National Conference.

Csikszentmihalyi, M. 1975. "Play and Intrinsic Rewards." *Journal of Humanistic Psychology* 15(3): 41–63.

Davis, Don Jack. 1990. *Behavioral Emphasis in Art Education.* Reston, VA: NAEA.

Ewens, Thomas. 1990. "On Discipline: Its Roots in Wonder." *Art Education* 43(1): 6–11.

Ewens, Thomas. 1994. "Rethinking the Question of Quality in Art." *Arts Education Policy Review* 96(2): 2–15.

Greene, M. 1995. *Releasing the Imagination: Essays on Education, the Arts, and Social Change.* San Francisco: Jossey-Bass Publishers.

Greene, Maxine. 1987. "Creating, Experiencing, Sensemaking: Art Worlds in Schools." *Journal of Aesthetic Education* 21(4): 22.

Greene, Maxine. 1994. "The Arts and National Standards." *Educational Forum* 58(4): 391–400.

Gruber, Donald D., and Hobbs, Jack A. 2002. "Historical Analysis of Assessment in Art Education." *Art Education* 55(6): 12–17.

Mager, Robert F. 1975. *Preparing Instructional Objectives.* Belmont, CA: Fearon.

National Art Education Association. *Position Paper: The Essentials of a Quality School Art Program.* Reston, VA: NAEA.

Rollins, Jeanne. 1994. *The National Visual Art Standards.* Reston, VA: National Art Education Association.

Siegesmund, R. 1999. "Reasoned Perception: Aesthetic Knowing in Pegagogy and Learning." *Arts and Learning Research* 15(1): 35–51.

Walker, Sydney. 2004. "Understanding the Artmaking Process: Reflective Practice." *Art Education* 57(3): 6–12.

WEB RESOURCES

An assessment guide by Marvin Bartel to assess students' art criticism, art history, and aesthetics discussion and writing is at:

http://www.goshen.edu/art/ed/rubric3.html

Part 3

Integrating Art into the Classroom

$\mathcal{A}$ngelica Kauffmann's 1794 *Self-Portrait Hesitating Between the Arts of Music and Painting* shows a young woman whose body seems to want to go in one direction and her head in another. We often have to make choices among interests, subject matters—even friends. Students might use this picture as a motivation for their depiction of a dilemma in choices of interests to pursue.

Oil on canvas, 58- × 86-inches. Reproduced by permission of the Winn Family and the National Trust. This painting hangs in the Nostrell Priory, Yorkshire, England.

*M*ost art has content—that is, it is about something. Perhaps it is about a flower garden filled with buzzing insects, or an early culture's celebrations, or us in our community. It can be about geometric designs or visual fields, or about a visual response to music. Art often has rapprochement with fields such as science, social studies, reading and math, as well as the other arts. It is often enriched by that relationship. Can anyone think of art that has no content?

Making the case that art should be part of the common curriculum designed for future nonspecialist citizens, the National Art Education Association (NAEA) recommends one-hundred minutes of art class time each week in the elementary school, with art taught as a subject in itself. Arts-based goals are essential in arts education. But art is also a critical element in the general classroom.

Unfortunately, the relationship between art and other disciplines is not always a happy marriage. Because some school systems lack understanding about art learning and consider it less important than the "academic" disciplines, frictions can occur, and teachers can be reluctant to correlate art with the other subjects they teach. On the other hand, art teachers can be reluctant to devote some of their often limited teaching time to "non-art" subject matter.

But the truth is, teaching content through art can only make that content more accessible and more meaningful. When art considerations are serious and fused to the theme, significant art can result—and so can significant learning about traditional academic subject matter. The following chapters explore that synergy.

Chapter 6

Integration in the Three Domains: Cognitive, Affective, and Psychomotor

*B*efore turning our attention to art education's relationship to various academic subjects, let us first consider a simpler way to consider education: in the affective, the cognitive, and the psychomotor domains. These domains comprise the three major categories of a system titled Bloom's *Taxonomy of Educational Objectives* (1954)—an approach to learning that is widely used in many schools that require written lesson plans. Briefly, the cognitive domain deals with the factual information that students learn in school, as well as with higher-level skills such as analysis and synthesis. The affective domain deals with the role that the emotions play in learning. The psychomotor domain deals with how the movement of the body is involved in learning.

One of the main virtues of the Bloom system is that it calls attention to the affective and psychomotor domains, which tend to be neglected in schools. The system also emphasizes higher-order thinking, which is less amenable to simple measurement and is more like the thinking done in art. The three domains cut across the disciplines. Because the fusion, like many experiences we encounter in "real" life, combines knowledge, body movement, and emotions, fusing all three into any one subject or lesson makes the learning in that subject very powerful. To ignore two of the three areas may make what remains "just boring facts," "just jumpin' around," or "just a bunch of talk about our feelings."

Each domain is considered to have several levels, or stages, within it, ranging from basic to advanced. For example, in the affective domain the levels are, from lowest to highest, as follows: receiving or willingness to

Courtesy of Lawrence Stueck.

Fourth-grade children converted their classroom into a model city. They designed and constructed their own buildings: a bank, court, post office, newspaper building, etc. Subjects were taught through an integrated curriculum.

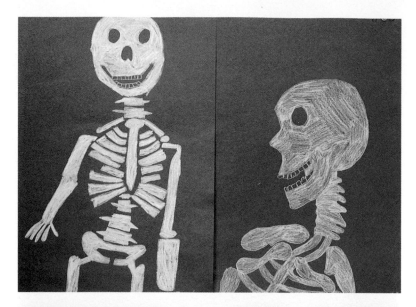

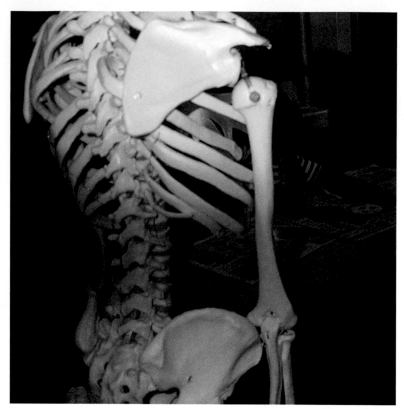

Cognitive learning is evident as fourth-graders analyzed the skeleton's three-dimensional structure and synthesized this knowledge into their two-dimensional renderings. Language arts integration occurred when the art teacher featured the celebration of Dias de las Muertos in the hallway display.

attend, awareness, responding or willingness to participate actively, valuing, and organizing values. When education critics say that too many "low-level objectives" and not enough "high-level objectives" are used, they are referring to Bloom's Taxonomy.

We begin by examining the cognitive domain.

THE COGNITIVE DOMAIN

Much of schooling centers upon cognitive objectives. Indeed, some teachers of art would say too much, particularly of the lower-level skill of know-ing, as evidenced through rote memorizing, identifying, and matching. However, most educators also feel that too little emphasis is spent on the higher cognitive levels, such as applying knowledge to new situations, ana-lyzing, synthesizing, and evaluating. Teachers are often at a loss as to how to evaluate such higher-level thinking. Art activities offer wonderful oppor-tunities for demonstrating application of the higher-level skills. Numerous examples of such opportunities will be given in the following chapters dealing with art's relation to cognitive objectives in literacy, math, social studies, science, and the related arts. Cognitive objectives within the field of art—especially in art history, art criticism, perception, and aesthetics—will be discussed in Part 5.

Kids can leap like frogs. Note the kids in different poses: side view, back view, seated. Psychomotor reenactment of catching frogs may have preceded the making of this delightful watercolor painting. One color, blue, predominates. Four tints and shades of green, from blue to yellow, are used for the carefully observed leaves and frogs.

The teacher models how the tree branches move in the wind.

The teacher leads the Hokey Pokey.

THE PSYCHOMOTOR DOMAIN AND MULTISENSORY AREA

Some educators and many students believe that children spend too much elementary school time sitting at desks or tables. By doing so, they miss out on opportunities to learn through their bodies. Moving our bodies and using our other senses can stimulate learning in all subjects, including art production and art criticism activities. For example, a lesson plan objective might be as follows: "Students will be able to take the exact pose and facial expression of Van Gogh's Dr. Gachet, and they will tell the class something that he might be thinking about Vincent."

Psychomotor approaches also can be used for aesthetic experiences in and of themselves. Acting out a picture is one way in which kinesthetic awareness can trigger artistic awareness. For example, one objective is that, by using their bodies, students will be able to stimulate awareness of what they have perceived. For example, they might be given the following instruction: "Show with your body how cats clean their bodies. How can we show this tongue licking the paw in our drawing?"

The Bloom Taxonomy lists these psychomotor stages:

1. perception,
2. readiness to act,
3. ability to copy an instructor,

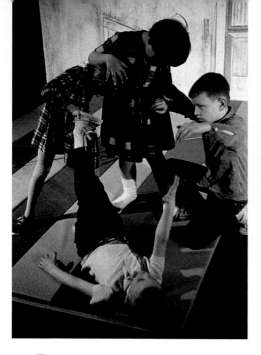

Far Left: *Courtesy of David W. Hodge.* Middle: *Courtesy of Beverly Barksdale Mallon.* Far Right: *Courtesy of Robert Clements.*

Psychomotor acting out of the motions before beginning the drawing enhances the children's kinesthetic knowledge. ***Far Left:*** Students "freeze" into a living sculpture, for classmates to draw. ***Middle:*** Arms are flung high, and legs leap into the air in these two collages of a New Year's Eve celebration, which used decorative foil papers and confetti from the school's holiday giftwrap sale samplers. ***Far Right:*** Energetic boys dance to the music with marimbas while decorating the large paper with paint on their feet.

4. and 5. ability to carry out simple, and then complex, movement patterns with confidence,
6. ability to modify and adapt established patterns to meet special situations, and
7. ability to create new movement patterns.

Can you conceive how these stages relate to art teaching?

Psychomotor exercises are used in many progressive children's programs at museums to arouse interest in artworks. They have children respond nonverbally to the artworks, using their bodies and creative movement. Using an art reproduction, you can use many of these same ideas in your classroom:

- Using your imagination, place yourself in the picture. Move the way the people shown are moving.
- With a friend, act out a dramatic skit showing what the subjects are saying and doing.
- Show what you see through sounds, impromptu drama, human sculpture, and free movement.
- Take the exact pose and facial expression of the subject, and tell what you are thinking.

- Re-create the sounds you think you might hear, using your voice and hands for drumming.
- Imagine the smells that are in the air.
- With your friend, go on a "treasure hunt" around a room in the museum to find the pictures that depict certain items on a list the teacher has prepared.
- Become human sculptures, and use free movement to re-create the essence of the picture.

Multisensory stimulation, such as olfactory awareness of aromas, also can be a strong motivator of art and learning. ("Sniffing a jar of ground cinnamon, students will show in their artwork the events of which the smell of cinnamon reminds them. Show how the figures looked as they mixed ingredients, did the baking, and ate the baked goods.") A popular auditory stimulation is painting to music. ("Painting to the rhythm of *The Nutcracker Suite,* students will represent the music's measured regularity and variation in their paintings of dancers and soldiers in motion.") In fact, some art teachers make calm, classical music a staple feature during working periods.

Left: Children twirl scarves overhead to awaken their awareness prior to depicting the Olympics' rhythmic gymnastics event. The twirls in the chalk background echo the twirling scarf. First period, pencil drawing; second period, chalk background; third and fourth periods, paint. Note the girl's strong body, arms, and legs. **Middle:** Whitney Leet's "Proud of" picture shows the child's pride in doing handstands on the bars. Note the unique U-shaped arms and legs and the hair hanging down, also the thorough all-over marker coloring. **Right:** Using a brayer to ink the surface of the fish and make a "gyotaku" print is an unparalleled multisensory experience, also providing psychomotor and perceptual stimulation.

THE AFFECTIVE DOMAIN

Why bother with feelings in a book about teaching art? Just phrasing the question in this way suggests that emotions are something bad, something regrettable to be pushed aside, something that gets in the way of productive working and living.

Yet just the opposite is true. Feelings are the engine that drives us as we decide what actions to take. Emotion is a state of aroused feelings or agitation. The creative imagination needs to have access through art, fantasy, play, and daydreams to affect-laden thoughts—even though they may contain frightening and puzzling sexual and aggressive content. Fred Rogers of *Mr. Roger's Neighborhood* teaches his young audiences that "it is okay to have scary, bad dreams." Indeed, the role of dreams in our psychological functioning is just beginning to be understood.

Affect is a broader concept than emotions; affect includes emotions, drives, and feeling states—those that are temporary and those that are pervasive. Concerning the identification of pervasive feeling states in children's development, L. S. Vygotsky urged educators to attend less to the child's ideas and more to the child's internalized, private speech; that is, ask Is the child giving himself or herself a positive message of "I think I can"? or a negative message of "I always mess up"? Or, is the child conveying an emotional deadness, an inability to say "Whoopee!"? In educating for affective growth, cultivate students' ability to experience affect itself by asking them questions such as the following: "How did the person feel when the event happened?"

Likewise, cultivate the ability to take affective pleasure in the challenge of solving art problems or making art products. Feelings often motivate art and sustain its production over the long periods necessary for creation. If something is important in an emotional sense, then the creation of art

Courtesy of the Art Education Archives, School of Art, University of Georgia, Athens, GA.

Affective goal: "How did you feel at the event?" The wedding of an older sibling made an emotional impression on this upper-elementary-grade artist, who then captured the ceremony's sacred feeling in her tempera painting.

becomes a way of taking action to share the importance of the experience. Many artists root their art in concerns of life and death, nature and living beings, and the expression of feelings. Art can give voice to our inner needs and desires. It can give shape to our hopes, fears, ideals, and our very sense of self (see section on psychology in Chapter 14).

Few would disagree with affect's importance in art, yet many novice teachers have a particularly difficult time conceiving of affective objectives. Perhaps this difficulty comes from their having been taught to keep feelings to themselves. In order to help a teacher overcome this difficulty and wed affect to art learning, five kinds of affective objectives are described.

Affective Objectives in Art Lessons	Representative Statements by Teacher or Students
Students will express personal feelings in their art production.	The feeling I'd like to put in my mask is one of super power.
Students will express feelings common to their age.	Fear of scary things in the closet was something I felt strongly when I was your age.

Affective Objectives in Art Lessons	Representative Statements by Teacher or Students
Students will show feelings about external events in their art.	Mary's being in the hospital makes me want to do something to try to make her feel a little better.
Via art criticism, students will indirectly express their personal feelings.	The people in the picture appear to be afraid of the storm that's approaching, as though bad things might happen.
Students will express feelings by sharing art as gifts.	What will you say when you give your art to someone special to you? What do you think that person might say to you?

Courtesy of Joyce Vroon.

Affective goal: Personal feelings can be expressed in a picture of one's dream. In sixth-grade student Paul Freschi's dream picture, the figure confronts devils, flames, a dead end, and a maze of high yellow walls.

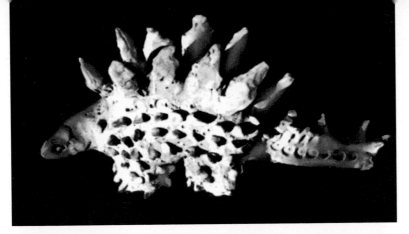

CLAY DINOSAURS: A SAMPLE LESSON PLAN COMBINING COGNITIVE, AFFECTIVE, AND PSYCHOMOTOR OBJECTIVES WITH ART OBJECTIVES

Education should focus on the integration that occurs within the child—the integration of the child's emotional, psychomotor, intellectual, perceptual, and aesthetic experiences. Here is a sample lesson plan containing eight types of objectives. Such a rich, integrated plan enables students with a wide variety of learning styles, emotional needs, and life needs to become involved in producing quality artwork. It also enables them to understand how their art is to be evaluated:

Clay Dinosaurs, Primary Grades	Enabling Activities
1. Art production (specific art skills to be learned)	Students will pull head and leg forms from a ball of clay to construct a dinosaur. Students will form eyes, ears, mouths, and tails.
2. Artistic perception (where we see specific art elements in daily life)	Students will describe similar structural forms in nature, such as other animals, tree branches, tables, and post-and-lintel construction.
3. Art history (interpretation of similar artworks by artists of other times)	Students will describe animal forms shown in reproductions of Aztec pottery, tell how the legs were made, and describe the animal's expression.
4. Art criticism (discussion and interpretation of students' works)	Students will describe differences in each other's creations, identifying those that look delicate, ferocious, or strong.
5. Aesthetics (discussing ideas about art)	Students will discuss whether scary and ugly things can be art, even though some people think art should be only about what is beautiful.
6. Affective (dealing with emotional needs)	Students will describe how their dinosaur makes them feel, their dinosaur's personality, how it interacts with friends or enemies that try to hurt it, whether it has any children, and what the children are like.

Top: *Courtesy of* Emphasis Art, *Second Edition, University Elementary School, Iowa City, IA.* Middle: *Courtesy of Robert Clements.* Bottom: *Courtesy of David W. Hodge.*

Top: Many kinds of instructional objectives can relate to this third-grade clay dinosaur lesson. **Middle:** Psychomotor motivation occurs through doing a "Dinosaur Dance" and making dinosaur sounds. **Bottom:** This prickly dinosaur is perfectly protected from others' perceived onslaughts.

Courtesy of Beverly Barksdale Mallon.

A sad, mad, disgruntled pot.

Courtesy of Beverly Barksdale Mallon.

Affective goals can be involved through children giving artworks they have made as gifts.

Clay Dinosaurs, Primary Grades	Enabling Activities
7. Cognitive and functional (correlated to important knowledge about our world and our functioning in it)	Students will be able to match their dinosaurs to photos of actual dinosaurs. Students will be able to describe how their dinosaur's diet and defense mechanisms relate to those the students use themselves.
8. Psychomotor and multi-sensory (dance, music, vocalization, role-playing, taste, smell, hearing)	Students will mimic the sounds and movements of their dinosaurs, then use these motifs to organize a dinosaur dance.

FOR FURTHER READING

Bloom, Benjamin S. 1984. *Taxonomy of Educational Objectives: The Classification of Educational Goals.* New York: Longman.

Ohio State University TETA Mentors. 2002. "Integrated Curriculum: Possibilities for the Arts." *Art Education* 55(3): 12–22.

Phillips. L. C. 2003. "Nurturing Empathy." *Art Education* 56(4): 45–49.

Russ, S. W. 1993. *Affect and Creativity, The Role of Affect and Play in the Creative Process.* Hillsdale, NJ: Lawrence Erlbaum Associates.

Sorri, Mari. 1994. "The Body Has Reasons: Tactic Knowing in Thinking and Making." *Journal of Aesthetic Education* 28(2): 15–26.

Szekely, George. 1995. "Circus." *Art Education* 48(4): 44–50.

WEB RESOURCES

For resources in drama, music, dance, and interrelated arts, see:

  http://www.princetonol.com/groups/iad/lessons/middle/comparts.htm

For a list of plans sorted by grade, see:

  http://www.getty.edu/artsednet/resources/grade.html

Chapter 7
Art and Literacy: Reading and Language Arts

*L*anguage arts share much common ground with the visual arts: Both subjects focus on means of expression; both use symbols; both employ similar methods of critical analysis and interpretation. At the beginning of the nineteenth century, Frederich Froebel, often referred to as the father of the kindergarten, eloquently wrote of the important connection between drawing and writing: "The drawing properly stands between the word and the thing, shares certain qualities with each of them, and is therefore, so valuable in the development of the child. . . . The word and the drawing, therefore, belong together inseparable, as light and shadow, night and day, soul and body do" (1974, originally published 1826).

Drawing before writing forces the child to recall and decide on the details that enrich the writing—how many windows, a chimney, trees, a fence. Drawing precedes writing and is an important element in the "prehistory" of children's writing, just as hieroglyphic pictograms probably preceded written alphabets, and drawing continues to be a valuable supplement and complement to written language in more sophisticated communication. Art and writing can be meaningfully combined, for example, in capturing a recalled experience—time spent with a loved one or a pet, or in a special place. Not only does drawing come first, but encouraging children to draw assures that their early writing process is authentically rooted in their own personal experiences. Drawing is how many—perhaps most—young children communicate ideas, since they may not yet have the words to describe events, or they may simply be too shy to talk. In children's earliest representational drawings, they will employ their natural narrative impulse: the desire to create stories in their drawings and to talk about the drawing event.

At every possible moment, encourage this in your classroom. Have children draw a picture showing something that is meaningful to them, on a topic they have chosen—a funny thing I saw, something that surprised me, a great day I had. Then ask them to write about it. (Children learn to read most easily when they themselves have authored the text.) Their first

texts will emerge in the captions and stories that they dictate to accompany what they have drawn. Furthermore, children's interest in one another builds as they are able to talk with each other about their drawings. The drawing and the accompanying talk give the naturally curious young child access into other children's minds and feelings.

Unfortunately, many teachers have students draw a picture to go with their story after the writing is completed; the art is just decoration. Even worse, some teachers, who think drawing is just "fooling around," scold children when they are drawing instead of writing. In fact, the interplay of the two forms of communication is a powerful motivator for both drawing and writing. Both the artwork and the written passages offer representations of the same cluster of things—each provides a window into the child's world.

Drawing, then, is critical to the early development of language and narrative. But even after we learn to write, drawing is essential, for we learn through representation. We construct meaning by formulating our own representations. While these representations are usually verbal or written, they may also be diagrammatic or pictorial: Art and language are both communication vehicles by which ideas are transmitted. Learning to draw requires close observation skills—skills that catalyze thinking skills. Certainly, the development of civilization is largely based upon the ability to communicate in many ways—verbal and written, but also visual, musical, and mathematical.

THE VOCABULARY OF ART

Vocabulary development is a major factor in success in reading. The more words a child knows, the better his or her word recognition skills; the more meanings, the better the comprehension. In language, the properties of objects are conveyed by adjectives: the *yellow, striped* tiger. Translating this

Courtesy of Jessica Crosby, Reading for Life Project, Claiborne County, MS, and the Mississippi Cultural Crossroads, Port Gibson, MS.

Reading and art can augment each other. Famous quilter Hystercine Ranking passes on quilting skills to students as they participate in the Reading for Life Literacy Program, illustrating in quilt form their own stories inspired by books of African-American authors. From a theme in the book, children develop their own story, with the teacher asking questions such as Who, What, When, and Where.

into the terminology of art, "yellow" is a color or hue, and "striped" describes the surface pattern. Thus, the tiger can be described verbally, using adjectives, or visually, using art elements. The whole panoply of art's formal elements (line, color, texture, pattern, shape, space) reflects simply another potential vocabulary for description or representation. Children's writing and their artwork are both enhanced by their learning to think, talk, write, and draw in terms including the following, which are drawn from four of art's design elements.

Top left: *Courtesy of Betsy Lilliston.* Top right and bottom: *Courtesy of Joyce Vroon.*

Draw and then fill in the background with a story. **Top left:** A self-portrait is enhanced by a background story, "What I did last summer." **Top right:** After drawing a guitar, Tyler Grubb adds song lyrics, written in successive rows around the guitar's outline. **Bottom:** In this picture, called "Word Processing," after making a careful line drawing of an old Corona typewriter, student Eleanor Siegel then wrote a story that she lettered in the background.

Top: *Courtesy of Beverly Barksdale Mallon.* Bottom: *Courtesy of Mary Lazzari.*

Make a decorative border of words explaining the picture. **Top:** "Me and my Dad and my neighbor Casey eating a watermelon with a bluebird watching." By kindergartner Annabelle Barbe, with Faith Ringgold's art and the lovely spring weather as the motivation. **Bottom:** A third-grader wrote Reverend Martin Luther King Jr.'s "I Have a Dream" speech around his illustration.

Lines Lines make up the shapes of letters. Before alphabets were invented, ancient peoples—Egyptians and Native Americans, for example—used hieroglyphics, or sign language. Lines also describe shapes, and they can themselves have names: straight, curved, arched, wavy, fish-scale, jagged, zigzag, made of dots or dashes. And lines have characteristics; a line may be described as delicate, nervous, bold, static, flowing, rhythmic, hesitant, or energetic. Lines can be created spontaneously, or with thoughtful, deliberate motions.

Ask your students to describe the characteristics of lines in nature—tree roots, bark and branches, spider webs, water ripples, lightning, leaf veins, feathers, wood grain, and insect wings. Listen to the vocabulary they can find to talk about something as simple as a line.

Shape Shapes are the building blocks of letter forms; children must learn to identify them before they can learn to read. Shapes may be square, rectangular, round, elliptical, oval, triangular, or amorphous. Each letter of the alphabet has a distinct shape or combination of shapes. These can be thought of as having both a positive shape, formed by the outline of the letter, and a negative shape, which is the empty space inside and outside of the outline. Shapes are created by lines merging, touching, and intersecting one another.

The shapes of objects or figures in a composition, such as trees, houses, people, animals, furniture, and vehicles, generally are called positive shapes. The empty area around them is referred to as negative space; this negative space often includes objects with a quality of emptiness, such as ground, water, and sky. Primary-grade children often use formulas (in art terms, "schema") for the shapes of human figures and trees and birds and houses; more natural representations develop at later ages.

Shapes are often flat and two-dimensional (squares, circles) but they can also have or suggest volume and three-dimensions (rectangular solids, cubes, cones, pyramids). Shapes with volume are sometimes called forms.

Ask your students to talk about the difference between a circle and a ball. Listen to the complexity of their language.

Left: *Courtesy of Joyce Vroon.* Right: *Courtesy of Dahria McClelland.*

In art, as in letter shapes, the negative shapes are as important as the positive shapes. **Left:** "Black Beauty," an exciting story, is here illustrated by third-grader Devin McGillivary with exciting background shapes. **Right:** Note the attractive background shapes in a third-grader's Oriental brush painting.

Left top: *Courtesy of Shirley Lucas, first grade.* Right top: *Courtesy of ICCA, Milner Library, Illinois State University.* Right middle and bottom: *Courtesy of Melody Milbrandt, primary grade and first grade.*

Left top: The king's powerfully patterned robe, and **right:** the snowbird's staccato snow pattern, the proud girl's dress of equal-sized stripes, and the barnyard's rough, bumpy texture vividly describe the situations.

Texture and Pattern The surfaces of objects like clothing or trees, or natural occurrences like clouds and water, can be described using many different adjectives: rough, smooth, bumpy, jagged, fluffy, and so on. In art, texture is often considered an adorning or secondary feature that adds richness and variety to shapes. Similarly, pattern adorns shapes and has helpful descriptive terms: regular and irregular, stripes or bands, zigzag or chevron, scallop or fish scale, plaid or cross-band, checkerboard, notched or crenellated (like the tops of castle towers). In art, patterns are often created by setting up a series of parallel lines or lines that intersect. (For more about the language of art, see Chapter 2.)

In the complex interplay between language and art, adjectives can be used to describe what is seen—and art (line, shape, texture, pattern) can be used to give visual expression to what adjectives express verbally. And more: Not only do objects have formal properties (the dark grey clouds), but they can also be said to have emotional properties (the *angry* dark grey clouds). Drawings can express the same intensity of emotion.

A kindergartner recounts her Disney World trip: one, the cover; two, leaving home; three, staying at a fancy hotel; four, on the roller coaster; and five, on leaving, I was sad.

IN THE CLASSROOM

Writing and Art

Having a notebook or sketchbook in which to record their visual and written impressions permits kindergarten and primary grades language arts students a way to give voice to their feelings and ideas. Encourage them not only to write and draw in combination, but also to use diagrams and pictograms. Have middle-school students write in their journals about photographs they take. Encourage them to show in their writings and drawings such major modalities as the passage of time, movement, and different concepts of space. Cartoon art can provide useful models here, with its use of close-ups, distant views, framing through close objects, silhouettes, high views and low views.

Ask older students to make detailed drawings of their rooms at home and diagrams of how they might organize their "stuff" more efficiently; have them draw their rooms from the doorway and again while sitting on the bed. A written description to go along with the drawing can give the students a different kind of perspective. Whetting students' interest to use their imaginations in both writing and making art can be done through stimulating their senses and memories—for example, by the scent memories of bread baking or of flower fragrances. If you can, let the real scent pervade the classroom while you share a story and artwork with your students. Ask them to represent in pictures and words what this motivation provoked in their imaginations. Finally, have them tell one or two other students about their work by describing the picture and reading the words.

Top right: A time capsule book, to be stored away unopened for a decade.
Bottom right: Aspirations of learning how to do Japanese anime cartoon stories.

Making art and talking about what they have made allows children to expand their ability to communicate in almost endless ways. In describing what they have created, children will find themselves using not only adjectives, but virtually every part of speech—in particular, verbs ("The dog in the picture is running") and adverbs ("The dog is running wildly to get to the little boy")—as well as complex narrative structures. Making art, then, is one of the most important tasks you can provide for the students in your classroom.

SPEECH, THOUGHT, AND ART

Speech plays an essential role in developing children's thinking. Cognitive psychologists noted this relationship of speech and learning and therefore recommended that children be encouraged to work interactively in pairs and groups. We form thoughts into speech at the same time as speech forms our thoughts. Thus, language is an important mediator between learning and development. This concept is applied in good art lesson plans, which almost always allow for a time to talk about the art produced, to share the art's meaning with others in the class. Much research supports the idea that verbalization improves retention of art concepts. But research suggests that art can be used to promote language arts goals as well. Here are some ways.

- *Illustrate a story.* Language can be facilitated by primary-grade children's illustrating a popular story like "Rotten Ralph." Let each child pick a character to draw, or divide the story into scenes and give each child a scene to illustrate. Then tape all the drawings together to make a visual narrative that can be put up for hallway display and for students to discuss.
- *Keep a journal.* Have students in the intermediate grades keep journals, and encourage them to both write and draw. Give them opportunities to talk about how writing and drawing can work synergistically.
- *Write a poem or an essay.* Ask students to write a poem about an artwork—their own, or a reproduction that you show them—empathizing with the figures depicted. Or ask them to choose from several reproductions and write a reflective piece about why they made the choice they did. Suggest that they answer questions about the feeling they had when they saw it and the elements of the work that attracted them.
- *Talk about a memory.* Talking can lead to both drawing and writing. Have children start with something simple—sights on the school bus, for example. A brief discussion can lead students to create word pictures and drawings describing the experience. Or word pictures can describe a remembered place, such as "My Bedroom" or "At the After-School

Courtesy of Joyce Vroon.

Third-graders Elizabeth Nellis and Jill Reid illustrate a scene from favorite stories, "Rotten Ralph" and "Corduroy."

Courtesy of Joyce Vroon.

Sixth-grader Sarah Hipp illustrates a poem by Langston Hughes about a broken heart.

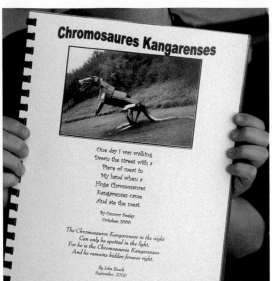

Young children's drawings can communicate more than their words. Kindergartners wrote and illustrated "The Further Adventures of Peter Rabbit." **Left:** The child dictated the story, "Peter Rabbit and Flopsy, Mopsy, and Cottontail look at a rainbow while waiting to take a ride on an airplane." First period, learning how to draw a rabbit; second period, pencil drawing the scene; third period, watercolor; fourth period, markers. **Middle:** Children wrote poems in response to a sculpture field trip. **Right:** The rabbits play in the rain.

Rec Program." Young children can collaboratively come up with remembrances, which the teacher can record on the board; then children can individually do their drawings and writings.

- *Write a story.* Acquiring more skill, children in the intermediate grades can first outline a story, using only a few words or short phrases. Then they can work these words or phrases up into sentences. After the basic writing is done, then they can polish the piece. Tell them to save an area near the top of the page for an illustration of a scene in the narrative. Or alternately, have them make a colorful, decorated border using relevant symbols.
- *Learn to "read" pictures.* Literacy is broadly defined as the ability to read and write. But more and more, the texts that students are being asked to understand and interpret are not simply words; they are words and pictures. Advertisements, Web screens, illustrated magazines and brochures, film, product design, television images—these things are part of our everyday lives. **Visual literacy**—the ability to analyze and interpret visual images—has become a vital component of learning to be a critical thinker. Some writers call this concept aesthetic literacy or cultural literacy. Creating and talking critically about art and learning the basic principles of art criticism provide students with necessary tools for today's world.

A self-written, self-illustrated story about a fantasy memory. "Walking in a magical forest, I saw these three trees with weird hands, bowties and necklaces, going to a party, and they invited me. We partied all night long."

THINKING CRITICALLY ABOUT AND THROUGH ART

Speech development as well as the ability to think critically are fostered by conversations about art. Children can be guided both to give verbal form to their thoughts and to understand the language of art. Students should learn to point to evidence in the work itself to support their interpretations. Give them a chance to tell you what they see and feel. During the primary grades, encourage children to ask questions about visual phenomena, to list special eye-catching items in a picture. Children will spontaneously put forth their explanations of the artwork's meaning. Using art reproductions to encourage speech development can free children from the fear of making too personal a revelation, yet at the same time allow them to express their personal feelings. When a teacher asks, "What do you think the lady looking in the mirror is saying to herself?" students often can share from their personal experiences.

Working in groups facilitates language development. Primary-grade children in pairs or small groups can do any number of tasks. Ask them, for example, to sort art postcards into categories: those showing different emotions; those showing realistic or abstract art; those showing past and current

Courtesy of Barbara Thomas.

The teacher urges her students to illustrate the book, "The Red Chameleon" in their own colors and patterns.

Courtesy of ICCA, Milner Library, Illinois State University.

The design principle of repetition gives power to this Near-Eastern child's crayon engraving of the story of the old man, his grandson, and his donkey.

times. Students can describe the similarities and differences between artworks depicted and describe overall concepts that a group of cards have in common. Or give each group a set of cards that have already been sorted, and ask them to describe why one of the items in the set does not belong. Listen to the discussion of categories, themes, and art elements that almost always follows. Older students in small groups can sort art history cards in more sophisticated ways—by chronological order, or by style, or by medium, for example. Or have a group create a narrative around the set of art postcards they have; the only rule is that all the cards must be used.

Courtesy of Joyce Vroon.

Many symbols are evident in this personal myth written and painted by fifth-grader Mary Radford Wyatt. The yellow-and-green striped boat with dark sails seems to portend danger; green-faced spirits blow the wind away from the sailboat; Atlas holds up the boat on the watery globe.

Encourage questions. In leading class discussions about art reproductions, listen for questions like, "Why is that weird thing supposed to be art?" Students will always wonder about art. Encourage them, so their wondering can be transformed into significant thinking about aesthetics—into thinking about the nature of beauty, realism vs. abstraction, and art's purpose.

An easy game that promotes both speech fluency and critical thinking is to have one student face the class and describe an art reproduction that only that student can see. Ask the other students to imagine what the art looks like while the student who is "it" describes the artwork as thoroughly as possible. Then turn the artwork to face the class and see how amazed the students will be to see something that is often very different from what they have envisioned. We begin to understand, then, how complex artworks can be, and how much they demand from language.

THE ART OF LANGUAGE: COMMONALITIES BETWEEN DESIGN STRUCTURES IN LANGUAGE AND ART

As we have seen, language and art can both complement and supplement one another in a variety of ways. Certain design principles are powerful and effective in both language and art. Theme and variation and focus, for example, are principles of art design that are mirrored in the design principles of language, called figures of speech. These include metaphor, repetition, variation, symmetry, dominance, and emphasis. Metaphors and similes can actually be depicted through art. (The girl danced as lightly as a bird. The ocean frowned up at the rain clouds.) Alliteration—repeating the same sounds for effect (Hortense honked the horn to hurry us.)—is akin to making an artwork with a repeated color family or just one type of shape. Balance or symmetry in artworks are the same principle as making sure that structures within sentences are parallel.

Making your classroom an integrated environment for learning the dual methods of communication—language and art—will help your students become more adept at both methods.

FOR FURTHER READING

Bitz, Michael. 2004. "The Comic Book Project: The Lives of Urban Youth." *Art Education* 57(6): 33–39.

Catterall, J. "Does Experience in the Arts Boost Academic Achievement? A Response to Eisner." *Art Education,* July 1998, 6–11.

Cohen, Elaine, and Ruth S. Gainer. 1984. *Art: Another Language for Learning.* New York: Schocken.

Eubanks, Paula. 2003. "Codeswitching: Using Language as a Tool for Clearer Meaning in Art." *Art Education* 56(65): 13–18.

Galvin, S. "Scent Memories; Crossing the Curriculum with Writing and Painting." *Art Education,* March 1997, 7–12.

Hubbard, R. 1989. *Authors of Pictures, Draughtsmen of Words.* Portsmouth, NH: Heinemann.

Johnson, P. 1997. *Pictures and Words Together; Children Writing and Illustrating Their Own Books.* Portsmouth, NH: Heinemann.

Olson, J. L. 1992. *Envisioning Writing: Towards an Integration of Drawing and Writing.* Portsmouth, NH: Heinemann Educational Books.

Richards, Allen G. 2003. "Arts and Academic Achievement in Reading: Further Implications." *Art Education* 56(6): 19–24.

WEB RESOURCES

For helping kindergartners develop preemergent writing skills:

http://www.pbs.org/teachersource/prek2/issues/index.shtm

For lesson plans for older students about text in art, see:

http://www.getty.edu/artsednet/resources/Sampler/e-aintro.html

For a lesson on writing haiku and ukiyo-e prints:

http://edsitement.neh.gov/view_lesson_plan.asp?ID=305

Pieced and appliquéd cotton embroidered with plain and metallic yarns, 69 × 105 inches. Bequest of Maxim Karolik. Courtesy of the Museum of Fine Arts, Boston, MA. Photograph © 2004 Museum of Fine Arts, Boston, MA.

It is not necessary to be able to read or write to tell a wonderful story! Even though Southern society banned slaves from learning to read and write, Harriet Powers (a former slave from Athens, GA, 1837–1911) still could tell a powerful and beautiful story about biblical stories and events in her own life.

What could have more power and charm than her collage-like quilts, which now hang in our nation's most important museums? She described the lower left square, "Cold Thursday, 10 of Feb. 1895. A woman frozen while at prayer. A woman frozen at a gateway. A man with a sack of meal frozen. Icicles formed from the breath of a mule. All blue birds killed." Can you find the dead blue birds, woman praying, man with sack, and the mule with icicles?

What makes the piece so beautiful? A large checkerboard pattern gives unity. Color is restrained to mostly white and very dark. Tints and shades in a very limited palette are used. The almost abstract figures create bold positive and negative shapes and speak in such a naive, mysterious way about the human condition.

For artists who use text, including Jenny Holzer and Barbara Kruger, see:
  http://www.princetonol.com/groups/iad/lessons/middle/art-text.htm
For sketching the setting of a story:
  http://artsedge.kennedy-center.org/content/2235/

For how to tell stories about paintings:
  http://www.getty.edu.artsednet/resources/Stories/intro.html
For how Jacob Lawrence's paintings are examined for their stories:
  http://www.getty.edu/artsednet/resources/jacoblawrence/index.htm

Chapter 8
Art and Mathematics

Over the doors of Plato's academy were written these words: "Let no one enter who is lacking in geometry." And Leonardo da Vinci announced, "Let no one read me who is not a mathematician."

Mathematical skills and concepts—measurement, estimation, scale and ratio, proportion, symmetry, perspective, working with plane figures and three-dimensional figures—can be employed in any number of art projects. Every day, math lessons can be enriched by art, and art can be used to teach mathematics. By helping your students realize how interrelated mathematics and art are, you can give them profound insight into both the seen and the unseen nature of the world.

MATH SKILLS

While students are producing art, they can be using a variety of the same skills that they need to use in solving mathematical problems, including measurement and estimating.

Measuring Measuring is a skill so important that Leonardo da Vinci wrote, "To measure is to know." Measuring is used in many art and design projects. Perhaps the most familiar for the primary grades is weaving with paper strips. On stiff paper folded in half, have students measure and mark lines $\frac{1}{2}$ inch to 1 inch apart (you may want your students to paint on the paper first) and then cut the paper into strips along the lines, beginning at the fold and stopping one inch from the paper's open edge. This creates the *woof*, or vertical part of the weaving. Colorful *weft* strips—gaily painted or cut from magazine pictures, or made from yarn, cloth, or feathers—can then be woven through the woof. For Mother's Day, have children use 18- × 24-inch paper for the woof to make a tablemat, using their mothers' favorite colors.

Courtesy of Barbara Thomas.

The joy of working with geometric shapes shows in this first-grader's face.

Courtesy of Baiba Kuntz. Seventh grade.

Quadrilateral symmetry is shown in these designs. Patterns are cut from clay-coated Chroma papers, pasted to a 13- × 13-inch stiff paper ruled into a 1-inch grid. Begin in the middle and work out.

Left: *Courtesy of Barbara Thomas.* Right: *Courtesy of Beverly Barksdale Mallon.*

Measuring is an important math skill to be taught. **Left:** Quadrilaterally symmetrical designs can be made from patterned papers cut into triangles and squares. **Right:** A kindergarten project involving measuring is paper weaving. Kindergartners first make abstract designs on colored paper; then they measure and cut both the strips and the mat. Finally they weave the strips over and under.

Measuring borders to a preselected dimension such as 2 inches × 2 inches is another way for primary students to incorporate math. First, students paint (perhaps to music) colorful abstract designs. When the paintings are dry, have students measure and cut them into 2-inch squares. These can be shared with classmates and pasted around a painting to make a beautiful, decorated border.

Estimating Estimation, a basic concept of mathematics, can be taught in connection with art criticism by having students look at art reproductions and estimate how many figures, animals, or buildings are shown, or the size of objects. In a studio activity, have students estimate the number of scissors or papers available, or the number of 2-inch squares they can make from a sheet of paper.

Students can also use estimation to figure out the areas of rooms and shapes in the school building in square feet. Have students pace off the length and width of their classroom or walk around the school, sketching what they see—for example, triangular pediments, columns, arches, fan windows, foyers, and courtyards—and later estimate the size of the various design elements.

Another more personal use of estimation is for students to pace off the length of a hallway and estimate how many of their artworks might be hung there.

MATH CONCEPTS

Many concepts that are basic to understanding mathematics can be reinforced through art lessons. These include scale and ratio, proportion, symmetry, and perspective.

Scale and Ratio Grids can help students learn about scale and ratio, the relationship of numbers of one size to those of another size. These principles can be employed in enlarging pictures. Have students rule a grid of 1-inch lines onto a student's artwork or school portrait photograph, or a magazine picture of a masterwork, and then number each square. Then mark a grid with 4-inch squares on a much larger piece of paper, and ask students to reproduce the smaller picture one square at a time. Or create a giant mural by marking 1-foot or larger squares and assigning each student to paint one square. The slight discrepancies give charm to the mural.

Courtesy of Mary Lazzari.

Scaling: A picture of Mona Lisa was ruled into 1-inch squares and cut apart. Students enlarged this to 1-foot square and imaginatively painted their designs.

Top: *Courtesy of W. Robert Nix.* Bottom: *Courtesy of Joyce Vroon.*

Top: The Fibonacci number series is widely used in nature. Thirty-four skinny petals and thirteen curved sepals are shown here. **Bottom:** The Golden Ratio appears in these third-grade paintings derived from Piet Mondrian's work.

Proportion Drawing the human figure in correct proportions does not, in itself, make art. Often, children's art with incorrect proportions has a charm quite lacking in proportionally correct art. But for those who do want to learn the visually correct proportions, Leonardo's writings contain many proportional ratios, such as 1 to 7 for a human figure's head to body. Leonardo's most famous drawing is his Vitruvian man, an illustration of the mathematician Vitruvius' observation that the navel is the center of the human body, and that outstretched arms and legs will touch the perimeter of a circle drawn with the navel as its center.

Middle-school students may be interested in the mathematical basis for pleasing proportion for forms in both nature and artworks. In architecture and art, pleasing proportions occur when the shorter side of a structure or drawing is about two-thirds the length of the longer side. Your books and writing paper have approximately these proportions. Dividing things into perfect squares or very skinny rectangles is not as attractive. In drawing a landscape, for example, your picture will be more pleasing if you divide the sky and land use two-thirds and one-third of the space, rather than half each.

The precise ratio, called the Golden Ratio, is actually not exactly two-thirds but rather .618. Try measuring photocopied front views of architectural masterworks like Phidias' design for the Parthenon, or the United Nations building, or important buildings in your own town. Do their height and width conform more or less to the Golden Ratio?

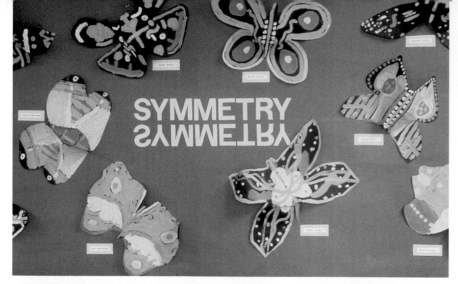

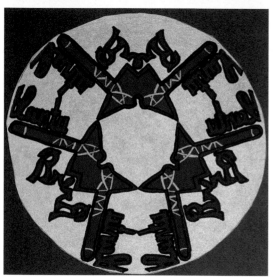

Top left: *Courtesy of Joyce Vroon and Marlee Puskar.* Top right: *Courtesy of Barbara Thomas. Student Nikki Foster, Grade 2.*
Bottom left: *Courtesy of Mrs. Smith.* Bottom middle: *Courtesy of Nancy Eliott.* Bottom right: *Courtesy of Barbara Thomas.*

Symmetry: Bilateral in butterflies; three- or six-fold in a design of one's initials; quadrilateral in designs from insect shells and circles.

This is such a pleasing and correct proportion that nature uses this same ratio in a series of numbers called the Fibonacci series. Each new number in the series is the sum of the last two (1, 1, 2, 3, 5, 8, 13, 21, 34, 55, and so on). Count daisy petals and the spiraling sections in a pineapple skin to confirm that the result is usually a Fibonacci number.

Symmetry The symmetrical nature of a math equation means that the two halves of an equation are the same. A common art method of showing symmetry is to paint on a folded piece of paper one half of a form, such as a butterfly, and then (quickly before the paint dries, or else dampen the paper) fold the blank side over and press.

Explore bilateral symmetry through paper dolls. Fold a long strip of the paper about four times, and then draw half the figure (or the whole figure with hands and feet outstretched) touching the side borders. Carefully cut out the row of figures without cutting the folded touching parts. Allow students to express themselves through drawing different emotions on the figures' faces, along with the different clothes we might wear when we have those feelings. Further personalize the figures by adding accessories cut from paper, such as musical instruments, ballet tutus, and softball mitts and bats. In other words, fuse the mathematical means to expressive ends to kindle the imagination. The figure chains can become borders around a wall or ceiling.

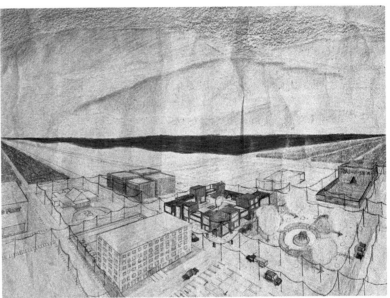

Top: *Courtesy of Joyce Vroon. Student Michael Selik*. Bottom: *Courtesy of Lawrence Stueck.*

One-point and two-point perspective are explored. The idea that lines in depth recede to vanishing points on the horizon was a Renaissance discovery. To make it art, add the unique and individual.

Perspective The development of perspective brings together math history and art history. So important to Renaissance artists was the concept of perspective, wherein forms recede into depth, that Leonardo wrote "Perspective is the rein and rudder of painting." The earliest reference to perspective is in mathematics, however, not art. In 300 B.C., the mathematician Euclid wrote about geometrical optics, and the Roman architect Vitruvius in 25 B.C. described "a way of sketching with the sides of a building withdrawing into the background," a technique used in ancient

Courtesy of Dahria McClelland.

Eight-fold symmetry shows in this design based on Australian aboriginal art.

Roman wall murals. The Greek mathematician and scientist Ptolemy wrote about optics A.D. 140, and the Iraqi mathematician Alhazen advanced his ideas a thousand years later.

It was the Italian Renaissance artists and architects Brunelleschi, Alberti, and da Vinci who brought these theories of mathematical optics into art, and later artists like Mantegna, Albrecht Durer, M. C. Escher, and Salvador Dali played with perspective in imaginative ways. Students can find and discuss the concepts of the horizon line and vanishing points in works by these and many other artists. Because of its complexity, perspective drawings is best saved for the upper grades, and, as with all art lessons, students should be encouraged to use their own personal imagery, however fantastic.

Using Computers to Learn About Symmetry, Scaling, and Proportion Computers bring almost unlimited possibilities to the integration of art and math. Designs drawn on the computer can be copied or flipped to show bilateral symmetry, copied four ways into quadrilateral symmetry, or "dragged" and copied into a whole repeated series. Proportional scaling can be taught through shrinking or enlarging the sizes of images in specified percentages. By greatly diminishing the pixel size and resolution of scanned photographs, students can gain an understanding of how size and resolution are related, and by specifying on the computer proportions of a color's hue, value, and intensity, students can understand the meaning and interrelationships of hue, value, and intensity.

LEARNING ABOUT SHAPES AND SOLIDS: STUDYING GEOMETRY THROUGH ART

Patterns, shapes, and three-dimensional solids are the basic "building blocks" of geometry—a mathematical discipline that most students don't study until high school. But a wide range of art lessons can help young children begin to understand what these shapes and figures are and how to manipulate them.

Shapes A number of materials can be used to teach children about shapes, including parquetry blocks, tangrams, American quilts, and a simple piece of string, a board, and some nails.

Parquetry Blocks Colorful parquetry blocks teach how shapes can be combined into larger shapes. Forms of beauty and power can be created by nesting forms within or adjacent to each other: Triangles can become squares and six-pointed stars, squares can build rectangles, and triangles and squares together can form isometric, three-dimensional illusions. Frank Lloyd Wright attributed his lifelong design ability to his using parquetry

Courtesy of Robert Clements.

The math concepts of how three-dimensional shapes are made from other shapes and how three-dimensional shapes fit together can be learned through block play.

shapes when he was an eight-year-old. This kind of geometric pattern especially characterizes his stained-glass window designs.

Polyhedral Shapes and String Art Intermediate students can use mechanical drawing instruments like compasses, 45-degree triangles and 30/60-degree triangles, and T-squares to make beautiful geometric designs. Older students can also use measurement to create geometric shapes in string art lessons. On a board covered with cloth, have students measure out a geometric pattern and carefully pound tiny tacks into the board at regularly spaced intervals. Then have them weave string from nail to nail, back and forth across the design, creating mandala-like designs.

Quilt Designs Plane geometry is artfully and imaginatively shown in early American quilts. Bring actual quilts from home, if possible, or show pictures and encourage students to talk about design and history. Like quilters, students can construct six-pointed stars or other designs through combining geometric shapes and patterns. Show students how the same designs occur in nature—as in snowflakes, for example. Discuss how nature's snowflake designs illustrate the principle of fractals.

Bisecting Shapes Children can create new shapes by bisecting shapes—triangles from squares, for example. Use folded paper airplanes or origami to let students explore how to bisect surface planes diagonally. But, to allow for true expression, bring in the imaginative, the fantastic,

Top row: *Courtesy of Beverly Barksdale Mallon.* Bottom: *Courtesy of Jenni Horne.*

Top row: Third-graders' knowledge about mathematical symmetry is applied in these swirling hex designs of eight-, six-, and sixteen-pointed star forms. Shapes can be combined to form other shapes; arcs are combined to create circles; rectangles reside inside triangles. **Bottom:** Pre-kindergartners learn about squares fitting together in a quilt design.

and the personal. For example, have students tape the folded construction onto a drawn picture to show the child's personal relationship to the subject—"This is a jet plane for my friend and me to fly," for example, or "These are swans on the lake where my family goes for picnics."

Tangrams Shape perception and spatial pattern recognition can be learned through tangrams, an ancient Chinese puzzle in which a square has been cut into seven triangular and quadrilateral pieces; the student then combines these to represent people, animals, and objects. Oxford math professor and "Alice in Wonderland" author Lewis Carroll was a great fan of tangrams.

Tiling Tiling or tessellation is a design made up of congruent regular polygons—that is, polygons whose sides are all the same length. Tessellations can be created only from polygons whose interior angles can be evenly divided into 360. This pattern technique appears in Islamic mosaic temple decorations from a half millennium ago and resurfaces in the twentieth century in the prints of M. C. Escher. One way students can make their own tessellated designs is to trace around cardboard templates. A more exciting method is to cut sponges into regular polygons and dip the sponges into paints. Use two different colors and pack them together into overall patterns.

Coloring Maps Believe it or not, coloring is a profound mathematical topic with many multimillion dollar applications. Mathematicians have proven that four colors are sufficient to color the countries on any map with no adjacent countries being the same color; have students try to replicate this famous proof.

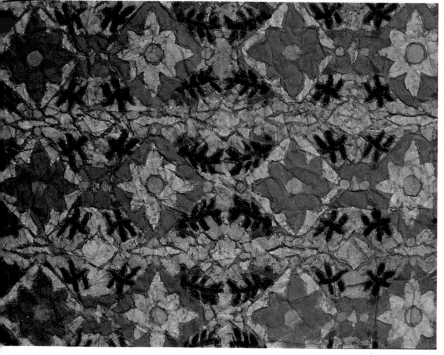

Top: *Courtesy of Mary Lazzari*. Bottom: *Courtesy of Barbara Thomas*.

Top: Tessellation or tiling creates amazing patterns and awareness of positive and negative space, here by a fifth grader. **Bottom**: The repeating patterns of symmetrical shapes in rows and columns and reversing colors creates a rich effect.

Top: *Courtesy of Joyce Vroon*. Bottom: *Courtesy of Reuben Williams*.

The four-color problem is an important math concept. For example, only four colors are needed to color maps with no states adjacent being the same. **Top:** A first grader tries to avoid adjacent colors being the same. **Bottom:** The mathematical proportion phi and Fibonacci number series are in sculptor Reuben Williams's metal sign and sunflower design for the school's water retention pond bog-garden.

WORKING IN THREE DIMENSIONS

A hands-on way to integrate free expression and math is to have students paint to music on posterboard, old file folders, or cardboard, and then have them measure, cut, and tape to construct three-dimensional models of square and cubic inches, centimeters, and meters out of attractive parts of the painting. Another way to show two-dimensions transformed into three-dimensional objects is to have children sketch the floor plan of their house or of a fort, then tape to that a frontal view of the proper size and fold it up. Two- to three-dimensional thinking can be fostered by having them look at plans and views of their school building; older students can discuss how a dome can be considered either an arch rotated 360 degrees or as a bisected sphere. Buckminster Fuller's geodesic domes can make this shape real. Students can design three-dimensional paper sculptures and then write descriptions of their sculptures, listing the shapes they used. Then have students try to figure out which description is of which sculpture. Or simply have students list the geometric shapes shown in architecture (the St. Louis Arch, the Eiffel Tower, and other examples from modern and ancient architecture), in nature (snowflakes, beehive cells), in art and design over the centuries (Chinese lattices, Moorish mosque tile designs from the Alhambra). Find geometric shapes in nearby community buildings to give this subject a tangible presence for your students.

Solids The Platonic solids are the cube, the tetrahedron (a three-sided pyramid, with four triangles), the octahedron (a figure made with eight triangles), the dodecahedron (with twelve pentagons), and the icosahedron (with twenty triangles). Students can find examples of all these forms in photos of architecture, in box design, and in chemical and cell structures. From the Renaissance forward, artists have been fascinated by these forms.

Youngsters who play soccer will enjoy making a large soccer ball from thirty-one pentagons and hexagons, cut from black-and-white oak tag or posterboard, with tabs on the sides to staple, tape, and/or glue them together. Have students cut the shapes out and draw their own sports exploits, using white chalk on the black shapes and black markers on the white shapes. Then put the ball together. The soccer ball is the same shape as the man-made buckyball (composed of clusters of sixty carbon atoms, C_{60}, and only a billionth of a meter in diameter), which transmits fiber-optic communications.

In a small-group project, students can build solid, three-dimensional structures from toothpicks and gumdrops. These will be stable because they are built of triangles, the most stable shape. A tetrahedon requires four gumdrops and six toothpicks; an octahedron, six gumdrops and twelve toothpicks; an icosahedron, twelve gumdrops and thirty toothpicks. Bring

in subject matter: For example, little cut-out figures can suggest an ancient Egyptian scene, a soccer game, or outer space explorers.

Mobius Strips The continuous curving transitions and ribbon edges of Mobius strips can imaginatively become the basis for depictions of fantastic amusement park rides. Alternately, a sequence of steps in an action scene can be drawn on both sides of a strip of paper and folded into a Mobius strip, to make a continuous, never-ending story. Cut a Mobius strip in half lengthwise to see what will happen. Other examples of "endless" design occur in Middle Eastern arabesques, Leonardo da Vinci's knot designs, the Celtic Book of Kells, M. C. Escher's prints—and tying shoes.

Spirals A spiral is a curve in a plane or in space that runs around a center. Mathematical formulae produce many types of spirals. Archimedean spirals, which resemble the neat peeling of an orange, can be cut from paper and hung over a lamp; they will rotate, just as the thermal currents on which birds and gliders effortlessly float upward. To decorate an artwork, make spirals cut from a thin strip of paper pulled between the edge of a knife and the thumb. A dandelion floated in water with its stem cut lengthwise into strips will form spirals. Spirals can be found in fingerprints, in the Chinese yin yang symbol, and in the tops of Ionic columns. Tornadoes, which spin counterclockwise in the Northern Hemisphere, have a corkscrew structure called a helix, a shape also found in spiral staircases, rotary lawnmowers and grain harvesters,

---

IN THE CLASSROOM

A Classroom Museum of Math, Nature, and Art

Encourage your students to bring in examples of math in nature or art to display or share. Look for mathematical principles in architecture, fabric design, boxes, and computer art. Look for relationships between snail shells, sliced sections of whelk shells, and photos of spiral staircases. Call attention to both the design structure and the mathematical and scientific explanations of nature's phenomena. Consider the following shapes, patterns, and principles, commonly found in nature:

- Symmetry in five directions (as a starfish or snowflake)
- Radial patterns (as in daisy petals)
- Spiral patterns (as in spiral whelk shells and the series of leaves going up a stalk)
- Fractal patterns (in which the part recapitulates the structure of the whole, as in dried mud flats, branching trees, and meandering rivers)

Left: *Courtesy of Jenni Horne.*
Right: *Courtesy of Storm King Art Center, Mountainville, N.Y. Gift of the artist. Photo: Jerry L Thompson.*

$C = \pi D$. The circumference of a circle is a little over three times the circle's diameter. This kindergartner's paper strips will need to be a little over three times the width she wants the circles to be. Her circle sculpture can hint at this relationship. **Right:** This knowledge can be applied at a large scale. Circles are piled 32 feet high in Alice Aycock's painted steel sculpture.

Courtesy of Joyce Vroon.

The mathematician Benoit Mandelbrot figured out the mathematical formulas for nature's branching and dividing forms. Now, using these formulas, computer programs can draw branching trees, meandering streams, and forming clouds. Artists and people sensitive to nature have long intuitively sensed these relationships. Sixth-grade student Michael Selik's photo shows the fractal branching of tree limbs creating dramatic silhouettes against the heavy winter sky.

the metal waste from a drill cutting soft metal, and the DNA double-helix molecule.

Math and art are two ways of knowing about the world. Especially during the Golden Age of Greece and during the Renaissance, math and art came together. You can help your students to see these interrelationships in a variety of art and mathematics lessons based on measurement, shapes, and proportions.

FOR FURTHER READING

Bickley-Green, Cynthia. 1995. "Mathematics and Art Curriculum Integration: A Postmodern Foundation." *Studies in Art Education* 37(1): 6–18.

Calter, Paul. 2004. *Squaring the Circle: Geometry in Art and Architecture.* Emerysville, CA: Key College Publishing. Calter is designer of the MATC (Math Across the Curriculum Project) at Dartmouth College.

Martinello, M., and Cook, G. 1994. *Interdisciplinary Inquiry in Teaching and Learning.* New York: Macmillan.

Courtesy of David Harvell.

Eight-fold symmetry shows in yarn designs popular in Mexico, called Ojos Dios (God's eyes). Rather than sticks, long cardboard strips were used for supports, making it possible to staple the class's work together for a magnificent hallway display. Another lesson conveyed is that, through combining our individual efforts, we can achieve greater goals than anyone can achieve individually.

Top: *Courtesy of Barbara Thomas.* Bottom: *Courtesy of Pat Kerner.*

Top: A school hallway display of math art. ***Bottom:*** Pillows with Adrinkra symbols contain many examples of symmetry.

Moore, Michael. 1995. "Towards a New Liberal Learning in Art." *Art Education* 48(6): 6–13.

Perkins, David. 1994. *The Intelligent Eye: Learning to Think by Looking at Art.* Champaign: University of Illinois Press.

Tolley, Kimberly. 1994. *The Art and Science Connection.* Reading, MA: Addison-Wesley.

Vonderman, Carol. 1999. *How Math Works.* Pleasantville, NY: Readers Digest Association.

WEB RESOURCES

See search engines for terms "math" and "art activities" and "elementary school."

For general information on art and math:

www.artsednetm.org/actmedia.html

www.artsednet.getty.edu/artsEdnet/Links_ed.html

Paul Calter (pcalter@sover.net) has researched how artists and builders (including Leonardo and Piero Della Francesca) have brought art and math together over the centuries to build the Great Pyramids, domes, and to figure out perspective and geometry. See this research at

www.Dartmouth.edu/~matc/math5/unit5.html

along with other units at

geometry/unit2/unit2.html#golden%20ratiomath5.geometry/unit5

For another excellent geometry site:

http://euler.slu.edu/teachmaterial/hyperlinks_for_geometry.html

For symmetry, go to:

http://log24.com/theory/dd/NetsVersion.html

For a good internet site on math:

http://www.internet4classrooms.com/math_elem_htm

For a student-made website on Fibonacci numbers:

http://www.thinkquest.org/library/
site_sum.html?lib_id=2872&team_id=5906

For Fibonacci numbers in nature:

http://library.thinkquest.org/5906/nature.htm

http://math.rice.edu/~lanius/Geom/index.html

For fractals:

http://archive.ncsa.uiuc.edu/Edu/Fractal/Fractal_Home.html

http://math.rice.edu/~lanius/fractals/WHY/

For learning geometry through art:

http://mathforum.org/~sarah/shapiro/

For mapping and the four-color theorem:

http://mathforum.org/~sarah/shapiro/shapiro.color.mapping.html

For geometry and art vocabulary:

http://mathforum.org/~sarah/shapiro/shapiro.gradefive.html

For finding polygon shapes in triangular graph paper:

http://math.rice.edu/~lanius/Geom/pol.html

For a math lesson using paper folding:

http://mathforum.org/alejandre/escot/folding.html

For a teacher-designed first-grade lesson bringing numbers and design together:

http://www.princetonol.com/groups/iad/lessons/elem/artmath.htm

For a lesson plan for computer art tessellations:

http://syrylynrainbowdragon.tripod.com/tes.html

For a lesson plan for tiles:

http://syrylyrainbowdragon.tripod.com/tiles.html

For more about string designs:

www.geocities.com/SoHo/workshop/9155/instructions3/designs.html

For more about tangrams:

www.enchantedmind.com/puzzles/tangram/tangram.html

www.tangram.i-p.com

For more about three-dimensional structures:

www.dpgraph.com/janine/mathpage/platonic.html

For more about spirals:

www. mathematische-bastelien.de/spiral.htm

Chapter 9
Art and Social Studies

Culture is the common possession of a body of people who share the same traditions. It is that complex whole that includes knowledge, beliefs, art, morals, law, and customs. One important way for transmitting, maintaining, and analyzing any culture is through the visual arts; hence, art plays an important role in social studies education. (One current elementary-school social studies textbook includes 600 reproductions of artworks, for example.) The arts are integral to the study of culture, and they are a common denominator in world civilizations. And, vice versa, topics from social studies can be used to learn about the art of art: light and dark, texture and color, dominance and subordinance, carrying through a motif and varying a theme.

This chapter suggests ways in which art can be integrated with the teaching of social studies concepts such as self-determination, location, and human/environment interactions. We will look first at general strategies for integrating art into social studies lessons. Also included here is a discussion of how art relates to the six basic social studies disciplines (from anthropology to sociology), and finally, an exploration of the role of art in multicultural understanding, an important movement in today's schools, and a topic that cuts across all of the social studies disciplines.

GENERAL STRATEGIES FOR ART AND SOCIAL STUDIES INTEGRATION

Some strategies are applicable in any of the specific social studies disciplines, and at almost any grade level.

Personalized Responses Because social studies/art integration projects often center on some *other* person or some remote event, always seek to motivate the student's *personal* response. "If you had been there, how

Courtesy of ICCA, Milner Library, Illinois State University.

Pride in his farm family's golden fields of grain, windmill, pond, animals, house, and flowers radiates from this Capetown, South Africa, primary-grade child's picture.

would you look, how would you solve it, who would be with you, what objects would you take with you, what clothes would you wear?" Seek the rapid involvement of both thought and feeling. Since art often involves the expression of personal feelings, urge students to put themselves and their daily activities into their representation of the earlier culture's figures.

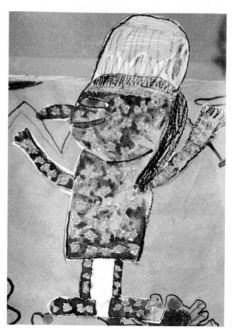

Left: *Courtesy of David Harvell.* Middle and right: *Courtesy of Alice Ballard Munn and Diane Barrett.*

When art considerations are serious, integrated art and culture lessons are of value for learning in both areas. The study of ancient Egyptian culture comes alive through art expression. **Left:** Life-sized paintings of mummy sarcophagi create a display of grandeur and majesty in the elementary school's entrance hall. **Middle:** Glazed ceramic sculpture of the Egyptian ibis-headed scribe deity, Thoth. **Right:** A first-grade student's painting of Nut, the star-studded deity of the night.

Courtesy of Melody Milbrandt.

The third- and fourth-graders' personalities shine through this mural showing Native-American styles of dress, artifacts, housing, and decoration.

Begin with their own beliefs, values, and community, rather than your giving out information. Combining their personal experiences and multicultural perspectives is primary.

Strive to make the classroom a more democratic place by incorporating the neglected group's subculture. Ask students from differing cultural backgrounds to explain why they like the art that they do—but be careful not to stereotype cultures by expecting students to express particular preferences, or suggesting that all students from a particular culture will like the same thing. The art program you provide your students can help them to feel pride in and connectedness to themselves and their own cultural backgrounds, to other people, and to other cultures.

Hands-on Art Activities Creative, hands–on activities can promote both social studies knowledge and cross-cultural understanding in many ways. One of the best hands-on projects to promote multicultural understanding is mural-making. Mural projects help students gain not only knowledge about art and about the mural's topic, but also another kind of knowledge: social intelligence, or how to plan and execute a project in a team. When individuals collaborate, whether in a family, a classroom, or later in a job, their self-esteem grows and they feel less alienated.

Individual projects also encourage both social studies learning and cultural understanding. For example, students can paint cultural celebrations and discuss diverse customs. Puppet plays and dioramas can illustrate clearly what students know about other cultures, or about their own cul-

Paintings: *Courtesy of Melody Milbrandt.* Repoussés: *Courtesy of Joyce Vroon.*

Medieval life is shown in these artworks. Third graders show their understanding of medieval life from the girls' and boys' perspectives: the need for protection, and the thrill of battle and metal clanging on metal. Themes of protection, death, and territory are brought out. A maiden awaits her knight outside her well-protected fortress. Death lies outside a closed-up castle. The repoussés remind us that subject matter and art media came together in this medieval age when both armory and metalworking were at their heights.

Courtesy of Jackie Ellett.

Multicultural understandings are acquired as these students from many ethnic backgrounds become friends, working together, side by side, creating a mural.

ture at an earlier time. Students can construct and draw; they can manipulate ideas through art construction—by drawing their understandings of things, by cutting out labels and pasting them onto their drawings, by constructing models and dioramas. For example, these can be models of artifacts, buildings and communities, land forms, coal mines, off-shore oil-drilling rigs, or open-pit mines. Students can exhibit sewing, soap carving, paper bag or straw dolls, baskets, jewelry, pottery, playhouses, tie-dyed fabric, block printing, bulletin boards, posters, knitting, or quilting. Other media might include photography, computer art, collage, sculpting, and constructions of two- and three-dimensions. But keep in mind that the art activity should be thoughtful—not simply a rote assignment. For example, a poster should be done in conjunction with a serious study of poster design—the work of Ben Shahn, perhaps, with its bold lettering and simple design.

Doing an artwork in the style of another culture can teach students about that culture's way of looking at phenomena. When doing a contemporary version of an earlier culture's style, however, be sure to discuss the sociopolitical issues of that culture. Help students bring out what they already know or can research about the culture. Just making a kachina doll will not necessarily result in multicultural understanding; without discussing the culture, such an activity may be considered a mere pastiche of surface appearances.

Drawing Still-Life Arrangements About a Culture Study a culture through a still-life arrangement that you and your students put together. Collect or borrow from a children's museum or curriculum-materials center artifacts from particular countries and regions to give a feeling about their design motifs and indigenous art materials. Perhaps students' parents have masks, wood carvings, costumes, textiles, ceramics, toys, dolls, fans, puppets, and kites to loan for the still life. To bring out more fully the nature of a culture, have the students not merely draw an object from it, but also discuss how the culture treated groups such as children, women, captives, and the elderly, and how it accumulated its wealth.

Early Americana still lifes might include travel posters of cities' historic buildings, colorful bedspreads or quilts hung or draped, and historic farm implements. Student models can even sit or recline within the still life, wearing old-fashioned costumes, while other students photograph or draw the whole scene.

A wide variety of cultural artifacts can facilitate learning about diverse cultures. Often students and their families will be willing to loan such artifacts, or parents may be willing to come in and talk about them. Consider sending a letter home early in the year describing what you plan and asking for parent volunteers or loans. Here are some possibilities:

Central American pottery

Colorful paper umbrellas from Japan

Kites, fans, and bells from the Orient

Masks: African, Indian, Malaysian, Indonesian, Mexican, Chinese opera, Mardi Gras, clown, Japanese Noh or Bugaku, Greek drama

Eskimo sculpture in soapstone or whalebone

Top left and right: *Courtesy of Baiba Kuntz.* Bottom: *Courtesy of David W. Hodge.*

Nineteenth-century clothing design is studied as students took turns modeling, a half period each turn. Fifth-grader Laura Richart captured every ruffle with eight colors of Sharpie® markers. **Bottom:** Make nineteenth-century culture come alive through a still life of early Americana.

Top: *Courtesy of Deborah Lackey.* Center and Bottom: *Courtesy of Joyce Vroon.*

Knowledge of a culture's materials and customs. ***Top:*** Through drawing a still life of artifacts from the Southwest Native-American culture, fifth-graders' learning about styles of decoration is integrated with their knowledge of the culture. ***Center:*** Oriental costume is studied as a student model coyly poses wearing a richly patterned silk kimono, with fan and umbrella and pussy willow flowers. ***Bottom:*** Watercolor landscape painting is studied along with the use of the fan in East Asian culture.

Indian kachina and Japanese kokeshi dolls

Navaho rugs and San Blas Indian molas

Musical instruments from around the world

Puppets, toys, dolls, and wood carvings from around the world

Using Models and Speakers When studying a certain region of the world, see if you can invite someone from that region to come and talk while wearing ethnic costumes. They may even be willing to pose for your students for drawings and photographs. Invite them to share the cultural artifacts from their collections. While drawing the visitor in costume, students can ask about the country's current problems and successes. Also invite guests and parents with interesting occupations and hobbies and work costumes to model while they chat with the students. If you teach in or near a large city, the country's consulate may be able to put you in touch with people who have objects they would be willing to loan for school use, or who would be willing to come and talk while modeling. Or have the students themselves take turns wearing special hats or clothing, such as Indian and African tie-dyed shirts or firefighters' uniforms.

Sketching Trips Sketching trips can help students gain insight into issues of historic preservation, trade, technological innovation, and community growth. Before you go, discuss the background or sociopolitical issues you want them to understand, and while you are at the site, point out its aesthetic qualities. Use this occasion to help them understand how to create an attractive drawing—for example, the appropriate use of foreground, middle ground, and background. Of course, you will want to visit the sketching site before class to check on hazards and procedures and to secure field-trip approval from authorities. Some possible sketching sites might be:

Museums of art or natural history	Construction sites
Manufacturing facilities	Fair or arts festivals
Bus and train stations	City halls and fire stations
Historic buildings, monuments, or statues	

Using Art Reproductions You can use art reproductions in many ways to help children understand social studies content. Use art posters or large art reproductions to generate ideas about concepts like loyalty, conflict, equality, tolerance, power, and control. Ask, "How does the artist convey who is in control? What conflicts might be on the characters' minds? Are the males and females or people of different races treated differently?" When showing materials to the class, share with the students what you know about the artist's life, class, and ethnic origin, but let the students hypothesize on how issues such as life circumstances, gender, and ethnicity might have affected his or her art.

Hypothesizing, evaluating, and synthesizing are skills at the top of Bloom's Taxonomy of Educational Objectives, and they can be readily practiced using art reproductions. "What happened before? What will happen afterward? What culture practice changed before or after this scene we are looking at? Was the cultural practice shown good or bad for the society? Is this a *good* picture? Why or why not?"

Art reproductions and postcards are easy to handle and store, although real objects, of course, have a more tangible presence. Using postcards, photographs, or other reproductions of artwork, ask children to sort the artworks into the region or society from which they originated. Then, ask them to look for and describe the overall stylistic concepts that a group of cards may have in common. Facilitate learning about the art of a particular region or time through sets of art-reproduction cards made for playing an artistic version of Old Maid. "Find all the artworks made [for example] in the Orient, or during the Industrial Revolution, or in this century."

Since an art reproduction is "just a picture," students often can interact easily and reflect on their own lives as they interpret the art, without feeling personally threatened. Teams of students from diverse backgrounds can discuss how the values of other cultures are shown in the artworks and compare those values to their own. Let students who have finished a hands-on activity early play games like Go Fish with the reproductions, where students must try to acquire sets of related pictures.

A DANGER OF SOCIAL STUDIES/ ART INTEGRATION

Keep in mind an important caveat: Both bad art instruction and bad social studies instruction can easily result from the thoughtless integration of these two subjects. Stereotypes emerge all too readily from carelessly planned lessons, and hasty assignments result too often in look-a-like exercises such as sketchily colored-in outlines of one's palm and fingers for a Thanksgiving turkey. It goes without saying to eschew stereotyped, impersonal activities, such as photocopied patterns of pilgrims and presidents' profiles, wherein the art method (uncreatively coloring patterns) violates

Left: *Courtesy of David W. Hodge, Collection of the Neville Museum, Green Bay, WI.*
Right: *Courtesy of Joyce Vroon.*

Left: Take the students on sketching trips to where different cultures may be studied. Here, Amish wagons are captured by art professor David W. Hodge, who contributed many pictures to this book. ***Right:*** A discussion of the last century's attitudes toward death, its sentimentality, and its love of classical culture might be sparked by sixth-grade student Billy Welsh's photograph.

the social studies goal (assimilating into oneself something about the personal, creative initiative of the subjects studied). If no art instruction is provided, little or no art learning will occur; art materials will just be used up. Do not use art exercises just as a way to fill an unplanned fifteen minutes.

On the other hand, art/social studies learning experiences in which the teacher sets higher standards than those students will meet naturally, and that require both more effort and longer periods of time than routine work, can result in students' most memorable experiences. In such projects, students sense the unity of thought, personal feeling, and expressive action that results from an aesthetic experience. Hence, teach the social studies/art integrated lessons suggested here in tandem with the qualitative art instruction principles and methods given throughout this book. Rigorously guide students, and they will then be seriously involved.

The activities suggested here are not intended to supplant a regular art instruction period, but rather to supplement it. The National Art Education Association recommends that in addition to 100 minutes a week for art, more time should be devoted to art that is related to other subjects.

THE SOCIAL STUDIES DISCIPLINES

In the section that follows, we will explore how to integrate art with the goals specific to seven of the social studies disciplines: anthropology, economics and vocations, geography, history, political science and law-related education, psychology, and sociology.

Left: *Courtesy of Marlee Puskar and Joyce Vroon.* Middle: *Courtesy of Mary Lazzari.* Right: *Courtesy of Barbara Thomas.*

Cultural anthropology studies a culture's traits and artifacts. **Left:** Egyptian artifacts and wallpaper design accompany the students' Egyptian work in this display of students' Egyptian paste jewelry. **Middle:** Studying Anasazi pottery of the Ancient Puebloans, third-graders created these ceramic pieces decorated with black-marker Native-American designs. **Right:** African culture is examined through a papier-mâché constructed mask decorated with beans and broomsedge.

Anthropology Anthropology is the study of a people's symbols. Cultural anthropology analyzes cultural traits and artifacts. From examining and making drawings of artifacts, students can imagine what life was like in another country. When studying objects, ask, "What are the artifacts made of? For what purpose? Compared with today's artifacts, how well do you think the old objects met the need?"

Some issues to be sensitive to:

* It is disrespectful to emphasize just one aspect of a group's culture, such as weaponry (tomahawks) or inhumane practices, while neglecting a culture's nurturing and civic contributions.
* It is not helpful to exoticize a culture or people or to label them primitive. This only makes them strange or foreign. Emphasizing the "grossness" of foods or "weirdness" of clothing teaches that "they're strange from us."
* Just as the concepts of race and racial characteristics lead to false stereotypes and harm, likewise there are dangers in homogenizing many national groups into one; for example, lumping Puerto Ricans, Mexican-Americans, and Cubans into a single category of Hispanic or Latino.

With sensitivity, art activities can bring anthropology and the study of cultural beliefs and artifacts into any classroom. Here are some possibilities:

* Fold a piece of paper in half lengthwise. In one column, list schooling or coming-of-age rituals in some place or time; in the other column, list the practices in your own community. Compare and discuss the two lists.
* Illustrate the activities that people perform and the objects used at various times of the day and in different seasons. Likewise, reinforce concepts of time in early primary grades through a display showing the students' illustrations of their own activities at different times of the day.
* Have kindergarten students sort sets of artwork reproductions of the civilization into time categories: now/then, first/second/third, nighttime/daytime, summer/fall/winter/spring, before/after, or in the morning/at noon/in the evening.
* Make drawings of today's artifacts, such as fancy sports shoes, and generalize about our society from the artifacts that are drawn. The crafted objects of a society reflect its values.

Courtesy of Joyce Vroon. Left: Student Edgar Crosset. Middle: Student Taylor Dryham

Eighty percent of America's job wealth comes through the service sector; shown here vocations of pet store operator, cleaning services, and advertising.

Economics/Vocations Economics deals both with the structures that exist to provide jobs and services and also with the distribution of wealth. Examine artworks to see in them economic concepts. Discussing artworks such as George Caleb Bingham's "Fur Traders Descending the Missouri" (which the artist had first titled "French Trader and Half-Breed Son"), Honoré Daumier's "Third Class Carriage," François Millet's "The Sower," or Duane Hanson's life-size polyester resin and fiberglass figures such as "Tourists" or "Cleaning Lady" can bring out the interrelationships of resources, suppliers, consumers, and economic needs.

Here are some possible activities for supporting economics learning:

- Have students illustrate an individual plan of economic action—draw or make a collage of what you would invest in "if you won $20,000." Draw and discuss make-believe choices of "being given an amount of money to spend to buy presents."
- Assemble a drawing still life using objects of scarcity, exchange, and consumption.
- Look at advertising art and talk about how art is used to motivate buyers.
- Sketch at a local business or construction site and show types of resources: natural resources, capital resources, and human resources.
- Illustrate through drawings and diagrams how rail lines, highways, airports, industrial complexes, and geographic factors interact.
- Fold a page from the help wanted classified ads into fourths. In each of the four quarters, draw a career choice you know about and then categorize these career drawings: people who make things, fix things, create, serve, and work with ideas.

- Ask discussion questions relating to aesthetics and economics, such as "Are costly things more beautiful than inexpensive things? Why?" or "Can richer people get cooler things?"

You can readily use art lessons to let students discuss art-related career choices—mention, for example, that "these ceramic animals you made this week are as interesting as those I saw at the downtown art fair last weekend that sold for $50." Career choices become an increasing concern as students get older. Help students identify options by asking "Can you describe some occupations that use the skills found in this lesson [for example, measuring, designing, color choices]?" or "Did you know that many people make their livings by designing things like the racing automobiles that you have drawn?"

Geography Making maps helps students to learn both specific geography and general map skills. When students design maps, create fantasy countries, and develop their own personal map symbols, they will often be more interested in map reading in general. Some suggestions:

- Make neighborhood maps. Group together students who live near each other so their knowledge will inform each other as they locate fun places to go, fast-food restaurants, and playgrounds, and their own homes. Teach about symbols by letting students invent their own symbols for houses, streets, trees, and government buildings.
- Have students draw maps showing how to get from their homes to a favorite location and decorate them with personally significant details of what they see along the way, such as places to throw rocks, pick flowers, and tease barking dogs.

98 • **Part 3** Integrating Art into the Classroom

Left: *Courtesy of Claire Clements.* Right: *Courtesy of Lavonne McPherson.*

Left: Working in a group, students sewed and quilted the individual states into one United States of America, e pluribus unum. *Right:* Consideration of architectural differences between contemporary homes and this Pueblo adobe home occurs when a model is made.

- In the intermediate grades, make maps of regions and transportation arteries around your city or town. Experiment with out-of-the-ordinary art materials, such as cut yarn pieces or cardboard relief, to encourage a different type of artistic thinking. With these regional maps, encourage students to wonder about how major rivers, landforms, and highways affect urban growth.
- For a very large map, students working in small groups in an out-of-the-way corner of the room can use a mixture of sawdust, glue, vermiculite, plaster of Paris, and water on a large piece of cardboard or plywood to make a raised relief map of a part of the world.

Moving beyond maps, to make comparisons between geographic areas, students can draw differences in climate, transportation, foods, customs, and home architecture on a paper folded in half. After studying the street names in the area, students can draw imaginary portraits of the individuals, or creatively illustrate the name of a famous place to show something about it. While studying about transportation, have students sketch vintage automobiles in the school parking lot or bicycles brought into the classroom, with a student modeling as the driver. In their picture backgrounds, have them draw from photographic views of modern cloverleaf intersections or historic photos of city streets and bridges.

Art reproductions can be examined regarding the land forms, and aesthetic concepts of the beautiful and ugly can be discussed in looking at photos of highway views, landscape design, and urban development.

History Make history vivid in students' minds through art projects. To foster creative thinking about peoples' motivations at a certain time in

history, such as prehistoric peoples' cave art, have students hypothesize about the prehistoric artists' intent while reenacting the painting in the dim light inside a cast-off refrigerator carton. Students can draw scenes showing themselves in historical events and add their own captions, for example, as a character in Gustav Leutze's "Washington Crossing the Delaware." Using these pictures or art reproductions, have students sort them into chronological order and interpret what is happening in the picture. Have students draw and describe public buildings in the community, sort them into chronological order, and discuss the values conveyed by the architecture, or ask them to illustrate a problematic situation, such as a slave's dilemma to run away or not, or an immigrant's dilemma, or an army general's dilemma, and draw your own personal solution.

Any number of specific art lessons can illustrate history for students.

- In two clay figures or on two halves of a sheet of paper, contrast your life with that of a person from a historical period.
- Make applehead dolls, with yarn hair added and dressed to represent historical figures, and add an accompanying illustration of an event in that famous individual's life.
- Put on a puppet play showing two varying scenarios of how an event may have taken place, and enact contrasting feelings toward the event.
- Illustrate what you may have been doing, in reality or in fantasy, when a great event occurred.
- Make a mural depicting historic events, and tell another class about it.
- Make illustrated time lines showing the development of tools, inventions, and the arts, or illustrated grids showing, for example, names of cultures down one side and headings such as houses, headdresses, and food across the top.
- Make models of ancient monuments, castles, cathedrals, kon-tiki rafts, dioramas and displays, masks, embroidery, engravings, and costumes for role-playing to stimulate students' imaginations, especially when personalizing occurs and art principles are emphasized.

Political Science and Law-Related Education Law-related education deals with concepts such as equality, fairness, honesty, justice, power, property, responsibility, and tolerance. Students can relate to issues such as family law (e.g., beatings), community-safety law (e.g., bike helmets), and consumer law (e.g., shoplifting). Political science is concerned with examining rules, both good and bad, and taking the rights of others into account. Students can illustrate examples from their lives of their own legal awareness, from raw power to group values to a belief in principles. Many art reproductions illustrate such issues. Students can debate the merits of the issues, both from the artist's point of view and in the students' own personal opinions concerning how such issues play out in their own communities. For example, Diego Rivera's contrasting murals "Night of the

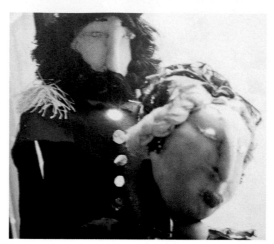

Courtesy of Barbara Thomas.

Civil War issues of human rights vs. states' rights are brought to light through this puppet project.

Rich" and "Night of the Poor" and Luis Cruz Azaceta's "Oppression III" illustrate issues of corruption and humans' cruelty to each other.

Other related art lessons include:

- Do figure drawings of a police officer who models while talking about community law problems, or from a uniformed member of the military who talks about issues of international law.
- Make puppets during the primary grades to enact issues involving classroom rules, such as raising one's hand to speak, or in mock trials conducted on law-related issues, such as a trespassing trial of Goldilocks vs. the Three Bears.
- Draw and discuss how people on the playground show that they do not approve of certain behavior.
- Make posters in elementary classrooms to illustrate rules for safety on the playground swings, and in middle-school classrooms to illustrate the pros and cons of community issues, such as gun control and airport or city dump relocation. Combine drawings and text in balloons, as is used in cartoons.
- Draw political cartoons about politicians or world issues, after examining the symbols and stereotypes in published cartoons and discussing them.
- From the intermediate school years to young adulthood, children's law and order orientation is strong; older students can research and debate the rightness or wrongness of actions in art history episodes such as Michelangelo's breaking his contract with the Pope and running away from painting the Sistine Chapel ceiling.

Courtesy of Joyce Vroon.

Political issues of fairness and power may be discussed following sixth-graders making political cartoons characterizing leaders' features, here President Carter and a general.

Psychology Psychology is concerned with how an individual perceives the world or behaves based on those perceptions. Social roles (such as leadership, aggression, and submission) and personal social needs (such as acceptance and belonging) can be brought out through students making artworks on topics like sibling relationships, relationships with school peers, or what I do to please my parents. Topics like "I am happiest when . . ." or "What I value" may be too broad and require narrowing during

 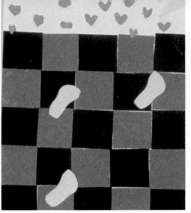 

Psychology: Goals, relations with siblings, dealing with happiness and sadness, self-examination of personal and social goals are some ways psychology and art can come together. ***Top left:*** Combining the expressing of a personal goal or favorite activity with a study of Stuart Davis's art, a student produced this exuberant soccer design. ***Top middle:*** The ability to transcend what life throws at us is metaphorically shown in the piece explained by the artist: "I am walking through the checkerboard of life's moods and feelings, stepping through the red of happiness and the black of sadness." ***Top right:*** Issues of being on endless display may be metaphorically suggested in Michael Selik's dream drawing of himself rapidly proceeding through an endless hall of mirrors. ***Left center:*** Dealing with one's feelings of love, anger, and frustration (towards one's brother) is shown in the "Brother Killer Machine." ***Left bottom:*** Doing her self-portrait lets fourth-grader Johanna Siska think about her appearance, dress, and values.

the motivation period—for example, "What (*about siblings, about food, about the playground*) makes me feel happy, sad, or mad?" Self-expression as a goal can be brought out through eliciting and praising unique expression. "Because you are a unique individual, your art should not look like anyone else's. Make it your own way."

One goal of social studies education is to help students learn to respect others—and first, to respect oneself. Creative expression in the arts is an excellent way to build self-respect and positive self-concept.

Individual differences can be brought out through self-portraits that show personal interests, values, likes, and dislikes (see the section on self-portraits on pp. 256–258). Psychology exercises on peer understanding ("Find out three things about your partner") can easily be integrated with the art task of drawing a classmate. Have students illustrate what-will-happen-next endings to situations of value conflict (individual freedom vs. the common good, for example). Motivate thinking about value-based problems by having one student draw a problem situation on half a folded paper and another student draw the solution on the other half.

Top left: *Courtesy of Teacher Susan Whipple and the USSEA art collection of Dr. Anne Gregory.*
Top right: *Courtesy of Barbara Thomas.* Right middle: *Courtesy of Melody Milbrandt.*
Right bottom: *Courtesy of ICCA, Milner Library, Illinois State University.*

Sociology: ***Top left:*** Society's institutions of home, government, and church try to affect the blue bird flying upwards. ***Top right:*** Nineteenth-century American village life is shown in this first-grader's drawing. ***Right middle:*** Many group social interactions occur at a first-grader's birthday party. ***Right bottom:*** A 13-year-old Indian girl showed the teamwork required in making a mural.

The relativity of perception can be shown by asking for different interpretations of art reproduction. "Does anyone think it means something different?" The meaning of a painting such as Edvard Munch's "The Scream" can be debated—what might have provoked the feelings depicted in the painting, and what strategies might be used for dealing with such emotions? Brainstorming for alternate solutions to a problem can also be used for art teaching—for instance, have students work in pairs and discuss how to make their designs attractive and eye-catching.

Sociology Sociology is the study of how people function in groups. Art can provide an easy way for many students to understand the sociology of their family and community. In early grades, have students draw their families and what the family does on special days. In middle grades, illustrate the contributions of the people who live in your city or state. Focus on the outstanding contributions made by immigrants from a particular country or region.

Sociology and art come together when students think about questions like these: Why do the people in our community do art? How and why is our art different from art in other lands and at other times? In our area,

how does art bring about a sense of community? How are the varied cultural customs around us shown in the art of our community? How have people in our community and elsewhere, and at other times, made art to mark life transitions and other social purposes?

Use art to explore abstract concepts by first examining artworks reflecting those concepts and then having students make their own drawings. In upper grades, encourage students to think about such concepts as norms, society, values, competition, status, and change. Ask them to draw "If I could change this city (or this school) in some way . . ." or "If I were the teacher. . . ." Try illustrating a concept or an event working only from a verbal description, such as whether child labor laws are fair.

Art reproductions can spur discussions of sociological issues. For example, Jacob Lawrence's "Migration Series" documented the changed lives of African Americans in the 1930s as they moved from the South to the North seeking work. Or use sociological strategies to encourage art: Have students use the polling methods of sociological studies to interview friends and family about art-related issues—for example, whether a new public building is attractive or not. Students can poll their neighbors on the design merits of a new playground, public sculpture, or community recreation center. Try illustrating a concept or event such as the urbanization of an area, child labor in a clothing factory, or the making of steel, working only from a verbal description. A group of students can each draw one event in a sequence, and the whole can be pasted together. Students can then label the drawing and take turns explaining them. To bring out the idea of multiple group memberships (recreational, community, religious), have students make drawings of themselves doing an activity in each of several different groups, and then combine the resulting artworks into a large display. Stimulate career thinking by drawing people in uniforms or work-related clothes: police officers; firefighters; nurses; performers such as clowns, dancers, musicians with their instruments; scuba divers; and athletes in uniform.

Students can write or give oral reports on a family member, relative, or neighbor engaged in the arts in an activity that integrates not only social studies and art but also language arts. Use photography and videotaping to document individual interviews with artists or community persons, or to explore the community's eyesores and attractive sights.

MULTICULTURAL UNDERSTANDING THROUGH ART

Multicultural understanding is part of and also transcends many of the ideas presented in this chapter. Multicultural understanding is not a passing trend: It is a new approach to our nation's "melting pot" concept, a way of thinking about what defines an American and how our various cultural

Courtesy of Jackie Ellett.

Notice in their artwork how students from different ethnic backgrounds become friends as they create art side by side.

heritages can accommodate one another. Will the melting pot, in which all cultures assimilate into a single American identity, be replaced by a salad bowl, in which each culture retains its particular individuality?

As American schools become increasingly multicultural (many districts are already close to 100% nontraditional in their ethnic makeup), art teachers are building curricula that promote the appreciation of diverse artistic heritages. Art is a natural area in which to combat ethnocentrism and monoculturalism. The goal is not to add "multicultural" ingredients to education but to make education itself truly multicultural—not to abandon an existing curriculum but to expand it to include cultural plurality.

We can help children to understand and acquire the shared knowledge, beliefs, and attitudes common to members of both our nation's culture and their specific group. When you are a source of positive energy concerning students' ethnic heritages, your art program can motivate and develop confidence in at-risk students. Yet, while education should help students understand the cultures in which they live, it can and should also free them from their cultural boundaries. Art can help teach students to respect those who are different from themselves, those who lead their lives in different ways. Not only are our society and our schools incorporating new cultural perspectives, but so also is the art world.

Multiculturalism in the Postmodern Art World In recent decades, the art world has increasingly moved away from abstract art elements and toward exploring social, political, and environmental world problems

Courtesy of Dahria McClelland.

Coral reefs, built over hundreds of years around the world, are endangered by mud and pollution from development. These artworks may help call attention to this problem.

through combining historical and popular images and new mixed-media techniques. Art for art's sake—once a cutting-edge contemporary idea—has been eclipsed, and formalism—the idea that the formal elements and principles are art's central issues—is under attack as irrelevant and even oppressive. In the early twentieth century, the Modernist movement dealt with issues such as abstraction and abstract expressionism and avoided sociopolitical commentary. The Modern period was characterized by rational, traditional, absolute, and universal values. Postmodernism, on the contrary, is characterized by relativity and conflict.

Art's new emphasis is "Aboutness." Art is about the society in which it is made. It is about a particular culture's values and political beliefs, to which its creator either acquiesced or resisted. Especially nowadays, there are numerous notions of the nature of art, reflecting less a unified worldview and more a minefield of conflicting notions about the nature of art. Art imagery can be a battleground of meaning. It can be a weapon of competing groups in their quest for influence and power. Certainly, it is true that art can be an agent for social change. Some would even go so far as to say that all art is political. Artworks such as Nancy Spero's and Leon Golub's works about brutality, Judy Chicago's and Mary Kelly's pieces about women and motherhood, Kara Walker's cutouts of African-American stereotypes, or Nam June Paik's and Joseph Beuys's video

about whales show this renewed sociopolitical activism. Of course, this increased activism is not entirely without precedent: Many artists over the ages have been political, and many periods have been dominated by political art. During the Modernist period, the artworks of George Grosz, Max Beckmann, and Kathe Kollwitz, for example, criticized Nazi Germany.

Multiculturalism Through a Thematic Approach A thematic approach to multicultural art focuses on cultural differences and commonalities through exploration of concepts such as adaptation, survival, environment, time, space, and motion. Students explore a variety of resources, and consult references on the Internet, and in books and magazines. Groups of students from diverse cultures can work together arranging art reproductions about such issues into a bulletin-board display. The teacher and students pick an issue to be explored historically through analysis of artworks. For example, today's ecological crises have pointed up the merits of less technologically intrusive ways of living. The Native Americans' sense of stewardship for the earth addresses these needs, and our recognition of this has resulted in an increased interest in Native-American culture. In teaching such thematic units, relate the material to the students' own life experiences, their own understanding of the current

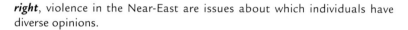

Contestable issues bring out dissenting opinions and help to make individuals aware of other points of view. **Left**, ctting down old-growth forests, **middle**, preserving air quality, quality of life in the inner-city, housing, and, **right**, violence in the Near-East are issues about which individuals have diverse opinions.

We can help students understand and respect the Native-American ethnic heritage by representing persons from that culture in their traditional dress. **Top left:** Here fourth-grader Shelly Jones paints a Native American in traditional costume using the skillfully coordinated shades and tints of Indian red and earth colors with accents of bright colors. **Top middle:** Is all art political? The plaintive expression on this clay figure seems to tell volumes about America's historic mistreatment of Native peoples. **Top right:** Detail of a 12- × 12-foot cultural mural showing figures in Native American and African dress circling the globe. **Bottom left:** Patterns of crosses, thunderbolts, stripes, dots, and a parade of animals and birds make this full-size replica in acrylic paint of a Plains Indian teepee by fifth- and sixth-graders an object of wonder and beauty.

Top: *Courtesy of Tainan Schools.* Bottom: *Courtesy of Beverly Barksdale Mallon.*

Your art program can help students feel pride in and connectedness to their cultural backgrounds. ***Top:*** Here, elementary-school children from Tainan, Taiwan, have depicted their culture's traditional river festival. ***Bottom:*** Surely, part of America's strength is its ability to integrate the cultural contributions of its diverse population. Fourth- and fifth-graders painted this stage backdrop for a social studies pageant. Shown are famous American Freedom Fighters who have changed our society, set against a starry, fireworks-filled sky. In this detail, clockwise from the top: Abraham Lincoln, James Madison, Thomas Jefferson, Susan B. Anthony (in red dress), Frederick B. Douglas, Eleanor Roosevelt, and Cesar Chavez.

situation in the students' community. Still another way to promote multicultural education is through exchanges of child art between schools here and in other countries.

Multiculturalism Using Contestable Issues Another way to approach multiculturalism through art is to use issues about which students can debate. This teaching method fosters the examination of cultural assumptions, a critical attitude towards the status quo, and a nurturance of social change. Present the students with a real-life dilemma related to art and social studies and discuss how to solve it. An "Art News" bulletin board on current events related to social science/art topics can trigger discussion. The controversy might be about a piece of public art, or about an artist's actions or financial predicament, or an art theft or forgery, or the return of artwork to the country or tribe of its origin. Inform students about the situations and feelings behind the real-life controversy.

In artworks, students can look for evidence of oppression and social structure inequality. They can find images that maintain the dominant culture, and show another group or gender in subservient roles. Students can try to find artworks showing positive or negative attitudes towards such ideas as the following: that people have the right to live in different ways, that power should be equitably distributed among groups, and that social justice should exist for all. You need to be aware, of course, that some school administrators and communities may not be sympathetic to the contestable issues approach.

Jean Piaget, an influential psychologist, believed that students and educators should be searching for conflict, since conflict is a part of all life and is necessary for development. A plant's roots become strong by pushing against the soil. Art criticism, using art reproductions, affords a forum to debate the merits of the values shown in artworks. For example, ideas about the power of the state can be debated using Max Beckmann's "Departure" as a starting point toward a discussion of the equitable administration of justice to all people in a community. Important skills to learn include how to respond to conflict—by acquiescing to the dominant point of view or assertively advocating for one's own or minority points of view—and how to express disagreement agreeably, in a patient, rational manner. Students can do their own artworks about their perceptions of inequities in the community or nation.

The art/social studies program that you provide your students can help them to feel pride in and connectedness to themselves and their own cultural backgrounds, as well as to other people and other cultures. Social studies and art have much in common; they share a common interest in perceiving the distinctive attributes and amounts of things, and in grouping and generalizing things by shared properties. Values education can be promoted through art making and art viewing. And there are larger goals, even beyond learning specifically about art and social studies. The study of the arts and humanities enriches daily life, helps one to understand oneself, helps maintain civility, and develops a sense of community.

FOR FURTHER READING

Billings, Mary-Michael. 1995. "Issues vs. Trends: Two Approaches to a Multicultural Art Curriculum." *Art Education* 48(1): 21–24, 53–56.

Chalmers, F. G. 1996. *Celebrating Pluralism: Art, Education, and Cultural Diversity.* Los Angeles, CA: Getty Education Institute.

Chandra, Jacqueline. 1993. "A Theoretical Basis for Non-Western Art Historical Instruction." *Journal of Aesthetic Education* 27(3): 73–84.

Congdon, Kristin. "Multicultural Approaches to Art Education." *Studies in Art Education* 30(3): 176–184.

Delacruz, Elizabeth. 1995. "Multiculturalism and Art Education: Myth, Misconceptions, and Misdirections." *Art Education* 48(3): 57–61.

Garber, Elizabeth. 1995. "Teaching Art in the Context of Culture: A Study in Borderlands." *Studies in Art Education* 36(4): 218–232.

Katter, Eldon. 1995. "Multicultural Connections: Craft Community." *Art Education* 48(1): 8–13.

Kauppinen, Heta, and Diket, Read (eds.). 1995. *Trends in Art Education from Diverse Cultures.* Reston, VA: NAEA.

Leshnikoff, Susan K. 2003. "Teaching Art and Moral Conduct; John Dewey for Today." *Art Education* 56(6): 33–39.

Lippard, Lucy. 1984. *Get the Message? A Decade of Art for Social Change.* New York: Dutton.

McFee, June K. 1988. "Art and Society." In Getty Foundation for Education in the Arts. *Issues in Discipline-Based Art Education: Strengthening the Stance, Extending the Horizons.* Los Angeles: The Getty Center for Education in the Arts.

McFee, June, and Degge, Rogena. *Art, Culture, and Environment: A Catalyst for Teaching.* Belmont, CA: Wadsworth.

Neperud, Ron (ed.). 1995. *Context, Content, and Community in Art Education.* New York: Teachers College Press.

Purser, R. E., and Montouri, A. 1999. *Social Creativity.* Cresskill, NJ: Hampton Press, Inc.

Saunders, Robert J. (ed.). *Beyond the Traditional in Art: Facing a Pluralistic Society.* Reston, VA: National Art Education Association.

Wasson R., Stuhr P., and Petrovich-Mwaniki, L. 1990. "Teaching Art in the Multi-cultural Classroom: Six Position Statements." *Studies in Art Education* 31(4): 234–246.

Young, Bernard. 1991. *Art, Culture, and Ethnicity.* Reston, VA: NAEA.

WEB RESOURCES

For lists of civic, historical, economic, and historical social studies concepts:
http://www.michigan.gov/mde/
1,1607,7-140-6525_6530_6568-19452--,00.html

For a guide to art careers:
http://www.princetonol.com/groups/iads/lessons/middle/careers.htm

For a guide to many lesson plans and ideas related to social studies topics:
http://www.getty.edu/artsednet/Search/map.html

For sources in Chicano art and culture:
http://mati.eas.asu.edu:8421/ChicanArte/html_pages/
Protest-home.html

For Navajo art lessons:
http://www.getty.edu/artsednet/resources/Navajo/index.html

For multicultural prints and lesson plans on topics such as African-American art, Mexican-American art, women artists of the Americas, or India art:
http://www.getty.edu/artsednet/resources/Maps/index.html

For social studies lesson resources and website references:
http://smithsonianeducation.org/educators/index.html

For material on Japanese art and people:
http://www.smithsonianeducation.org/educators/lesson_plans/
japan_images_people/index.html

For a lesson relating Harriet Tubman, freedom quilts, and the Big Dipper:
http://artsedge.kennedy-center.org/content/3501/

For a lesson on art jobs, especially using computers:
http://www.princetonol.com/groups/iad/jobs/artjobs.html

Chapter 10
Art and Science

Both science and art are ways of knowing, both provide students with a grasp of new similarities and contrasts, and both go beyond traditional categories to yield new visions about our world. Both can show the principles that underlie nature's phenomena. Science and art also share many of the same goals:

- Development of curiosity
- Building a knowledge base
- Visualizing mental images
- Investigating, fantasizing, and combining objects and ideas in new ways

Courtesy of Frank Wachowiak.

Art and science are two complementary approaches to understanding nature. Here, a Japanese upper-elementary-grade child envisions the famous French entomologist Jean-Henri Fabre as a boy pursuing his hobby.

To show art/science integration in action, this chapter covers many of the concepts taught in the elementary-school science curriculum.

DRAW AND SEE AND THINK

We never see a thing so clearly and vividly as when we draw it: hence, draw as often as possible in science lessons—draw specimens, maps, charts, and experiments. Urge careful observation in doing the drawing. Discourage students from using visual stereotypes, such as lollipop trees and V-shaped flying birds. Let the students' vivid imaginations help them to see, feel, and represent their own reality, sparked by the phenomena before their eyes. (For specific recommendations on drawing animals, still lifes, and the outdoors, see Chapter 23, Drawing.)

Encourage your students to think about what they see, to see analogies between what is observed and what it brings to mind—ask "What does this remind you of?"—for what we see depends greatly upon the connections elicited from memory. Let our immediate visual experience be supplemented by what our imagination brings to mind.

TEACHING SCIENCE THROUGH ART

Animal Life Enthusiastic artistic responses can be evoked by bringing to class live animals as well as terrariums and aquariums with coral and seashells. Bleached animal skulls or skeletal bones make excellent studies for line drawings, as well as vehicles to promote an understanding of anatomy. When studying vertebrates and invertebrates, classify and draw a wide variety of animals both with and without backbones, such as crickets, butterflies, snails, and earthworms. Draw birds' nests, birds in cages, and mounted birds, fish, and animals. Bring from the students' homes, or

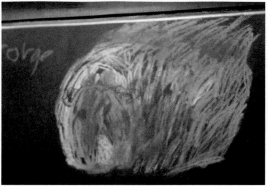
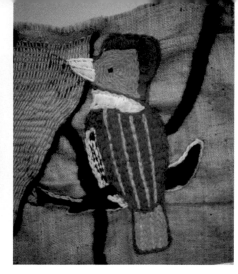

Top left, top middle, bottom middle, bottom right: *Courtesy of Joyce Vroon.* Top right: *Courtesy of Claire Clements.* Bottom left: *Courtesy of Barbara Thomas.*

Top left and middle: The class's live hamster was drawn. Second-grader George Sheerer drew in pastel on dark paper. **Top right:** For a very different art medium, this perky bluebird was rendered in stitchery. **Bottom left:** This display uses both three-dimensional and two-dimensional Antarctic penguins.

Bottom middle: A chalklike artists' material, conté crayon, was used by third-grader Quincy Smith for his animal drawing on grey paper, a favorite drawing technique of Renaissance artists. **Bottom right:** Second-grader Bingham Jamison drew a trio of sand birds in pastel.

keep as pets in the room, turtles, rabbits, and guinea pigs, and draw these in a variety of art media. Include drawings of the animals and birds along with nature studies of birds' nests, feathers, and making casts of animal tracks. Ecology, camouflage, and types of claws and beaks can be studied by using magazine photos for drawing animals and plants in their native environments. In connection with a study of weaving, try to weave a bird's nest or other container. Use puppets to engage in artistic and fantasy extensions of science and to illustrate concepts of one species preying on another, one species using another yet not harming it, or two species

deriving mutual benefit. Sketch the life stages of the brine shrimp, frog, or salamander, and include sketches of the plants and animals that are found around a pond.

Create an imaginary, three-dimensional insect using a variety of materials, then write a description of the creature, describing the physical features that it uses to find food and to defend itself. Draw ant farms and insect and butterfly collections. Using tempera resist or on a dark paper, draw pictures of oneself catching fireflies at dusk, of an expedition collecting nature specimens, or of yourself in a butterfly garden.

  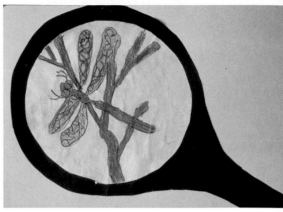

Arachnids, hemipterans, and lepidopterans: **Left:** The millions of varieties of insects, awesome in their natural beauty, have unlimited art possibilities, as illustrated in this crayon engraving by an intermediate-elementary-grade youngster. It was enhanced in the final stage by oil pastels on the background areas; borders of black lines should be preserved around each form to unify the composition. **Middle:** A second-grader used white clay to construct a spider on its web. **Right:** A dragonfly (odonate) seen through a magnifying lens.

IN THE CLASSROOM

Learning Science Through Art
Before or after a lesson of drawing animals or living things, an art/science card game can be played wherein small groups of students, using art reproductions, categorize the art reproductions (depicting, for example, spiders, fish, mammals, microorganisms) into the taxonomic categories of the animal and vegetable kingdoms—as well as into the various art styles.

Astronomy and the Solar System
Using a pattern of the star points in the Big Dipper, Big Bear, or Orion (on black paper and using chalk), students can draw their own superheroes or objects in the sky, creating "new" constellations. Have students draw views of the Earth and Moon in space, imagining they are inside or outside space-travel vehicles and confronting our spiral-shaped Milky Way galaxy.

Climate
Students can draw their own family members *as if* they were people from different climates, in native dress and in their homes. In artworks, show the climate through such features as the northern lights and wavy convection currents above a fire; ask "Where was it? What else can be seen? How does it feel?" Study the art of people from hot and cold climates—for example, African and Eskimo art.

Effects of climate and the environment on people: In this multisession art lesson, fifth-graders drew and watercolored themselves in their winter coats. **Left:** Sarah Wampler added her cat and dog, a squirrel in a nest in a white snow-covered tree, and white marshmallows floating in hot chocolate. **Right:** Betsy Ure captured the reflective sheen of her jacket, her multitasseled cap, and her love of basketball.

Nutrition and vitamins and minerals in foods can be studied through drawing still lifes. ***Top:*** Fruits and vegetables in crayon resist by second-grader Juliana Ramus. ***Bottom:*** Autumn harvest in pastel on dark paper and showing effects of light.

Foods and Nutrition Have students draw themselves gardening or harvesting or eating favorite foods and berries or at a fast-food restaurant. In the background, ask them to list the foods and their minerals, number of calories, and grams of fat. Make charts of the different kinds of food that we eat in a week. On a large piece of cardboard—the side of a mattress box, perhaps—draw a giant food pyramid; onto the pyramid, students can tape or pin their illustrations of favorite foods in each of the food groups. For this, they could draw from a still life of fruits, vegetables, nuts, breads, and cans and boxes of prepared foods.

Geology Take a sketching trip, perhaps to a nearby eroded gully, to draw unusual earth and rock formations. Point out the color and surface textures of sedimentary and igneous rocks as well as the effects of water and wind erosion or past glacial activity. From photos, draw cave interiors with stalactites and stalagmites, and imagine an exciting "Tom Sawyer-like" story of students in a cave, finding prehistoric cave art such as that found worldwide on rocks under cliffs. From small still-life arrangements of colorful rocks and minerals, draw their shapes, textures, patterns, and colors and label them. Discuss the chemical elements that

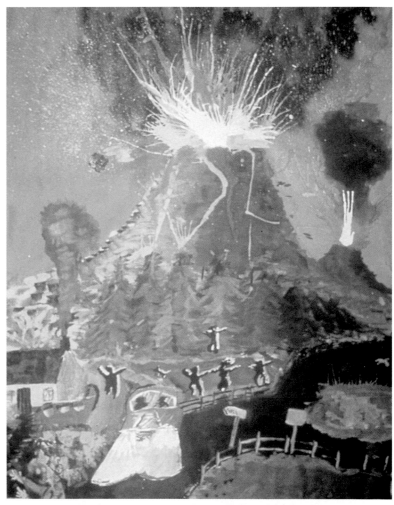

Geological knowledge of earth's molten interior magma layer is apparent in David Williams's use of a straw to blow paint.

make up pigments—iron red, chrome green and yellow, cobalt blue, lead white, cadmium orange. When studying fossils, make plaster bas-relief casts of current everyday objects.

The Human Body, Anatomy, and Growth After seeing anatomical drawings by da Vinci and Vesalius and first making a figure drawing, students then can use tissue paper or plastic wrap to enable them to see through to the original drawing below. Then they can imagine, draw, and label the locations of the muscles. Then, on top of that layer, on another sheet, have them locate and draw the (real and imaginary) organs inside one's body. Insights into human growth can be gained by having students draw themselves from baby pictures or from imagination, doing the good and bad things that they did at that age. Also students can draw an imaginary view of themselves when they are old and doing some favorite activity.

Light and Perception Just as telescopes and magnifying lens revealed many of nature's mysteries four hundred years ago, perception-enhancing devices today can likewise foster science/art integration—microscopes, prisms, kaleidoscopes, holographs, magnifying lens, fiber optics, telescopes, microscopic projectors, X-rays, cameras, computers, mirrors, and black lights. A study of reflections and shadows can be tied in with a study of Monet's water-lily pond paintings and Impressionism, as well as Seurat's Pointillism.

IN THE CLASSROOM

Understanding Light
Encourage students' interest in the properties of light by having them arrange crystals and bottles of different colored glass on sunny window sills or against a light source. Fill some of the bottles with dried flowers or branches, some clear ones with colored water, and others with strips of aluminum foil. Have a ROYGBIV spectrum hunt!

Study spectrums in nature by finding rainbows after a shower and then painting rainbows. The concept of mirror images can be tied in with a unit on printmaking, in which the images are reversed. Take students outside on a sunny day and have them draw each others' shadows on the asphalt playground or concrete, and then decorate these distorted images. Distortion through a convex lens can be seen using narrow olive jars, clear glass marbles, or magnifying glasses. Students can draw the distortion seen in chrome hubcaps, shiny bowls, and other polished, convex surfaces. Study distance perception (Leonardo called it the perspective of disappearance) by

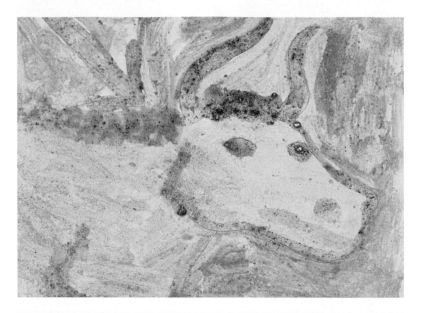

Courtesy of Jackie Ellett.

Geology and minerals: ***Top:*** Earth pigments of iron oxide, charcoal, and kaolin clay, with white glue added, are used in this fifth-grader's study of cave art animals. ***Bottom:*** Prehistoric peoples' pictographic representations of figures and animals in cave art are studied by third-graders in their re-created, crumpled paper cave into which the youngsters could crawl.

making drawings of mountains that recede into the distance. Pinhole cameras and shadow-puppet plays also are useful for studying light.

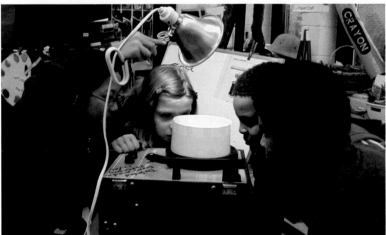

Courtesy of Frank Wachowiak and Mary Sayer Hammond.

Top: *Courtesy of Joyce Vroon.* Bottom: *Courtesy of Mary Lazzari.*

Top: Perception of light is shown in sixth-grader Alex Davis's photo of sunlight on rocks. ***Bottom:*** Children gather round to view their Zoetrope "movies" and experience the magic of bringing a series of two-dimensional drawings into motion.

A science perception objective might be: "Students will be able to identify and draw a variety of leaf forms." Leaf terms to be learned might be opposite and alternate, simple and compound, and with margins: entire, serrate, or dentate. Children used a bold contour-line technique, emphasizing the veins but not coloring in the spaces solidly. They filled up the white paper in an allover design, with leaves turning in all directions and some overlapping. Then, they applied transparent watercolors over and between the leaves.

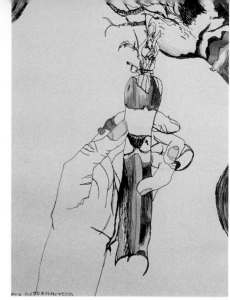

Left: The camellia's leaf veins and petals, stamen, and anthers are drawn in pastel over a freely painted background. **Middle:** A riotously energetic picture of leaves and butterflies by third-grader Kristin Dudley. **Right:** Eighth-grader Laura Gutterman drew an amaryllis bulb in her own hand.

Magnetism To illustrate magnetism in connection with a study of photograms and light, make photograms of iron filings. Along with an explanation of the photochemical phenomena of photograms, the edges of objects such as fern leaves and lacy objects also can be discussed.

Molecular Structure Models of the elements can be made from Styrofoam, gumdrops, colored modeling clay, or table tennis balls, and toothpicks; then make fantasy sculptures of as-yet undiscovered, fantasy elements.

Plants and Botany Still lifes of plant specimens can be used to call attention to the ecological devastation faced by plants and animals—for example, the fact that 250,000 of today's plant species will vanish within the next few years. Large potted plants of assorted foliage can be used for teaching both botany and art. To draw how insects help flowers, use a magnifying lens to examine and draw flower pistils, stamen, and anthers. Have students draw their favorite tree and then draw and label the tree's visible and underground parts; attach a close-up sketch of its leaf. Using a fast-growing plant like a sweet potato or bean, draw its stages of growth each week. Properties of leaves, leaf edges, and shapes can be studied by matching and identifying those with different edges and shapes and then making a composite drawing to show this variety. Along with a discussion of the concept of photosynthesis, both live and dried flowers and plants, such as Indian corn, decorative gourds, locust pods, and fall weeds, make a wonderful autumnal still life to be drawn.

Simple Machines See if you can borrow "props" from nearby museums or historical societies, or perhaps from students' families. Arrange still-life setups of antique Americana hand tools and farm implements, or of contemporary objects such as a bicycle or a wheelbarrow. Arrange simple objects like lanterns, lamps, clocks, and musical instruments. While studying machines and how they work, have students use hand tools for craft and sculpture projects. For a study of balance, fulcrums, and levers, draw children on a teeter-totter. While studying axles, draw or make toy vehicles. While studying energy-creating machines, make pinwheels and draw windmills and waterwheels.

Technology and Energy Encourage students to explore the opportunities for creating art through technology. Show the class examples of sophisticated computer art, and have them create their own. Use videotaping to record scientific phenomena, such as pollution in the neighborhood. Or videotape interviews with peers and parents about their reaction to new technologies. Make drawings of facilities and equipment associated with energy, such as power plants and hybrid autos.

Courtesy of Joyce Vroon.

Top left: Old-fashioned telephones are drawn—where else?—but on telephone book pages. *Top right:* Toxic waste is the subject of fourth-grade student Eliot Brusman's modern-day adaptation of Grant Wood's *American Gothic.* *Bottom:* After discussing Claes Oldenberg's sculptures, Sahra Robinson made a soft sculpture of a boom box radio cassette player.

IN THE CLASSROOM

Flying Machines

After a study of the principles of flight, have students decorate, make, and fly paper airplanes, parachutes, and kites. After a study of early American weathervane designs, make windvane designs (perhaps of animals, such as a favorite cat or dog). A whirligig and a figure can be cut from oak tag and attached to both ends of a soda straw, which is then pinned, through a bead that can revolve, to an upright dowel rod (or the eraser of a pencil, sunk in a spool glued to cardboard).

Courtesy of Joyce Vroon.

Wave action on the surface of water is shown in sixth-grade student Elizabeth Leaque's impressionistic painting in complementary tints and shades of orange and blue.

Water View Paul Klee's paintings of underwater life, and make artistic charts of the ocean food chain using a combination of real objects (such as preserved dried fish) and photos of microscopic life, large fish, and mammals. Draw from a still life of sea creatures and objects that float on or in the water or are found on the beach (coral, seaweed, and seashells), then add figures and other sea life and paint the sea in the background.

Using crayon resist, draw a *20,000 Leagues Under the Sea* picture of what can be viewed from an underwater-exploration vehicle. When studying water evaporation, make watercolor paintings while outdoors on a sunny day. In relation to topics of water pollution, oil spills, and Brownian motion, students can make marbleized papers that later can be used in other art projects.

Courtesy of Joyce Vroon.

Oceanic exploration is shown in these imaginative underwater themes, á la Jules Verne, by Japanese children. When youngsters are capable of producing such rich visual statements, why allow them to settle for stereotyped, minimal results?

Top: *Courtesy of Jackie Ellett.* Bottom: *Courtesy of ICCA, Milner Library, Illinois State University.*

Top: After a look at Currier and Ives winter scenes, this snowy scene of the student and friend ice skating on a frozen pond was painted. **Bottom:** A blustery winter wind whips the huddled birds.

Cloud formations, shown in Virginia Simm's photo of a figure silhouetted against the heavy clouds, are one of the most visible manifestations of wind and air.

By using imagination, wind can be shown indoors where there is little; on a table, three girls pose as if holding kites. (Notice also the beautifully organized, stimulating classroom environment.)

Weather, Wind, and Air After showing Leonardo da Vinci's drawings and Turner watercolors of clouds and storms, draw a storm and/or cumulus, stratus, and nimbus cloud formations. Draw the snow plows, road-clearing equipment, and sandbagging used to ameliorate the weather's effects. Include in the weather drawings activities that children do under adverse and pleasant weather conditions. Along with discussing artworks showing umbrellas in use, make a still life by hanging a variety of colorful and overlapping umbrellas and raincoats from the ceiling and walls.

Tornadoes, which spin counterclockwise in the Northern Hemisphere, have a corkscrew-structure called a helix, also found in the metal waste from a drill cutting soft metal, in grain harvesters, in the thermal currents on which birds and gliders float upward without effort, in the spiral staircases of historic works of architecture, and in the DNA double-helix molecule.

In summary, scientific knowing and artistic expression can be enhanced by each other in a myriad of ways. Each casts light and insight back upon the other. Our goal herein is not that our students will become

The interactions of water and wind, light and shadow, swan and reflection are poetically shown in sixth-grade student Mary Margaret Murphy's photograph.

artists or scientists, but that their perceptual, cognitive, and expressive capabilities will be developed, and that they will sense in the world some unity of natural phenomena.

The wrath of Hurricane Hugo and its effects on beach surfaces and structures are captured in sixth-grade student Kempton Mooney's series of photos.

FOR FURTHER READING

Tolley, Kimberly. 1994. *The Art and Science Connection*. Reading, MA: Addison-Wesley.

WEB RESOURCES

For lessons from the Smithsonian Institution on science and social studies:

http://smithsonianeducation.org/db/list.asp?museumid=
-1&supplierid=-1&pamphletcategoryid=-1&statusid=1&mediaid=
-1&contenttype=3&gradeid=2&categoryid=-1&KEYWORD=

For science topics:

http://www.i-a-s.com/PostWrap+index-page-Science.phtml

http://www.getty.edu/artsednet/resources/Ecology/index.html

For a lesson on stormy weather:

http://www.arts.ufl.edu/art/rt_room/sparkers/stormy/storm.html

For a lesson for drawing yeast cells reproducing:

http://artsedge.kennedy-center.org/content/2290/

For a lesson on the Japanese art of fish printing:

http://artsedge.kennedy-center.org/content/3436/

Chapter 11

Art and the Performing Arts

Courtesy of Beverly Barksdale Mallon.

Before drawing, fourth-graders danced to imitate festive New Year's revelry and blowing of celebratory horns. One can almost feel the excitement and hear the cacophony of the celebration!

*A*ll of the arts foster the growth of cognition. The arts develop children's sensitivity to the symbol systems and ways of thinking employed in each art form. Each art form has its own symbol system, grammar, and syntax with which children can express themselves and their understandings of the world. For example, a tree might be represented in art as a lollipop form; in dance, by upraised arms waving; in music, by gently blowing sounds; in drama, by an overshadowing protective being with a deep voice. Finding relationships among these forms of representation can facilitate learning, and children's early arts experiences will later coalesce into sophisticated reasoning and problem solving.

The visual arts deal with form and images and use vision and tactile sensory systems. Dance is a kinesthetic art form. Music is predominantly aural, using sound and hearing, but it also employs bodily or kinesthetic experiences. Drama is sometimes considered the most integrated form, using action and behaviors that employ aural, kinesthetic, tactile, verbal, and visual ways of knowing. Children's literacy in all of these symbol systems and modes of thought should be developed.

Particularly in the early years of schooling, many "cognitive" activities occur as physical activities—drawing, moving, or enacting. Perception rather than logic governs children's early views of reality. Children relate to the arts as media for expression and communication at a time when their verbal skills are not fully developed. For young children especially, the arts must be thought of as total and integrated experiences.

Interweave the various arts.

Left: *Courtesy of Joyce Vroon.* Middle: *Courtesy of Gwenda Malnati.* Right: *Courtesy of Beverly Barksdale Mallon.*

Left: Sixth-grader Kristie Stephens drew a portable cassette player and head-set on a musical sheet. **Middle:** A student performs on her guitar beside Jake Rakestraw's musician sculptures. **Right:** This fifth-grader decorated her self-portrait with musical notations—symbols of her interest in music. A study of American primitive portraits preceded the drawing and painting. Notice the sophisticated rendering of the hair, eyes, and nose.

IN THE CLASSROOM

"Stormy Weather"

For a truly integrated experience, have students dance, waving scarves, to reflect the gusting movements of wind and rain. Their dance can be accompanied by appropriate musical sounds using their voices for the howling wind and shaking a sheet of metal to simulate the thunder. They can enact a skit of a family reacting to the storm's approach. They can use chalk and paint to depict the storm's fury. Of course, language arts activities might also be involved as children write a script of the storm's approach.

Integration in the arts is legendary—material often moves easily from one medium to another. Consider, for example, that Mel Brooks's *The Producers* started as a film, became a Broadway musical, and will soon become a second film based on the musical. And innumerably books are adapted for dance, film, stage—and even as the basis for paintings.

Elementary classroom teachers in the primary grades can easily integrate the arts and move from one art form to another as children make music, act, dance, and draw. For example, after reading the story, "Jack in the Beanstalk," ask:

For music: "What kind of musical sounds can we make with our voices that sound like an angry, running giant? This half of the class will be the giant; this half will show Jack's fright. I will be the conductor."

Courtesy of Sharon Burns-Knutson.

The arts are integrative in many African cultures. Both drama and dance, along with religion and art, employ masks. Here, a student's metal-embossed mask takes its motivation from the magnificent metalwork of the Benin kingdom.

Courtesy of Beverly Barksdale Mallon.

The art teacher was asked to have her class make a backdrop for the school Holiday Multicultural Musical Festival. The fifth-graders arrived at a circular design of "People from Around the World," to be shown in their nation's costumes. The 8- × 8-foot multicultural mural was painted flat on the floor with acrylic paints on a primed painter's drop cloth. Prior to designing their figures, children consulted costume books and the encyclopedia.

For drama: "What would the characters say when the maid hid Jack? Can you make up words to show why she risked losing her job to help a thieving kid?"

For dance: "How could we show the chase by moving our bodies around the front of our classroom? Use all the parts of your body and all the ways you can think to move your body to show the characters' personalities and the chase—your knees, your elbows, the height of your body. Row 3 be giants; Row 4 be Jacks."

For art: "What scene will you show in your artwork? Make the figures large so we can see the expressions on their faces. How will their fingers be?"

DEVELOPING MULTI-ART CREATIONS

In many of the world's non-Western cultures, the arts are now and always have been connective and integrative. In some African and Asian dance and dramatic enactments, the colorful costumes look like sculptures. Drumming and other instruments create the exciting rhythmic music. Festivals combine music, dance, theater, and visual arts in a symbiotic way.

Likewise, the teacher who is interested in art may be called upon to have students make backdrops for school plays and festivals. Perhaps special costumes and props will be required. After becoming a famous sculptor, Henry Moore talked fondly of the great satisfaction and happiness he had felt working with his school buddies on such integrated drama/art activities. Even Leonardo da Vinci staged multi-arts festivals as a regular part of his responsibilities as a resident court artist in the Renaissance.

Multi-arts exhibits can combine an art display with students' musical or dramatic performances. At these, students can demonstrate their special art skills in the hall or foyer. School arts festivals can be made more special by having students wear costumes, bring special theme-related food to be served at the opening, or by having a joint exhibition of parent and child art.

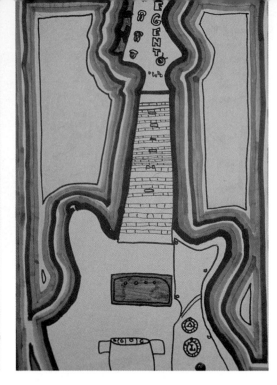

Top and bottom left: *Courtesy of David W. Hodge.* Top middle and right: *Courtesy of Joyce Vroon.*

Top left: Sounds inspire art; here, students recorded the sounds of bees, which then motivated this seventh-grade linoleum print, containing the word, "BUZZ." ***Top middle and right:*** One way musical ability and art interests can be integrated is by drawing musical instruments. Fifth-graders Courtney Clinkscales and Eleanor Siegler carefully draw an electric guitar and then outline it in repeated bands, which seem to echo the guitar's reverberative strumming sound. ***Bottom left:*** Musicians in a still life motivated this marker line drawing.

MUSIC

Some modes of expression studied in music include: listening, chanting, singing, playing, improvising, moving to music, and symbolizing through music.

Children love chants and chanting (think "Ring Around the Rosie" and jump rope double Dutch rhymes). They can sing similar chants and songs in round form, or act them out, and then draw the events with much vigor. Because of the rich motivation of aural and motor stimulation, they may reach new levels in drawing ability, being able to draw the figures connected to each other.

Music has as its "vocabulary" beat, rhythm, meter, tempo, repetition, contrast, structure, tone color, and accent. Just as students learn about line and shape in art, they can learn about using musical elements, and one can reinforce the other. For example, students can describe repetition and variation in Ravel's *Bolero.* Teach them to look for repeated elements in artworks.

One of the most accessible ways of integrating art and music is to have children paint to music of very differing tempos and tone colors. For example, Respighi's "Fountains of Rome" lends itself to paintings of fountains splashing water. Marches by John Philips Sousa stimulate paintings of Fourth of July parades. Mussorgsky's "Night on Bald Mountain" engenders more mysterious creations. As an experiment, have the students fold a

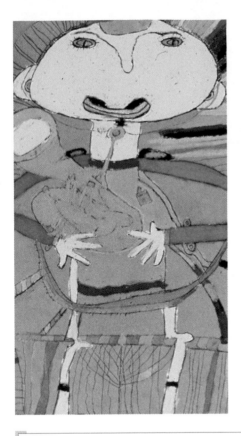

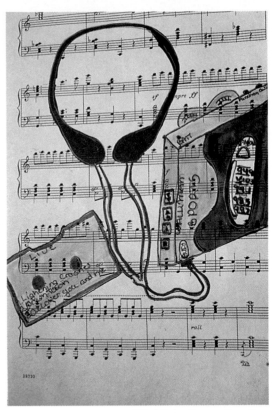

Left: *Courtesy of Frank Wachowiak and Mary Sayer Hammond.* Middle: *Courtesy of Dahria McClelland.* Right: *Courtesy of Joyce Vroon.*

Left: A seated student holding a baritone horn is depicted in a highly original way, especially in how the artist met the challenge of showing foreshortened legs. *Middle:* A video cassette movie of jitterbuggers was played to motivate a figure drawing and painting project. *Right:* Fifth-grade student Alexandra Robinson drew cassette and CD players onto old music score sheets.

paper in half and paint one side to fast music, the other to slow music. Can you tell which halves were painted to each kind of music?

Have students bring in musical toys. Play the toys. Then arrange them into a still life and draw and paint the still life. Draw musical notational symbols in the background. Have students draw and paint musical instruments using old sheet music as the background.

Courtesy of Beverly Barksdale Mallon.

"I Believe I Can Fly" music was played while students made their designs. Faith Ringgold's book was inspiration for this third-grader's idea, "One night, in a dream, the sun was smiling at me, and I felt so happy, I felt like dancing on the moon." Children took turns lying on the art tables to see how their bodies looked outstretched. The project required five class periods and used: (1) a pencil drawing, (2) gone over with heavy marker so it could be (3) traced through a sheet of paper with (4) white oil pastel for the (5) water-color resist.

Far left and middle right: *Courtesy of Dahria McClelland*. Middle left and far right: *Courtesy of Beverly Barksdale Mallon*.

Far left: The student captured the strong X-shape of the dancers criss-crosssed in space. ***Middle left:*** The essence of femininity is captured in this frilly-skirted dancer. ***Middle right:*** Great effort is required to lift one's dance partner overhead. ***Far right:*** Dancing imbues this beautiful self-portrait, beautiful patterned dress, and staccato flailing legs with the spirit of life.

Rather than painting to music, integration can also work in reverse—creating music to painting. For instance, Mussorgsky's famous "Pictures at an Exhibition" was painted in response to seeing paintings a friend had made hanging at an art display. In response to seeing a few art reproductions, students using instruments can create a musical mood akin to the mood depicted in the visual artwork.

Using drumsticks or their pencils, students can tap out the rhythms of groups of objects in artworks, for example, the pattern of clouds, of the swaying grasses, of the soldiers marching. Then have students apply this knowledge of rhythm in their own artworks. Symbols used in paintings and in music can be compared. For example, investigate how darkness and scariness are shown in art and music. How are emotions such as happiness and sadness conveyed in the two art forms?

DANCE

Dance actually occurs in three domains: composing, performing, and appreciating. With young children, focus on the hands-on activities of the first two, and especially the second. Older students can be made aware of the elements used in dance. Watching a video of a dance performance, have them identify when instances of the following elements occur:

- Space: How are the stage's space and the spacing of the characters used to represent emotions and actions?
- Time: Are key events repeated several times?
- Effort: Where and how is great effort portrayed?
- Abstraction: What movements depict the essence of the characters?
- Representation: How do costumes and props affect the dance?
- Alignment: How are figures aligned—parallel, diagonally, or in some other form?
- Axial movement: Do figures move straight to the front, rear, across, or diagonal of the stage?

An exercise in composing can use a simple, familiar story everyone knows, such as the "Three Little Pigs." Students, working in small groups, can discuss how to use the dance elements to plan out a dance telling the story.

DRAMA

Drama incorporates a wide range of elements: silence, singing, darkness, light, time, surprise relationships, character, style, variation, pace, rhythm, space, movement, mood, symbol, meaning. When students make drawings about a play, urge them to incorporate some of these concepts in their representations.

Make students aware of theater's art-related professions: costume design, makeup and hair design, set design, lighting design, advertising design, website design, and program design. Set design is similar to a common art activity, that of building dioramas. Typically a shoe box is used as the stage. Children decide which play or story to build a set for (this way, there would be several plays portrayed), and where different scenes of the play will occur.

To give an introduction to lighting design, they can darken the classroom or go into a dark enclosed area and use a flashlight, with or without colored cellophane over it, to show how the stage is lit during certain scenes. Other students can be deployed to develop accompanying music to introduce certain scenes. Using paint or watercolors, students can paint

papers in colors that indicate the atmosphere and lighting of certain scenes. Another day, using black markers they can draw the scenes on the papers. Another day they can use oil pastels and crayons to color in the characters' costumes.

To understand costume and prop design, have students sketch out the costumes, special hats, and props to be used in a play created from a favorite or vivid story, employing the symbols denoting the characters, that is crowns, scepters, and tools. These can then be cut out and placed in the diorama sets. Disregard scale.

With kindergarten and primary-grade children, a big box of top hats, cowboy hats, firefighters' hats, wedding gowns, fancy ball dresses, cowboy boots, spiked high heels, and props, borrowed from a used-clothing store or drama department, can be used for reenacting scenes. Older students can model for figure drawing, using these costumes. They can then add special features and balloon captions to their drawings to further clarify the dramatic character they have depicted. Another day they can paint in an appropriate background, showing the time of day or night, room interior or outside scene, and animals and props.

Left: *Courtesy of Robert Clements.* Right: *Courtesy of Margaret Hodge, Bergstrom Art Center, Neenah, WI.*

Left: Drama: Acting out the scene of witches stirring a boiling pot (of dry ice) to motivate a scary art lesson. **Right:** An extraordinary hat gives one "special powers."

Courtesy of Robert Clements.

To motivate a lesson, dramatize a scene of Native Americans gathered around a fire.

Courtesy of Beverly Barksdale Mallon.

First-graders dramatized the poses that Olympic athletes would take when bringing home their trophies to their countries' rulers. Annabelle Barbe's picture shows the three gold medalists, met at their nation's shoreline, wearing great smiles of pride in accomplishment.

Courtesy of Robert Clements.

Borrowed fire department gear and sounds stimulate exciting reenactments.

PLANNING FOR INTEGRATION

In developing related arts activities, as in all your educational planning, try to identify the unique strengths of your students and have them do special work in that area. Are there two or three students who have shown special interest in dance or music? If so, have them work as a team to develop it using their special strengths. One way to think of special strengths is through Howard Gardner's eight forms of intelligence. Think about how multiple intelligences can be supported by the integration of visual and performing arts.

Gardner's Multiple Intelligences and Performing Arts

1. Language	understanding dialogue
2. Logical and mathematical	seeing plot line structures (conflict, resolution)
	watching patterns in dance
	hearing repetition in music
3. Interpersonal	understanding the development of characters through dialogue.
	noting dancers' relationships to one another
4. Musical	scoring and performing music
5. Spatial	designing sets
	creating choreography or blocking
6. Bodily-kinesthetic	participating in dance or drama

7. Intrapersonal   interpreting personality through dialogue

8. Naturalistic   creating props of animals, birds, and trees

                                     painting sets to represent the out of doors

Each of the arts is certainly wonderful in itself. By bringing them together along with other disciplines, you can give added value and fun to the academic curriculum, to art learning, and to children's lives. While planning an activity in a different discipline, ask questions like the following:

- How would this idea be shown in music? Let's make appropriate sounds to accompany the artwork.
- If this was a play, what colors of lights would you use on the stage?
- If we were frozen living sculptures, what pose would we be in to suggest this action?
- Can anyone think of a story, or movie, or TV show, or a painting that is sort of like this play? How do the plots differ?

By demonstrating such interrelated arts thinking, you are modeling attitudes that foster a rapprochement and interplay of the arts. You are laying the groundwork for skills so essential in America's great industries such as

Courtesy of Beverly Barksdale Mallon.

To be able to leap into the air and touch one's toes is an acrobatic feat! After enacting such movements, children drew and cut out their figures and traced the pieces onto vinyl letter scraps from a sign store. These were then pasted down to comprise the entire figure. Leftover gift wrap samples, from the school's fundraiser, added exciting patterns.

Courtesy of ICCA, Milner Library, Illinois State University.

The circus is a multisensory extravaganza involving all the performing arts.

advertising, web design, TV production, and filmmaking. At the heart of learning in the arts is the blending of form and feeling, giving form to an experience, while at the same time using our emotional awareness. This may occur through composing or playing music, writing a play, choreographing or dancing a dance, or creating an artwork. Learning in the related arts lets students use the arts' formal elements to express something about their feelings, knowledge, and life experiences.

FOR FURTHER READING

Edwards, Linda Carol. 1997. *The Creative Arts, A Process Approach for Teachers and Children*. Englewood Cliffs, NJ: Prentice Hall, Inc.

Kinder, A. 1987. "A Review of Rationales for Integrated Arts Programs." *Studies in Art Education* 29(1): 52–60.

O'Brien, Bernadette C. 1978. *Tapestry: Interrelationship of the Arts in Reading and Language Development*. New York: New York City Board of Education.

WEB RESOURCES

For many related arts lesson plans:

http://artsedge.kennedy-center.org/teach/
les.cfm?subjectID=&otherSubjectId=&gradeBandId=2&x=15&y=
6&showDescriptions=true&sortColumn=

Chapter 12
Teaching Art to Children Who Have Special Needs

*A*pproximately 12 percent of students in American public education are in special education programs, and they are entitled by law to instruction in art as well as other content areas. Children with mental and physical disabilities (in learning, hearing, vision, and mobility), as well as those who use mental health services, now are integrated into classrooms of children without disabilities. Given this, every public school classroom teacher and art teacher is increasingly called upon to serve in his or her classroom youths who have disabilities; currently, 85 percent of teachers teach children with disabilities. Hence, all art teachers must be prepared to respond to the needs of students with a broad range of abilities.

EIGHT CONCEPTS IN SPECIAL EDUCATION

In this chapter we will discuss eight important concepts in the area of special education: inclusion, people-first language, developmental disability, normalization, age-appropriateness, partial participation, empowerment, and human worth.

Inclusion After the passage in 1975 of Public Law 94-142, the Education for All Handicapped Children Act (renamed in 1990 the Disabilities Education Act) was passed. It mandated the regular education initiative for students with milder disabilities, and it promoted the integration of children with severe disabilities. The law mandates testing, individualized educational plans, parental consent, confidentiality, least restrictive environment, and educational programming for youths with developmental disabilities. Students must be served within the regular classroom unless specific social or physical barriers interfere with the child's learning. In more and more art classrooms, inclusion is being implemented to the fullest extent possible; students with significant mental and physical dis-

Courtesy of Beverly Barksdale Mallon.

This dynamic painting of a cat was created by a student who was diagnosed with behavior disability and learning disorders and who was mainstreamed into a third-grade class.

abilities are taught in regular classes with nondisabled students. Over a third of students with disabilities spend from 60 percent to 90 percent of their time in regular classrooms.

People-First Language In your speech, use people-first language. Do not refer to "the blind" or "the retarded," thus implying that these individuals belong in a class that is set apart; instead, speak of "persons with disabilities in seeing or learning." It is a matter of human decency and

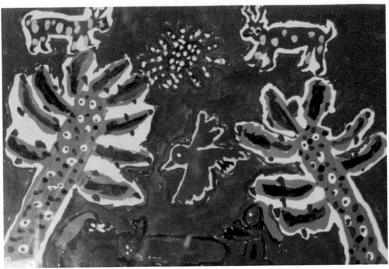

Courtesy of Beverly Barksdale Mallon.

A fifth-grade girl in special education painted this marvelous design titled "The Healing." Perhaps some of the child's African-American artistic heritage and Pentecostal religious beliefs are evident in the artwork's rich patterning and religious power. At the center bottom can be seen a moving scene of two small figures ministering to a prostrate figure in bed. Stags and sun fill the painting's upper portion. Even the trees bow to the heavenly bluebird's power.

respect. As another example, "persons who use a wheelchair for mobility" is more respectful than "crippled people." Further, do not focus on what someone cannot do, such as a child who "can't draw." Instead, focus on capability, such as a child who can "vocalize about the patterns he or she draws." Negative language continues old attitudes of exclusion and a "them vs. us" perspective. Likewise, positive language fosters positive attitudes and helps to promote independence, self-help, and community integration. Terminology changes rapidly, but at this time the term "with disabilities" usually is preferred to "exceptional, challenged, or handicapped." Even more important than terminology, however, is having an attitude of acceptance and faith in the individual.

Developmental Disability

A developmental disability is a severe, chronic disability of a person that:

- Is attributable to a mental or physical impairment or combination thereof
- Is manifested before age 22
- Is likely to continue indefinitely

- Results in limitations in three or more areas of life activity: self-care, language, learning, mobility, self-direction, capacity for independent living, and economic self-sufficiency
- Reflects the need for individually planned treatments of long duration

Normalization

Normalization is the use of means as culturally normative as possible to establish personal behaviors that are as normative as possible. It does not mean that all people should be the same. Normalization is the idea that all people in a society should have, as far as possible, equal opportunity to live, work, and play. It means that students with disabilities in your art class should be treated as much like all other students as possible.

Age-Appropriateness

A concept related to normalization is age-appropriateness. Teachers of art frequently have been criticized for having older special education students do activities that are deemed to be "babyish." Strive to keep your choice of topics and media age-appropriate. For example, do not have older students do pudding painting; instead, use an adult material such as paper pulp. Test whether an activity is too childlike by asking yourself whether nondisabled persons of the same age would want to do it. When using art materials such as crayons, which some people may associate with primary school, emphasize how they have been used by famous artists, such as Picasso. (This is a good strategy even for persons without disabilities.)

Printing designs and shapes with potatoes, sponges, and erasers provides an unusual experience in aesthetic discrimination and fine-motor coordination. In addition, the decorative patterns that result can then be used for gift wrap, for greeting cards, and for covering boxes.

Partial Participation For students with especially severe disabilities, keep in mind the principle of partial participation. Is there some way in which the student with a disability could participate in the lesson? Perhaps a student without language could hold up the art reproduction that the class discusses. A student without sight could work with another child in cleaning the paintbrushes with soap. Even if a student cannot do all of the steps in a process, you or another student can arrange for the individual to do those that he or she can. However, because the child may need longer to do a certain step, the sequence may need to be changed.

Empowerment Another important concept in special education is empowerment. It is very easy for helpers to "overdo" for individuals with disabilities. In fact, many children both with and without disabilities are masters at getting extra services from adults, using the familiar refrain "You draw it for me." To foster independent achievement, the less assistance the teacher or aide offers, the better.

Human Worth Every individual is a human being of worth. Each child presents potential, and it is the teacher's job to unearth that potential. As teachers filled with openness, patience, and belief, it is our job to unlock the potential within each person. Art teachers especially, charged with nurturing creativity in the individual, must model and teach respect for human diversity. Humanistic education's goals are to value people and to believe in every human's potential.

GENERAL TEACHING STRATEGIES

For most children in elementary and middle school, the teaching guidelines proposed in this book should prove to be adaptable and effective. For children with special needs, however, other teaching strategies may be needed. This chapter provides some practical approaches to help teachers meet the challenge. First, the good news: The art class or studio atmosphere is the best of all possible environments in which to work with children having developmental disabilities. Each child is accepted, and his or her potential is respected. Each child can excel in some way, and every child can be an achiever.

The importance of the teacher and his or her role cannot be emphasized enough in the context of teaching children with special needs. All attributes of the dedicated teacher that we have spelled out so far—empathy, knowledge, tact, confidence, resourcefulness, understanding, equanimity, and patience—are important in the successful management of a classroom that includes students with disabilities. Precedence, if any, must be given to the qualities of understanding and patience. Some general strategies for teachers who are experiencing inclusion for the first time include the following:

Courtesy of Knox Wilkinson.

Knox Wilkinson, an artist with mild mental challenge, has successfully shown his work in museums throughout the nation and world. He is involved in efforts to help others achieve through art, and his design of two birds here is an announcement for a Very Special Art Exhibition.

1. Accept the children as they are.
2. Familiarize yourself with the disabilities of special children assigned to your class. Use the student's out-of-school interests as guides for suitable activities.
3. Ascertain whether a progress chart has been recorded on the students by a previous teacher. Note the art experiences and projects with which they have been successful.
4. Help the parents to promote their child's life-enriching recreation and leisure skills by advising them regarding art materials their child enjoys using. Suggest art and hobby materials they might acquire for use in their home and inform them of community arts class offerings.
5. If teacher aides are assigned to help you with the students with disabilities, involve the aides appropriately. Do not let the aide sit idle, but, more importantly, do not let an oversolicitous aide do the project for the individuals.
6. Keep your own progress report on every child with disabilities. In a few school systems, the art teacher must write and implement individualized educational plans (IEPs) for each student with developmental disabilities. This involvement in the IEP process is a valuable educational practice in making art fundamental for all students.
7. Consider carefully your teaching procedures for students with disabilities. Will you use free-choice projects, in which children choose

Projects that may be undertaken successfully with children with some kinds of special needs. **Top:** Three-dimensional animals constructed with folded and cut tagboard. **Bottom:** Stabile constructed of found materials.

their own subject matter, materials, and time limits? Will you employ the unit or project method, in which the same art activity is planned for students both with and without disabilities? The latter approach usually calls for individual adjustments to meet the needs and abilities of the student with disabilities.

8. Ask the child if there is something that could be done to facilitate his or her participation in the activity. ("How can we make it easier for you to do the project?")

9. Enlist the aid of students without disabilities—especially those with proven abilities and stable, pleasant personalities—to help their classmates with disabilities.

10. Above all, do not permit those children with disabilities to participate in copying or tracing artwork. Help them to create their own imagery, even though this imagery may differ from that of the other students in the class. Even when children's graphic expression consists of scribbles, they have feeling for the patterns their marks make. They have made something that did not exist earlier in the world.

The following sections describe specific teaching strategies and tactics to follow in working with students who have developmental disabilities. Keep in mind that even if the students with disabilities have normal or above-average IQs, they probably will require some nontraditional teaching strategies and adaptation of materials.

Teaching Students with Learning Disabilities or Hyperactivity

In teaching the child with learning disorders or hyperactivity, at all times proceed deliberately, methodically, and calmly. Give directions or instructions slowly and clearly, using simple language at a rate that the children can assimilate. Make sure, if possible, that you have the child's attention when explaining something. Students with learning disabilities often look as if they understand, when in fact they are confused. In spite of very clear instructions, assume that misunderstandings may exist.

Prepare lessons to meet specific needs—hand-eye coordination, fine or gross motor skills improvement—and to meet identifiable objectives such as color or shape naming. Demonstrate more, and talk less. Employ visual symbols and models. To hold the child's attention, speak in a well-modulated tone of voice. (Certainly, all students could benefit from such a tone.) For youths with attention deficits, use colorful teaching materials.

Although the teaching materials should be colorful, the room surroundings should show a calm, ordered environment. A teacher can help in this by doing the following:

- Keep changes to a minimum.
- Consider limiting opportunities for choice.
- Consider minimizing the number of materials used.
- De-emphasize group activities.
- Give immediate reinforcement.

Students having problems in math, such as dyscalcula, may find measuring a challenge, for example, when measuring a mat.

Be prepared for emotional outbursts. Heed when a child may be close to losing control, and change the situation before that point is reached. Give "road markers"—notices that an activity will terminate or change in a few minutes. These signal a student that he or she must get ready to move on to another activity.

Consider reordering seating arrangements so that a child is not distracted by viewing others. Working in a carrel may help a child to concentrate. The student could sit up front in a corner or behind a partial screen. Likewise, a temporary folding screen could be placed on a child's desk to form a baffle or cubicle. Try to create seating arrangements and projects that encourage staying in the seat—for example, looking at an art history book while seated in a beanbag chair out of view of most distractions.

Teaching Students with Vision Deficiencies Most students with vision deficiencies in school classes will not be totally blind, but rather will have some residual vision. As a teacher of art, a subject involving considerable visual/motor coordination, you may be among the first to notice that a student in your class might have a vision deficiency. If you suspect something may be amiss, notify the school nurse or parent. The following behaviors or conditions might be indicative of a vision deficiency:

putting head close to artwork to see it

tilting head or thrusting head forward to see artwork

squinting or frowning

rubbing eyes

focusing with difficulty

becoming irritable when doing precision art assignments

red rimmed or encrusted or swollen eyelids

watery eyes

crossed eyes

recurring sties

Also listen for the following complaints:

complaints of not being able to see well

complaints of headache following close work

complaints of eyes itching, burning, or feeling scratchy

complaints of blurred or double vision

To encourage a child's participation to the maximum extent possible, the following approach can help to achieve success. Increase the amount of contrast between the drawn lines and background. Broad-line markers of vivid colors and brightly colored crayons are preferable to markers and crayons of more subdued values. Some media, such as puff paint and glue-line prints, will leave a raised line that can be felt. Black paint can be added to white glue for drawing on white paper, and a bold raised line will be left when dry.

For those who supplement vision with touch, use large contrasting (black-and-white) sheets of paper. However, some students will prefer tinted paper, which minimizes glare. Other techniques, such as printing on plastic-foam meat trays and drawing on heavy aluminum foil with a dull pencil, will leave a recessed line. Art media that make noise, such as squeaky brayers and markers, or that smell, such as scented markers and paste, can add interest.

An emphasis on three-dimensional work is often beneficial, employing projects such as jewelry making, weaving, and pottery.

Figure sculptures of pipe cleaners or wire and polymer clay can be used to emphasize good posture. Topics such as "a call for help" can foster the expression of feelings. Making texture maps and box sculptures can communicate the individual's concept of himself or herself as a person capable of moving around the home and community.

Teachers can help by asking a child whose vision is deficient what light level is most comfortable for him or her: near a window, in bright light, or in subdued light. Provide optical aids such as magnifying glasses. Allow the child extra time for eye rest. Your school may permit printed material that can be photocopied at a greater magnification. Make eye contact as you address the students. Sit on a chair or stool so that your face will be nearer to the child's eye level. Do not address the class while facing the chalkboard or standing in the glare from a window.

Consistently storing supplies in the same place helps students with vision deficiencies to find what they need. In order to foster independence, require students with vision deficiencies to help care for the art materials. For students with partial vision, light shows can use colored gels and projectors.

Encourage interpersonal interactions between blind and sighted peers; for example, assign a sighted student to serve as a helper. In looking at art reproductions, have the partially sighted child sit close to the front of the room and be given the opportunity to examine the print at the distance and in the light level that is best for him or her.

Teaching Students with Neurological and Orthopedic Disabilities Students with neurological and orthopedic disabilities are likely to have frequent absences. If the child is hospitalized, send work home but don't make demands that the child cannot meet. Provide the parents with suggestions about possible art projects. And, on the child's return to school, make the student feel welcome. Spend time helping the class to develop realistic attitudes about infirmities and teach the students how to interact with peers with disabilities.

School absences can affect not only academic performance, but also social and emotional development—especially self-esteem. Students may be excluded from class activities or rejected by peers. Hence, treat these students as worthwhile, competent students who have interests and needs similar to their classmates.

Because students with neurological and orthopedic disabilities may have received pity or overprotection, never expect them to do less than that of which they are capable. Develop reasonable objectives and expect their attainment. However, recognize that, because of fatigue, they may not be able to do all activities or to finish activities on time.

Borders, boundaries, and holding devices may help students with disabilities perform various tasks. Plastic meat trays can hold clay and small objects, and cafeteria trays can be clamped with a C-clamp to a wheelchair work surface. Masking or duct tape can be used to tape down water containers and to tape a brush to a child's hand. Individuals with severe limitations in movement can pull a string to move a mobile and can make patterns in salt, sugar, or millet on a colorful tray. Further, using a rasp to carve blocks of balsa wood can provide both exercise and an art experience. Also, students can press papier mâché into a greased mold to create sculptural forms.

An occupational therapist on the IEP team can be a resource in knowing how to secure and in getting adaptive equipment.

Teaching Students with Hearing and Speech Disabilities For students with hearing and speech disabilities, emphasize art projects such as self-portraits to help them overcome their self-consciousness. Likewise, working with a buddy on a joint project will help to reduce feelings of insecurity. To encourage their use of residual hearing, have students sit on a wooden floor and bang on a drum, or paint to music. Develop language skills by staging plays with puppets and masks, using a model grocery store to serve as a setting.

To promote normalization, remind nonhandicapped students that 30 percent of school-age youngsters are likely to have relatives with hearing disabilities.

However, some students with hearing disabilities may be indistinguishable from their nonhandicapped peers in behavior. A child with a hearing impairment may appear to be inattentive and to daydream, seeming reluctant to participate in class activities. Another child with a hearing disability might have developed mannerisms such as looking as though she understands when, in fact, she does not. Students with impaired hearing may have frequent absences from school because of earaches or sinus congestion, which can be a source of temporary or permanent hearing loss. Likewise, allergies and head congestion also can temporarily reduce hearing.

Allow students with hearing disabilities the opportunity to move their chairs as needed in order to hear better or to see the teacher's face for speechreading. Speak naturally for students who are speechreading. Don't slow down or exaggerate mouth movements. Recognize, though, that they may need to hear a term repeated many times and in many ways. Help students with hearing disabilities to find seats away from humming fans or boisterous students, and try to keep background noise to a minimum. Give students with hearing disabilities an outline of the art assignment, or have a classmate take notes using carbon paper.

Encourage students with speech and hearing impairments to talk about their artworks, perceptions, and out-of-school activities. When they are speaking, listen attentively and show your active interest through facial expressions. Don't inadvertently look away while they are speaking. Also, don't finish their sentences for them. To promote their talking, ask open-ended questions including *How, why, where,* and *when,* rather than questions that can be answered *yes* or *no.* And, to overcome their shyness about speaking and to help them understand their assignments, encourage them to ask questions. Positive self-esteem comes from full participation in the student art community. The key is to minimize discrimination, stigma, and difference.

Teaching Students with Mental Impairment Levels of mental impairment vary, from mild to severe to profound impairment. Each stage has its own requirements. At the stage of profound impairment, an appropriate goal is that the student be aware of movement and sensation and be able to handle art materials with enjoyment.

Strive for projects that are both age-appropriate and ability-appropriate. Repeat instructions and procedures frequently. Use multilevel approaches, sequencing, adaptation, and much reinforcement. Plan projects that may be broken down into sequential, manageable, and explainable steps. Then do the project one step at a time, finishing one step before explaining the next

Courtesy of Beverly Barksdale Mallon.

A twelve-year-old boy diagnosed with mild intellectual disability did this cheerful artwork to the Beatles song, "Here comes the Sun, I say it's alright." In the first period, the sun was drawn with hot colors. Then oil pastels were used to color the artwork. Circular shapes, triangular shapes, and serpentine shapes were emphasized by the teacher.

Courtesy of Beverly Barksdale Mallon.

This unique composition of a kicking judo athlete with his head going off the page was the original idea of an intermediate-level student diagnosed with mild intellectual disability. His proudly earned black belt dominates the picture's center.

Courtesy of Beverly Barksdale Mallon.

Wonderful jumping action is shown by the outstretched legs and the bouncing braids in this primary-level special education student's basketball scene. She wears two gloves, so much the better to catch the ball. During the first period, motivation consisted of jumping and using hands to catch; also, the figure was drawn in pencil. In the second period, a fantasy background was painted in with neon watercolors. In the third period, markers were used to add detail.

step. Allow sufficient time for the completion of each stage; it may be necessary for early finishers to do filler activities while others complete a step. Do not begin a new step, however, until the previous one has been completed.

In an inclusive classroom, you must help all the students. If a lot of repetitive one-on-one instruction is necessary, then a teaching assistant is indicated. You cannot devote all your time to one or several children.

Teaching Students with Behavioral Disorders Let the students, especially those with behavioral disabilities, know you expect reasonable standards of conduct in art class. Communicate your expectations clearly and firmly. Then, provide consistent consequences for inappropriate behavior. When students feel connected to what is going on in the art classroom, they are more likely to engage in responsible behavior. Hence, devote classroom meeting time to establishing and discussing standards of behavior. This is what inclusive schooling strives for.

Courtesy of Beverly Barksdale Mallon.

A student with behavior disorders and mild intellectual disability made this thrilling geometrically dynamic painting. Note the visual push and pull of the rooftops as shapes alternately advance and recede. Objects that are on top of, behind, and beside other objects optically shift from moment to moment. The teacher showed the class a crazy quilt, which students then sketched in chalk. In the second period, the students painted in the squares. In the third period, the students painted in the patterns and details. This child was particularly involved, "because my Gramma makes quilts."

Behavioral psychologists urge teachers to try to "catch children being good" and to reinforce their good actions. Some teachers object on ethical grounds to the use of behavioral techniques, such as token economy, contingency contracting, and group-based contingencies, while others believe such procedures are a humane way to help students to achieve in the classroom. How do you feel about this issue? Use unexpected rewards, such as displaying artwork outside the principal's office. Provide reinforcements such as letting the child arrange a bulletin board, pronounce the art vocabulary words, or sketch a tray of toy figures.

Empathize with the students and show that you understand the lesson's difficulties: that the classroom space is cramped when students are doing large pictures, that the temperature in the room is uncomfortable, that hard work is required to color in the whole background.

It can be helpful to students who have problems for the teacher simply to be empathic and to listen passively, acknowledging their concerns. Saying "I see," nodding, and smiling are ways to communicate your attention and understanding. If you suspect the problem may come from a home situation, however, take the child aside and encourage the student to tell you about it, asking him or her, "Would you feel comfortable sharing what it is?" When a teacher discovers a problem that is beyond his or her area of expertise, it should be referred to the school counselor or psychologist. Knowing when to refer is very important.

Rather than issuing blaming "You" messages, express your feelings using "I" messages. For example, "Because your noisy, out-of-seat behavior showed disrespect for and ignored the art class rules, I am angry." Three steps in giving effective "I" messages are: (1) a nonblaming, nonjudgmental description of the behavior; (2) a description of the tangible effect the behavior is having on you, the teacher, and on other students; and (3) a description of how this behavior is making the teacher feel.

To prolong attentiveness, consider using projects that might imply monetary value (glazed ceramics, leather work, crafts). Tools should be manual arts tools (hammers, gouges). Art media should offer active resistance (linocuts, carving). In addition, the project should have three dimensions. Emphasize experiences that deal with kinesthetic manipulation and multisensory stimulation.

Students with disabilities may have difficulties in tolerating changes in routines. Further, recognize that some students are easily distracted and have short attention spans, and that many require constant praise and encouragement. Brief, one-session projects demanding minimum memory recall may be necessary. Longer projects may be appropriate as well, but only if broken down clearly into separate steps, presented one at a time. Also, remember that, like all students, those with disabilities respond more enthusiastically when their art experiences are successful.

Courtesy of Robert Clements.

Materials that involve real tools and give active resistance, here, making crayon scrapings, can appeal to youngsters.

USING ART FOR COMMUNITY AND SCHOOL INTEGRATION

Persons with disabilities are not a separate group from the community at large. They are citizens with the rights of all citizens. Congress has passed the Americans with Disabilities Act, guaranteeing these individuals rights to equity in employment, housing, and community services. Some ways the art program can promote positive community attitudes follow:

Encourage these students to participate in community activities so that they may see themselves as, and be seen by others as, active members of their community. Involve them in activities about their own cultural heritage in particular.

Be alert to opportunities such as art exhibitions in which your students with disabilities can participate. A Pilot Club or similar civic organization in your community or state may sponsor activities in which your students could receive recognition. Make arrangements for students with disabilities to attend community art openings and art festivals.

Display the students' work attractively and elicit supporting response from their peers. Remember that their projects, which may differ in appearance from the art of students without disabilities, can bring pride to the school, delight to parents and visitors, and an enhanced sense of self-worth to the participating students.

From "The Problem with Martin Ramirez," Clarion, *Winter 1986. Collection of Gladys Nillson and Jim Nutt.*

Famous Hispanic-American artist Martin Ramirez hid his artwork behind the radiators in the mental institution where he spent his adult life, until the artistic power and rhythm of his works were discovered by an art teacher.

Ascertain whether the student, parents, or caregivers are being served by community organizations whose purpose is to provide support for them. For example, perhaps there is a support group in your commu-nity for young people requiring mental health services. Phone nation-wide *211* to reach the quasi-governmental, centralized resource with a name such as "Help Line" or "Community Connection" that, in turn, will put people in touch with social service agencies and support groups appropriate to their needs. Certain community service organi-zations may provide special equipment as well. (For example, the Lions Club offers services to people with vision difficulties.)

Be an active advocate for accessibility. When setting up art exhibitions, have certain pieces designated for touching. Position large-print labels at the proper height. Integrate alternative forms of communication, such as Braille and Blissboards (boards with pictures to which a person points to communicate). Art teachers can help children without speech to draw their own "talking books."

Line illustrations from Art and Mainstreaming, *a textbook dealing with art instruction for exceptional children in regular classrooms, by Claire B. Clements and Robert D. Clements. Courtesy of Charles C. Thomas Publishers, Springfield, IL.*

Children in a variety of art activities that build self-worth. Left to right, top: Construction with wood scraps from lumber yard, costumes and hats designed for a parade; paper masks. Left to right, bottom: Simple cardboard-and-string mobile; train engines and trucks constructed from discarded gro-cery cartons.

IN THE CLASSROOM

Experiences and Objects That May Appeal to Students with Physical or Cognitive Disabilities

Painting

Cutting

Pasting

Rolling beach balls

Opening packages

Toys

Construction (wood, boxes, found objects)

Meat-tray boats

Weaving

Balloons

Fingerpainting

Figure drawing

Pets and animals

Flowers and trees

Dressing up, costumes, and uniforms

Kinesthetic activities

Decorating the classroom

Puppets

Piñatas

Fanciful hats

Marching and parading

Printmaking (with vegetables and found objects)

Big cardboard cartons to hide and play in and to transform into vehicles

Fish in aquariums

Clowns

Making music with assorted and thickened concocted instruments

Bright colors in paper, cloth, yarn, cellophane, and ribbons

Noisemakers and horns

Modeling mixtures

Singing

Masks

Face makeup

Drums

Pantomime

Painting to music

Use of mirrors

Mobiles

Kaleidoscopes

Kites

Specialized Materials

Familiarize yourself with the many specialized devices, tools, and materials now used in art classes by children with significant physi-cal disabilities. The school's special education coordinator may be able to help you in requisitioning the following materials for your students:

Four-holed scissors that both student and teacher can manipulate simultaneously

Fat-handled brushes (1- or 2-inches wide) or brushes that have handles wrapped with masking or surgical tape to provide a better grip

Giant color crayons, felt-nib markers (water-based), kindergarten-size pencils with soft lead

Glue sticks (which may be easier to use than squeeze bottles of white glue)

Painting stretchers assembled together and placed on desks around the perimeter of the in-process projects so that students can judge their work's boundaries; other possibilities are plastic meat trays and cafeteria trays

C-clamps and duct or masking tape to hold artwork onto wheelchair trays; specially designed art boards for wheelchairs

Duct tape for taping a brush to a child's hand

Forehead pointers

Mouth wands or rubber spatulas with brushes or markers taped to them

Posters and instructional signs with giant-size letters and numerals

Cameras and computers adapted for special use by those with disabilities in vision, movement, and coordination

Touch table, touch box

Flannel boards and pegboards

Building blocks in assorted shapes and sizes

Magnifying glasses and colored gelatins

Wood or plastic colored beads and sticks in assorted sizes

For additional found or recycled materials useful in art classes, see Appendixes A and B

FOR FURTHER READING

Blandy, Doug. 1994. "Assuming Responsibility: Disability Rights and the Preparation of Art Educators." *Studies in Art Education* 35(3): 179–187.

Blandy, Doug; Pancsofar, E.; and Mockensturm, Tom. 1988. "Guidelines for Teaching Art to Children and Youth Experiencing Significant Mental/Physical Challenges." *Art Education* 41(1): 60–67.

Clements, Claire, and Clements, Robert. 1984. *Art and Mainstreaming: Art Instruction for Exceptional Children in Regular School Classes.* Springfield, IL: Charles C. Thomas.

Guay, Doris. 1994. "Students with Disabilities in the Art Classroom: How Prepared Are We?" *Studies in Art Education* 36(1): 44–56.

Thorne, J. H. 1990. "Mainstreaming Procedures: Support Services and Training." *NAEA Advisory.*

Putting on real snorkeling goggles for simulating "diving under the water" to examine the plastic fish models in the pan is just the ticket for a fun "Deep Sea Diving Lesson."

WEB RESOURCES

For links to sites on mental retardation and developmental disabilities including autism:

http://www.dddcec.org/Links.htm

For more Internet resources concerning special children:

http://www.irsc.org/

For information on art therapy and how it may help children with special needs:

http://www.irsc.org:8080/irsc/irscmain.nsf/sub?readform&cat= Rehabilitation&subcat=Art+Therapy&type=Web+Pages

For behavior modification:

http://www.proteacher.com/030001.shtml

For lesson ideas for students who have hearing impairments:

http://www.pbs.org/wnet/soundandfury/lesson1.html

For an article on mental retardation:

http://www.medterms.com/script/main/art.asp?articlekey=20174

For helping students with sight and hearing to become aware of those without:

http://pbskids.org/arthur/parentsteachers/lesson/communication/ index.html

For helping middle-school children understand about disabilities:

http://www.pbs.org/wnet/religionandethics/teachers/lp_special.html

For living with limiting physical conditions:

http://www.pbs.org/wnet/religionandethics/teachers/lp_special.html

For children using a wheelchair:

http://pbskids.org/anne/tclesson04.html

For a glossary of disability terms:

http://www.rescare.com/web/Main/Glossary.asp

http://www.ldonline.org/ld_indepth/glossaries/ld_glossary.html

For an article on mental retardation:

http://ericec.org/digests/3637.html

Chapter 13
Teaching Art to Students Who Are Gifted

This chapter discusses giftedness in general, relates general-intelligence approaches to artistic giftedness and creativity, gives strategies for the teacher, and offers suggestions for outreach into the school, home, and community. Gifted and talented students are part of the greater school community and should have appropriate adaptations and challenges made for them in the regular art class setting. Admission into a school's gifted programs often requires a score on the Stanford Binet Intelligence Test of 120 to 130 points, as well as teacher recommendations, high grades, and acceptance by a review committee. Some experts feel the intelligence test is overly weighted toward skills in math and reading comprehension, with areas such as art ability going unmeasured. One alternative to the IQ test is the Torrance Test of Creative Thinking, which considers four aspects of creativity: fluency, flexibility, elaboration, and originality. As a teacher, you can nurture these four desirable characteristics for all children by talking with and questioning your students as they create their artwork and by urging them to produce lots of different and unlikely ideas:

Fluency: "How many can you show?"

Flexibility: "Can you think of another way to look at it?"

Elaboration: "Can you tell about this in more detail?"

Originality: "Show your special idea in your own way."

However, since creativity is so domain specific, and it is not a trait or a capacity that pervades all of an individual's activities, it is doubtful that creativity can be assessed. To characterize creativity as simply a set of abilities that incorporate fluency, flexibility, and originality leaves many other aspects of creativity unaccounted for. In your life experiences, you undoubtedly know individuals with remarkable gifts in some areas, but who are sadly deficient in other areas.

Likewise, Harvard psychologist Howard Gardner does not believe that there is one monolithic kind of intelligence. Instead, he describes eight distinct forms of intelligence, or ways of "information processing" (1990):

- Linguistic
- Logical and mathematical
- Interpersonal (knowledge about other people)
- Musical
- Spatial
- Bodily kinesthetic
- Intrapersonal (information about oneself)
- Naturalistic

Gardner does not consider artistic thinking to be a separate form of intelligence. However, these forms can be directed to artistic or nonartistic ends. For example, language ability can be used by a poet or a lawyer. Kinesthetic ability can be used by a dancer or a surgeon. Spatial ability can be used by a sculptor or a sailor. You can bring these concepts into your classroom for all students in the following ways:

- Linguistic intelligence can be related to art through discussions of art criticism, art history, and aesthetics. Encourage students to give their artwork a title and to write about it. See Chapter 7, Art and Literacy: Reading and Language Arts.
- Mathematical intelligence can be related to art through the study of geometric forms such as icosahedra in three-dimensional constructions, fractal geometry in computer art, linear perspective, and topological surfaces in mapmaking and Escher prints. See Chapter 8 on math and art.
- Knowledge of other people (interpersonal sensitivity) can be shown by empathically discussing the art of others. Students can give encouragement to peers for their art and can depict interpersonal relationships in their own. See Chapter 6.

Courtesy of Baiba Kuntz.

Top left: Fifth-grade student Kristen Richardson paints her imaginary bird. **Bottom left:** A branch in bud and one bird are silhouetted against the full moon while another watches after a nest of eggs and a hatchling. **Top** **right:** School has ended for the year; everyone has gone home for the summer, and two gifted students paint on, intent on finishing their tempera birds. **Bottom right:** Pride can be taken in the finished artwork.

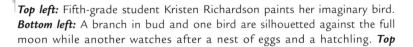

- Musical intelligence can be related to art through painting while listening to music, creating music to accompany a certain painting (such as Mussorgsky's *Paintings at an Exhibition*), and studying how various cultures have expressed themselves through music and art. And bodily kinesthetic intelligence can be fused with art creation and appreciation

by, for example, dancing out of the feeling depicted in a work of art. See Chapter 11, Art and the Performing Arts.

- Spatial intelligence is the area that is related most closely to visual art. It can be cultivated by exploring ways of creating and analyzing space in art, especially in architecture and sculpture, but also in all art ideas dealing with space—for example, perspective. See Chapters 29 and 30 on sculpture and architecture.

- Intrapersonal intelligence is awareness of the subtle interplay between cognitive and emotional processes that guide one's behavior. This form of intelligence can be given expression in art classes by discussing the meaning of one's own art or of masterpieces and by considering questions of aesthetics. See Chapter 6, particularly the section of psychology, for ideas on how to direct energy in individuals' unique emotional makeups toward productive art ends.

- Naturalistic intelligence can be related to art by the artists' experiencing and depicting observed natural phenomena. Examples are the notebooks of Leonardo da Vinci about natural phenomena, John James Audubon about American birds, and J. M. W. Turner about cloud formations. The photos by Romain Vishniak of microscopic life are another manifestation. See Chapter 10, Art and Science, for examples of student projects.

CREATIVITY

New studies in creativity focus on problem solving, problem finding, and on the creation of products. The four stages in the creative act are preparation, incubation, inspiration, and verification. Creativity is no longer seen so much as an individual activity conducted more or less in isolation. Instead it is increasingly being viewed more as an interactive dialectical process among talented individuals, domains of knowledge and products, and the judges. No person, act, or product is creative or noncreative in itself; judgments of creativity are made by knowledgeable judges.

When people are involved in creative activity or play, self-consciousness disappears, the sense of time becomes distorted, and the activity becomes

Courtesy of Beverly Barksdale Mallon.

Gifted students frequently go beyond the assigned project, doing extra work on their own. This depiction of Olympic athletes was done by a fifth-grade student independently following her completion of the class project shown on the top right. To create a feeling of ancient marble, she created marbelized paper using chalk floating on water. She then traced her figure drawings from the artwork she did in art class and combined them with Grecian columns. Three Olympic events are shown in the pictures: rhythmic gymnastics, soccer, and volleyball. The bottom picture shows her first paintings of the figures, cut out and applied onto a background of interlocking pastel shapes. On doing a second version of her picture, perhaps she felt that a more classical style of depiction could more adequately capture the Olympics' classical ideals.

Left: *Courtesy of Baiba Kuntz.* Right: *Courtesy of Saga Prefecture, Kyushu Island, Japan.*

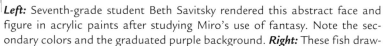

Left: Seventh-grade student Beth Savitsky rendered this abstract face and figure in acrylic paints after studying Miro's use of fantasy. Note the secondary colors and the graduated purple background. **Right:** These fish draw-ings are by primary-grade children. What imaginations these youngsters possess to invent and elaborate so skillfully.

enjoyable in itself. A balance of challenge and skill is achieved, action and awareness are merged, and distractions and worry are put aside. Psychologist Mihalyi Csikzentmihalyi found that adults' play (such as mountain climbing, gardening, chess, or art making) had the following characteristics: (1) able to concentrate on a limited stimulus field, (2) in which individual skills can be used to meet clear demands, (3) thereby for-getting personal problems, (4) and one's own separate identity, (5) at the same time obtaining a feeling of control of one's environment, (6) which may result in a transcendence of ego-boundaries and consequent psychic integration with metapersonal systems. This sixth point can also be stated as creativity being based on the belief that the individual can transform the world.

CHARACTERISTICS OF STUDENTS GIFTED IN ART

In the qualitative approach to art, all students are encouraged to develop many of the characteristics possessed by persons talented in art. Talented students have greater persistence and are able to work both longer and with greater concentration. They find pleasure by encountering complex, challenging problems. They can become absorbed for hours in a medium. Worries and cares drop away and they derive deep, personal satisfaction from their art involvement. Some or all of the following characteristics are true of people gifted in art:

- First reveal giftedness through their very early drawings and may develop a personal style of representation early in their school years.

Collection of Frank Wachowiak.

A superb pen-and-ink drawing of lush foliage by a gifted sixth-grade Japanese girl.

- Use a greater amount of detail, pattern, and texture in their artwork than do most children. Some of this elaboration is observed and some develops out of a sheer love of patterning.
- Possess a richer store of images and ideas from which to draw, heightened by their acute observation.
- Often possess a photographic mind, with vivid recall of events engaged in or observed that distinguishes their efforts, which are characterized by a richness of details.
- Master certain technical aspects of drawing—perspective, foreshortening, volume, shading, overlapping, spatial handling, movement—much sooner than do their peers.
- May choose subjects of fantasy for their art compositions, with complex themes involving intricate structures and a host of participants.
- Are open to new experiences with new media, techniques, and tools.
- Show great interest in the art world and the lives of contemporary artists and craftspeople. They may visit art museums and some even may carry a sketchbook to record their impressions.
- Rather than merely reacting to occurrences in the world, their creativity may lead them to take a proactive stance toward them.
- Learn quickly to employ the vocabulary of art both effectively and confidently and to criticize and evaluate their art production for design.
- Usually prefer drawing, painting, printmaking, and collage to step-by-step craftwork.
- Use color imaginatively, making up their own palette by combining the hues provided to the class.
- Are oblivious to distractions when engaged in their art, and often resent interference.
- Generally are highly self-motivated and driven by a need to fashion art products on their own—after school, at home, and even during other classes.

TEACHING STRATEGIES

The teacher can encourage gifted students by providing a supportive environment. Students feel this is more important than any instruction they receive. Often in artists' biographies we read of how one teacher took the child artist aside and pointed out how his or her gifts could benefit the world. Overpraise is to be avoided, however, because it can lead to peer resentment. Be aware that learning occurs from "Novice to Expert"; by analyzing experts' performance, novices can see differences among them. This is a familiar idea in arts' education where, centuries ago, the apprentice system was used. Perhaps you are the expert role model who can guide a child, or perhaps you can put the child in contact with an expert.

A good approach is the minimal one of leaving the student to follow his or her special direction—in effect, underteaching. The teacher can provide challenges through multimedia techniques and subject-matter assignments that demand imaginative solutions and interpretations. For example, an assignment might be to depict a famous person when young, experiencing the first intimations of her or his future role in life. Although a teacher should provide challenges, on no account should you rush the gifted child into advanced forms of expression.

Letting the child pursue his or her own endeavors may pose problems for the teacher who uses the project method, in which all students in class engage in the same subject-matter assignment using the same technique. To allow gifted children the special privilege of working on their own subject choice, at their own pace, while their classmates are required to stay with the assigned project, is not recommended. A wiser procedure is to challenge gifted children to stretch the possibilities of the assigned project or theme to their fullest. Remind gifted students that there are many moments outside of class when they can soar creatively and imaginatively in subjects of their own choosing, and encourage them to share with you some of those outside efforts.

Model creativity yourself in your teaching. To keep the creative spark alive, each day surprise the students in your class with something new. Each day, ask, "What would happen if . . . ?"

Courtesy of Barbara Thomas.

Model creativity in your teaching. Each day somehow surprise your students.

Gifted students can stretch the possibilities of the assigned project to the fullest. A middle-school student did this colorful simulated mosaic employing cut and torn colored paper for the tesserae. Note the gradations of blue in the harbor's water. The subject is Sakurajima Park, with a view of an erupting volcano on a nearby island, Kagoshima, Japan.

EXTENDING INTO THE SCHOOL, HOME, AND COMMUNITY

The teacher can foster students' creative growth not only in the art class but also in the school at large, the home, and the community. Find ways to extend art activities into the community and the individual's ongoing daily life. Community integration may be especially helpful to creative students because of their tendency to be more socially reserved, aloof, and distanced. They also are more questioning, skeptical, and opinionated. People may express negative attitudes toward them, and both peers and adults may perceive them as smart alecks.

To foster the creative and social growth of talented students, consider forming a club or an organization for your gifted students, who might find kindred spirits in such a group. Together, they can discuss and share their artwork and go to special events, such as museum openings. They can contribute artistically to the school's special functions, perhaps by painting a set for an assembly program. Middle school youths can be organized into a chapter of the National Art Education Association's National Junior Art Honor Society. Because males and females need role models with whom to identify, provide gifted students with role models from both genders and from diverse cultural backgrounds. Do not enter gifted elementary and middle school children's art into competitions, however, because such external competitions can undermine creative interest and performance. For the one child who is reinforced by a prize, 10 or 100 children will have confidence in their nascent ability undermined. Especially shun coloring contests of pictures drawn by adults.

The home environment is extremely important in encouraging creativity. Studies of creative individuals reveal that often at least two generations had participated in the particular creative field. Creative adults report that when they were young they were exposed to environments in which they were encouraged to ask questions and to test their ideas by active experimentation. (Note that these also are the tenets of the constructivist educators.)

At a parent conference, share with the child's parents your notice of his or her special giftedness. Direct parents' awareness toward community art enrichment programs for children. An art specialist with hundreds of students each year might use a letter to parents to give notice of artistic giftedness and offer suggestions for how to nurture it. An example of such a letter follows:

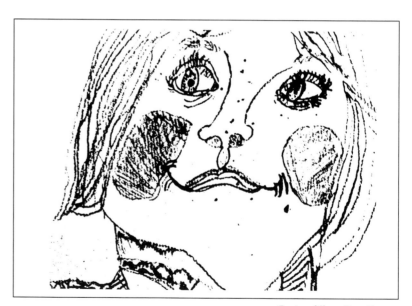

Courtesy of Sharon Burns-Knutson.

The teacher of art should call parents' attention to gifted students' abilities so that the children may receive enrichment instruction and the gift be nurtured. Gifted first-graders have produced these detailed contour-line drawings. They reveal once again what youngsters are capable of achieving in drawing skills when they are encouraged to become aware. First-grade children can notice jewelry details, barrettes, freckles, eyeglass hinges, creases of skin around the eyes and at the mouth's sides—even the oval on the upper lip below the nose and the wrinkles in the lips.

Left: *Courtesy of Saga Prefecture, Kyushu Island, Japan.* Middle: *Courtesy of Frank Wachowiak and Mary Sayer Hammond.* Right: *Courtesy of Beverly Barksdale Mallon.*

Left: This gifted second grader from Japan is imbued with an intuitive understanding of nature's fractal growth patterns. **Middle:** Art enrichment in the community can help gifted students learn to take their time and create works of beauty. **Right:** Gifted student Annabelle Barbe adds watercolor with gay abandon over an equally free pencil sketch of a daffodil bouquet.

To the Parents or Guardians of :

Teaching at Anniston and Mayberry Elementary Schools for the past two years, I have had the opportunity to observe the art achievement of over a thousand students. You probably are already aware of your child's giftedness in art; however, I felt it to be my professional responsibility to bring to your attention my notice of and appreciation for the quality work your child does in art. Giftedness is rarely loudly announced; many geniuses as adults showed no spark of giftedness when young (for example, Einstein, Churchill, Tolstoy, Kafka, and Proust). Picasso was poor academically. As a general trait, artistic giftedness in children is shown by their being able to concentrate longer, having a lot of ideas to express, and including a lot of detail to make their drawings more elaborate. They are more self-directed, draw more realistically earlier than other children, and use art materials more creatively.

Some talented children have profited from several art-enrichment programs in our community. Although as a school employee I cannot endorse any one program, I wanted to bring their existence to your attention if you wish to look into their suitability in meeting your child's needs:

Mayberry Recreation Department, Lyndon House Art Center, classes for children ages 4–12, Tuesdays and Thursdays, 3:30 to 5:30 PM, 10 sessions, cost $40 a term. The YMCA has art classes for members, Saturday, 10–12 AM. Alachua County Junior College has a gifted program on Saturday mornings that sometimes has classes focusing on the arts (546-9990). Private art teachers of whom I am aware in the community are Martha Menendez, 546-7783, and James Jackson, 543-3454. In addition, there are probably more programs of which I am unaware.

Please contact me at school at 543-9087 (between 2:30 and 3:30 PM is best) or at home at 548-4543 (between 7 and 8 PM) or by e-mail: fjones@_, if I can be of help to you concerning how we might work together to further your child's artistic creativity.

Art Teacher, Anniston and Mayberry Elementary Schools

Teachers who discover talented children are fortunate. They witness what children can do in art when they extend themselves to their fullest potential. Teachers can derive clues from the creative solutions that gifted children employ to help them motivate other classmates. What teachers see and learn from the characteristics and working habits of talented children is what they emphasize in a qualitative art program. They see keen, sensitive observation; rich imagination; persistence, patience, and concentration; and above all, art that is engaged in by the child both seriously and purposefully.

FOR FURTHER READING

Clark, Gil, and Zimmerman, Enid. 1987. *Educating Artistically Talented Students.* Syracuse, NY: Syracuse University Press.

Csikszentmihalyi, M. 1996. *Creativity: Flow and the Psychology of Discovery and Invention.* New York: HarperCollins.

Dunnahoo, D. E. "Re-thinking Creativity: A Discipline-Based Perspective." *Art Education* 46 (July 93): 53–60.

Feldman, D. H.; Csikszentmihalyi, M.; and Gardner, H. 1994. *Changing the World: A Framework for the Study of Creativity.* Westport, CT: Praeger Publishers.

Gardner, Howard. 1983. *Frames of Mind.* New York: Basic Books.

Getzels, J., and Jackson, P. 1963. "The Highly Intelligent and Highly Creative Adolescent. A Summary of Some Research Findings." In C. W. Taylor and F. Barron (eds.), *Scientific Creativity: Its Recognition and Development.* New York: Wiley, 166–172.

Getzels, Jacobs, and Csikszentmihalyi, Mihalyi. 1976. *The Creative Vision: A Longitudinal Study of Problem Finding in Art.* New York: Wiley.

Greene, Maxine. 1995. "Art and Imagination: Reclaiming the Sense of Possibility." *Phi Delta Kappan* 76(5): 378–382.

Hurwitz, Al. 1983. *The Gifted and Talented in Art: A Guide to Program Planning.* Worcester, MA: Davis.

Piaget, J. 1982. "Creativity." In J. M. Gallagher and D. K. Reid (eds.), *The Learning Theory of Piaget and Inhelder.* Monterey, CA: Brooks/Cole. (Originally published in 1972.)

Runco, M. A. 1997. *The Creativity Research Handbook.* Vol. 1. Cresskill, NJ: Hampton Press, Inc.

Szekely, George. 1988. *Encouraging Creativity in Art Lessons.* New York: Teacher's College Press.

Torrance, E. Paul. 1966. *Torrance Test of Creative Thinking.* Bensenville, IL: Scholastic Testing Service.

WEB RESOURCES

For ideas from the American Association for Gifted Children:
http://www.aagc.org/enrich.htm

For information on how we are all gifted:
http://pbskids.org/georgeshrinks/caregiver/outreach.html

For a guide to websites of organizations for gifted children:
http://www.gifted.uconn.edu/parentws.html

For student- and teacher-built websites on educational topics:
http://www.thinkquest.org/

For one school's gifted and talented program over the curriculum:
http://www.bcps.org/offices/gt/elementary_curriculum041602.htm

For a description of a school's gifted program:
www.bcps.org/schools/CES/cromwell/pdf/GT-fact-sheet.pdf

For information on gifted students with learning disabilities:
http://www.homeeducator.com/FamilyTimes/articles/9-5article8.htm

For a glossary of gifted terms including IQ scores:
http://www.gtworld.org/index/html

For the ERIC database to educational research:
http://www.eric.ed.gov/

Part 4

Creating an Art Curriculum

"Rain Storm over Shono" by Japanese artist Ando Hiroshige (1797–1858) is the most famous of a series of woodblock prints called "53 Stations on the Tokaido," showing scenes along the hundred mile Tokaido Road from Edo (now Tokyo) to Kyoto. Regional leaders (shoguns) traveled the road frequently to pay homage to the Emperor, whose palace was in Kyoto—and to visit their wives and families, who were required by the emperor to live there. Hiroshige accompanied a shogun on one such tribute trip and sketched the rest stops and inns along the way. This print shows coolies and their clients near the inns at the Shono station, coping as best they can with a sudden cloudburst. Two coolies use bamboo mats to shield themselves from the driving rain, while two porters carry an official in the covered, two-man conveyance. Running downhill in the opposite direction, a servant shields his master with an umbrella. The storm's hasty transition can be seen in the color gradients of the print's several wood blocks: the ground from blue to grey, the sky from black to grey, the rows of storm-tossed pine trees each successively lighter, but with each individual row shifting from dark to light. Bending from the fury of nature, some travelers press on, others turn back. If you were there, which course of action would you chose? As you go about developing and implementing your art curriculum, may your days be sunny and the showers brief.

Private collection, Athens, GA.

he following chapters address students' development during kindergarten and then during two-year periods: primary Grades 1 and 2, intermediate Grades 3 and 4, upper-elementary Grades 5 and 6, and middle-school Grades 7 and 8. For each period, you will find:

- A list of developmental characteristics of the age group and their implications for the teaching of art
- A description of children's typical artistic development in terms of their use of shape, size, color, space, shading, ways of drawing objects, the human figure, and favorite subject matter
- A description of art production teaching strategies, including specific activities, that are particularly effective for the age group under discussion
- An overview of teaching procedures for art criticism, art history, and aesthetics

- A list of suggested topics or subjects to inspire students in these grades (or, for kindergartners, a set of guidelines about teaching young children)

In each case, the developmental characteristics are general and approximate; every child is an individual, and you will always find children in these grades who do not display these characteristics. Good teachers modify their approaches and strategies based on the individual needs of the children in their classroom.

But first, the five specific grade-level chapters are preceded by Chapter 14 discussing overall cognitive and psychological factors in children's learning and creative development.

Cognitive and Psychological Factors in Children's Learning and Creative Development

$\mathcal{M}$ind, eye, heart, hand, or context (used as metaphors)—which of these controls the art learning process? Do children draw what they know, or do they draw what they see? Is it knowledge or vision that guides the drawing process? In general, young children draw what they know. Older children in our culture tend to draw more of what they see. Young children tend to pay little or no attention to the object and instead use a scheme, a product of individual cognition. During elementary school, children increasingly do attempt to draw objects more as they appear. Cognitive and developmental psychologists have made the

Moving beyond the scribbling stage, the young child begins to use geometric shapes to make representations. *Butterflies in the Garden* shows a wonderful, intuitive use of color in the multihued flower petals and cheerful use of background washes. White crayon lines are especially effective in crayon resist.

case for a connection between children's art and their intellectual growth. Yet even older children may rely upon visual constancies—the remnants of their earlier cognitive schemes—for representing an object. These stereotyped "ideas" must be overcome for the child to "see" and draw an object with a degree of accuracy in representation. Young children can be exposed to drawing the figure or still life; however, teachers must accept the efforts of those still employing their own fixed schema of how to represent something, rather than attempting to capture its visual appearance.

Educators concerned with perception have emphasized children's ability to see, and especially to see differences. They stress vision, figure-ground relationships, and seeing, describing, and depicting differences within art's formal elements and principles. The "hand" as metaphor is especially relevant in the primary grades, when some youngsters may require a longer time to develop eye-hand coordination. The "mind" is foremost as cognitive psychologists emphasize the mental processes in the child's constructing knowledge. Our metaphor of "heart" goes in tandem with mind; in our representations we show both our cognitive and emotional knowledge. Contextualist educators place importance on the making of choices within a given societal context. These orientations are *not* mutually exclusive, experts, as well as new teachers such as yourselves, have differing degrees of acceptance of any of these orientations. Indeed, powerful thinkers such as Jean Piaget have provided theories that account for several of these orientations.

CONSTRUCTIVISM

Piaget's psychological theory of intellectual change, *constructivism,* refers to the self-constructed nature of knowledge. Children are to be seen less as

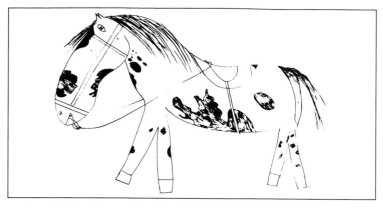

Learners can find ways to create meaning from art experiences. Here, the bright and varied colors of insects and gardens are fused into a personal representation. Art criteria of varied shapes, informal balance, and border-touching are applied. ***Top:*** This first-grader's tissue collage is given movement and unity by colors moving from a red area in the upper left to a white area on the right edge. ***Bottom:*** Colored tissue is applied by a fifth-grader to a marker drawing on 18- × 24-inch white construction paper.

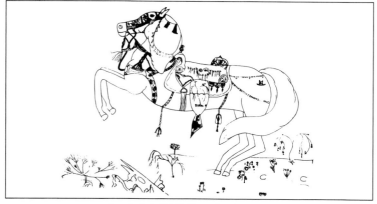

These drawings, made by the same girl at ages 7, 9, and 10, illustrate increasing refinement in drawing horses.

problem solvers and more as problem seekers or raisers—developers of strategies for manipulating information. That is, when students are tied to facts, we prevent their inventing and discovering for themselves. Education's value is measurable largely in terms of how well it permits the learner to go *beyond* the information given. Learners need to discover the means by which to make meaning out of experience and the knowledge they have gained. (For some art examples, see Chapters 9 and 10 on social studies and science integration.) Through art representation, the child can find new ways to represent meaning.

These ideas gave rise to *discovery learning,* which focuses on creating the possibilities for the child to invent and discover knowledge. One variation of such ideas was in A. S. Neil's school, Summerhill, where the learning decisions were made by the students, who were considered to be innately wise and realistic. Effective discovery learning requires emphasizing objectives constantly and asking reflective, "springboard" questions—those that contain an element of controversy or contradiction. Identifying contradiction, identifying novel problems, taking risks in problem solving, and building a representation of the world are central in art making and art criticism. When a child seriously draws an object or writes about a concept, discoveries are made; writing and drawing are aids to learning. Discovery learning is not about haphazard, aimless goings on.

Piaget's theory focused on how the changes in children's thinking come about. The large changes in children's development are the sensorimotor period, the period of concrete operations, and the period of formal operations. These bear a rough resemblance to stages in art education: scribbling and manipulation of materials, learning how to represent things and ideas through art media, and, in middle school, increased intellectual examination, such as in art criticism, art history, and aesthetics.

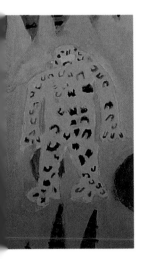

Left and middle: *Courtesy of Joyce Vroon.*
Right: *Courtesy of Debra Belvin and Crayola® Dream-Makers®, a registered trademark of Binney and Smith.*

Left: A meaningful, personal learning base can be exemplified by students' drawings of personal myths. This integrated art lesson was done after students studied Greek mythology and wrote their personal myths in language arts class. Here, sixth-grader Burton Dodd's Hulk-like blue monster is seen through the eyes of its adversary's dragon-like teeth. **Middle:** Meaningful learning, the personal expression of a learned skill, is shown in second-grader Martin Tilson's depiction of "Something I Am Proud Of," here, the joy of achievement in soccer. **Right:** Achieving personally meaningful goals is shown in this fifth-grader's oil pastel, "I Become a Hero on That Special Day."

Piaget emphasized the rational mind's central role in forming the knowledge structures necessary to bring stability and order in understanding the world. He believed there was at work in the individual's knowledge-gathering capabilities "an equilibration process," rational and conscious that was used by the individual to construct systems of order. The individual's mental change occurs not just from mental reflection, but also from the action, exploration, and interpretation; hence, the individual constructs knowledge. It is for this process that the constructivism theory is named.

In earlier times, a child had been considered to be a blank slate or empty tablet (tabula rasa) onto which the information was written. But constructivists view knowledge not as objective truth, but as transformative and changing. Rather than there being "one correct interpretation" to an artwork, an artwork's interpretation is more or less relative. Constructivists believe that, for true learning to occur, students must construct their own meaningful, personal knowledge bases under the guidance of a teacher who encourages active learning. Certainly, making an art representation of a thing is a clear way to construct and show to oneself and to the world what one understands about that thing.

Before the constructivists, the behaviorist psychologists had emphasized how the environment could shape the individual through positive and negative reinforcement. For the stimulus–response psychologists, knowledge was a passive kind of behavior, as in operant conditioning, and was elicited by stimulus and strengthened by response. The developmentalists, on the other hand, had a theory of innate biological unfolding, like a bud unfolding to become a flower. But the constructivists believed these theories were insufficient to explain how the sources of changes in interpreting the world came about. They believed it was through the individual's revising theories, based on the individual's experience in the world.

Matching the Child's Natural Way of Thinking Educational psychologist Jerome Bruner led the cognitive revolution that rejected behaviorism's constraints. His bold dictum, "Any subject can be taught effectively, in some intellectually honest way, to any child at any stage of development," pointed out how early learning experiences form the basis for later learning. The task in the early years of school, then, is to put the material into the child's natural way of thinking—that is, using the senses along with concrete objects. An outstanding example of this in architecture occurred when a second-grade boy, Frank Lloyd Wright, and his mother worked together with Froebel blocks. He and his mother worked together at the task for years. So strong was this influence that his final words were, "Put blocks in the young child's hands." Attendant to this developmental idea, Bruner believed knowledge was acquired in a spiral manner. Sequential art curricula that revisit art concepts year after year show an application of this idea.

ROLE OF THE SOCIAL CONTEXT

Piaget and another constructivist educational psychologist, L. S. Vygotsky, believed that teachers should encourage students' verbal interaction with peers to develop their thinking about issues. In so doing, the children are forced both to confront the views of others and to learn to express and defend their own ideas. They learn by interacting with a more experienced play partner, a peer, a teacher, or a parent. For example, Montessori education combines classes of three grade levels. There is little evidence that creative learning arises spontaneously and in isolation; the imagination develops especially well through pretend play with peers.

Although teachers traditionally have been accustomed to valuing the silent classroom of children working individually on tasks, the constructivists' ideas of social learning instead urge teachers to appreciate the developmental role played by guided communicative language interactions. This book's chapter on art criticism and aesthetics (Chapter 22) shows specific ways that this is done through questioning, generalizing, and hypothesizing what will happen next in the picture. In one method, *reciprocal learning,* the teacher and students take turns summarizing the main ideas in the picture.

Courtesy of Clarke Middle School, Athens, GA.

The three proud students pictured here collaborated to carve this huge wood bas relief.

Courtesy of Barbara Thomas

Students' peer-to-peer verbal interactions may help them to think about the sociological and artistic issues.

Courtesy of Baiba Kuntz.

The educational power of working in pairs (or dyads) is shown here in this pair of wrestlers. Seventh-graders Michael Schmidt and Matt Siegfried worked side-by-side on their wrestlers of Sculpey™ for weeks, finally putting them into the same wrestling ring.

Courtesy of Frank Wachowiak and Ted Ramsay.

Working in a Group: Students interact as they jointly develop their "jungle." Intermediate elementary grade children made the large (18- × 36-inch) group collograph. A paper punch created patterns in the leopard and on the bushes. Pinking shears were used to cut the palm trees. Additional cutout holes, as well as little squares and triangles of paper, also were pasted onto the cardboard plate.

Group Work in School, Art, and Life Educational psychology has swung away from thinking of the student as an isolated problem solver toward thinking of the student as learning in a social environment. Buzz groups, dyads, educational games, working in teams, and group mural projects are a few manifestations of this. Cooperative learning—an idea supported by constructivists—requires children to be dependent on each other to achieve a learning goal, for example, to prepare a report or mural or to construct a tower of a certain height.

Likewise, in the fine arts, attention is increasingly being paid to how learning and creativity operate less as the purview of the individual and more as within the verbal interaction of a social context. Some examples: While inventing cubism, Picasso and Braque felt "rather like two mountaineers roped together" (Berger, 1965). Paul Cezanne and Emile Zola, when young, were buddies. Mary Cassatt's creative genius was catalyzed by close friend and mentor Edgar Degas. Many of the abstract expressionist painters spent hours talking together in the evenings. Jacob Lawrence received his art inspiration in art classes at Harlem's first art center. Judy Chicago worked collaboratively with numerous women artists on The Dinner Table project. Such examples challenge the myth of a person-centered view of creativity and emphasize instead the social, family, and school context. As the student integrates give-and-take reciprocity of discourse, the student's consciousness is restructured by the social context.

Courtesy of David W. Hodge.

The social context can be a powerful catalyst for learning. Here busy upper-elementary youngsters work on a group project, a reduction linoleum print. Step One: In this variation of the regular lino print process, the students first cut away selected areas of the linoleum and pulled several prints using a red printing ink. Step Two: While the prints were drying, the youngsters gouged out additional sections of the block. Step Three: The cleaned plate was inked again in green and printed over the first red edition, with care taken to "register" or match the second printing over the first. Step Four: While the two-color prints dried, students cut away the final selected areas. Then they used black ink for the third and last impression.

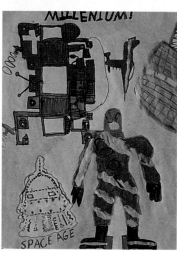

Top left and right: *Courtesy of Frank Wachowiak child art collection.*
Bottom left: *Courtesy of Beverly Barksdale Mallon.* Bottom right: *Courtesy of Joyce Vroon.*

Imagination is not just for frivolous fantasy. It also can set the stage for generating ideas useful in real contexts. ***Top left and right:*** Here, the world of the future is depicted by Saga, Japan, upper-elementary students. ***Bottom left:*** As robots and computers increasingly assist us, we are enabled to see the robotlike aspects of ourselves, here, a green monster missing a few teeth. ***Bottom right:*** In fifth-grader Brett Bessinger's scene of the future, a red spaceman interacts with jets, spaceships, and communication satellites.

Cooperation in the arts is more the rule than the exception. Murals would not exist without willing owners of walls; school symphonies wouldn't exist without a supply of instruments and taxpayers willing to hire the teacher. Advertising art would not exist without advertisers and advertising media. Creativity is not only culture dependent, but also domain specific and field specific. Domains and fields are sociological concept systems that either allow or thwart the development of the individual's conscious and unconscious functions. In other words, development moves from the outside in as well as from the inside out.

But operating in real-world contexts should not mean disregarding the positive role of the individual's imagination. Imagination is not merely frivolous fantasy of minor importance. Imagination assumes an important educational role when we think of it as students generating meaningful patterns of ideas that are useful in a real context.

ROLE OF THE EMOTIONS: THE INTUITIVE AND THE NONRATIONAL

In addition to seeing and knowing (the eye perceiving and the mind constructing reality and operating within a context), there is a third element that guides children's drawings and learning—the feelings, which we metaphorically call "the heart." Psychologists interested in the link between self-esteem and learning have found that youngsters with high self-esteem performed better. In viewing a class's drawings, one sees the children's distinct personalities infusing both the objects shown and the very different drawing styles. Educators who believe the expression of feelings is art's main purpose emphasize the emotional and psychological basis for art expression (see also Chapter 6 on the affective domain).

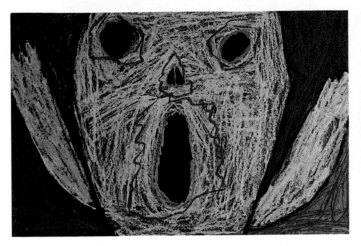  

Left: *Courtesy of Joyce Vroon.* Middle and right: *Courtesy of David W. Hodge.*

Left: A dissonant, chaotic situation appears in third-grader Josh Schaefer's scary white face of a Halloween mask. Students love the macabre. Oil pastel on black paper. ***Middle and right:*** Masks reveal more than conceal. They may tell us a lot about our feelings and personalities, here, a blonde-haired and a blue-haired mask.

Emotions do guide actions and are shaped by them. The elementary-school-age child must develop an emotion-filled eagerness to learn new skills and win recognition through successful performance, or the child risks developing a sense of failure and inferiority. This elementary-school-age crisis of a sense of industry inferiority was explained by psychologist Eric Erickson. His theory of psychosocial development stages explained how social factors influence feelings and behavior. (Erickson had been a high school dropout who wandered around Europe studying art until age 25, when he studied with Freud.)

Nonrational impulses, which may well be ill-defined, play an important role in the individual's change and growth. Piaget's equilibration mechanism accounted well for the human tendency to learn logical, rational, and stable structures, but it did not account well for the nonrational, or for innovations in the humanly crafted world. We "know" about things with *both* ideas and feelings. We understand with both the logical, linear, and rational as well as the emotional, intuitive, and nonrational.

Art can provide vicarious experiences in dealing with dissonant, chaotic situations, and these experiences, in turn, can help individuals deal with the dissonance they encounter in their everyday lives. Children's drawing violent monsters and Dungeons and Dragons superheroes and fighter planes while vocalizing "akakakakakak" give psychological voice to their creators' coping strategies.

Art and creativity are often considered functions of the right brain, while the left brain controls activities more amenable to tests, according to some researchers on brain functioning. Although many neurophysiologists

Left: *Courtesy of Joyce Vroon.* Right: *Courtesy of Joyce Vroon. Student Katherine Bell, Grade 5.*

Left: We understand experience with both our conscious and unconscious mind. Asked to depict a dream, fifth-grader Elizabeth Towles's picture of swimming seems to depict feelings of danger and helplessness. ***Right:*** Giving expression to one's personal myth. Set against a dark stormy sky, two enormous, dangerous lightning bolts crash at the bare feet of a calm young girl, dressed in a primitive style dress. Language arts, writing, art, and study of Greek myths were integrated.

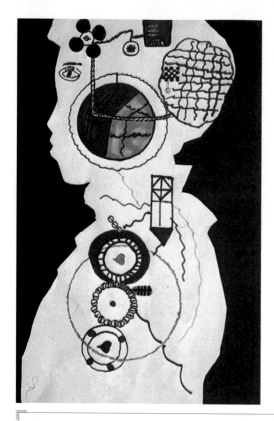
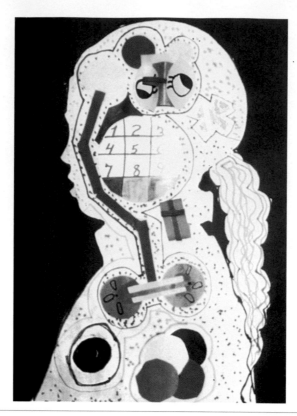
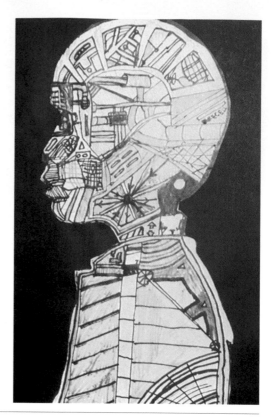

Fifth-grade students created these X-ray silhouettes, showing how the opportunities and challenges of technology—for example, radio transistors, motors, battery watchworks, cameras, computers, and television—have affected them. 18- × 24-inch white construction paper, watercolor markers and crayons, wallpaper samples, scissors, pencils, and paste were used. A film projector lamp helped to create the student's shadow silhouette. The completed drawings were cut out and mounted on dark-colored construction paper.

are skeptical about the hemispheric separateness of right and left brain functions, the notion may serve a useful purpose in highlighting the importance of educational activities such as art. Like other dichotomous systems from years past, such as Viktor Lowenfeld's visual/haptic dichotomy, this dichotomy widens the scope of what is legitimately thought of as education's proper role. Likewise, Howard Gardner's theory of multiple intelligences also opens the door for a respect for multiple ways of knowing about the world (see Chapter 13, on giftedness).

Transformation As art is made, the brain's different mental functions—the rational, the intuitive, and even the irrational—are brought together. The rational processes are complimented by the fluid, nonrational, noncategorical thinking that occurs outside of conscious awareness. Art's bringing together these different mental functions into harmonious interplay can serve to transform the individual as well as society.

Transformation and novelty are important goals of education. David Feldman calls this tendency of mind to provide novel constructions the "transformation imperative." Humans have a tendency to intentionally transform their physical and social world. They want to bring into the world new conditions that will make it a more satisfactory place. Crafted objects that have already been made serve as models for innovation. Art classes provide children with exposure to such objects and especially to the process of transforming things and ideas through art to make a more meaningful world.

Like young kittens, young children are curious, toying with the boundaries around them and engaging in novel activities. Children gain pleasure from the manipulation of symbolic forms. Our educational task is to keep this playful analogical thinking growing, rather than dwindling, throughout the school years. Analogical thinking reaches back into the individual's rational and nonrational thoughts and emotions. It combines previous experiences in unusual ways to generate new patterns of meaning. Teachers should try to develop in their students an equilibrium between both logical and analogical thinking. In this endeavor, art classes can help. Art classes catalyze the imagination as students generate ideas and designs to solve a problem in the context of art creation or art criticism. Art activities can stimulate students' imaginative, creative, and transformative potential—essential to our nation's greatness.

CHILDREN'S SIMILARITIES AND VARIABILITY

Children everywhere have much in common. They react in similar ways to their environment. They laugh, cry, play, act, sing, and dance. They delight in seeing and manipulating bright, colorful objects, in playing games, and in manipulating machines and vehicles. They respond to sympathetic, supportive voices and to loving, nurturing hands.

Scribbling Likewise, children everywhere draw in much the same manner during their early developmental stages. Long before we learn how to respond to the world cognitively, we respond to it aesthetically through touch, taste, smell, and sound. Preschoolers begin with random, haphazard marks and then move on to explore different types of scribbles. Acquiring more control and the desire for representation, children become

Courtesy of Beverly Barksdale Mallon.

Second-grade students transformed ideas of normal architecture into "funhouses"—fantasy creations designed for pleasure and delight. **Left:** A house shaped like a Coke® bottle, with a taco-shaped patio for outdoor cooking. **Right:** A riot of hearts and stars add excitement to this huge funhouse.

Courtesy of Baiba Kuntz.

By the eighth grade, children are quite differentiated and variable, as shown in their representations in Sculpey® modeling clay. **From left to right:** A strong, self-reliant cowboy with chaps, lasso, mustache, and rocks, by Jonathan Honor; a strong, green-haired, red-bearded figure wearing contemporary baggy jeans with yellow stitching, by Lucas Simpson; a one-eyed general with the Union Jack and sword, claiming new land for the kingdom, by Dan Millner; a very artistic girl painter with thick black braids, dotted overalls and shirt, completing work on her Miro-esque easel painting, by Amanda Ip; an old wizard in a beautiful star-studded cape parts the crashing waves, by Alison Eckenhoff; a young child, well protected with yellow slicker, rainhat, boots, and umbrella, accompanied by a duckie, by Dena Gilman. Magazine photos on the walls provided a vague sort of motivation and students worked for weeks on their characters.

able to shape their scribbles into simple, geometric shapes, which then develop into semirealistic interpretations. Contrasted with later stages, in which development is much more variable across cultures, the early stages of artistic development (up to 5 to 7 years of age for children without developmental disabilities) are universally determined; they are strongly similar across different cultures and times.

Later Variability
While universal patterns of development govern the early stages of expression, forces of the specific culture and its educational and enrichment programs play greater roles as children mature. Some students may have had abundant art experiences (just as some children may have been read to abundantly), while others have had few creative opportunities. Students in the same class may come from different backgrounds and have totally different day-to-day experiences. Because no two children are alike, it is difficult to generalize about them by age or gender. To understand and help children to grow through art, however, the teacher must be aware of those characteristics that have been identified with certain age groups.

Stages
Stage theory should be used only as a descriptive, however, and *not* as a prescriptive device. Stages are "external" not "internal"; a person does not "have" a stage. Rather, a stage is a commonly available structure of thought, like "gender" and "race." Like them, stages can be stereotyping and limiting. A teacher should keep in mind that stages may be skipped and even reversed. Even within one drawing, indications of several stages may be found. Lowenfeld's stages—the scribbling stages; the preschematic stage (first representational attempts, 4–7 years); the schematic stage (achievement of a form concept, 7–9 years); and the gang stage (dawning realism, 9–12 years)—have been criticized for these reasons.

Further, stage theory fails to account for how cultural influences can shape development. In school, the child is taught to accept culturally approved systems of drawing and to ignore those that the culture does not approve of or value. Artistic expression is not a driving force that seeks improvement, nor is it an unfolding of predetermined abilities. Instead, it is bound to the time and place of its creation, and it reflects the creative options available at that time and place.

U-Shaped Decline
Educational psychologists have documented "U-shaped declines" in creativity (although there is little unanimity as to when such decline occurs—in primary school, intermediate school, or middle school). Some researchers say the young child's early prowess in graphic symbolizations submerges by ages 8–11; this is called the U-shaped development in graphic symbolization. Perhaps this slump is due to inhibitions caused by the child's inner demands for photographic realism. Regrettably, after these slumps, only a few resume their creative efforts.

Except among those who go on to become adult artists or who have outstanding art teachers, often there is little development in drawing skills beyond this stage. Alas, education too often brings with it increased criticality. Some say that this critical preference for what is safe and conventional is not a loss, but instead shows an increase in evaluative skills. However, while mastery of rules obviously benefits an individual, in too many instances it simultaneously inhibits the individual's existing abilities and capacities. (For example, untrained folk artists' creations may have a raw freshness judged superior to educated artists' artworks.)

While art teachers may fret over a diminution in artworks' imagination, kids don't see it that way. Five-year-olds prefer the realistic drawings of ten-year-olds to their own. Eight- to ten-year-olds, in the conventional years of middle childhood, have as their main art goal to be as realistic as possible. Only on reaching roughly age twelve can children entertain the idea that there are other things in art besides realistic drawing skill.

Later is not better. Artwork from earlier stages in a child's life is not inferior to later work. A younger child's work, filled with exciting, unpredictable naiveté, may show more giftedness than that of an older child. The spontaneity, beauty, and naiveté of a child's artistic expression at age 10 may never again be seen in that unique form in that child's work. Just as with fine art produced over centuries, fine art from the distant past is not inferior to more contemporary artwork. Instead, the work from each time shows the distinctive characteristics of that time.

All courtesy of Frank Wachowiak; except Grade 1 girl, courtesy of David Harvell, and Grade 7 girl, courtesy of Baiba Kuntz.

Facing Page: Children's development in art is sequential. It generally moves toward showing more realistic proportion, more muscles, gender characteristics, and detail; however, there are numerous exceptions to the "typical" sequence. After leaving the scribbling stage, children at first draw tadpole-like figures in which single, straight-line limbs protrude from the head. By first grade, most children conceive of the head as a separate circle, from which hangs a body drawn with a triangle or square. Attached to this are straight limbs with two sides, rather than just being a stick (Grade 1 girl). Then, the phenomenon of bending limbs becomes graphically realized, and curved, sausage-type limbs are drawn (Grade 2 boy). Joints develop, and knees and elbows then are drawn as the locations of the bending (Grades 3 and 4 boys). The limbs become progressively more fused to the body (Grade 3 boy and Grade 5 girl). Overlapping of limbs over the body can be seen (Grades 2 and 4 boys, Grade 6 girl and boy). Proportions change from the three-heads-high figure (Grade 2 boy) to the five-heads-high figure (Grade 6 boy). The form of the neck, arising from the torso, becomes more clearly realized. Hips and muscles become more clearly represented (Grade 6 girl and boy). Foreshortening appears (Grade 8 girl's writing arm), and three-quarter views may appear (Grade 8 girl's face).

Grade 1 girl

Grade 1 boy

Grade 2 girl

Grade 2 boy

Grade 3 boy

Grade 4 boy

Grade 5 girl

Grade 6 girl

Grade 6 boy

Grade 7 boy

Grade 7 girl

Grade 8 girl

Courtesy of Beverly Barksdale Mallon.

Later is not better. Many adult artists would give a lot to be able to design like this kindergartner. It seems almost unbelievable that a kindergartner could create this rhythmic collage design of Matisse-like doves with such sensitivity to positive and negative shapes. In three 35-minute periods, kindergartners learned how to put triangles together to create diamond shapes and how to draw doves. First, they drew triangles and doves. Next, they traced over and over these shapes (to develop facility in writing). Then they cut them out, arranged them, and glued them down.

The spontaneous and intuitive visual expressions of young children are so wonderful and so filled with wonder that they have influenced many noted artists such as Jean Dubuffet, Juan Miro, Paul Klee, and Karel Appel. Pablo Picasso said, "Once I drew like Raphael but it has taken me a whole life to learn to draw like a child" (de Meredieu, 1974).

FOR FURTHER READING

Arnheim, Rudolf. 1966. *Art and Visual Perception: A Psychology of the Creative Eye.* Berkeley: University of California Press.

Dewey, John. 1934. *Art as Experience.* New York: Minton Balch.

Edwards, L. C. 1990. *Affective Development and the Creative Arts: A Process Approach to Early Childhood Education.* Columbus, OH: Merrill Publishing Co.

Erickson, Erik. 1963. *Childhood and Society.* New York: Norton.

Feldman, David H. 1986. *Nature's Gambit.* New York: Basic Books.

Feldman, David H. 1987. "Developmental Psychology and Art Education: Two Fields at the Crossroads." *Journal of Aesthetic Education* 21(2): 243–259.

Freeman, Nancy H., and Cox, M.V. (eds.). 1985. *Visual Order.* Cambridge, England: Cambridge University Press.

Gardner, Howard. 1990. *Art Education and Human Development.* Los Angeles: Getty Center for Education in the Arts.

Hamblen, Karen. 1986. "Artistic Commonalities and Differences: Educational Occasions for University-Relative Dialectics." *Visual Arts Research* 12:2.

Harris, Dale. 1963. *Children's Drawings as Measurements of Intellectual Maturity.* New York: Harcourt, Brace and World.

Kindler, A. M. (ed.). 1997. *Child Development in Art.* Reston, VA: NAEA.

Krathwohl, David; Bloom, Benjamin; and Masia, Bertram. 1984. *Taxonomy of Educational Objectives, Handbook 2: The Affective Domain.* New York: New Directions.

Lowenfeld, Viktor. 1947. *Creative and Mental Growth.* New York: Macmillan.

Pariser, David. 1995. "Not Under the Lamppost: Piagetian and Non-Piagetian Research in the Arts: A Review and Critique." *Journal of Aesthetic Education* 29(3): 93–108.

Parsons, Michael. 1987. *How We Understand Art: A Cognitive Development Account of Aesthetic Experience.* Cambridge, England: Cambridge University Press.

Piaget, J. 1959. *The Language and Thought of the Child,* 3rd ed. London: Routledge and Kegan Paul.

Reiff, J. 1991. *Learning Styles.* Reston, VA: NAEA.

Rush, Jean C. 1984. "Bridging the Gap Between Development Psychology and Art Education: The View from an Artist's Perspective." *Visual Arts Research* 10(2): 9–14.

Sarason, Seymour. 1991. *The Challenge of Art to Psychology.* New Haven, CT: Yale University Press.

Vygotsky, Lev S. 1962. *Thought and Language.* Cambridge, MA: MIT Press. (Originally published 1934.)

Vygotsky, Lev S. 1978. "Mind in Society: The Development of Psychological Processes." M. Cole., V. John, S. Steiner, and E. Souberman, eds. Cambridge, MA: Harvard University Press.

Wilson, Brent, and Wilson, Marjorie. 1981. "The Use and Uselessness of Developmental Stages." *Art Education* 34(5): 4–5.

Winner, Ellie. 1982. *Invented Worlds: The Psychology of the Arts.* Cambridge, MA: Harvard University Press.

WEB RESOURCES

For the ERIC database to educational research:

http://www.eric.ed.gov/

For an illustrated account of children's stages of art development:

http://www.arts.ufl.edu/art/rt_room/teach/young_in_art

*I*n general, you will find that kindergartners:

- Are interested in new things and eager to learn, but have a limited attention span and are easily fatigued. *Preserve and stimulate their natural curiosity. Expose the children to many manipulative materials and encourage their interest in using art materials. Provide for changes of pace and location. For example, begin by doing art, then sit and discuss each others' art.*
- Are prolific workers for a short period of time and want to see immediate results. Can sustain ideas from day to day. *Plan brief, stimulating lessons. Break lessons into parts, but make sure each part produces a result.*
- Can answer speculative questions, such as "What would happen if . . . ?" *When talking about an art reproduction, ask children to speculate about what happens before or after.*
- Can sing complete songs from memory; can chant and move rhythmically to a beat. *Have your students paint to music, or sing while making art.*
- May play alone or cooperatively. The typical developmental sequence is:
  - *solitary* play (no awareness or interaction with another)
  - *onlooker* play (near others and aware of their play, but not entering into the other's play)
  - *parallel* play (independently working on a common activity, such as putting puzzles together and building with blocks)
  - *associative* play (using each other's toys and asking questions)
  - *cooperative* play (for example, playing hospital requires defined roles and a division of responsibilities of doctor, nurse, and patient)

  Do group projects only when each child can do his or her individual part independently. Use large boxes as houses, stores, boats, planes, and trains, to provide venues for cooperative play. Encourage play with puppets; provide a simple puppet stage.
- Learn social and interpersonal skills while playing. Can understand the need for rules and fair play. *Let children help around the room. Teach them how to give encouragement to each other about their art.*

Courtesy of Beverly Barksdale Mallon.

The newness of drawing the school's butterfly garden with chalk outdoors motivated this kindergartner's painting of three powerful bluebirds soaring through a garden of beautiful tall flowers reaching up to the sun. Another day the children worked indoors painting the 14- × 18-inch artworks.

- Like to do pretend play. Like to engage in make-believe stories about the characters in their pictures. *Seek opportunities to do pretend play activities, since they develop both cognition and imagination. Use puppet plays and made-up stories. Ask, "What would this character in your picture say?"*

Using mirrors and guided instruction, kindergartners are capable of drawing self-portraits. They drew in pencil first and painted on a second day: a girl with thick black braids; a figure with circular blue earrings, eyes, and mouth; a boy with stick-up hair; a girl with a huge smile, neat hair, and a white floral-patterned dress; a girl with a perfect triangular dress with head perched atop; and a girl with surprised eyes and lush eyelashes.

- Desire the approval of classmates and teachers. Have a strong need to get and give love. *At sharing time, have the children tell about their pictures. Encourage them to comment on things they like in peers' pictures. Ask "Who is there with you in your drawing?" Show that you respect their art.*

- Have a playful attitude toward the environment, its objects, and experience. Like to use an object in several ways; have an easy and rapidly changing interchange between what is real and what is fantasy. *Encourage the interplay of reality and fantasy, and accept the dreams of grandeur shown in their art. Don't belittle their shows of grandeur (for example, "I am the strongest").*

- Can imitate movements of animals, evoking associations and imagination. *Use movement to motivate an art experience; for example, moving like a rabbit can stimulate drawing a rabbit.*

- Delight in fantasy and imaginative games. *Use psychomotor games and role-playing exercises and fantasy to stimulate their art. For example, ask, "If snow were like jelly beans, how would my yard and house look?"*

- Are developing awareness of their bodies; are interested in moving and using their bodies. Like to climb into large boxes and under tables, run and hide from someone, play ring-around-the-rosy, and put together and take apart objects. *Use games ("Simon says touch your head, tummy, ears") to encourage children to represent body parts in their artwork. Involve the child's sense of body. Ask, "When you're swinging on a swing (or riding a bicycle or climbing a tree), which parts of your body feel it?"*

- Can manipulate objects appropriately; for example, know to rock a baby and push a car—not vice versa. *Develop desirable work habits: Teach*

The 12-inch-square mirror tiles, which can be purchased at any home decorating store, had their edges taped with duct tape for safety and were then taped together at the top to form a tent shape so that children on each side of the table could draw their self-portraits. Note how the premixed colors of tempera paints were distributed.

the proper way to use a paint brush, markers, and clay, as well as how to clean a table.

- Can spend hours in sand and water play, dredging rivers and sailing boats, constructing mountains, and making small boats to sail. *If possible,*

Courtesy of Beverly Barksdale Mallon.

Children painted and cut out the first letter of their first names and combined them with their self-portraits. This boy's anger and anguish over his home situation may be reflected in his self-portrait.

provide a sand table, a water table, and props to use. Encourage children to play together and to talk and listen to each other.

- Desire to discover and to test their conceptual and physical powers. Can be self-reliant in expressing their ideas. *Avoid projects that need to be "one right way," such as a Pilgrim or a turkey, for example. Praise students when they have arrived at their "own way" of drawing something.*
- Have feelings that are easily hurt. May experience a lack of confidence by determining that another child is the "class artist." *Respect their artwork; don't "correct" their drawings for being visually inaccurate. Accepting their art expressions and treating them with respect can build feelings of self-worth. Likewise, showing respect for their verbalizations about the meaning of their art can build self-respect and confidence. Praise children for arriving at their own unique solutions. Praise individual expression.*
- Need outlets for wishes to dominate, destroy, or make a mess. *Provide opportunities for manipulating blocks, wood scraps and the like and for playing in water, mud, and clay. (But teach good housekeeping—don't let objects get broken, and make sure children clean up.)*

ARTISTIC DEVELOPMENT

Drawing development is highly variable, especially during kindergarten. Some kindergartners will be scribbling or just coming out of the scribbling stage. Many will draw using diagrammatic forms somewhere

between scribbles and symbols. And children whose ability at making graphic representations is advanced will make symbolic representations more like those typical of first- and second-graders.

Preschoolers begin with random, haphazard marks and then move on to explore some of several kinds of scribbles (Kellogg, 1970). Following random manipulation comes controlled manipulation, as the child discovers more consciously the ability to repeatedly go back and forth, up and down, diagonally, and around in a circle. Rather than thinking of these manipulations as *scribbles* (a term that has negative connotations to some people), we can think of them as *presentations,* in contrast to children's later *re*-presentations. These presentations may include:

- Patterns of marking in strokes
- Patterns of dots
- Vertical, horizontal, diagonal, circular, curved, and waving lines
- Placement of patterns on the page, such as overall, quarter page, centered, in halves, along a diagonal axis, and following the shape of a two-corner arch, a one-corner fan, or a two-corner pyramidal form

As children acquire more fine motor control and the desire for representation, they move beyond scribbling's back-and-forth scrubbing

Some common configurations seen in kindergartners' art range from disordered scribbles, to ordered scribbles, to geometric configurations, to combining these into tadpole-like figures, to a clearer understanding of trunk and limbs.

motions and learn to draw simple geometric, schematic diagrams. They begin to introduce geometric symbols—circles, squares, triangles, and rectangles—into their artwork. (In fact, the telephone doodles of some adults often are of such diagram-like presentations of nonobjective, geometric markings.)

These shapes have a multitude of uses. A circle may be used for a person's head, the sun, or a flower blossom. Radiating lines from the circular forms represent limbs and sun rays. Common at this stage is the tadpole figure—a circular or oval form with sticks protruding to represent limbs. Some writers call such post-scribbling diagrams presymbolic or preschematic; that is, the child has not yet settled upon one defined symbol for or method of drawing a person (or house or animal). At this stage children confidently and proudly give their drawings titles; one minute afterward, however, they are likely to rename their artwork.

Kindergarten students exaggerate the sizes of things and people important to them. They often draw themselves bigger than their parents. Hands, arms, and legs may be omitted. Drawn objects usually are not in correct size relationship. Don't focus on size or omission of arms, hands, and legs—these will be learned later; instead, enjoy such disparities. Most children pass quickly through these early stages of visual representation;

enjoy your students' ability to create in this spontaneous flowing development from scribbles to conceptual symbols to a more naturalistic representation. All too soon, the harsh standards of realism will destroy the child's satisfaction with the symbols. Rather than forcing children in the manipulative stage into "higher" stages, help them to feel good about their artistic efforts.

Also enjoy the nonnaturalistic use of color. Kindergartners choose colors imaginatively, not realistically. Children this age use color without regard to its local use or identity—it is so related to feeling and expression. Urging children to use realistic color representation is to deny them their own feelings. Whatever color strikes the child's fancy suffices; a blue or green face is as beautiful as a "flesh-colored" one. In fact, many mature artists have striven to emulate the kindergartner's freedom in selecting colors nonnaturalistically. Relish and praise this wild color imagination, for it will not last long.

As figure drawing ability progresses, the idea of a body that is differentiated from the head develops. Limbs move downward to grow from shoulders rather than heads; fingers appear at the ends of stick arms. Gradually, each limb grows to comprise two lines, suggesting the arm's or leg's inner form. In creating a way to depict a figure, each student's combinations of symbols may differ greatly from those used by his or her classmates.

Some kindergartners also arrive at the concept of using a baseline at or near the bottom of their picture. Rather than depicting figures floating freely, these children develop an awareness of a ground-line—a line upon which figures and objects can stand, which may be the bottom of the page itself, or a separate drawn baseline.

TEACHING ART

Kindergartners require little or no motivation from a teacher to create art. Your role is two-fold: to encourage and guide individual expression, and to help children understand appropriate behaviors in working with art materials. Help children to be inwardly motivated and to use personal symbols. Avoid asking questions that may divert their attention from their work. Indeed, suggesting what to draw may confuse some children, who find inspiration when pencil hits paper. If children run out of ideas, suggest that they review their past drawings. As they look, you can ask, "What is that?" to spur their recollections. When a child simply does not know how to begin—an unusual circumstance—you might motivate her by saying, "What is it you want to make? Which color would you like to begin with? Do you want to make it big or small?" Avoid giving your own ideas as corrections—"The sky should reach the ground," for example—or commenting on size disparities.

 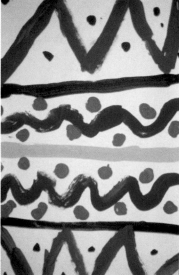

Left: *Courtesy of David W. Hodge.*

Left: This child intently works to develop her way of representing human figures. **Right:** An understanding of triangular and curved shapes can develop into zigzag and wavy lines in bands, along with decorations, to create an attractive artwork.

Courtesy of Beverly Barksdale Mallon.

A 2-inch border was drawn on the paper first to be saved for a later decorated border. This four-period lesson involved pencil drawing on the first day, going over the figures with markers on the second day and also writing; watercoloring the figures and making watercolor experimental patterns to be used for the border on the third day; and pasting on the border on the fourth day. Kindergartner Eduardo Rojas drew "Hermano and Me Going for a Walk with Papa and Mama," accompanied by a watermelon, a baby, a picnic, and unique sawtoothed grass.

While it is important not to dictate or over-direct the creative efforts of the kindergartner, teachers must demonstrate how to handle art supplies and finished work appropriately and reinforce proper classroom behaviors: "I like how you always put your brush back in the right jar of paint. I like the way you share materials." However, although it may take self-control to withhold feelings about paint being wasted, colors mixed to "mud," and paintings messed over, be careful not to inhibit individual creativity by demonstrating a negative attitude about messiness.

Try to avoid cute, follow-the-directions, gimmicky assembly projects geared to impress parents. Although such projects often are shown in kindergarten teaching magazines, especially at holiday time, they typically teach next to nothing about artistic expression. Instead, they reinforce in children's minds the idea that adults "own" the correct way to do things and that children cannot arrive at their own solutions but must simply copy patterns. Such "one-right-way" projects frustrate children because they condition them to accept adult concepts that children simply cannot produce on their own; they teach children to regard their own ideas as unacceptable. They deprive children of opportunities for decision making and individual expression.

An art project that is not at the child's stage of visual representation is a subtle lie—a plagiarism. In many "tricky" projects, for example, the teacher does inordinate amounts of cutting beforehand (a task from which the children would benefit by doing it themselves) and then requires the children merely to assemble the pieces in the right order. While "following directions" is doubtless reinforced through assembling a head with features, or a body with limbs, such projects involve little creativity. Follow-the-directions projects promote doing without thinking; they are the antithesis to creative expression.

Although you may want to demonstrate a method for assembling, for example, a figure, other approaches should also be shown or encouraged. Or you might ask children to come up with alternative ways to put together the figure (perhaps by placing three eyes on the face). Representation should come from the child, with the teacher's guidance, and should reflect the child's ability in conceiving of the human form. In fact, some educators believe teachers should never show art examples to children, since the goal is to develop the child's self-confidence—not to imitate an example. With kindergartners, however, examples may be helpful if they are introduced casually and briefly as just one of many possible ways to do the artwork and followed by encouragement and praise as children discover their own approaches. Children *do* learn by imitating, but the danger of copying is that it leaves the kindergartner feeling insecure about his or her own powers.

When the project is finished, how should it be displayed? The general rule to follow is: The younger the child, the more attention should be placed on process and the less on display of the final product. If you do display artwork, always display the work of all the children in the group or class. With kindergartners, do not emphasize taking the work home; instead, let the child make that decision.

Help every child think in positive self-statements: "I am able to think of new ideas. I am a capable person. I enjoy drawing in my own special way." Note, however, that it is not necessary to praise every product. Lavish and constant praise can be as harmful as criticism, in that it can communicate falseness and misunderstanding. Indiscriminate praise does not recognize individual accomplishment and does not build a sense of self-worth. Excessive praise can lead children to want to please adults rather than to please themselves. Respect the product, but don't overemphasize it.

More helpful and encouraging are descriptive comments that recognize or ask about what the child has done: "You were really concentrating on that" or "What an interesting way to use the brush—like a bird hopping around" or "Green!" or "You mixed all those colors together and made the color of tree trunks" or "What a big strong shape!" or "You invented a new color. Can you give it a name?" or "What a lot of circles!"

Top: *Courtesy of Barbara Thomas.* Middle: *Courtesy of Melody Milbrandt.*
Bottom: *Courtesy of David W. Hodge.*

Top: In kindergartner Derek Looney's illustration for "The Rainbow Fish," an initial pencil drawing was then outlined in marker, after which watercolor and a touch of sparkle were applied. **Middle:** This kindergartner boldly used black paint to draw the figure and snowman. The legs, arms, large boots, gloves, snowman's twig arms, and tassel hat show excellent awareness, perception, and representational skill. **Bottom:** This kindergartner knows a way to draw an elephant and repeats it throughout the picture.

Whenever possible, encourage parents to show interest in their child's work. Suggest making comments such as, "So many different kinds of lines in it! I enjoy having a chance to see your work." "How did you do it?" since they focus attention on the process rather than on the product. To share these ideas with parents, you may want to write them a letter, reminding them that their reactions may influence how their child feels about himself. Caution them against both ridiculing questions and indiscriminate praise. Instead, urge them to commend their child for what she has done—not for what she is. Separate the child from the act and praise the act, not the child. Urge parents to provide a safe climate in which their children can feel relaxed and accepted in their artistic expressions.

Teaching Drawing Drawing clarifies, focuses, and increases children's comprehension. It communicates to the world some idea of the child's understanding. Discourage erasing, and help children develop confidence in their ability to put their ideas down on paper. Thick kindergarten pencils, markers, and ballpoint pens are good for drawing; regular-sized crayons can cramp kindergartners' hands, so use the extra stout crayons, if possible. Teach children to store a marker's cap on the marker's end and to replace the cap over the felt tip securely. (Because of harmful fumes, do not use permanent markers, especially with young children.)

Students draw things intuitively as they know them: the sky as a ¾-inch-wide blue band across the top of the picture; the yellow sun that appears in part or whole in the upper corner of almost every drawing. In such symbolic representations, the symbol prevails over what is visible to the eye. Even kindergarten students who are advanced in their representational skills usually show little awareness of overlapping (or representation of things behind or blocked from view); that is, they draw both the outside and the inside, as in a transparent house or in legs visible through pants or a skirt. Kindergartners who are advanced in visual representation will devise a variety of interpretations for the human figure, a house, a tree, and animals. They discover the relationship between objects and color and seek colors close to those they know flesh and tree trunks to be. Like many children in first and second grades, advanced kindergartners develop a way to portray a front-view figure, a side-view figure, a sitting figure, a

Courtesy of Jackie Ellett.

Four kindergartners prepare to discuss their paintings. The two students in the background probably can tell stories about the shapes they have created; the two students in the foreground appear to have achieved a concept of a girl figure and an animal.

Courtesy of Melody Milbrandt.

Notice the precocious artist's larger size, the body schema of a tapering rectangle for the torso with bent elbow arms, the lollipop tree with apples, and the use of sophisticated analogous colors.

girl, a boy. Don't dictate adult forms, but encourage children to perceive and discover.

Teaching Painting Kindergartners typically love to paint with large, ½-inch brushes that allow them to convey boldly the strong, clear configurations they have created. If space permits, let children sit on the floor and use 18- by 24-inch paper, which allows them to get their whole bodies into the act of painting. Easels can help children appraise their art from a distance; they may take up too much room, however, especially in the crowded, "temporary" trailer-classrooms in which art is sometimes taught.

Consistency of the paint is important: To minimize drips and spills, it should be like heavy cream, not water. One good way to provide paint for children's use is to put four jars of different colors in a cardboard box (shoeboxes work fine), with a different brush for each color. Or small shallow dishes or trays, even glass furniture-leg casters, may be filled with a tablespoon of each color and held in a larger tray. Fill paint jars only to the depth of the brush bristles, ½ inch to 1 inch, to help prevent paint on hands. Teach children to tap their brushes against the inside of jars to control drips. Smocks—adult shirts do fine—protect clothing, and using

Courtesy of Beverly Barksdale Mallon.

First this watermelon-eating family scene by kindergartner Annabelle Barbe was drawn in yellow chalk. Next, watercolor, and then black marker and other marker colors were added. In the fourth period, squares made during the watercolor experimentation were shared with classmates and used for the decorative border, interspersed around the text, "Me and my dad with my neighbor Casey eating watermelon with a bluebird watching."

plenty of newspapers to keep paint off floor surfaces will keep custodians happy. Have several buckets of warm soapy water ready so children can wash brushes and soak trays. The brushes should be rubbed on the hand or on soap to remove paint from their metal ferrule and then placed upright to dry.

Painting a box or a board a solid color can be an appropriate challenge for kindergartners. When dry, the board or box can be decorated with patterns, using oil pastels or paint. With holes drilled into it, a small box can be used as a pencil holder; a large one can hold books or toys; and an even larger one can become a playhouse or part of a puppet theater.

Teaching Cutting, Pasting, and Collage By 4 to 4-½ years of age, most children can cut along lines without much failure or frustration. (A six-year-old who has trouble with this task may have a perceptual motor problem. See Chapter 12 for help with this.) Tiny hands are too often asked to use scissors with which even adults would have difficulty, with blades that do not contact each other well. To assure a pair of good scissors per child, some schools encourage the parents to send a good pair to school. Have a few pairs of left-handed scissors available. (If your scissor supply is inadequate, try teaching a lesson that uses paper tearing. Show children how to determine whether the paper has a grain that makes it easy to tear in one direction but difficult to tear in the other direction.)

As they cut, urge children to press the finger-hole handles together with sideways pressure, so that the blades are pushed together and make a clean cut. Children have a natural tendency to snip a tiny shape right from the center of a new piece of colored paper, leaving the rest for the scrap heap. To prevent such waste, emphasize the need to find an appropriate size scrap from which to cut a desired shape (and, along the way, let children know about the frugal use of resources and the beauty of recycling!). Always teach scissors-safety. Remind students to hold scissors carefully and to put them down before waving to get the teacher's attention.

Kindergartners often need to be taught the mechanics: how much glue or paste to use and on which surfaces to apply it. Many children delight in squeezing out great streams of white glue onto the paper, using much more than is required—or than is desirable for stacking the final product. White library paste can be used in lieu of glue, or you can create a nontoxic homemade paste. A simple recipe for homemade flour paste is ½ cup flour and ⅔ cup water mixed with ½ teaspoon powdered resin (which can be purchased at any art supply store). Cornstarch paste can be made by bringing ¾ cup water, 1 tablespoon light corn syrup, and 1 teaspoon white vinegar to a full boil, then mixing ½ cup cornstarch with ¾ cup cold water and adding it to the boiling mixture, which should then be removed from the heat and left to stand overnight. A few drops of oil of wintergreen or oil of peppermint will preserve the paste for about two months.

"We're NOT gonna' make a real cat!" was the motivation for this "Crazy Cats" project, which emphasized the differences between realistic cat colors and fantasy colors. In the first period, the teacher directed the kindergartners' drawing of the trunk, legs, etc. In the second period, playful patterns were painted to decorate the body. In the third period, the animal was cut out and glued onto an 18- × 24-inch contrasting colored paper.

Collages are always fun to create. To facilitate collage activities, organize trays or shoeboxes of found treasures: wallpaper and cloth scraps, metal foils and textured papers, feathers, and yarn with which to adorn pictures help children become aware of contrasts in solid versus patterned papers, dark and light coloration, and rough and smooth surfaces.

Teaching Fingerpainting Fingerpainting is a wonderful way to help children discover types of lines. When we talked about scribbles earlier, we noted that children may draw fan shapes and parallel lines. You can guide children to use not only their fingers but the edge of their hands, their palms, and so on as they paint.

Fingerpainting can be done directly on washable Formica-type table surfaces as well as on paper. Surfaces may be dampened to facilitate the paint's movement. Protect the floor with newspapers, and have the children wear smocks. Keep soapy water available to rinse hands as children finish.

Prepared fingerpaint is available, but homemade fingerpaint is easy to make; the simplest way is just to add paint to liquid starch. Another formula combines equal amounts of liquid starch and soap flakes, such as Ivory®, with color. If using powdered starch, dissolve ½ cup of it in cold water, then add 4 cups of boiling water, along with ¼ cup of soap flakes, the color, and ½ teaspoon glycerin. Likewise, wheat paste can be used: add 1 ¼ cups nontoxic wheat paste and ½ cup soap powder to 4 cups of water, beat, and separate into jars to which you add powdered or liquid tempera paint colors. Three or fewer colors are sufficient.

To create records of the fingerpainting experience, make monoprints by pressing sheets of slightly dampened newsprint or wallpaper sample-book pages onto the painting before it dries. Enhance the learning experience by pointing out the various kinds of lines and movements made by the children's fingers and the edges of their hands. Finally, children may find that cleaning up is as much fun as making the painting: Use a bucket of soapy water, a big sponge, and a rubber squeegee for the task.

Teaching with Chalk Chalk is easy to use and can be used outdoors on a sidewalk or playground, so messiness is not an issue. In fact, some school districts specifically prohibit the use of chalk inside a classroom by an entire class due to the amount of suspended particulates generated. If you are using chalk for an indoor project, reduce the level of dust by first sponging the paper with water or starch diluted to half strength and then having children draw on the paper with thick chalks. Another way to "fix" chalk and prevent its getting onto clothing is to dip it into buttermilk while drawing. (To prevent this dipped chalk from getting hard and unusable, rub its ends on a piece of screen or concrete to clean it when the project is complete.) Using dark colored paper gives chalk drawings a dramatic effect.

Teaching Three-Dimensional Art Because of its three-dimensional "realness," clay is a particularly good medium for drawing out shy children and encouraging them to talk about what they have made. For kindergartners, clay activities should primarily provide a touching and feeling experience, so be particularly careful about the clay's consistency. If it is too sticky, it will be difficult to model and may also be unpleasant for the squeamish child. Rolling out the wet clay on a piece of burlap or heavy cloth quickly removes the excess moisture. Note, however, that clay that is too dry will be difficult to model. Clay may remind some children of too-recent toileting conflicts; colored and scented claylike doughs and manufactured claylike products (see below) can avoid the problem.

Clay can be pulled apart and smoothed together repeatedly, knocked down and rebuilt, punched with holes or pinched and built up. Clay can be made into a snake, a cup, or a dinosaur. As with all art projects, however, clay products should not be contrived by the teacher. Don't hurry children through the exploration; rather, give them the freedom to represent their own experiences. Children love to make tubes (snakes), balls (eggs), and concave shapes (bird nests) and to tell stories featuring their clay creations. Children who are able to make figures can be taught how to attach appendages, such as legs, onto their forms by scoring and smoothing the pieces together. Volcanoes of clay can ooze red streams of lava. Children can shape animals, pumpkins, chickens, and ornaments to hang from a tree

Courtesy of Beverly Barksdale Mallon.

Kinderartners love to roll clay into spheres and attach the forms to make figures, here with fancy hats. Then, after exploration, the clay can be rolled back and re-used.

branch in the classroom. Do not feel that all pieces must be saved or fired; if clay is limited, better to reuse it.

For cleanup, use a piece of moist clay to pick up pieces that have fallen to the floor or are scattered about on the table; only after you have gathered up all the loose bits of clay in a dustpan should water be used on the table. Damp sponges and dry paper towels can help clear the inevitable thin film of clay. (For additional suggestions about clay maintenance and clay finishes, see Chapter 32.)

Many clay substitutes are available commercially, but a Playdough®-like mixture can easily be made by combining 1 cup of salt, 2 or 3 cups of flour, and 1 teaspoon of salad oil to alleviate stickiness. Cook the mixture in a saucepan on the stove, adding just enough water so that it releases from the sides of the pan but not so much that it sticks to the hands when cooled and kneaded. For a salt and cornstarch dough, heat 1 part water and 3 parts salt; slowly add 1 part cornstarch; stir well and knead. You may want to color the doughs, or add oil of peppermint and cream of tartar to preserve the mixture for several months. New wet-setting clays and other modeling formulations are also available at arts and crafts stores; although more costly, they are clean and easy to use and clean up.

After being modeled, leave the mixture to dry and set. Baking it for one hour at low heat will lend additional hardness. This mixture, called baker's clay, often is used for ornaments. For ornaments, give each child a golf-ball-sized piece of baker's clay to model. Remember to insert a hole at the top of the child's ornament, through which a string or ribbon can be threaded to hang it.

Courtesy of Barbara Thomas.

After studying Matisse's paper cutouts, kindergartners cut out and arranged the shapes of fish, seaweed, and water.

Puppetry is also an excellent way for children to overcome shyness and develop public-speaking ability. Puppets can be made in many ways, the simplest of which are:

- a paper plate painted to be a face and stapled to a tongue depressor stick;
- a paper lunch bag painted with a face and put over one's hand, or, alternately, stuffed with newspaper to make it three-dimensional and then tied to an inserted stick that is held;
- a face drawn onto a finger with marking pens, with a scrap of cloth loosely tied around it for a scarf.

More complex puppets can be made from a stuffed sock, a styrofoam ball, or a little tube fitted to the finger. Other three-dimensional activities that also are recommended for developing perceptual discrimination and eye-hand coordination include construction with boxes and tape, parquetry designs, stringing of beads, and building with blocks and Legos.®

ART CRITICISM, ART HISTORY, AND AESTHETICS

Art Criticism   At the kindergarten level, helping children learn how to talk about art can be considered a part of learning to perceive and conceive. Visual awareness is a hallmark of general intellectual development.

Not only can children sort, they can describe categories for sorting. They look through the art to vicariously experience the art's content. They pay little heed to style, composition, or multiple meanings—awarenesses that come in later grades. As kindergartners, however, they can attend to and question the nature of visual phenomena, such as color and shape.

Art criticism is a term used to describe a way of talking about not only fine arts but also one's own art and that of classmates. At the kindergarten level, art talk can deal with what we see, what it is called, how it appears, what colors and shapes and textures it has in it, and what ideas it brings to mind. As the children talk about art, accept their approximations and their weaknesses in logic. Time permitting, some of them can report on their painting or clay work at the daily reporting period. They can name the colors, the shapes, the objects and forms, and use fantasy in telling stories about their works. Likewise, they can learn to appreciate the work of others through the teacher's encouraging them to "Tell what you like in others' work."

Needless to say, art criticism is not a license to make *critical* remarks about an individual's artwork. Making comments to a kindergartner such as "Don't you know that the sky meets the ground?" or "Can't you see that the arms come from the body, not from the head?" would discourage that child.

Art History   Children like to look at pictures, to hear the teacher tell about them, and to tell about them themselves, so showing and talking about art reproductions can be a simple way to introduce art history to kindergartners. However, teachers should take care not to overly influence students' work. You may want to simply say, "Here is how an artist, J. B. Murry, did his artwork about water. He used long lines and decorations of other colors. I'd like to see how you make art in your own way." Not all art educators agree that art should be shown to young children as a drawing motivation, lest the children come to feel that their effort is insufficient. If fine art is introduced as a drawing stimulus for the children, use art that appears to be near the children's stage of visual conceiving, such as folk art or art from prehistoric civilizations, which may bear a surface similarity to young children's ways of representing forms. The teacher who obviously values each child's unique way of drawing and can reinforce individuality in expression can benefit children through the brief, matter-of-fact use of clear, appropriate exemplars.

Aesthetics   Discussions about aesthetics are not beyond kindergartners. For example, the teacher may ask, "Is it okay for art to show scary things and ugly things, or is it better for it to show mostly nice things and pretty things?" Or, in relation to a discussion of pattern in clothing, a teacher might ask, "Can decoration be called art, or does art have to show some real thing, like people and animals?"

The teacher briefly showed the kindergarten students a painting by folk artist J. B. Murry, which she determined was at the children's general stage of visual comprehension. A child then made this beautiful painting, full of pattern and smiling faces.

In this painting of a tree in a snowstorm, the kindergartner carefully observed how tree limbs diminish in size.

IN THE CLASSROOM

Teaching Kindergartners

With kindergartners, usually no suggestions are necessary; the child is eager to make art. Allow freedom in choice of subject matter. Children should not be dependent on teacher motivation, but, rather should be able to focus independently on personal ideas to express. Because some children will be in the scribbling and presymbolic stages, avoid unnecessary domination: Don't dictate that they draw a horse one day, a tree the next, a snowman the next. If children need something to get started, suggest common experiences such as playing on the playground, or with a pet, or with "the person who takes care of you," common sights such as suns, birds, houses, and trees, or exciting occasions, such as a heavy snowstorm, fall leaves, and a field trip to the fire station. Think about offering wide-open motivations like "A Favorite Way to Use Water": spray it at a friend, jump in ocean waves, splash in the tub, walk through rain. Kindergartners will reward your suggestions with wonderful, individual creations.

 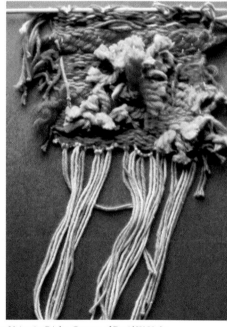

Left: Encourage children's drawing from their own personal experiences and imaginations. Note the beautiful complementary colors used. *Right:* A weaving by a kindergarten child, using a variety of yarns of different sizes and with some cut loops extending forward.

FOR FURTHER READING

Brown, Eleese V. 1984. "Developmental Characteristics of Clay Figure Modeling by Children: 1970–1981." *Studies in Art Education* 26(1): 56–60.

Cherry, Claire. 1990. *Creative Art for the Developing Child.* Columbus, OH: Merrill Publishing Co.

Colbert, Cynthia, and Taunton, M. 1987. "Problems of Representation: Preschool and Third-Grade Children's Observational Drawings of a Three-Dimensional Model." *Studies in Art Education* 29: 103–115.

Danko-McGee, Katherina, and Slutsky, Rushan. 2003. "Preparing Early Childhood Teachers to Use Art in the Classroom; Inspiration from Emilio Reggia." *Art Education* 56(4): 12–18.

Flannery, Merle. 1986. "Art as a Neotenizing Influence on Human Development." *Visual Arts Research* 12(2): 34–40.

Froebel, F. 1974. *The Education of Man.* W. N. Hailman, trans. Clifton, NJ: Augustus M. Kelley. (Original work published 1826, published in England 1887.)

Gaitskell, Charles D. and Margaret R. 1952. *Art Education in the Kindergarten.* Peoria, IL: C. A. Bennett.

Gardner, Howard. 1980. *Artful Scribbles, The Significance of Children's Drawings.* New York: Basic Books.

Jenkins, P. D. *Art for the Fun of It: A Guide for Teaching Young Children.* Englewood Cliffs, NJ: Prentice Hall, Inc.

Kellogg, Rhoda. 1970. *Analyzing Children's Art.* Palo Alto, CA: National Press.

Kindler, Anna M. 1977. *Child Development in Art.* Reston, VA: National Art Education Association.

Piaget, J. 1959. *The Language and Thought of the Child,* 3rd ed. London: Routledge and Kegan Paul.

Pile, Naomi F. 1973. *Art Experiences for Young Children.* New York: Macmillan Co.

Schiller, Marjorie. 1995. "The Importance of Conversations about Art with Young Children." *Visual Arts Research* 21(1): 25–34.

Thompson, Christine. 1998. *The Visual Arts and Early Childhood Learning.* Reston, VA: National Art Education Association.

WEB RESOURCES

See search engines for terms "kindergarten" and "art activities."

For more resources for teaching art to kindergartners, see:

Task Force on Children's Learning and the Arts:

Aeparta.org/tfadvoc/taskforces/younger childrenpdf.

National Association for Young Children:

www.naeyc.org www.artsed.net.getty.edu

For kindergarten art lessons:

http://www.princetonol.com/groups/iad/lessons/early/early.html

For one thousand kindergarten art lesson plans:

http://www.kinderart.com/

Chapter 16

A Sequential Curriculum for Grades 1 and 2

*A*lthough children are all individuals and vary from the norm, children in first and second grades typically:

- Are active and easily excited. *Use almost any topic as motivation.*
- Enjoy working with their hands. *Use hands-on art activities as vehicles for correlated learning.*
- Take great pride in their work. *Display work in the hall.*
- Exhibit strong feelings of possessiveness. *Be aware that some children may cry if their work is kept for an exhibit.*
- Are eager to learn. *Teach them many ways to see and draw. Do not underteach.*

Courtesy of Frank Wachowiak and David W. Hodge.

First-graders use geometric shapes to construct the human figure, here, squares, circles, and rectangles. Very large paper is helpful, as seen in both the figure and the collaged lion.

- Want to be first. *Assign special responsibilities: "You may be the scissor monitor today."*
- Have a limited span of interest and are easily fatigued. *Give a series of objectives throughout the lesson rather than all at the beginning.*
- Have feelings that are easily hurt. *Point out several alternative ways to draw something, with each conveying different qualities, rather than just one right way. Praise when students arrive at their "own way" of drawing something.*
- Are alternately cooperative and uncooperative. *Give "road signs" to foreshadow how long each phase will be, when the phase will stop, and what the next phase will be.*
- Usually can grasp only one idea at a time. *Give instructional objectives throughout the lesson instead of all at the beginning.*
- Delight in imaginative games, dances, stories, and plays. Like to pretend and engage in make-believe. *Use psychomotor games and role-playing exercises. Use puppet plays and made-up stories about the characters in their pictures. ("What would this character in your picture say?")*
- Desire the approval of classmates and teachers. *Encourage the children to tell about their pictures at sharing time.*
- Enjoy fantasy; often create "secret worlds" in which they enjoy living. *Use fantasy as a motivation. ("If I were a . . . , what would I be like?")*
- Are interested in new things to touch and taste. *Use tactile motivations, such as rabbits, toys, turtles.*
- Are fascinated by moving and mechanical devices. *Arrange wind-up toys as still lifes. Use visual-perception devices such as kaleidoscopes.*
- Enjoy TV, illustrated books, movies, picnics, school field trips, new clothes, pets. *Ask children to do art criticism of book illustrations. Have them draw after field trips and draw pictures of pets.*

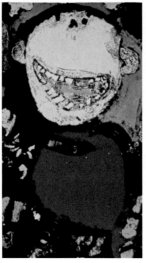

In these very large, first-grade tempera and India-ink portraits can be seen the characteristic features: circle heads; the figures from 2-½ to 3 heads high; the bodies comprising circles, squares, and triangles; and the sausage limbs.

ARTISTIC DEVELOPMENT

The information below shows how children ages 5 through 7 typically employ various art elements. These are stages of enormous variability and change. Instructional objectives are given but are not meant to be prescriptive. Beauty and expression can be achieved in many ways—not through only one teacher-prescribed "right way." Representations consisting of scribbles can be as expressive as those depicting clearly defined objects, such as houses: Skills developed at later stages are not necessarily "better."

Shapes Five- and six-year-olds will typically:

- draw the geometric symbols of the circle, square, triangle, oval, and rectangle.
- employ a basic symbol, such as a circle, to depict varied visual images— the sun, the head of a person or animal, a table, a flower blossom, a tree, a body, and even a room.
- use combinations of symbols that very often differ from those their classmates use.
- depict simplified representations and are not too concerned with details.

Some six-year-olds and most seven-year-olds will typically:

- change slowly from geometric, symbolic interpretations to more specific characterization and delineation.

- use more details in depictions—hair ribbons, buttons, buckles, eyeglasses, necklaces, rings, shoelaces, purses, fingernails, patterns, and wrinkles in clothes.

Size Five- and six-year-olds will typically:

- use emotional exaggeration of size, enlarging things that are important to them and omitting features that are not. For example, children may draw themselves bigger than their parents or omit arms and hands if they are not needed in their depiction. Size also may be determined by the need to fill an empty space or the desire to show a clear relationship.

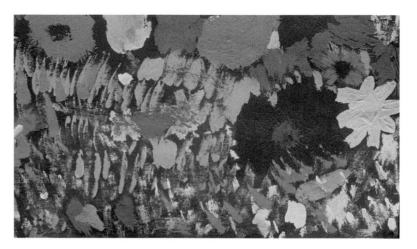

Changing colors on the teacher's signal in a game of "Pass the Paint Please" is a clever way to maintain young children's attention. A good topic for this rotating color painting is "A Flower Garden from Above." Note the teacher's attention to the mostly analogous colors she mixed.

Courtesy of Sharon Burns-Knutson.

This remarkable self-portrait is a contour drawing by a second-grader. She patiently delineated what she observed. Guide children to look carefully and see freckles, collar stitchery, and patterns in the hair. This portrait reveals what drawing skills youngsters are capable of when the teacher encourages them to become aware, observe details, and draw slowly and deliberately.

Some six-year-olds and most seven-year-olds will typically:

- approximate more representative proportions, although figures still may be three heads high (the proportions of the Peanuts cartoon character, Charlie Brown) rather than the subsequent five heads high.

Color Five- and six-year-olds will typically:

- use color in a personal or emotional context without regard to its local use or identity. For example, a face may be painted blue or green.

Some six-year-olds and most seven-year-olds will typically:

- use color in a local, stereotypical way. For example, tree trunks are brown, and the sky is blue.

Space Five- and six-year-olds will typically:

- employ a baseline as a foundation on which to place objects such as a house, a tree, or a figure. The bottom of the page sometimes substitutes for the baseline.

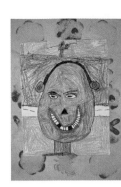

Left: *Courtesy of Mary Lazzari.* Right: *Courtesy of David W. Hodge.*

Left: Children will exaggerate features that interest them. Even though lots of baby teeth fall out at this time, it does not take away from one's happiness. **Right:** Note the exaggeration in this boy's strong arms. Popeye would be jealous. This first-grader shows the typical three-heads-high figure, with the proportions of Charlie Brown in the cartoon, "Snoopy."

Courtesy of Sharon Burns-Knutson.

A still life of flowers motivated second-grader Kate Rethwisch's crayon and watercolor painting.

- draw both the outside and inside of a place, a person, or an animal, as if in an X-ray or transparency. Later, students may use a second or third baseline higher on the page.

Some six-year-olds and most seven-year-olds will typically:

- begin to place distant objects higher on the page, although distant objects often are drawn the same size as closer objects.
- use a foldover technique, turning their papers completely around as they draw, to show people on both sides of the street, diners around a table or a picnic lunch, people at a swimming pool, or players on a baseball field.

Objects Five- and six-year-olds will typically:

- draw things intuitively as they know them: the sky as a band of color at the top of the page, the sun that appears in part or whole in an upper corner of almost every picture, the railroad tracks that seldom converge,

Courtesy of Joyce Vroon.

The tiny figures in the background give the scene a feeling of great distance. For her "What I am Proud of" painting, second-grader Samantha Bubes depicted her pride in her roller-blading. Notice the charming way that the sun's cheerful face echoes her own face. Also note the careful, allover use of markers.

Courtesy of Joyce Vroon.

Mixed Plan and Elevation Drawing: Here, the walking figures and cabin cruiser are seen as if from the side, while the rowboats and sidewalk are seen as if from the top. Showing both the top and side views in one scene is called mixed-plan-and-elevation drawing. This, and foldover drawings, which show the events upside down on the other side of the street, are charming ways by which artists represent what is known rather than what is seen. Conception and perception work together in this Taiwanese primary-grade child's telling about events at the water's edge.

the leaves that are wider where they attach to the branch or stem, the tree with a very wide trunk to make it strong, the eyes high up in the head, and the mouth as a single, curved, happy line.

Some six-year-olds and most seven-year-olds will typically:

- draw objects as they know them to be rather than how they see them at the moment, such as a table with four legs when only two are visible from their vantage point, or a house with three sides when only one is visible from their sketching station.

The Human Figure Five- and six-year-olds will typically:

- devise a variety of interpretations or schemata of the human figure, house, tree, animal, and so on, depending on their experience.

Some six-year-olds and most seven-year-olds will typically:

- begin to use characteristic apparel and detail to distinguish sexes, such as skirts and trousers, and differences in hair styles.

TEACHING ART

Something big, something small.
Something short, something tall,
Something dark, something light,
Help to make your drawing right.

This rhyme helps remind young children to add variety to their compositions. In most instances, the *more* images, shapes, or ideas the students incorporate, the more unified their drawings become. "Who else was there?" and "What else might have been on the ground?" are helpful prompts.

Teaching Drawing As children join the community of picture makers, they begin to understand the demands of representation. They like to paint simple images, using themes such as a favorite toy or "What I like to do when it rains." For children whose abilities have developed beyond the scribbling stage, discourage their rushing to finish or scribbling in backgrounds haphazardly. Children love to use their pictures to tell stories, and both pictures and stories can change over time. Children often make several representations of the same subject—for example, the family's new baby. Some can write their own titles and stories; some will need help to put their ideas into words.

One common sequence for first- and second-graders is to draw a house, then a tree, then a flower, then a person, and then a pet. Drawing the chimney at right angles to the slanted roof shows that, while children can recognize the correct vertical orientations, they prefer the perpendicular orientation in their drawings. During this period, floating objects gradually will diminish, replaced by figures on a stand line or a baseline. Later, the children may move to the use of multiple stand lines. At this age, however, it is too early to introduce overlapping.

Introduce your students to various tools for making linear images, including pencil, ballpoint and felt-nib pens, crayon, oil and chalk pastel, brushes, school chalk, a nail for crayon-engraving projects, or fingers for finger painting. Praise their discovery of various line patterns: stripes, plaids, circles, stars, spirals, radiating lines, and zigzags.

Children this age like their pictures to show clear and vivid relationships. One good way to achieve this is to use large brushes: ¼-inch, ½-inch, or larger. Another way to show clarity is to draw objects against an empty background. Passing the paint containers every few minutes also works well, since it encourages students to add something new to their drawings.

Fold-Over Drawings Some children will show figures arranged in a circle or on both sides of the street and upside down on one of the sides—representations known as foldover drawings. Games such as ring-around-

Courtesy of Frank Wachowiak and Ted Ramsay.

This busy child is not a slave to realism. Four eyes are called for—two to keep track of the hair brushing and two to keep track of the simultaneous teeth brushing. What could be more expressive! Figure schemes are energetically explored. This Picasso-like black crayon self-portrait, 12 × 18 inches, is by a first-grade girl.

the-rosy can be used to stimulate these charming representations. For young children, foldover is a quite satisfactory method of design representation, because it tells very clearly what is occurring.

X-ray Drawings Another pleasing representational device often used in these drawings is X-ray drawing or transparency—seeing the figure through the clothes or seeing through the walls to what is inside the house.

A first-grade child uses the circle-square figure schema in her drawing of pets and friends. Figures are shown with no elbows and no shoulders, which would distract from the figures' crosslike forms, but the cat has well-defined elbows and shoulders. Pattern in clothing is depicted by stripes, plaids, and even a floral design. This multicolor crayon engraving technique requires considerable patience. Because it calls for the application of several layers of crayon, use a small size of heavy oaktag. Begin with a light hue, such as yellow or pink, and build layer on layer through darker colors to a final brown, dark blue, or black.

Transparency does not mean that children think clothes are transparent; instead, it comes about because they draw the figure first and then dress it, like using paper dolls. As children grow older, this way of representation diminishes, although it is a common device in some cultures, such as Australian aboriginal art, which can be employed as a motivational material.

Introduce first- and second-grade children to line drawing, the variety of shades, light and dark value, color, and pattern. Encourage drawing based on their personal experiences and observations, but welcome and praise imaginative expression as well. In addition, provide many opportunities for them to draw from real objects—plants in and around the school, pets brought to class, flower arrangements, toys and dolls, classmates, self-portraits, depictions of the family in various settings, community helpers, and subject matter observed on field trips. Provide large-size paper or newsprint so that details the children consider important can be

X-Ray View: The outside shape and the insides of rooms, from basement to attic and complete with pictures, furniture, and staircases, are shown in Millie Rhodes's cross-section, see-through drawing of her house.

shown. In figure drawing, the size of the drawn head often determines the size of the body. Encourage the children to fill the page.

Teaching Cutting, Pasting, and Collage Students in this age group need to develop their scissors skills. Invite them to cut simple, basic geometric shapes out of construction paper. Make sure to have some left-handed scissors available. Encourage the beauty of torn paper edges. Offer the use of pinking shears and scissors with scalloped and patterned edges as a privilege to reinforce this.

Provide opportunities that involve pasting little shapes onto big shapes, such as those cut with a hole-punch. Point out how contrast is achieved by pasting a light-colored shape over a dark-colored shape and vice versa. Demonstrate how to use paste and glue economically and effectively. You may want to use a felt board to introduce children to the countless possibilities of cutout shapes and how they can be juxtaposed. Cooperative murals employing the cut-and-paste technique, in which each child contributes one or more parts to the whole, are very satisfying projects (see Chapter 26). Almost any theme lends itself beautifully to collage making at this stage: flowers in a garden, animals in the jungle, fish in the sea, birds in a tree, and butterflies in flight.

"On Our Street" was the subject of this colorful colored construction paper collage by a first-grader. The class first discussed shapes of houses, garages, churches, synagogues, and stores, then of trees, bushes, hedges, fences, sidewalks, telephone poles, traffic signs, billboards, mailboxes, pets, cars, and trucks.

Teaching Printmaking Simple repeat prints result in colorful, allover patterns. These can be made with vegetables, found objects, clay pieces, erasers, cellulose scraps—or hands and fingers. In most instances, colored construction paper works best for the background printing surface; other possibilities include colored tissue paper, newsprint, wallpaper samples, brown wrapping paper, and fabric remnants. Printmaking activities with children at this age are somewhat limited because first- and second-graders do not possess the necessary skills for complicated techniques. Emphasize

For primary-grade children, delightful prints can be created using plastic foam meat-trays as the printing plates. Trim off the curved part of the tray. On the tray, first make a preliminary drawing with a felt-nib pen or soft-lead pencil. Then make the impression by pressing a blunt-pointed pencil into the tray. Water-base black printing ink, rolled out on the engraved tray with a brayer, may be used to print.

space-filling when trying plastic foam meat-tray prints with incised relief created by pencil pressure. Monoprints, too, are wonderful projects for this age group.

Teaching Ceramics   Clay is a wonderfully satisfactory medium for children at these ages. Make sure ample supplies are available—a ball of clay about the size of a grapefruit is recommended for every child. The clay must be properly malleable. If it is too sticky, leave it to dry a while. Allow the children to discover clay's potential. Encourage them to squeeze, pinch, poke, and stretch the clay. Show them how to make coils and how to form the clay into small balls or pellets. Guide them in the creation of simple, familiar forms. Suggest they hold the clay in their hands as they manipulate it into the desired shape; this strategy discourages the tendency of some

Top left: An animal with a figure or with its young is a wonderful ceramic theme. This Japanese child's figure on a horse was additively constructed, that is, each separate part was first constructed separately and then smeared well into the body; thus, the piece may stay intact. With additively constructed pieces, emphasize heavy and firmly attached legs by roughening and smearing of the clay at the points of attachment. **Top right:** A stronger way to model clay is to pull the parts out of the lump of clay. **Bottom:** A pancake shape of clay has coils added, the cheeks stamped, and feathers added.

children to pound the clay flat on their desks. Primary-grade children can control the relatively simple sculptural forms of an elephant, hippo, cow, horse, rabbit, turtle, pig, dog, cat, whale, or resting bird. They enjoy manipulating the clay by adding or subtracting. Teachers tend to prefer the subtractive way (pulling features out), because the resulting form is less likely to fall apart.

Construct simple pinch pots from a lump of clay the size of an orange, and bisque-fire the pots if a kiln is available. Ask the children to hold the clay ball in the palm of one hand and to insert the thumb of the other hand into the middle of the clay ball about halfway down. As the children rotate the clay ball, they should push and pinch their thumb and fingers along the inside and outside of the ball in overlapping pinches. Caution them not to make the wall or bottom of the pot too thin. Also, because the marks of their fingers and thumb often add an attractive texture in itself, discourage the use of water to smooth their clay.

ART CRITICISM, ART HISTORY, AND AESTHETICS

By ages six and seven, children are beginning to try to figure out what an artwork is, and to make their first interpretive efforts. Of course, their ideas of what is logical may not conform to the standards of adult logic. They look through the visual rendition. They do not see the style, or the composition, or the multiple meanings that things can carry. They begin to develop a language for art criticism, with the names of the formal elements. For example, they can match photos of textures to real textures. They can describe how things are the same and different.

You should try, at this stage, to expose students to as much material as possible in order to establish a knowledge base. The goal is twofold:

1. to teach students how to experience the delight and values shown in the arts; and
2. to contribute to the students' general perceptual and conceptual knowledge that operates tacitly in a broad range of situations in and out of school.

One caution: Avoid the reductive bias of presenting only clear instances, rather than showing the complexity of knowledge. Require students to examine their own knowledge to come up with answers. This approach is in line with education's shift from being curriculum-centered to being learner-centered.

"Do you like this painting? Why?" are appropriate critical questions for students in Grades 1 and 2. For children at this age, subject matter is most important. For example, in responding to Albrecht Dürer's drawing of a hare, children generally say they like it because it's cute or because they like rabbits. Children do not differentiate between the world of pictures and

Courtesy of Barbara Thomas. Student Courtney Daniel.

Three-dimensional Vincent van Gogh's *Starry Night* was the motivation for this first-grade student's cut-paper and crayon-resist version of the radiating starlight.

Courtesy of Barbara Thomas.

Help students learn a language of art criticism, "Do you like this painting? Why?"

what the pictures represent; they like pictures of things they like and reject pictures of things they dislike or fear. Indeed, understanding the difference between appearance and reality develops gradually. For example, one first-grader, needing to assure himself that he had not created a frightful lion, told the class with some uncertainty in his voice, "It's not a real lion."

Courtesy of Barbara Thomas.

Studying the artist William Johnson's use of enlarged body parts, third-grade student Kelisha Scott did this colored drawing of the cook skillfully using his hands to flip pizza at the school's partner Pizza Hut.

Children at this age also like pictures that are clear and vivid. Clarity of perceptual cues and orderly organization of elements are very important. Their perceptions are limited to a single interpretation. Talking about art reproductions helps to develop their skill in drawing inferences. They can scan and take in whole scenes to figure out situations, characters, and narration. They can predict what a scene would be like if they were there and how they would feel about it. But because they cannot imagine the scene in an alternative way, art inquiry is limited to what is shown rather than also incorporating how what is shown could be changed. By the second grade, children's preferences typically begin to grow beyond like or dislike of a subject, and personal experience becomes a relevant factor.

Children between ages 5 and 7 are particularly drawn to the effects of color. From the first class meeting, begin teaching this age group perception of the art elements, especially color awareness. Emphasize the child's

Courtesy of Joyce Vroon.

Using mirrors, these primary-grade students draw and paint themselves in fancy hats. Art by third-grader Natalie Long.

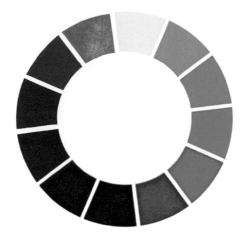

Complementary colors are those opposite each other on the color wheel; analogous colors are those side by side.

everyday surroundings: the classroom, clothes, books, artwork, and posters on display. ("If you have anything turquoise around your desk—maybe a notebook or a bracelet—hold it up.") Help them to identify the primary and secondary colors. Introduce the warm, sunny colors such as yellow, orange, pink, and red, as well as the events associated with them—the circus, county fairs, parades, Mardi Gras, autumn harvest. Likewise, talk about the deep, cool colors such as green, turquoise, blue, and blue–violet and the images they evoke—the mysterious night, the ocean depths, the rain–wet jungle, and the deep, dark forest.

Take advantage of the many stimulating games, toys, and devices available for developing color awareness: the prism, paint chips, the color wheel, and the kaleidoscope. Use the appearance of natural phenomena like rainbows as the basis for a discussion of the color spectrum. Encourage color matching and sorting exercises using found materials such as scraps of art paper, wallpaper, magazine illustrations, cloth, and yarn. Store the color collection in shoe boxes, one box for each color. When the children are using paints, encourage them to create new colors by mixing colors on their wet or moist paper and naming their new color inventions.

Have children explain the meaning and contribution of the following terms: color, shape, line, pattern, repeat, and texture. Encourage them to describe pattern and texture in clothing, in school surroundings, and especially in nature's bark, fur, fish scales, and plumage. Just as talking about art helps to promote their artistic creativity, artistic creation helps them to talk about art.

Teachers should exploit all means at their disposal, including the marker board and bulletin board, to call the child's attention to art-project-related vocabulary.

Children between ages 5 and 7 should know the following basic art terms:

black	glue	pink
blue	green	pinch pot
bright	grey	purple or violet
brown	hammer	rectangle
brush	ink	red
cardboard	kiln	ruler
chalk	light	scribble
circle	manila paper	shape
clay	mural	square
coil	nail	stripe
construction paper	newsprint paper	tempera paint
crayon	orange	tissue paper
dark	oval	triangle
dot	overlap	watercolor
drawing	paste	weaving
easel	pastel	white
eraser	pen	yellow
fingerpaint	pencil	

IN THE CLASSROOM

Suggested Subjects or Themes for First- and Second-Graders

Playground games	What my parent and I like to do together
Fun in the snow	
Fun in the fall leaves	My make-believe wish
A flower garden with insects	Skipping rope
My pet and me	Our community helpers
Stuffed animals	Butterflies in a garden
Animals in the zoo or jungle	Fish in the sea
Farm animals	Land of make-believe
Noah's ark	My favorite toy
Kings and queens	Clowns (for pattern)
What I like to do when it rains	

This first-grade student painted her fantasy wish to be able to fly like a bird.

FOR FURTHER READING

Dalton, Kimberly, and Burton, David. 1995. "Children's Use of Baselines: Influence of a Circular Format." *Studies in Art Education* 36(4): 105–113.

Erickson, Mary. 1995. "Second-Grade Students' Developing Art Historical Understanding." *Visual Arts Research* 21(1): 15–24.

WEB RESOURCES

For lower–elementary sequences:

http://www.getty.edu/artsednet/resources/Scope/Developmental/level1.html

http://www.princetonol.com/groups/iad/lessons/

http://www.arts.ufl.edu/art/rt_room/teach/young_in_art

For figure schemas and baselines:

http://www.arts.ufl.edu/art/rt_room/teach/young_in_art/sequence/symbolism.html

In this first-grader's painting of a clown, an initial crayon drawing in a light color was then gone over with watercolor.

Chapter 17

A Sequential Curriculum for Grades 3 and 4

*A*lthough children are all individuals and their development will necessarily vary, third- and fourth-grade children typically:

- Have improved eye–hand coordination. *Students will draw from peers posing as models.*
- Have better command of small muscles. *Students will draw details of clothing and features.*
- Are becoming aware of differences in people. *Students will show differences among figures and objects in their artwork.*
- Are gradually learning to become responsible, orderly, and cooperative. *Ask students to share, distribute, and collect art material.*
- Begin to form separate-sex groups. *Find art motivations that speak to both boys' and girls' interests.*

An intermediate-elementary-grade boy, who incidentally was in need of braces, did this fantasy oil pastel resist of an imaginary creature; part animal, part bird, part fish, and part insect. The white shapes of the head and ears are repeated in the spirals of the tail and hind legs. Star, flower, and leaf forms fill the background.

Courtesy of Sharon Burns-Knutson. Students Elizabeth Browning, Caleb Rucker, and Jenna Lindberg.

These fourth-grade students were encouraged to observe details in their oil pastel self-portraits. Is our skin really the same color throughout?

- May start to join gangs and cliques. *Students will depict their friends in their art. Use peer approval to modify behavior.*
- Enjoy comic books and other visual texts. *Have students create their own comic book characters and superheroes.*
- Are growing in critical skills, self-evaluation, and evaluation of others. *Ask students to evaluate their work based on instructional objectives.*
- Are able to concentrate for longer periods of time. *Projects may span more than one period, especially if new objectives are set.*
- Are developing an interest in travel. *You can ask students to describe how historical artworks relate to a culture.*
- Are interested in the life processes of plants and animals. *Have students draw from life, taxidermy models, and pictures of flora and fauna. Ask them to describe how their drawings show the specific features of plants or animals.*

- Are developing a sense of humor. *Students can discuss aesthetic issues raised by cartoons—for example, how is the powerful person depicted?*
- Are becoming avid hobby fans and collectors. *Students will discuss their collections in terms of art criticism: "The picture shows his batting strength."*

An especially important developmental issue at this time is whether the child develops feelings of competence or inferiority. Elementary students need generous amounts of encouragement to complete assignments and generous praise for their good performance. While regular classroom activities develop children's skills in reading and math, children may develop feelings of inferiority about their drawing ability if they are not given encouragement and instruction. Don't be afraid to teach art skills; these can help students win recognition and praise through their artwork.

ART DEVELOPMENT

Although children's art at all developmental stages has a unique beauty, the third-grade and fourth-grade years often seem to be the "golden age of child art." Just as roses are most beautiful at the moment halfway between bud and full flowering, children at this time create art that reflects the charm of newly discovered representational concepts along with signs of a move toward realism. Abstraction and realism are in a state of happy coalescence, and children's belief in their expressive powers is not disturbed by the anxiety about "not looking right" that comes later. By this time, most children have developed methods of drawing that satisfactorily communicate their meaning to adults. Their schemas may be based partly on concepts and partly on perception. Early forms—the lollipop tree that once seemed okay—yield under increasing perceptual input to become more novel, fresh forms. Beneath the surface, however, the conceptual model still has an influence, and the child who uses a conceptual scheme should not be made to feel inadequate. This child's vision may be driven more by intuitive design decisions. Rather than settling for stereotypes, the teacher should instead encourage students to put visual discoveries into representational forms. For example, the teacher might

Courtesy of David W. Hodge.

Experiment imaginatively with a range of colors. Do not be a slave to natural appearance. How wonderful are the orange and purple eyes, purple and green fingernails, and green lips and eyelashes! The key to these third-graders' successful artworks includes mixing a varied range of tempera hues, making sure the children devote time to doing preliminary sketches, working on very large (18- × 40-inch) paper, and encouraging the imaginative use of color.

say, "Does anyone see anything around the mouth that we could draw? Juan says he sees half-circle lines at the edge of the mouth. How can we draw these?"

Once again, we should note that later is not better in children's art—the skills developed as a child matures are no better, and in some ways less interesting, than those of younger children. But in general, third- and fourth-graders demonstrate the following skill levels in art.

Shapes Third- and fourth-graders will typically:

- Draw and compose with more conscious, deliberate planning, and they will show more naturalistic and realistic proportions.
- Select and arrange objects to satisfy their compositional design needs.

Color Third- and fourth-graders will typically:

- Mix and experiment with an expanded range of colors, including tints and shades.

Courtesy of Jackie Ellett.

Fourth-grade students learned about overlapping, perspective, and pattern in architecture as they drew from slide-projected city scenes.

- Discuss the mood and effects of warm and cool colors, both within a painting and in the environment.
- Use analogous colors (those adjacent to one another on the color wheel).
- Neutralize (dull a color) by mixing it with the complementary hue (opposites on the color wheel).
- Describe the effect of subdued colors next to bright, intense colors.

Space Third- and fourth-graders will typically:

- Create space and depth by employing vertical placement, diminishing size, and overlapping shapes.
- Describe how the horizon line can be used to show distant space.

Objects Third- and fourth-graders will typically:

- Select and arrange objects to satisfy their compositional design needs rather than realism.

The Human Figure Third- and fourth-graders will typically:

- Show action in their drawings of people and animals.
- Draw with more naturalistic and realistic proportions; more will use the five-heads-high figure.

Courtesy of Joyce Vroon.

The fascination that uniforms hold can be seen in fourth-grader Jessie Maxwell's marker drawing made from a newspaper photo.

TEACHING ART

At this stage, and certainly by the fourth grade, children can be introduced to observational drawing and basic contour-drawing techniques. For an immediate visual stimulus, begin with simple, easily recognizable, objects: fruit, vegetable, shoe, glove, helmet, cap, cowboy hat, baseball mitt, football, or water pitcher. As the students' skill and confidence in contour drawing increase, introduce a combined arrangement of several objects in which the items overlap. Guide the children to look carefully and intently at the objects and to draw very slowly and deliberately.

Teaching Drawing, Designing, and Painting Children like to depict clothing—their favorite outfit or occupational clothing, such as a police uniform. Group projects comprising students' individual works can demonstrate the power of working together to create projects of large size and scope. Continue to call attention to the immediate and visually stimulating subject or image for drawing. On sketching excursions, scout for the unusual site—the pictorially exciting vista with multifaceted structures, interesting towers and spires, and varied foreground and background breakup. In representing distance and overlapping, children often change color and size to show space and its vastness. Suggest new directions in design such as the following:

- Overlapping shapes
- Achieving distance through diminishing sizes and placement of objects higher on the page

Courtesy of Sharon Burns-Knutson.

Fourth-grader Caleb Rucker's leopard marker drawing shows keen observation in the changes in size and direction of the leopard's spots on this decorative plate.

Courtesy of Barbara Thomas.

Pattern was the focus of this third-graders' cat drawing. Interest is created by the bold black-and-white diamonds in the floor, the patterns in the cat's fur and the wall moldings, and, for a finishing touch, the background three-dimensional dot pattern using T-shirt paint.

- Creating pattern and textural effects contrasted with quiet or plain areas
- Drawing the lines with varied weights and in varied ways

Explain about inner contour lines. For example, with a flower, suggest that the children begin in the middle with the core, adding one petal at a time, rather than with a hasty and general outline of the entire flower. In other instances, such as with a banana or okra, begin with the outer contour line and then add inner contour lines to clarify the form. A few children can even draw oblique planes and use overlapping.

A soft lead pencil is best for contour drawing. Kindergarten pencils are recommended. Erasures should be discouraged; instead, a second, corrective line more carefully observed is suggested. The students may stop at critical junctures, reposition the drawing tool, and then continue drawing.

Courtesy of Joyce Vroon.

For her stuffed animal still life, Christy Kelly will use many premixed containers of paint in a variety of tints and shades.

Direct the children's attention to nature and its variety of lines, shapes, textures, colors, patterns, rhythms, and contrasts. Help them see examples of radiation, emphasis, and unity in natural forms. Urge students to bring interesting natural objects (taxidermy specimens, roots, weeds, fossils, honeycombs, bird's nests, pods, pinecones, seashells, and coral) into class to be used in discussions about artistic perception and for inspirational still lifes.

Teaching Color Awareness Introduce art projects that demand multiple color choices:

- Make collages using colored construction paper, colored tissue paper, wallpaper samples, paint chips, and assorted color fabrics and felts.
- Weave with colored papers.
- Color with crayon or oil pastel on colored construction paper.
- Make mosaics with colored tesserae on a colored or black background.
- Create a color environment or happening in the classroom, combining, for example, crepe paper, balloons, beach towels, hula hoops, paper fans, colored cellophane, ribbons, scarves, umbrellas, posters, and fabrics.

Encourage students to mix and experiment with an expanded range of colors, including tints and shades. Discuss the mood and effect that warm and cool colors give within a painting and in the environment. Call attention to the analogous colors (those adjacent to one another on the color wheel). Now students often are ready to tackle the intricacies of color neutralization (dulling a color) by mixing a color with its complementary hue (opposites on the color wheel). They also can appreciate the subtle contrast of subdued colors next to bright, intense colors.

Teaching Collage Introduce cut, tear, and paste projects that require the creation of texture and low-relief effects. These can be accomplished by

Courtesy of Joyce Vroon and Marlee Puskar.

A collage display is made from third-graders' brass fastener action puppets.

folding, crimping, pleating, fringing, weaving, braiding, and curling the paper. Direct the children's attention to positive and negative shapes. Suggest how the positive shape—obtained by cutting a motif (star, leaf, heart, cross, diamond) from a piece of paper—and the negative shape—the paper that remains after the shape is cut out—can be juxtaposed in a collage design. Introduce colored tissue paper, either cut or torn, as a collage medium. Urge the use of light-colored tissues first, building up later to the sparing use of darker colors as accents. Encourage color discovery by suggesting that students build several tissue layers. Collage projects in tissue lend themselves beautifully to nonobjective designs and depictions of dreams and moods. Children also can make collages interpreting sounds: whisper, shout, swish, rattle, squeak, roar, and thunderclap.

Teaching Printmaking The vegetable, clay stamp, and found-object print media introduced in the primary grades now can be augmented with oil pastel as a final, rich embellishment. Likewise, a variety of printmaking processes, which are explained fully in Chapter 27, now are manageable. These include the glue-line print, the collograph or cardboard relief print, and the string or cord print, in which string is glued to a cardboard plate, inked, and printed. An excellent medium for greeting-card designs is the plastic foam meat-tray print (with sides cut off to make a flat surface). On the foam tray (or similar ¼-inch thick polyurethane foam insulation material from a building supply store), lines are engraved with a pencil and the tray is inked and printed. The engraved lines will appear white in the completed print. In the monoprint technique, a sheet of plastic laminate or of glass (with edges taped) is inked with a brayer. The composition then is created by scratching through the paint with a stick, Q-tip, edge of a cardboard piece, eraser end of a pencil, or wood chopstick. Then a sheet of paper is placed over the inked surface, pressed down, and pulled off carefully.

Teaching Ceramics Review with third- and fourth-grade children the knowledge that they have gained in earlier school years about clay: where it comes from; its properties, such as plasticity; its possibilities; and its limitations. Describe the importance of ceramics in the everyday life of both ancient and contemporary cultures. An exploratory session in clay manipulation is again recommended to help students appreciate the following:

- Clay that is too hard is difficult to model.
- Clay that is too moist sags if the supports of clay or rolled paper, or the "fifth leg" under the stomach of an animal, are not sturdy enough.
- Appendages break off when the clay piece dries unless they are securely joined to the main structure with clay-scoring or slip-cementing.
- Textures, patterns, and details can be made in clay with fingers, pencils, and assorted found objects.
- Solid clay pieces over ½-inch thick may explode in the firing kiln unless openings are made through which the air inside can escape.

In pottery making, children can make the basic pinch pot into a larger container or an animal's body by joining with clay-slip two pinch pots of the same size. Cut out openings, and add feet and spouts for more complex pots.

ART CRITICISM, ART HISTORY, AND AESTHETICS

The third and fourth grades are the stage of beauty and realism. The child believes the purpose of art is to represent something. He or she wants objects to look real, with clarity and good definition. Indeed, the more realistic and clear the artworks, the better the artworks are liked. Children in these grades feel that artwork should be recognizable pictures of handsome, valuable, interesting items. They do not care for pictures showing anything weird or ugly. In responding to realistic art, children comment, "I wish I could draw like this." In fact, this hankering after realism is so strong that, when confronted by abstract artwork, the children try to find a specific image in it.

Second- and third-grade children take a longer time to look at art. They now have the linguistic skills to express the concept that artworks are different from the thing itself. ("It is a picture of a rabbit" rather than "It is a rabbit.") Students can identify events depicted in artworks, and they can describe both likenesses and differences between pictures. They can accept their peers' differing representations as being valid art expressions and recognize style in each other's works. They can tell about the colors, shapes, lines, and textures in an artwork. In addition, children this age can recognize different media and techniques in various works of art. Likewise, they can identify the forms of artwork: sculptures, ceramics, landscapes, portraits, and architecture. In discussing artworks, they can identify objects

Courtesy of Barbara Thomas.

Studying Henri Matisse's paper cutout pictures, fourth-grader Amy Wallace made this joyous collage.

Courtesy of Joyce Vroon.

Third-graders studied Piet Mondrian's paintings before making their own designs.

The following words can be added to the children's growing art vocabulary:

background	engraving	pyramid
balsa wood	foreground	radiation
batik	form	rasp
brayer	found material	scoring of clay and paper
cellophane	hue	shade
ceramics	inking slab	sketch
collage	intensity	slab
collograph	landscape	slip
color wheel	masking tape	spiral
complementary colors	monoprint	staple
composition	mosaic	still life
cone	negative shape	stitchery
contrast	papier mâché	tie-dyeing
contour line	plaster	tint
crafts	plywood	unity
cube	positive shape	value
cylinder	poster	

and make associations about them. For example, they can rank in order a series of objects, such as figures by age, or animals by power. They can describe some criteria for art (e.g., "pretty," or "bold"), and they can plan an art exhibition. Of course, many of the above abilities depend upon exposure and education, such as found in a quality art program.

IN THE CLASSROOM

Suggested Subjects or Themes for Grades 3 and 4

These topics are suitable for children of ages 7, 8, and 9.

Inside me (imaginative X-ray)	Totem poles	The pet show or pet store	Still life of interesting objects
Fun on the jungle gym	Action poses	A magic forest	Flower market or fruit market
Sports poses and still lifes	Design in nature: radiation	The wedding	The toy store or Santa's workshop
The circus parade	A tree house	Western objects	The circus in action
The merry-go-round	Tree of life	Here come the clowns!	Space voyage
The house where I live	Imaginary animals	Washing the family car	Self-portraits
Rare birds	Prehistoric animals	Food we like to eat	Sunken treasure
Animals and their young	Teddy bears	Boarding the school bus	A special place to go
Flowers from above	The insect world	A quiet activity at home	
Autumn leaves and trees	Playing a musical instrument		

If I were a balloon seller, a juggler, a tightrope walker, a ballerina, a scarecrow, a skydiver, an astronaut, a clown. . . .

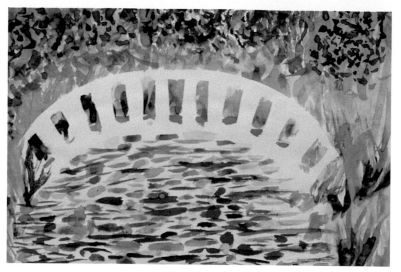

Courtesy of Barbara Thomas.

Studying Monet's paintings of his beloved lily garden and Oriental bridge at Giverny, fourth-graders first cut out a bridge stencil prior to making their Impressionist painting.

FOR FURTHER READING

Freeman, Nancy. 1991. "The Theory of Art that Underpins Children's Naive Realism." *Visual Arts Research,* Spring: 70–71.

Johnson, Andra. 1992. *Art Education: Elementary.* Reston, VA: National Art Education Association.

WEB RESOURCES

For elementary-school art lessons:

http://www.princetonol.com/groups/iad/lessons/elem/elemlessons.html

http://www.davis-art.com/textbooks/elementary/attc/main.asp

For hundreds of lesson plans, many correlated to academic subjects:

http://www.artsedge.kennedy-center.org/teach/les.cfm

For a development sequence:

http://www.arts.ufl.edu/art/rt_room/teach/young_in_art/

Courtesy of Frank Wachowiak and Mary Sayer Hammond.

Far left: Note the paint setup for students to use in painting outdoors. **Middle left:** Pulling the forms of wings, ears, and tails out of the clay body. **Middle right:** Adding the black paint over a previously mostly white crayon resist creates a whole new picture. **Far right:** To paint a box sculpture and make it appear three-dimensional, use organic shapes to cut across the box's rigid form.

Courtesy of Baiba Kuntz.

Fifth- and sixth-grade children created these sophisticated self-portraits with an animal or bird. The drawing was first done in gold or silver crayon on black construction paper. Then, oil pastel created the complementary and analogous color areas. Notice the sensitive handling of the eyes, eyelids, hair, and face planes.

Chapter 18
A Sequential Curriculum for Grades 5 and 6

*A*fter the strong beginning most children experience in the primary and middle elementary grades, when almost all children feel they can do art, a period of plateau or decline may occur during the upper elementary grades. Perhaps increasing critical awareness causes the self-doubt. To be sure, the best art, whether realistic or abstract or primitive, is characterized by assuredness and verve, and this confidence seems to be shaken in the upper elementary grades. Children's criteria of what is good in art outrace their abilities. They come to feel that their drawings are "not good enough," and they decide they are "no good in art." These attitudes underscore the importance of discussions about aesthetics, what makes quality in art, and whether realism is or should be the only goal.

We believe that the guidance and encouragement of a sympathetic, knowledgeable teacher can prevent students from languishing on the same creative plateau for years. Without a teacher's guidance and encouragement, children's cognitive and affective growth in art, employment of visual resources, command of the vocabulary and language of art, and use of formal elements may remain static or even retrogress. This eventually may lead to discouragement, frustration, and apathy. Children who are not taught art skills may develop into adults who feel limited in their ability to make and discuss art.

However, under the guidance of a teacher who helps them to create and appreciate the beauty they create and who gives them good reasons to try, children will grow in their ability to be careful delineators, to represent overlapping and receding spatial planes, and to use these concepts in their contour drawings, drawings of buildings in nature, and imaginative drawings of the fantastic. Another approach that is especially suited for those who doubt their art ability is to use art topics in which students express themselves and their values through symbols, dreams, and metaphors—in other words, art that expresses their uniqueness as individuals.

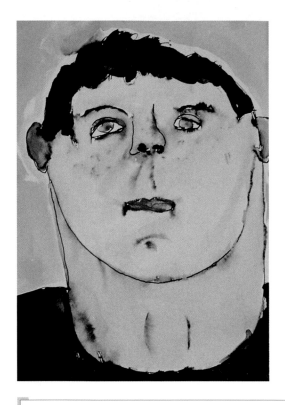  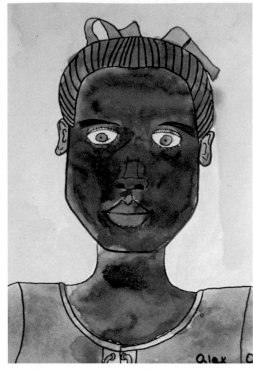

Left: *Courtesy of Melody Milbrandt*. Middle: *Courtesy of Baiba Kuntz*. Right: *Courtesy of Joyce Vroon*.

Left: Self-portrait of a fifth-grade boy in ink and watercolor. **Middle:** Fifth-grader J. Ryan Lapatka's self-portrait in conté crayon on grey paper.

Right: Fifth-grader Alex Owen's permanent marker and watercolor for his portrait of a classmate.

Although children are all individuals and their development will necessarily vary, fifth- and sixth-grade students typically:

- Begin to concentrate more on individual interests. *Students will depict their individual collections, their clothes for special occasions—for example, baseball uniforms, ballet costumes, scout uniforms.*
- Are now interested in activities that relate to their gender. *Students will use methods of art criticism to describe and interpret artworks showing preadolescents.*
- Vary in maturity, with girls more developed physically and emotionally than boys.
- Are becoming more dependable, responsible, self-critical, and reasonable. *Students will use their own evaluation of their artwork—describing both strengths and weaknesses—as a guide toward making changes in it.*
- Are interested in doing and making things "right"; try to conform to ideals of "good" behavior. *Students will explore using the methods of realistically showing deep space. Students will be able to conform to their group's behavior policies.*

- Develop interests outside home and school—in their community and in the world at large. *Students will describe how the arts are incorporated into their community.*
- Begin to criticize adults and anyone in authority. *Students will debate the art judgments of experts.*
- Are undergoing critical emotional and physical changes. *Students will depict their physical appearance and emotions in their art and writing.*
- Become more involved in hobbies and collections. *Students will create an art display or representation of a hobby.*
- Begin a phase of hero and heroine worship. *Using examples from art history, students will describe a favorite artist's life.*
- Often enjoy being by themselves, away from adult interference. *Students will create personal art notebooks/diaries showing their inner lives.*
- Enjoy working on group projects. *Students will cooperate with a group of peers in planning and executing a group project.*
- Are developing a sense of values, a sense of right and wrong. *Students will debate issues in art ethics. ("Who should own and display Native American art—big city museums or tribal museums?")*

- Are increasing their interest and work span. *Students will work on an art project for three or more hours.*
- Tend to form separate gangs or cliques according to their interests, sex, ethnicity, neighborhoods, and family status. *Students will identify and interpret historical art exemplars representing groups with which they identify.*

The principal developmental focus coming into play for children around this age is one of identity versus role confusion. Can the child find a meaningful place in the world and in the world of work? Promote their development of a sense of identity through group art projects that focus on community occupational roles, including the many occupations artists have.

ART DEVELOPMENT

The level of mastery that individuals achieve when developing expertise is closely intertwined with the effectiveness of the instruction they receive. Without a teacher's guidance, children's growth and interest in art and their use of formal elements, in the way they perceive artistically and in how they discuss art may remain static. Fifth- and sixth-graders do develop some unique abilities, to which the illustrations throughout this chapter attest.

The following table gives some general, stage-related descriptions of children's art development at this age.

Art Development	Enabling Activities
Become increasingly critical of their drawing ability and often are so discouraged with their efforts they lose interest in art class unless they are wisely and sympathetically motivated and guided.	Students will describe well-drawn and expressively drawn parts in each others' artwork. Students will describe and use design principles in creative crafts. Students will show more interest in art history.
Develop a growing curiosity to experiment with new and varied materials, tools, and techniques.	Students will use specialized tools and techniques, such as linoleum-cutting tools, plaster carving, weaving, and stitchery.
Experiment more with value contrast, neutralized colors, patterns, and textual effects.	Students will neutralize colors and create both pattern and texture effects.
Begin to use rudimentary perspective principles in drawing landscapes, buildings, streets, train tracks, fences, roads, and interiors.	Students will use vanishing area perspective as well as appreciate other ways to create depth.
Become more interested in their environment as a source for their drawings and paintings.	Students will draw scenes of historical interest and natural beauty in their community.

Top: *Courtesy of Suzy McNeil.* Bottom: *Courtesy of Joyce Vroon.*

The self-portrait of this upper-elementary-grade boy is a contour drawing, patiently delineated. Fifth-grade student Brian Davis decorates a piece of wood with collage for his Marisol-like sculpture of his sports hero, Deion.

Teaching Drawing, Designing, and Painting Students now can be careful, expressive, and observational delineators. They begin to include shadows and receding planes in paintings. Scout out challenging sites to draw, such as nearby building construction and demolition sites, Victorian-style homes, and gardens. Because it may be inconvenient or difficult to leave the school grounds, find interesting locations around the school to observe and draw: the lockers, halls, gym, entrance, kitchen, or playground. Students can be guided to create variety, space, and movement in their compositions by the imaginative placement of images, objects, or motifs within the picture plane. Encourage them to put figures or buildings on different foreground levels and to terminate them at varying heights in the background. Shapes can be juxtaposed or overlapped to create unity and space-in-depth.

Sadly, inability to achieve satisfactory realistic results leads some children mistakenly to conclude, "I am no good at art." Challenge this self-

Courtesy of Carole Henry.

An exaggerated play of light and dark, revealing exaggerated muscles, impresses middle schoolers.

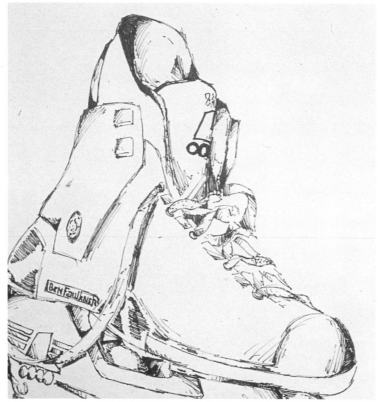

Courtesy of Joyce Vroon.

Rounded forms are carefully delineated as they turn away out of view in fifth-grader Ben Faulkner's roller-blade drawing.

doubt before it takes root. Continue practice in contour drawing, but introduce new approaches such as fantasy, nonobjective, and optical-art themes. Interest in the surreal shows up in the use of macabre and bloody images. Children can use metaphoric images—for example, an isolated tree for loneliness and despair. They can use metaphors in their designs for CD jackets. Lead students to discover the many different ways they can use line as pattern to enrich surfaces and vitalize backgrounds. Students become absorbed in the tricks of the trade; they like learning the conventions of comic book illustration, such as thought bubbles, overly defined muscles,

and stars and steam to depict violence. Reward and display their out-of-school independent efforts in drawing.

When your students paint with color, reinforce learning about complementary, monochromatic, and analogous color harmonies. Discuss tints and shades, the directions for neutralizing colors, the color spectrum, and the color wheel. Continue to build color awareness by calling the students' attention to color usage in their everyday world: magazine and CD jackets, athletic uniforms, storefronts, and automobiles. Use mood music as a background for free, expressive painting.

Teaching Collage Recapitulate previous learnings, such as the use of positive and negative shapes. Students like using partially three-dimensional effects of paper folding, fringing, pleating, spiraling, and curling. Introduce paper scoring to students who are ready for more skillful challenges. Demonstrate the scoring technique: Place paper to be scored on a thick pad of newspapers, use the blunt point of scissors, the pointed end of a wooden popsicle stick, or a similar tool to indent the curved line into the paper, then carefully fold along the indented line. To enrich students' collages, encourage them to scout for found objects such as wallpaper and rug samples, fabric and ribbon remnants, yarn, old greeting cards, and discarded building materials.

Collage-like techniques are possible with computer art that permits the instant scanning of photos or with clip art on the computer and the recombination of images in collage-like ways. Likewise, film images taken by the students themselves and photos from magazines can be combined in imaginative ways. Indeed, photography is a popular new medium to introduce at this age. Students love to take photographs of the environment, city scenes, and signs.

Teaching Printmaking Although the various printmaking processes introduced in previous grades—vegetable and found-object print, glue-line-relief print, polystyrene print, monoprint—can be repeated successfully at this age, the maturing students now will respond to more complex and challenging techniques. Linoleum printing is a favorite because of the opportunity to use a variety of gouges. Because more tools, materials, equipment, and time are required for advanced printmaking, see Chapter 27 for guidelines on inking, printing, and cleanup.

Courtesy of Joyce Vroon.

Metaphors can present a way to share one's feelings: wearing a false face (by Michael Selik); an intricate maze (by Grant Arnold); and a nest of snakes in a jungle of vines (by Matthew Parker).

Courtesy of Baiba Kuntz. Grades 5 and 6.

From a preliminary drawing, an attractive disposition of the basic shapes of an imaginary house is glued down, then architectural details and landscaping are added.

Courtesy of Joyce Vroon.

Sixth-grade students captured the texture of a billboard's multilayered torn surface, the expressive surface of a graffiti-covered wall, and the diagonal pattern of sunlight and shadows falling across a colonnaded entry. Students: Ashley Wagner, Catherine Overend, and Devon McClure.

Courtesy of Brian Baugh, Lyndon House Art Center.

New techniques fascinate students. This digital portrait photograph has been manipulated by hand drawing and re-photographing.

Middle: *Courtesy of David W. Hodge.* Right: *Courtesy of ICCA, Milner Library, Illinois State University.*

Left: This woodblock print of a child model playing a recorder shows carefully delineated fingers, and lines around the mouth to indicate the blowing. Cutting away the background created an attractive texture. Upper-elementary-grade student in Japan. *Middle:* Crafts are popular at this age; here, a sixth-grader's aluminum repoussé circus figure on a bike. *Right:* Maori chief by a New Zealand student, age 10.

Teaching Ceramics and Crafts Ceramic homes in clay relief are very successful at this age. Popular themes include animals and their young, animals in combat, portraits and self-portraits, clowns, acrobats, and mother and child. Students now place strong emphasis on realistic portrayals and the achievement of correct proportions and characteristic detail. Toward these ends, the teacher must be prepared to offer sympathetic and supportive guidance when called on. In most instances, recalled images alone will not supply the child with sufficient visual data. Build a library of photographs and slides showing exemplars of ceramics and crafts through the centuries. Neither overpraise the purely realistic approach they admire nor harshly criticize it; instead, introduce students to a variety of styles and interpretations. Many crafts are popular at this age. Creating simple jewelry also is a favorite activity.

ART CRITICISM

At this age, students can identify the major compositional features of an artwork. They can suggest alternative ways to make something and can express critical judgments about artworks. For example, one student said, "It needs to have a black dog in the painting." Encourage them to hypothesize about the motives that underlie behavior: "Why did the artist do it that way?" Fifth- and sixth-graders will be able to compare and contrast works in terms of both form and expressive meaning. They can describe how the elements work together to convey the ideas, and they can learn to see beyond the subject matter and use terminology to identify the style and mood. They can describe what things are like in art, although they do not use metaphors (e.g., "icy person") until later. They can identify symbols used in artworks.

The perspective lines (lines receding into depth) of tables, trucks, and buildings in this 11-year-old student's drawing of the Bilecik, Turkey, market do not go to one vanishing point. Instead, the lines head toward a general area in the upper right corner, in a method called isometric perspective. This technique, in which the perspective lines diverge as they go back in space, is also called inverse perspective and is used in much Near Eastern art.

Likewise, children at this age can describe artists in their community. Plan opportunities that promote independent action by students, such as interviewing community artists or other students. Promote their growing multicultural sensitivity by analyzing works from a wide variety of cultures.

Children also like to know about illustrators' tricks of the trade, such as zoom lines and ways of depicting muscles, and they are interested in studying how artists and illustrators use such conventions. For example, students might brainstorm about what is necessary to make a good depiction of a villain or a princess. A bulletin board, onto which students pin up examples they can bring in, can show symbols for power, violence, speed, and motion.

Fifth- and sixth-grade students should be able to use art terms such as the following in discussing artworks:

Design: motif, gradation, symmetry, asymmetry, emphasis, balance, composition, repetition, rhythm, simplicity, unity, variety

Shape: concave, convex, conical, pyramidal, exaggerated, geometric, biomorphic

Representation: foreshortening, proportion, symbol

Color: analogous, monochromatic, shading, harmony, spectrum, neutralization, transparent, opaque, translucent

Eye movement in a picture: circular, straight, spiral

From a linear design of the student's initials, an attractive design using trilateral symmetry developed.

Size: microscopic, telescopic

Space: narrow, wide, horizon line, perspective, vanishing point, vanishing area

Texture: granular, pebbled, regular, irregular, gradient

ART HISTORY AND AESTHETICS

In art history, students will be able to identify major figures and masterworks. They can explain how two styles of art differ and can arrange examples of historic styles into chronological sequence. Encourage them to think more deeply about experiences and about the motives that underlie behavior: "Why did the artist do it that way?" They will be able to explain different art criteria—those based on aesthetics, and those based on nonaesthetic criteria such as money or subject matter. Because students of this age tend to value things according to size, expense, complexity, and power, the teacher can present reproductions of artworks that are especially large, costly, or complex, or that depict powerful individuals.

The art preference of these children is for realism and "super" realism—a preference that peaks at age 11. In response to realistic artworks, students will say, "I wish I could draw like that." They are puzzled by pictures showing objects as they are not, or as they "should not" be. They call these depictions "weird" or "ugly." They feel that the things in pictures should be recognizable and valuable, neat, and interesting. At the same

Courtesy of Deborah Lackey.

Frank Stella's artwork motivated a team of four students who worked together on this cut-paper collage with craypas.

Top left: *Courtesy of Barbara Thomas.* Top right: *Courtesy of Jackie Ellett.*
Bottom: *Courtesy of Sharon Burns-Knutson.*

Top left: Studying Egyptian tomb figurines, fifth-grader Kristin French first rolled a slab of clay around a tube. Clay was then added for the arms and legs, and the tube's top was covered. A ball of clay was used as the head, and a draped covering and hieroglyphics were added. The piece was painted with green acrylic paint, a black wash was applied, and the figure was glued to a scrap of wood. **Top right:** Nigerian art motivated this project in aluminum tooling by fifth- and sixth-graders. Bold geometric designs have been used and stain has been applied to bring out the relief. **Bottom:** From a study of Nigerian art, fifth-graders used the counter repoussé metal-working process.

time, they are beginning to comprehend on an intellectual level (although often not on an emotional level) why an artist might show something other than a realistic rendering. They can and do use visual and verbal metaphors.

Students in the fifth and sixth grades are sensitive to the idea of "system," of a "right" way to do things. They try to adopt the rules and the codes necessary to survive in society. They want to know the right ways to count, read, and do math; the proper ways to play and to work; the codes of right and wrong. Because of the firmness of their convictions and their awareness of rules concerning the way things are supposed to be, their language contains many "shoulds." ("That's not what a good drawing of a car should look like.") The teacher of aesthetics can use these "shoulds" to

Courtesy of Baiba Kuntz.

Mirrors help students achieve success with projects like these life-sized plasticene clay-relief self-portraits. Upper-elementary-grade students are concerned with realistic portrayals showing correct proportions and details.

raise contested issues about the nature of art. ("Should good art take a lot of time to make?") Encourage students to think of questions about meanings and values. Ask them to clarify their statements, to give reasons to support their positions, and then to examine the reasons they gave.

FOR FURTHER READING

Churchill, Angiola. 1970. *Art for Preadolescents.* New York: McGraw-Hill.

IN THE CLASSROOM

Suggested Subjects or Themes for Grades 5 and 6
These topics are suitable for art projects for children of ages 9, 10, and 11.

At the gas station	A marching band
A view from a plane	A ball game or track meet
A bicycle race	An amusement park showing time, space, and motion
A horse show	
Warriors in armor	Consumerism at a shopping mall
Undersea marine life	
At the swimming pool or the beach	Motorcycles
Dreams	Renowned sports figures or celebrities
Values	Still life of musical instruments or sports equipment
Cartoons	
Winter recreation	Crowds at a street fair or county fair
Cities in outer space	
Portraits of self and classmates	Still lifes of watches, hair bows, computers, phones, old tools, and other old objects
Traffic jam	Still lifes of beach paraphernalia, diving equipment, or roller-blades
Landscape, cityscape, or seascape	
Nature study on a theme of adaptation or survival	Bags and packaging from fast-food restaurants

Moody, Larrie. 1992. "An Analysis of Drawing Programs for Early Adolescents." *Studies in Art Education* 34(1): 39–47.

WEB RESOURCES

For over one hundred art lesson plans for Grades 5 through 8:

http://artsedge.kennedy-center.org/teach/les.cfm?subjectId= &otherSubjectId=&gradeBandId=2&x=15&y=6&showDescriptions= true&sortColumn=

For the crisis of realism:

http://www.arts.ufl.edu/art/rt_room/teach/young_in_art/ sequence/realism.html

Chapter 19
A Sequential Curriculum for Grades 7 and 8

Vygotsky writes that adolescence is filled with the tension between intellect and affect, that is to say, between adolescents' increasingly self-critical attitudes and the emotional vicissitudes of puberty they are experiencing. Their overly critical attitudes lead many to abandon their creative efforts.

Middle-school students move into a changed academic world. For the first time, they may have a different teacher for each subject they take. If they come from the typical elementary-school situation in which the classroom teacher taught art, it will be their first contact with a specialist art teacher. In American schools, just a little over half of the students this age participate in visual arts classes. Regrettably, in some schools students involved in band or orchestra programs cannot take art. Also regrettable is that, in general, students draw less as they grow older. For a fair number of adolescents, however, a new synthesis occurs. Their newly developed technical facility is joined to their vision of what they need or want to express.

Middle-school students are experiencing a renaissance of intellectual inquisitiveness that in some ways may never be matched again. Although they are less inhibited than upper-elementary-grade children, they are highly critical of their own performance. Yet they are more willing to tackle new processes and new materials. They are technically more proficient. Their ability to capitalize on suggestions is heightened, and they can enter into critical discussions on art design and structure with a keener sensitivity and sharper argumentative skills. They are highly impressionable. Their cultural horizons are expanding, and they may carry with them for the rest of their lives the preferences and prejudices regarding art that they develop in these middle-school years.

All children are individuals, and their development necessarily varies. Students in Grades 7 and 8 typically:

- Have feelings of alienation and a need to be accepted by their peers. This acceptance often is more important to them than the teacher's

Courtesy of David W. Hodge.

This middle-school student is intent on his ceramic creation. For many youngsters, there is no greater satisfaction than hand building structures out of clay. The simple, basic pinch-pot form has been enriched by the addition of a foot, neck, handles, and an embellishing relief pattern.

In painting a design for a music cover, students can come to see how the artistic solutions of professional CD cover artists may apply to their own designs.

approval. *Students will work in small groups to determine a project, to carry out the project, and, subsequently, to discuss the project and related fine art examples.*

- Experience a change of identity, feelings of loss, and inner conflicts. Unpredictable behaviors may intensify. *Artwork and talking about art are ways to explore and even work through alienated and conflicted feelings.*
- Consider bad taste and what society considers good taste and vice versa. *In class discussion, students can critique fashion styles from different times and cultures.*
- Often are more inclined to daydream, to watch rather than perform. *From a study of art history books, students will describe an imaginary day in the life of an artist.*
- Need to begin considering vocational areas to establish a sense of their identity. *Point out vocations related to the arts, and have art history units on artists' personalities and careers.*
- May disparage or bully peers or, conversely, be bullied or disparaged. *Show art examplars of persecution and discuss the feelings of the people who are depicted.*
- Begin to emphasize their appearance and grooming. Popularity is now an issue. Intensely curious about the pubertal changes in their bodies. *Students will create a clay head in three dimensions of themselves or of a classmate. Study art's role in puberty rites, e.g., mask-making.*

Courtesy of David W. Hodge and Frank Wachowiak.

Circle self-portraits in oil pastel on colored construction paper by middle-school students. The circle format and imaginative use of color and form created a new artistic design challenge. Individuals shared their unique interests via flags, flowers, camouflage, and birds.

- Possess varying degrees of physiological and sexual maturity. *Students will interpret artwork showing persons of this age.*
- Are becoming more self-conscious regarding their changing physical characteristics. Feel that people are concerned about their appearance. *Students will be able to draw caricatures of their prominent features. Discuss famous stars' features when the stars were teens.*
- Are fascinated with their names. *Do name or initial designs as prints or collage.*
- Are in constant communication with their friends about dates, parties, TV shows, movies, music, classmates, and teachers' and parents' foibles. *From a personal record of phone doodles, students will describe the design variations and use these ideas as the basis for a T-shirt design.*
- May have difficulty in distinguishing between their own points of view and those of others because of an egocentric viewpoint. *Art criticism in which different views are expressed can help to lessen egocentrism.*
- Are unable to commit to decisions. May experience a loss of sense of identity and a snobbishness or scorn or rebellion against authority. *Use integrated learning experiences, challenging and exciting projects, and active and cooperative learning.*
- Model their behavior and appearance after sports stars, television personalities, rappers, recording artists, and movie stars. *Students will create artworks from photos of persons whom they admire.*
- Are developing their interest in sports, music, or other arts. *Students will draw their own collections of souvenirs and mementos.*
- Are unusually sensitive to other people's problems, but do not know how to help. *Students will create a work of art to share with another person and give emphatic feedback to another student about art.*
- Have a personal fable that normal laws of nature don't apply to them, and a belief in their immortal and unique existence. *Discuss art history examples of superheroes (e.g., Greek gods) interacting with normal people and discuss real-life consequences.*
- Are trying to develop a code or sense of values. *Students will interpret a work of art in terms of the moral dilemmas for the persons represented.*
- Form status groups and cliques, using "accepted," "tolerated," and "rejected" categories. *Students will interpret artworks by diverse groups, and, looking at pictures of alienation, explain what the artists were trying to communicate.*
- Seclude themselves from family and children. *As an out-of-school activity, draw one's room.*
- Have a growing desire for new and exciting experiences. *Students will be able to depict exciting, imaginary adventures through art.*
- Fluctuate between childhood and adulthood in their interests, insights, abilities, and judgments. *Students will describe art careers in the community.*

EMOTIONAL VULNERABILITY

Young adolescents have tender feelings, and direct criticism of students' artwork in front of their classmates can be humiliating. Avoid sarcasm and belittling remarks at all costs. Writing as an adult, Georgia O'Keeffe recalled the painful humiliation she felt when, at age 13, she was criticized by her art teacher in front of her classmates for drawing a plaster figure's hand too small. "At the time I thought she scolded me terribly. I was so

Courtesy of Davis Publications and Teddy Oliver.

A 12-year-old has expressed pain and humiliation in this oil pastel, "My Mother Just Spanked Me." From "Middle School Expressions," by Teddy Oliver and Robert Clements, *School Arts Magazine,* September, 1983.

Red Barn, Lake George, New York, 1921 (oil on canvas, 14-¼ × 16-¼ inches)
Georgia Museum of Art, Eva Underhill Holbrook Memorial, Gift of Alfred Holbrook.

Georgia O'Keeffe remembered for decades her middle-school teacher publicly rebuking the realism of her figure drawing in front of her classmates. Her paintings are acclaimed for their bold shape patterns.

taker, the methodical planner, the procrastinator, the idol seeker, the plodder, the perfectionist, the maverick, the dreamer, the braggart, the idealist, and the quiz whiz. The next week, a different role might hold appeal. Personalities depicted throughout art history (such as Albrecht Dürer's knight on a horse and Renaissance depictions of David and Hercules) can be related to some students' fantasies. Students' rites of passage are acted out in real fights, mock fights, and challenges to authority. This is a time of increased awareness and self-consciousness, sensitivity to the differences in others, identification with a peer group, and heightened emotional responses. Possibly as a means of self-searching, preadolescents like to draw portraits and self-portraits and capture their own and their peers' changing self-image.

Going steady, having crushes, engaging in sexual activity, and being subjected to physical and sexual harassment and abuse are emotionally charged situations in which some older students may find themselves. Other events fraught with the potential for creating feelings of guilt are the divorce of parents, an abortion, or the death of a loved one. Feelings of worthlessness, incompetence, ugliness, anger, guilt, and complicity interfere with the development of students' positive self-concepts. Teachers used to say that the schools' biggest problems were students' talking in class, chewing gum, making noise, running in the halls, and getting out of turn in

embarrassed that it was difficult not to cry" (O'Keeffe, 1988). Teachers may also embarrass students by praising their work too lavishly in front of their peers. To avoid public embarrassment whether correcting or praising students, give individual, in-process critiques.

Emotional swings and moodiness in children are common; some students may reject their own excellent artwork. Drawings of jeans, T-shirts, sneakers, and hairstyles considered as contrary to the adult culture's norms can express adolescents' need to be separate from the dominant adult culture. Especially if their art experiences in elementary school were limited, unsatisfying, or unrewarding, middle-school students may be apathetic or cool in their response to art. Once they become caught up in the excitement of a creative, productive, and qualitative art program, however, they become enthusiastic converts to art's adventures, challenges, and personally satisfying rewards.

During middle school, teachers really begin to see the personalities and idiosyncrasies of the students reflected in their behavior and their art. While students can be conformists, they also can be fiercely independent. They may try out a role for a week: the extrovert, the loner, the risk

Courtesy of Fay Brassie.

In a design for a jacket, this middle-school student has expressed yearnings for love, joy, and the banning of rules.

lines. Today, however, far more serious problems are endemic. By being a friend to the student and expressing personal concern, you may play a pivotal role in the student's life at a critical time. Through your teaching and encouraging, the art program may provide a vehicle for the student to express his or her conflicts or develop positive attitudes of achievement.

When students are going through emotionally trying situations, you may see a decline in their ability to concentrate on art expression. In their behavior, you may notice a shortness of temper or a lack of affect. For such students, art expression may serve as a beacon warning that a person is in trouble emotionally. Students' verbalizations during art criticism and art interpretation often provide a forum for other students to speak out about what is on their minds. Very general and wide-open art topics, such as "crying" or "oppression," may provide a way to express, through art, what formerly seemed to be unmentionable. The teacher of art may be able to help the young person cope with problems—not as a psychologist but as a caring friend with whom significant events may be shared. Through the school counselor, the art teacher also may be able to help individuals or their parents contact agencies skilled in dealing with serious emotional or family life problems.

The emotional side of middle-school art is shown in this soft firebrick sculpture and this driftwood sculpture. Here are seen the creators' sensitivity to others, their forming of significant relationships with others, their heightened emotional responses, and their self-searching.

Courtesy of Joyce Vroon.

Painting "A Dream" may be a way to gain insight into the messages from one's unconscious mind. Fifth-grade student Pierce Lowrey.

Not only can art announce to the sensitive perceiver an individual's distress, it can play a major role in restoring a person's balance after a traumatic situation. Art creation as well as discussions about art can help students feel better about themselves. Problem solving through art provides an opportunity for the "person within" to emerge. Interestingly, applying the principles of good design—balance, proportion, variation—seems to foster those same qualities in the artists. For example, during art creation, the individual may find help through being able to share visually, at whatever level is comfortable, the event that needs expression. Likewise, through talking about the art of others, the individual may be able to give voice to personal feelings and break out of his or her aloneness and grief. A student's art accomplishment can help others to see that person as an individual of worth. In turn, the achievement helps that individual acquire a sense of pride and self-worth.

ART DEVELOPMENT

Art Development	Implications for Instruction
Choose subject matter for art expression that relates to human-interest activities, community and worldwide events, and current projects in ecology, medical research, space, and undersea exploration.	Students will use current events as a springboard for their art expression. Students will explain the art principles they use to depict the sociological, artistic, or scientific event.
Attempt shading and cross-hatch techniques to make drawn forms appear solid, cylindrical, and believably realistic. Experiment with perspective drawing.	Students will use shading and cross-hatching to create the appearance of three-dimensional form. Students will be able to apply some perspective concepts.
Are self-conscious and self-critical about their drawing ability. Supportive instruction in contour and gesture drawing helps them to become increasingly skillful in figure and animal drawing.	Students will use gesture and contour drawing to capture the feeling and dynamics of the posed human figure.
Are ready to interpret complex compositions, such as richly orchestrated still lifes and multifigured events and celebrations.	Students will apply design principles of repetition and variation to draw an organized composition from a complex still life or from many figures in action.
Are mature and skillful enough to handle a variety of challenging crafts: photography, glazed ceramics, repoussé, plaster reliefs, sculpture in hard materials, and woodblock printmaking.	Students will use craft processes for personal art expression.

TEACHING ART

Teaching Drawing, Designing, and Painting Students like their work to have expressive content—to convey a mood and have a message. They are interested in finding a powerful means to convey an experience or an idea. Whereas younger students showed scenes, adolescents now use scenic natural forms to communicate their attitudes toward life. They can study symbols and work into their designs motifs for peace, freedom, evil, or envy.

Most students at this age have a love–hate relationship with drawing; while on the one hand they seek realism, yet, on the other hand, they are often frustrated by their inability to attain it. Elaborate still-life setups with models in expressive costumes stimulate their interest and, hence, their desire to accurately represent the model's positions and clothing. Line

Courtesy of David W. Hodge.

Through drawing classmates modeling, students can express indirectly something of their own nature. Here, a middle-school youth captures in a contour-line drawing a quality of openness and searching.

Perspective is shown in this 10-year-old girl's street scene from Tehran, Iran. Diminishing sizes are seen in the street vanishing around the bend, its dotted centerline, the curved fence, and the street-side buildings.

drawings of cartoon characters, mythical animals, and sports events are popular, as are cartoon portraits. Using shading, stippling, hatching, cross-hatching, and washes, they can begin to comprehend and depict the effect of spotlights on models. They will need guidance and reassurance, however, in handling color values and using cast shadows and reflections.

Students interested in creating depth in their pictures will begin to realize the importance of creating avenues into the composition. This is done by using lines and shapes that terminate at the boundaries or borders of the paper and lead the viewer into the picture. A bonus is that the more avenues created, the more opportunities the student has to employ a variety of colors, values, and pattern in the resulting shapes. Perspective may be introduced as just one of many ways that artists create the illusion of depth; however, only a tiny fraction of students can work out realistic perspective showing space and depth. Thus, unless a student specifically requests help, it is wise not to introduce regimented perspective rules or foreshortening techniques at this stage.

Inverted perspective sometimes now appears, and the beauty of this method should be pointed out—for example, in Persian art. Some students will want their drawings to "look right" and will request specific assistance in making their toppling, meandering fences stand straight. They want their sidewalks to lie flat and their roads to disappear believably over a distant rise or hill. To help them achieve these effects, show them that fence

posts are drawn parallel to the sides of the page, division lines in sidewalks are drawn at angles directed to a distant vanishing point, and roads or highways diminish in width as they move away toward the horizon.

Older middle-school students often are enchanted by the mechanical, mathematical aspects of perspective drawing. The illusion of space gives some students, especially those who do not like to draw, a feeling that they have done something of note. Their enthusiasm should not be dampened, but the teacher can point out the compositional limitations of a rigid reliance on perspective. Similarly, it is all right for students to strive for "right" proportions in their figures, but the instructor must help them to realize that drawing something "realistically right" does not necessarily make it "artistically right." Especially now, when the expression of feelings is so important, students can be shown that many artists throughout time who either did not know of or ignored the rules of perspective and proportion still produced art of great impact and beauty.

Middle-school students are mature enough to respond to the many subtleties and complexities of color harmonization. Review the processes for making tints and shades and the techniques for neutralizing colors. Challenge the students to use color principles in designing CD covers, monograms, posters, logos, book jackets, store-window displays, room decor, and stage designs. Call attention to how color is used in artworks for conveying emotion. Discuss the psychological effect of color on people, the colors emphasized in packaging and advertising, and the colors of ceremonies, celebrations, rituals, and rites of passage. Analyze how various countries and cultures use differing symbolic color meanings.

Taking ideas from contemporary color and light shows, students can be encouraged to construct their own color "happenings." They can use found materials such as ribbons, yarn, wrapping paper, kites, cellophane, balloons, hula hoops, confetti, crepe and tissue paper in assorted colors, giant paper flowers, fabric samples, and beach towels. Other exciting projects to stimulate color awareness can be motivated by examining such artists as Victor Vasarely, Richard Anuskiewicz, Marc Chagall, and Judy Pfaff. For example, students can construct toothpick-and-box sculptures painted in bold tempera or fluorescent colors and make miniature stained-glass windows using scrap colored glass, colored tissue paper, or stage gels.

Teaching Printmaking The simple prints that children enjoyed in earlier grades—vegetable and found-object prints, glue-line-relief prints, collographs, monoprints, linoleum prints—can be done with satisfaction and success during middle school. More complex subject matter and themes also now can be employed in a variety of printmaking processes. As always, the organization and monitoring of inking, printing, and cleanup are of special importance. At this grade level, sophisticated printmaking techniques such as reduction woodblocks can be undertaken if teachers are experienced in supervising advanced printmaking techniques. Use nontoxic, water-based inks rather than oil-based inks.

Teaching Ceramics and Sculpture Because students may come to middle school with varying backgrounds in clay experimentation and creation, provide for several sessions to review clay exploration. Discuss the importance of clay to the lives of people in other cultures.

Incorporate art history and social studies by discussing art visuals of ceramic pottery and sculpture from ancient as well as contemporary cultures. Include Greek vases of the Hellenic period, Chinese Tang figurines, the outstanding life-size ceramic warriors and horses unearthed at Xian, Japanese Haniwa creations, and clay vessels in the form of human figures from Mexico and Peru. Library copies of *Ceramic Monthly* can bring the students up to date on the newest developments in the field of ceramic pottery and sculpture. Put up a "potter of the week" display on the art-room bulletin board so that students will become familiar with pioneers and innovators such as Shoji Hamada, Dan Lucero, and Peter Voulkos.

Seventh- and eighth-grade students can engage in more complex and challenging clay construction and modeling than was possible in the early elementary years. If glazes and adequate kiln facilities are provided, students can experiment with safe ceramic glazes to give their works glowing color. A popular sculpture activity begins with metal rod and wire armatures that are attached to a block of wood for a base and covered with plaster-of-Paris strips to form expressive figures in motion: rock musicians, surfers, and sports figures, for example.

Courtesy of Claire Clements.

Hooking a rug can bring pride and satisfaction to middle-school students.

Larger-than-life clay portraits from Japan capture the human figure's expressive potential. Note the extra-heavy supporting neck and the freely applied dabs of clay used to create the form.

Teaching Crafts Crafts such as weaving, stitchery, hooked rugs, papier-mâché, puppetry, and simple jewelry are especially popular at this level (see Chapter 31). All of these hands-on activities should be included in a qualitative, progressive elementary- and middle-school art program. For example, weaving can progress from simple paper weaving in the primary grades to sophisticated, hanging woven panels in the middle school. The story quilts of Faith Ringgold and of Harriet Powers can motivate exciting sewn applique banners and quilts. Mask construction, simple puppets, and stitchery can be offered at all levels. Papier-mâché, paper sculpture, leather and metal tooling, marionettes, and jewelry are best reserved for upper elementary grades and middle school. Then, many students also are ready for challenging subtractive sculpture projects in soap, balsa wood, sandcore, leather-hard clay molds, plaster-of-Paris blocks, and soft firebrick. They will enjoy additive sculpture employing toothpicks, wood scraps, wire, metal, driftwood, and found objects. Specialized craft vocabulary terms such as the following should be taught: glaze, gouge, greenware, grog, leather-hard clay, mat, mat knife, mixed media, mold, raffia, reed, tesserae.

Teaching Collage, Photography, and Computer Art The collage process—which can be expanded to include montage and assemblage, and combined with new media—provides a host of opportunities to use the principles of art. These include variety in shapes, contrast in values and color, and overlapping to create unity. Collage allows students to express through art their personal concerns about attractiveness and intimacy as well as their social concerns about world problems such as ecology, hunger, drugs, and war.

Review with students the fundamentals of the collage process: how to identify and exploit positive and negative shapes, and how to create subtle space through overlapping. Show them how to achieve three-dimensional effects through paper folding, scoring, pleating, fringing, and curling. Preliminary drawings or sketches are recommended for collages when the subject matter deals with landscapes, figure studies, or still lifes. In themes from the imagination or in purely nonobjective interpretations, the direct cutting, tearing, and application of the shapes to the background may be encouraged. In both approaches, however, the pasting or permanent adhering of materials should be delayed until the students, with the teacher's guidance, can make those compositional changes—additions, subtractions, and revisions—that are necessary to enhance their creations.

Both new and found materials have expanded the range of collage creation immensely. Photographs taken by the students and images scanned into the computer, altered, and printed, as well as computer clip art, can be combined in imaginative ways. Explore the possibilities of colored tissue on white or colored cardboard, colored sections from magazine ads, wallpaper samples, and fabric remnants. Incorporate nature's store of colored and textured wonders: bark, leaves, sand, feathers, butterfly wings, dried flowers, seeds, and snake skins. The collage is an excellent first project of the year for middle-school art classes. It does not put as much pressure on the students as an assignment in drawing or painting, and it is not stressful to cut out elements and put them together to make a whole design. Every student in class can succeed in making a collage. See Chapter 28 for recommendations concerning photography, video, and computer art.

ART CRITICISM

A new and genuinely different way of thinking about art comes into being in the seventh- and eighth-grade years. The criterion of realism is replaced by those of intention and message. Given artwork containing expressive themes, students will talk about the expressive qualities of the artwork. They can recognize style and can contrast the treatment of theme in two or more artworks. They understand metaphor and mystery, and they can identify multiple meanings in represented objects. Students also can formulate and try many alternative hypotheses in explaining an artwork. For example, they can deductively reason: "Pretend to be (a famous artist) and address the problem of. . . ."

Accompanying the rapid changes in their bodies and their own search for identity is a shift in their understanding. Seventh- and eighth-grade students can recognize that expression of the experiences of others and of one's self is subjective. Reassure students that they need not share their own personal artworks publicly unless they so desire. Perhaps because expression characterizes this stage, there is less concern about realism and the beauty of a subject. Pictures now can be seen as metaphors for ideas, and emotions can be valued for their ability to inspire feelings. Social commentary art, such as that by George Tookers, helps them to express feelings of justice. Students can speculate on the artist's mood. They can imagine alternatives to what a picture shows and speculate on different scenarios. These exercises in expression allow students to feel an identification with accepted, mature artists. In another exercise, students can role-play contrary-to-fact propositions; for example, they can pretend to be an art museum director and make judgments about a variety of artists' works.

In addition, students will be able to discuss the aesthetic quality of an artwork or a utilitarian object. For example, students can judge the effectiveness of the designs of athletic shoes, T-shirts, and motorcycles, as well as analyze how such objects suggest ideas and feelings.

ART HISTORY AND AESTHETICS

Adolescents' ability to think abstractly and to reason about ideas increases dramatically at this time. Children in the seventh and eighth grades can consider the logical possibilities in a problem. They make guesses about what might be going on behind the depicted scene, and they can discuss symbolism, deeper meanings, and double meanings.

Students of this age also have the ability to conduct inquiry from several vantage points. That is, they can role-play different parts, such as art critic, artist, disgruntled client, or government official. Working individually or in small groups, students can report on artists' careers. In staged mock debates between artists they can address issues in art, such as whether paintings should show realism or depict emotion. Some terms to discuss are expressivism, realism, aesthetics, anatomy, judgment, value, art critic, censorship, metaphor, spontaneity, and craftsmanship.

During this new stage of aesthetic response, students can investigate questions of content and social significance. Because art is an expression of its creator, ask them to discuss how the artist uses color and design to show emotion. Students also are able to consider more abstract aspects, such as style and composition, and they understand that other students' perspectives can be different from their own.

To tap their interest in expressive works of art, expose them to Van Gogh's life and letters. Show them works about the suffering of women and children during wartime by Kaethe Kollwitz, Francisco Goya, and Max Beckman. Expand their knowledge and appreciation of master drawings and paintings by artists such as Leonardo da Vinci, Albrecht Dürer, Rembrandt Van Rijn, Rosa Bonheur, Paul Klee, Henri Matisse, Pablo

Exciting color projects to stimulate color awareness can be motivated by showing the work of Judy Pfaff, such as her 1986 *Apples and Oranges*. Mixed media, 113 × 72 inches.

Picasso, Louise Nevelson, Andy Warhol, Katsushika Hokusai, Georgia O'Keeffe, William Hogarth, Romare Bearden, Peter Brueghel, and Mary Cassatt. Students love the artworks of Red Grooms and Grant Wood.

Call students' attention to the cave drawings at Altamira and Font du Gaume as well, to Benin bronzes, and to the tribal-huntsmen renditions of African and Australian native cultures. Show them the sumi-e ink drawings of China and Japan and the expressive graphics of the Inuit and Native Americans. Students should be able to match artworks to styles. One appropriate task is to identify the artwork that does not belong in a group.

Middle-school students, coming as they often do from different elementary schools, will bring varied backgrounds in art vocabulary. Vocabulary words that have been suggested in previous grades should be reviewed and new words added as they are introduced:

Art history and criticism: expressionism, neo–expressionism, op art, pop art, African sculptures from Yoruba, Benin bronzes, Zaire nail art, Chi Wara antelope sculptures, surrealism, cubism, Renaissance art, impressionism, symbolism, double meaning

Drawing and painting: conte crayon, sienna, spectrum, stipple, umber, montage, ochre, watercolor wash, distortion, encaustic, fixative, foreshortening, gesture drawing, hatching, converging lines, crosshatch, caricature

Printmaking: baren, bench hook, burnish, etching, intaglio, printing press, proof, relief print

Photography, film, and video: negative, fixer, plate, tone, daguerreotype, cibachrome, playback, wipe, fade, establishing shot, zoom shot, soft focus, montage, slow disclosure, low-angle shot, freeze frame, long shot, pan, superimposition

Sculpture: armature, assemblage, bas relief, solder, sandcore, sepia, stabile, incised relief, repoussé, patina

IN THE CLASSROOM

Suggested Subjects or Themes for Grades 7 and 8

These project suggestions are suitable for children of ages 12, 13, and 14. Visual resources are absolutely necessary. For additional ideas, refer to the themes recommended earlier for Grades 5 and 6, which can be adapted to the middle school. Middle schools may comprise sixth through eighth grades, or even include the fifth grade as well, and this variation will affect the suitability of topics. Nonetheless, some themes, such as a bouquet of flowers, self-portraits, and animal pets, can be recommended without reservation through the eighth grades.

Environmental problems and solutions

The Olympics

I wish

Great moments in music or ballet

Great moments in theater, literature, or science

Great moments in sports

I would like/I would not like

Customs and costumes of the world

The weather's mood

Sadness in the world

Legendary heroes and heroines

Helicopters, planes, or air balloon races

A vivid dream

Skateboards and snowboards

Oppression and conformity

Landscapes

Illustrations of selected stories and poems

Dream cars, motorcycles, and boats

Historical costumes

Flying trapeze act

The electronic-game arcade

A cry for help

String quartet

Fashion show

Wrestling match

FOR FURTHER READING

Henry, Carole. 1996. *Middle School Art: Issues of Curriculum and Instruction.* Reston, VA: National Art Education Association.

Marcia, J. E. 1980. "Ego Identity Development." In J. Adelman, ed., *The Handbook of Adolescent Psychology.* New York: Wiley.

Michael, John. 1983. *Art and Adolescence, Teaching Art at the Secondary Level.* New York: Teachers College Press.

Stokrocki, Mary. 1990. "A Cross Site Analysis: Problems in Teaching Art to Preadolescents." *Studies in Art Education* 31(2): 106–107.

WEB RESOURCES

For a site with much information:

http://www.getty.edu/artsednet/Search/map.html

For lessons developed by middle-school art teachers:

http://www.princetonol.com/groups/iad/lessons/middle/

For junior high lessons:

http://www.getty.edu/artsednet/resources/Scope/index.html

For a year-long scope and sequence, with a multicultural social studies emphasis, for Grades 6 through 8:

http://www.princetononl.com/groups/iad/lessons/middle/yearplan.htm

Courtesy of David W. Hodge.

Vehicles are a popular topic with middle-school youths. ***Top:*** Students created collages from detailed drawings of an open-doored van parked on the school's premises. ***Middle:*** Translating the drawing into a collage. ***Bottom:*** Gas pumps and logos enhanced the compositions.

Part 5

Appreciating Art: Art History, Criticism, and Aesthetics

Van Gogh's "Starry Night" is one of the most beloved paintings ever made: its stars glow like moons, its moon glows like the sun, and its sun-filled "milky way" weaves through the heavens, making the earth roll in empathy. About this painting, third-grader Catherine Hodge wrote: "On a starry night, I feel like I could fly up to a star and use one for a merry-go-round. I think they would look beautiful on a summer night twisting and turning, rolling and tumbling in a yellow glow against the black sky." Writing about art is a wonderful way to develop both writing skills and art appreciation.

Vincent Van Gogh, "Starry Night" 20" × 30", Museum of Modern Art, New York City.

*D*espite a multitude of opportunities to appreciate art in the world about them, many children receive minimal training in learning how to think about, talk about, and do art. They leave school programs feeling like outsiders to the world of art, intimidated at the thought of visiting museums and art galleries. They feel that serious discussions of art ideas are something in which they have no business participating. They think that the study of art criticism, art history, and aesthetics is highfalutin, reserved for those going on for higher education. They have not recognized that art offers everyone a way to investigate the world and its meanings and values.

Toward Civilization, an influential report of the National Endowment for the Arts (1988), described the effect of this attitude on the nation:

> The arts are in triple jeopardy: they are not viewed as serious; knowledge . . . is not viewed as a prime objective; and those who determine school curricula do not agree on what arts education is.

Some educators believe that the activities of thinking and talking about art can give a new intellectual dimension to art appreciation, and they believe that fully implementing these activities would allow art to be accorded a higher place in the school curriculum.

Chapter 20

Teaching Art Appreciation: From Picture Study to Discipline-Based Arts Education

*T*he idea that students should study art masterworks and be given instruction in art appreciation is not new. In the mid–nineteenth century, German archaeologist and art historian Johann Winckelmann advised artists to dip their brushes in intellect. At that time in America, a new and distinctly American art was being advocated, one that would be pure, moral, and earnest—an alliance of art, religion, and nature. Educating the child's artistic eye was considered to be an integral part of moral and social education. At the end of that century, the "schoolroom decoration movement" worked to accomplish this by bringing plaster casts of antique sculptures into classrooms. Sepia art reproductions with a patriotic, religious, and moralistic orientation came into the public schools through the "picture study movement." From 1910 to 1920, this movement brought art prints into the schools. These pictures were filled with literary associations on which students could speculate. Works by artists such as Rosa Bonheur, Jean-François Millet, Raphael, and Winslow Homer were deemed to be suitable for young, impressionable minds, and some of these added prints, such as E. G. Leutze's *Washington Crossing the Delaware,* still hang in a few school hallways today.

During the 1920s, formal design elements gained more attention. These were spurred by interest in art movements such as cubism, Roger Fry's writings in aesthetics, and Arthur Wesley Dow's art education writings, which focused on the formal elements of line, value, and color. During the mid-1950s, four-color printing of large-size art reproductions

Courtesy of Gwenda Malnati and Eric Hamilton.

Primary-grade students researched and wrote reports on famous artists and delivered their reports in costume. **Top:** Ersatz Paul Gauguins and Polynesian friends. **Middle:** Mary Cassatts, Anna Ancher, and Claude Monet. **Bottom:** Leonardos and Michelangelos.

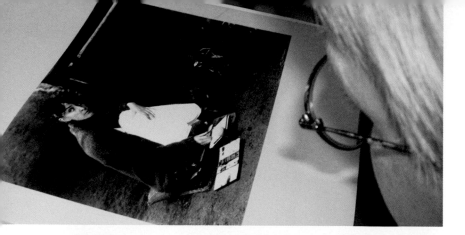

Top left: A student reads about Georgia O'Keeffe's life at age 29, when she was doing watercolors outdoors and teaching art to future teachers at West Texas State Normal School. **Bottom left:** A guest speaker, author, and story-teller Carol Sabbeth reenacted with the class Mary Cassatt's talking about her and her friends' paintings. **Top right:** Students examine the paintings of Grandma Moses, who, from ages 12 to 27, worked at neighboring farms as a hired girl, then married, had ten children, began painting at age 67, and was world famous at her death at age 101.

and 35-mm slides and slide projectors made it possible for masterpieces to be shown in the classroom.

Federal educational legislation also helped. The U.S. Office of Education, through its Arts and Humanities Program, sponsored programs and conferences on how to improve art education. Funds from a booming "Great Society" economy and federal educational enrichment programs (such as the Elementary and Secondary Education Act of 1965) purchased prints and slides for school libraries, social studies classes, art classes, and elementary classrooms. Innovative librarians, teachers, and administrators who sought enrichment sources realized the educational power of such reproductions. Major art museums throughout the nation printed inexpensive reproductions, and the National Gallery of Art in Washington, D.C., made available to the public schools a lending program for art slides, reproductions, filmstrips, and films.

Parallel with the development of printing technology and school enrichment programs was the rapid development in the nation's colleges

and universities of the disciplines of art history, art criticism, and aesthetics. Art educators looked at their own discipline and analyzed the elements in its structure. Some argued that art history and criticism were disciplines equally as valid as the actual creation of art. Hence, since the 1950s, national art education conference programs have addressed the question of how to incorporate art history and criticism into school art programs. University-level art texts made the case that art education's primary goal is to help students see art's role in giving meaning to human endeavor and in meeting daily living needs. Aesthetic education's goal was not only to teach students how they can experience the arts for their inherent values and delight but also to contribute to the students' general store of perceptions and concepts. The older term *art appreciation* came to be looked on merely as implying peripheral knowledge. Newer terms, such as *art criticism, aesthetics,* and *aesthetic education,* began to be used more widely (these are explained extensively in the following two chapters).

DISCIPLINE-BASED ARTS EDUCATION (DBAE)

Foundations took an interest in fostering school programs emphasizing a cognitive approach to art through art criticism, art history, and aesthetics. In 1982, the Getty Center for Education in the Arts was created to investigate the feasibility of having nonspecialist teachers and art teachers, in general classroom settings, teach students skills in the areas of art criticism, art history, and aesthetics side by side with the teaching of art creation. The director of the Getty Center wrote: "If art education is to become a meaningful part of the curriculum, its content must be broadened and its requirements made more rigorous." In 1984, Dwaine Greer gave this movement the label Discipline-Based Art Education (DBAE), by which it has come to be known. Its proponents stressed the need for balance among the four subdisciplines: art history, art criticism, aesthetics, and art production. Although it is not known if these four subdivisions will continue to be the main way that art learning is considered, the curriculum guides of several states have spelled out the content of art in a similar way.

Many art educators from the mid-1960s and after agreed on the importance of these endeavors; however, concern was also voiced regarding if, how, when, and to what degree such activities should supplant or supplement studio activities. Some worried that DBAE could have the effect of suffocating students' artistic creativity, because it emphasizes academic disciplines in which students might have little or no interest without a foundation of experience with art production. Others believed that DBAE did not account for many important functions of art, such as for healing, celebration, social protest, personal transformation, spiritual growth, exploration of the subconscious, and sheer play. In many of the world's non-Western cultures, the arts are connective and integrative. They do not readily fit into DBAE's four-part separation.

While DBAE was at first identified with the excellence in education movement, it developed in the midst of another powerful educational reform initiative—multiculturalism. The DBAE movement has been under pressure to incorporate multiculturalism and a global perspective, and it has made efforts to become more interdisciplinary, multiculturally child-centered, and issue-centered. Yet, by its incorporating multiculturalism, some DBAE proponents protest, saying that it has lost its main goal of helping students to understand and appreciate the meaning of works of art. And the debate continues about how to make DBAE more relevant to students' needs.

Art appreciation also is being fostered by the mass media. Television channels specializing in arts, history, and biography show wonderful programs on artists' lives and civilizations' artistic accomplishments. The Web can be used as an enormous resource for students' art research and reports. Yet, for students to benefit from these resources on TV and on the Internet, an adult's enthusiasm and guidance are usually necessary.

This textbook, *Emphasis Art,* has always strongly advocated the importance of serious, qualitative studio involvement. We believe that studio involvement—thinking and problem-solving in the media themselves—is primary and central in the elementary grades. The view of children as innate artists seeking expression, communication, and self-discovery, and having confidence in their own creativity and inventiveness, can be threatened by an overemphasis of academic study.

During the early years of this century, the "father of child art," Franz Cizek, taught that a child understands and enjoys art only to the extent that the child has acquired that understanding through personal efforts. Many art educators today believe that studio art is fundamental to the other disciplines, which are derivative. They believe that, in general education, studio art production represents the idea of the artist and that this concept should precede academic training in disciplines such as art history and criticism.

Thus, there continues to be a healthy professional debate on topics and emphases in art education. One conception for a sequential approach for aesthetic activities over the years is the following:

- In the early grades, the students should take *delight* in the aesthetic qualities of objects made by humans and in nature.
- In Grades 4 to 6, academic learning moves to the *perception* of artworks.
- In Grades 7 to 9, academic learning should center on the acquisition of *knowledge* of art history.

Below 10 years of age, production activities should always be central. This should be a time when children have hands-on involvement with the media. Especially during these early years, it is helpful to keep in mind Maria Montessori's dictum: do not give more to the mind than to the hand. When students are doing perceptual, critical, and historical activities, such activities should be closely related to, and, whenever possible, emerge from, the students' artwork.

GENERAL METHODS FOR ART DISCUSSIONS

The word *conversation* in Latin means change and exchange; *communication* means to share. Unfortunately, too often teachers tend to lecture rather than engage students in a conversational exchange. Your teaching methods will model for students ways to go about talking about art with their friends. These lessons can empower them for their lives, to enable them to feel comfortable going into art galleries, enjoying the artistic experience and sharing their responses with friends. The following classroom discussion strategies will be explained in the balance of this chapter:

- Questioning
- Arranging the room for discussions
- Leading discussions
- Focusing discussions
- Keeping discussions concise
- Relating to the students' conceptual stage
- Choosing topics that relate to children's developmental preferences
- Promoting confidence in thinking and talking about art

Questioning Questioning is a superb way to elicit students' input. Urge students to give reasons for their statements, ask them to disprove alternative explanations, and encourage them to generalize about their ideas. The interpretation of an artwork or thoughts about an aesthetic concept are, and always will be, issues that should be contested. One good way to promote discussion is by asking students "What's wrong with this picture?" This question demands that students put forth their criteria, which then can be debated or contested. Debating and contesting answers are central to the Socratic method of questioning, a method that has been acclaimed for 2500 years for its ability to give birth to ideas. Of course, avoid questions that get one-word answers, such as "This is an impressionistic painting, isn't it?" Instead, ask open questions, such as "Why do you think this might be considered an impressionistic painting?" Encourage the students to infer, generalize, analyze, and synthesize.

Arranging the Room for Art Discussions The environment—the climate for viewing the artwork—can help or hinder discussions. If possible, arrange the seating to provide each child with an up-front advantage. To see the reproduction up close, rearrange the chairs into a horseshoe shape, or seat the children on the floor. Urge the children to come up to the displayed art object and point out the area or detail they wish to discuss. A shy child can be asked to come up front to stand and hold the reproduction. A spotlight on the reproduction can focus students' attention. Avoid reproductions that are too small for class viewing; instead, these can be used for small group discussions.

Leading Discussions Skill in leading discussions is essential to get a whole class to contribute. Leading discussions can be difficult, especially in large classes and those containing students with behavioral problems. Some will want to monopolize the discussion, interrupting each other and talking over each other. Others will talk so quietly they cannot be heard and, by the softness and slowness of their speech, will invite interruptions. Check those verbose, verbally domineering students who, by monopolizing a discussion, prevent participation by quiet, shy students. Respond to, or even interrupt, a monopolizer by saying, "John is saying . . . and we'll discuss this aspect later, but now I'd like to know what some of the people who haven't yet shared their thoughts have been thinking about the idea of . . . (e.g., whether muscles need to be drawn to make a good figure drawing)." Make this a time not just to contemplate, but to interact dynamically with classmates and the art object.

Focusing Discussions A discussion can go awry if it is not kept clearly focused. Most children enjoy talking avidly about their experiences and reactions. There is no difficulty in getting them to express themselves

Courtesy of Barbara Thomas.

The teacher leads the class in an exciting discussion of the artwork. Notice how the teacher and the children are all seated on the rug, up close to see the art reproductions.

vocally about the art that you show to them; the main problem is to keep them on the subject, or "on track." If the discussion appears unfocused to the students, too wide-ranging to be helpful to their thinking and acting, they will tune it out. Use your leadership to keep the discussion on one central issue. For example, you might say, "Thanks, Juan, for bringing up this idea. It is a related idea, and an important one for us to discuss later, but for now let's see if we can put our minds to thinking about the issue of . . . ."

However, be sure to be open to the idea that curricula need not be imposed from above, but can arise spontaneously from the students. Avoid overdetermining the lesson. That students are allowed to take control of some situations builds their autonomy and feelings of empowerment.

Keeping Discussions Concise Another goal is to keep the discussion concise. Stimulate the raising of issues, but STOP the discussion before interest dissipates. Conciseness is important, because so little time is allowed for art in the school schedule. Some students in art classes think of art time as "a time when they get to make things" and resent other activities that seem to be tangential. Keep your art discussions from being boring. There are exceptional teachers, however, who can keep large audiences of students vitally engrossed for over an hour analyzing and talking about just one reproduction.

Relating to the Students' Conceptual Stage In motivating artistic expression, make sure that some of the historical artworks that you present are appropriate for the children's conceptual and developmental stage (see Chapters 15–19). This does not mean that only pictures of scribbles should be shown to scribblers; however, it does mean that artworks in a range that the child is comfortable with should be presented. In this way, you do not frighten the students into feeling inadequate, raising in their minds fears that their artwork will be woefully weak. Students should not feel that the teacher's expectations are unattainable. Using artworks that are visually and conceptually accessible can assist students in seeing alternative and attainable solutions that they can implement.

Artistic activity is a universal human attribute. Nothing in our society more effectively subverts and extinguishes artistic activity than the notion that the artistic product should be a copy of reality or someone else's version of reality. For this reason, often it is best to show historical examples as reinforcement *after* a student has reached a new conceptual and visual stage.

Choosing Topics That Relate to Children's Developmental Preferences When choosing reproductions and slides for study and appreciation, consider not just their representational ability, but also the natural preferences of the children. Paintings with realistic subject matter to which students can relate usually are more popular with upper-

Cat and Kittens, ca. 1872 (11 ¾- × 13 ¼-inches), anonymous, American. National Gallery of Art, Washington, D.C. Gift of Edgar William and Bernice Chrysler Garbisch.

Consider the children's natural preferences for picture study subjects. "What's wrong with this picture? Why is one kitten mad? In how many places do you see stripes? What does this picture tell us about what life was like over a century ago?"

Collection of Frank Wachowiak; photo by W. Robert Nix.

Young children are fond of representations of animals and their young. Pictures of a mother and child or animal with young can motivate children's creative writing about their family experiences with the birth of a sibling or a pet giving birth.

elementary children. Subject matter is the primary factor in young children's preferences, and there are strong differences between boys' and girls' preferences. Negative attitudes are expressed toward abstract works and those showing objects they do not like, such as still lifes of dead fish and birds. Young children prefer single subjects; older children can think in terms of more complex groups.

After subject matter, the next most important factor is color. Works that abound in color and contrast are appealing to primary-grade children; older children prefer tints and shades and subtle combinations. Middle-school students will respond to more complex art themes—to moody, muted colors and abstract, nonobjective compositions. Whereas showing just one or a few pictures is better for elementary students, a variety of examples usually will be more effective for middle-school students, because this multiple approach provides an opportunity to analyze contrasting styles and imagery.

Note that purposefully choosing nonpreferred artworks can evoke strong responses, which may lead to heated and stimulating discussions.

Promoting Confidence in Thinking and Talking About Art

Students should not be put on the defensive and made to feel that their verbalizations and artistic representations are incorrect. One goal of discussion is to give those students who have not yet grasped a concept—for example, realism—the "permission" to continue in their own intuitive way of artistic conceiving. ("How would you describe this 'different' quality that Marta's drawing has, and how did her depiction of the sun's personality help give that feeling?")

Avoid a "one right way" system. Discussion should be a bridge between thinking and acting. It should promote in the young artist a sense of integration and a feeling of self-worth as a thinking individual and as an artist. Bounce the discussion back and forth from "what we see" to "how we can make it." In this way, the discussion can reciprocally stimulate both intellectual thought and artistic creativity.

GAMELIKE EDUCATIONAL ACTIVITIES

While discussion is the major way to stimulate conversations about art learning, a second way is through gamelike educational activities. Although research shows games to be no more or less effective than traditional methods, students enjoy educational games as a change from the usual classroom routine. The game aspect should be easy, and students should first do a practice round. Games may require working together in small groups or pairs—a welcome relief from the usual routine of lecture, discussion, and individual seat-work routines. Students must understand the educational purposes behind the gamelike format, however, lest they feel they are wasting their time or "just playing." Following up with a short "debriefing session" discussion is critical in order that students understand what was the purpose of the game.

Most art games use printed reproductions. A principal source is postcards from art museums and galleries; sorting and matching of these can be done even on a small desktop. Also, the National Art Education Association has published a series of inexpensive art reproductions. Magazine-page-sized reproductions can be found in copies of many popular and art magazines, such as *Artnews* and *Art in America*. Museums and commercial firms specializing in art reproductions have large-size reproductions (approximately 20 × 30 inches) that may be purchased on stiff paper, stiff cardboard, or framed (see Appendix B).

Courtesy of Barbara Thomas.

Teacher-prepared educational materials such as "Art Bingo" and discussing solutions in small groups present these upper-elementary-grade students with a change of pace from the usual methods of learning about art.

Sets of art postcards can be used to meet art objectives in the following ways:

Art history: Two types of art history objectives are those requiring sorting and those requiring matching. Working in small groups, students sort the cards into chronological order, or match or group those of one art style, such as Impressionism.

Art history: Students match art critics' statements from the past to the art images shown on postcards. Some of the critics' statements may seem totally wrong, according to our judgments today.

Aesthetics and social purpose: Working in small groups, students decide on a single artwork they might theoretically acquire for the school. The underlying instructional objective is that the students will discuss the differences between artistic and societal values in selecting artworks.

Art criticism: Students identify and describe works by master artists.

Art criticism: Students describe the similarities and differences between artworks depicted and describe overall concepts that cards in a set have in common. Using cards that are sorted into prearranged sets, the learners describe why one of the cards does not belong in the set. This can lead into a discussion of categories, themes, and art elements.

Art criticism and social studies: Primary-grade children sort postcards into categories, such as those showing different emotions or those showing art from historical periods.

Art criticism and social studies: Students hypothesize about the artist's intent. As the students enter the room, the teacher gives each child a card with an artist's name on it. The student then must find the reproduction done by "his" or "her" artist and tell the class "why" the artist painted the picture.

Commercial sets of art reproductions are available for playing an artistic version of Old Maid; alternatively, sets can be made up by the teacher. The objective in playing is that students learn about an artist's personal style. ("Find all the Hokusais, the Romare Beardens, the pre-Columbian pieces, and the Georgia O'Keeffes.") Because such games can be played by students in pairs, they provide an easy change of activity in self-contained classrooms. Likewise, they promote friendships, provide activities for students who have self-directed time, and can be used in classroom learning activity centers.

In both discussions and games, keep in mind the level of the instructional objective. Is mere identification the desired goal? Always try to set some tasks in the upper levels of thinking, such as analysis and evaluation. For example, a higher level of objective—synthesis—can be attained by

IN THE CLASSROOM

Integrating Art Appreciation

With the students working in small groups, use sets of art postcards for integration with other subjects. In creative writing, for example, groups of students can make up a story using all of the cards in one set. Individual students will tell or write the parts of the story represented in each reproduction. In mathematics, students can describe the geometric shapes shown in the art reproductions—for example, domed architecture, pentagon shapes in Islamic architecture, and sculptures containing icosahedra. (See Chapters 9 and 10 for social studies and science suggestions.)

asking your students "Can you explain in your own words what makes this artist's style special?"

This chapter has overviewed the history and issues of art appreciation, described general strategies for leading art discussions, and listed some gamelike activities that promote talking and learning about art. We proceed in the next two chapters to think about specific ways to teach art history, art criticism, and aesthetics.

FOR FURTHER READING

Alexander, Kay, and Michael Day, eds. 1991. *Discipline-Based Art Education: A Curriculum Sampler.* Los Angeles: Getty Center for Education in the Arts.

Amdur, D. 1993. "Art and Cultural Context, A Curriculum Integrating Discipline-Based Art Education with Other Humanities Subjects at the Secondary Level." *Art Education* 46(3): 12–19.

Barrett, Terry. 2003. "Interpreting Visual Culture." *Art Education* 56(2): 6–12.

Batain, Margaret. 1994. "Cases for Kids: Using Puzzles to Teach Aesthetics to Children." *Journal of Aesthetic Education* 28(3): 89–104.

Blandy, Doug. 1988. "A Multicultural Symposium on Appreciating and Understanding Art." *Art Education* 41: 20–24.

Broudy, Harry S. 1972. *Enlightened Cherishing: An Essay on Aesthetic Education.* Urbana: University of Illinois Press.

Clark, Gil, Michael Day, and Dwaine Greer. 1987. "Discipline-Based Art Education: Becoming Students of Art." *Journal of Aesthetic Education* 21(2): 130–193.

Private collection.

Talking about pictures can develop thinking about both art and life. The painting *Road to Eternity* is by America's most famous folk artist, Reverend Howard Finster. Why do you think he painted the mountains with sad expres-sions? Why do you think the artist put pyramids in the background? Is writing all over a picture okay for an artist to do? How can we put the ideas in which we believe into our art?

Clements, Robert D. 1975. "A Case for Art Education: The Influence of Froebel Training on Frank Lloyd Wright." *Art Education* 28(3): 2–7.

Delacruz, E. M., and P. C. Dunn. 1995. "DBAE: The Next Generation." *Art Education* 48(6): 46–53.

Dobbs, Stephen. 1992. *The DBAE Handbook: An Overview of Discipline-Based Art Education.* Los Angeles: Getty Trust.

Efland, Arthur. 1990. *A History of Art Education: Intellectual and Social Currents in Teaching the Visual Arts.* New York: Teachers College Press.

Ewens, Thomas. 1990. "Flawed Understandings: On Getty, Eisner, and DBAE." In London, *Beyond DBAE: The Case for Multiple Versions of Art Education.* North Dartmouth, MA: Southeastern Massachusetts University.

Hamblen, Karen. 1989. "An Elaboration on Meanings and Motives, Negative Aspects of DBAE." *Art Education* 42(4): 6–7.

London, Peter, Judith Burton, and Arlene Linderman, eds. 1990. *Beyond DBAE: The Case for Multiple Visions of Art Education.* North Dartmouth, MA: Southeastern Massachusetts University.

National Endowment for the Arts. 1988. "Overview, Toward Civilization." *NAEA News* 30(3): 3–7.

Wilson, B., and B. Rubin. 1997. "DBAE and Educational Change." *Visual Arts Research* 23(2): 89–97.

WEB RESOURCES

For art games from the Albright Knox Gallery:

  http://www.albrightknox.org/artgames/index.html

For art games:

  http://www.princetonol.com/groups/iad/lessons/high/artgames.htm

Chapter 21
Teaching Art History

*A*rt artifacts provide a record of how people of that time acted and what they valued. They define the reality within which the individuals of that period operated. Rather than passing on the "fossilized" processes of cognition, through your teaching emphasize how cognitive knowledge evolves. As discussed here, art history refers not only to the discussion of artworks by masters and ancient civilizations but also to the objects that cultures recognize as having value, such as films, posters, and designed objects. And at the local level, it encompasses art expression by artists of one's own time who live in one's community. Some examples of instructional objectives in art history are:

- Compare the way you have depicted something—perhaps the design of clothing or a vehicle—with the way that two other artists in history depicted it. Have you used or shown something that did not appear in artworks of past eras?
- Describe works from art history and the humanities with well-known themes. Has the portrayal of the theme changed over time, or has it remained the same? For example, tell about different versions of the Tarzan, Superman, mad scientist, werewolf, vampire, or brute themes. Discuss how women have been shown as Eve or Cinderella, as beautiful and innocent maidens, or as evil stepmothers or witches. Try to imagine the intensity of feeling and pervasive belief system of a culture that is different from your own.
- Describe how symbolism has been used in art. For example, why was the ruler usually shown seated astride his horse? What ideas does the theme of the dragon express?
- Describe how different artists have given different meanings to the same themes.
- Discuss how ethnic groups, such as Native Americans, for example, have been portrayed in art.

- Describe why you think one artwork style was replaced by a different style. Describe world events that may have contributed to such changes in artistic representation. How does the art of an age say something about its character?
- Describe changing and constant elements in an artist's work, and relate these to changing and constant elements in your own art style.

When children talk about art, they grow not only in vocabulary describing visual phenomena but also in verbal sophistication. Students are weaned from relying solely on their ordinary speech and are helped to form a new art language. Use the vocabulary appropriately. Expand students' vocabulary from their ordinary speech and help them to build a new art vocabulary. New words and phrases such as those in the following list become part of their expanding vocabulary:

Action painting	Earthworks	Magic realism
African classical art	Environmental art	Mobile
Art nouveau	Expressive	Naive art
Assemblage	Feminist art movement	Op art
Bauhaus	Folk art	Painter's style
Caricature	Formalist	Painterly
Chiarosuro	Gallery installation	Patron
Critic	Genre	Pop art
Critique	Happening	Postmodern art
Cubism	Impressionism	Social conditions
Dadaism	Instrumental	

Ben Shahn (1898–1969) © VAGA, NY. "Liberation," 1945. Tempera on cardboard, mounted on composition board, 29 ³/₄ × 40". James Thrall Soby Bequest. Museum of Modern Art, NY, U.S.A. Digital image copyrighted by The Museum of Modern Art/Licensed by SCALA/Art Resources, NY.

Ben Shahn's painting "Liberation" shows a way that art portrays societal issues of destruction and renewal. The devastated bombed buildings indicate the failure of politics, economics, and the other social sciences to prevent World War II. Yet the three ragged children swinging on a playground's whirling tower, miraculously still standing, suggest youth's indomitable creative energy and spirit of transformation. When Shahn was five years old, his father was imprisoned in Siberia by the Czarist Russians for "revolutionary activities." This resulted in the artist maintaining a lifelong belief in the intolerable injustice of authority.

INTEGRATING ART HISTORY AND SOCIAL STUDIES

Perhaps you have just visited a museum or a Web virtual museum; perhaps you just watched a television program about an artist and you want to share with the students your excitement about her work. This is a simple way to make art history material both interesting and relevant—to be interested in the material yourself. Your interest will be infectious. Teachers have found certain specific strategies to be useful for adding interest, and we discuss several of these strategies below.

Presentations on an Artist's Life One teaching method, especially suitable for middle-school students who are beginning to look for adult role models, is to have students select an artist to research and role-play. The ability to imagine oneself out of the present and into the past or into another culture is an important aspect of understanding art history. Pretending to be the artist, and perhaps dressing up like the artist, the student tells the class the artist's life story. Then, the class questions the actor: What was the artist's personality like? What was the culture like? Where did the artist live? How did people of the time treat the artist? What was the artist's intention in making the art? These presentations can be videotaped and shared with other classes or at a PTO open house. Another teaching approach can be an interview show of a small group of these artist-actors at a supposed exhibition opening or panel discussion. One student acts as the emcee and interviews the participants; other students role-play critics and critique the artists' works.

Quizzes In a review of art history facts, interest can be spurred through a competitive game. Divide the class into two teams and ask cognitive questions of each team, for example, the name of the artist, the style of the

Top: An attractive display, along with three-dimensional objects suggestive of Native-American culture, is made of students' paintings seeking to emulate the empathy with which George Catlin captured the Native-Americans in their raiment. **Bottom:** Grant Wood's *American Gothic* was reinterpreted by Virginia Simms as a beach scene, complete with fun-loving youngsters, volleyball, Frisbee, sailing, and surfing paraphernalia.

artwork, or the century in which it was created. The team that gets the answer correct first then has its captain put an X or an O on a large tic-tac-toe game board drawn on the chalkboard.

Correlating Art History, Social Studies, and Studio Projects

Art making and criticism, art history, and aesthetics are most successful and most meaningful when they complement each other in an orchestrated, coordinated endeavor. Children's intense, purposeful studio involvement should be related to richly planned art motivations that include historical knowledge and art history examples. In this way, their critical faculties in knowing, appreciating, and creating art are synergistically enhanced.

Teachers have added to children's insights regarding African and Native-American art motifs through studio projects in mask-making. Others have coordinated the study of Egyptian tomb friezes with the making of group murals. Every phase of world art through the centuries can be given immediacy in an art studio environment, from the mosaics of Ravenna in Italy, to the Tang ceramics of China, the illuminated manuscripts of medieval Europe, the Benin bronzes from Africa, the marble sculptures from Greece, the ukiyo-e woodblock prints of Japan, or the wood sculptures of Louise Nevelson. Many teachers have imaginatively combined studio and art history to provide children with a growing treasury of knowledge about art, artists, art styles, and the permeating influence of art in our everyday lives.

It is best if the teacher has access to color reproductions, filmstrips, and color slides. If this is not possible, most public libraries have folio-size "coffee table" art books that contain pictures large enough to show to groups; note that large books are not shelved on the regular shelves, but rather on the "F oversized books" shelves. Sets of large reproductions can be ordered through the school librarian for use by the entire faculty. A few commercial sources of art visual aids are listed in Appendix B; the Web provides thousands more. Furthermore, most resourceful teachers have collected and organized their own extensive picture and color-slide files. The following table lists some familiar art-education studio projects, along with the names of a few artists whose works might serve as exemplars.

Suggested Art Project	Correlative Art Appreciation
Drawing-painting/ Helping at home or school	Genre paintings of Benny Andres, Thomas Hart Benton, Jean Chardin, Carmen Lomas Garza, Winslow Homer, Jacob Lawrence, Grandma Moses, Horace Pippin, Norman Rockwell, Lily Martin Spencer, Susanne Valadon, Jan Vermeer, Laura Wheeler Waring, Grant Wood, and Andrew Wyeth

4th grade

Matisse..the Master

Courtesy of Joyce Vroon.

Matisse display and related fourth-grade marker drawings that incorporate Matisse's lessons.

Suggested Art Project	Correlative Art Appreciation
Portraits and self-portraits	Portraits by Luis Cruz Azaceta, Mary Cassatt, Chuck Close, Domenico Ghirlandaio, Hans Holbein, Leon Golub, Amos Ferguson, Lois Mailou Jones, Margo Machida, Alice Neel, Nick Quijan, Sepik River/New Guinea shaman masks, John Valadez, Elizabeth Vigee-Lebrun, Leonardo da Vinci, Andy Warhol, Hale Woodruff, and Andrew Wyeth. Self-portraits by Max Beckman, Paul Gauguin, Frida Kahlo, Rembrandt van Rijn, Masani Teraoka, and Vincent van Gogh
Objects on a table, chair, or bench	Still lifes by Georges Braque, Bernard Buffet, Paul Cézanne, Jean Chardin, Janet Fish, Audrey Flack, Juan Gris, William Harnett, Margaret Angelica Peale, Pablo Picasso, and Odilon Redon
The landscape or cityscape	Pieter Breughel, Roger Brown, Paul Cézanne, John Constable, Raoul Dufy, Robert Duncanson, Richard Estes, Paul Gauguin, Vincent van Gogh, Edward Hopper, George Inness, Dong Kingman, Kerry James Marshall, Gabrielle Münter, John Marin, Georgia O'Keeffe, Mattie Lou O'Kelley, Maurice Utrillo, and Grant Wood

Suggested Art Project	Correlative Art Appreciation
Fauna	John James Audubon, Bambara Chiwara antelope figures, Rosa Bonheur, Cave paintings at Lascaux and Altamira, Chinese and Japanese animal drawings, Albrecht Dürer, Jean Louis Gericault, Franz Marc, Indian Moghul, Rembrandt van Rijn, Henri Rousseau, and Nellie Mae Rowe
Flora	Rudy Fernandez, Roberto Juarez, Patricia Gonzales, Maria Sibylle Merian, Lowell Nesbit, Georgia O'Keeffe, and Leonardo da Vinci
Figure composition	Benny Andrews, Paula Modersohn-Becker, George Bellows, Rolando Briseño, Pieter Brueghel, Mary Cassatt, Robert Colescott, Edgar Degas, Paul Gauguin, Francisco Goya, Gronk, Robert Gwathmey, Keith Haring, Joseph Hirsch, Clementine Hunter, Angelica Kauffman, Käthe Kollwitz, Marie Laurencin, Jacob Lawrence, Henri Matisse, Edvard Munch, Alice Neal, Juane Quick-to See-Smith, Bill Taylor, John Valadez, Diego Velasquez, and Elizabeth Vigee-Lebrun

Courtesy of Joyce Vroon.

A study of Georgia O'Keeffe's floral paintings with their dramatic value patterns and abstraction preceded the students' making these cut tissue-paper floral close-ups in many tints and shades.

Courtesy of Mary Lazzari.

Students will never forget Leonardo da Vinci's Mona Lisa painting after making this gigantic and imaginative scaled-up enlargement to grace their school gymnasium.

Suggested Art Project	Correlative Art Appreciation
The abstract, the nonobjective, the surreal, op, pop, and fantasy	Joseph Albers, Hieronymous Bosch, Marc Chagall, Georgio de Chirico, Salvador Dali, Sonia Terk-Delaunay, Arthur G. Dove, M. C. Escher, Minnie Evans, Helen Frankenthaler, Paul Jenkins, Frieda Kahlo, Wassily Kandinsky, George Longfish, Rene Magritte, Joan Miró, Piet Mondrian, Georgia O'Keeffe, Jackson Pollock, Martin Ramirez, Ad Reinhart, Bridget Riley, Tim Rollins and Kids of Survival, Mark Rothko, Frank Stella, Sophie Taueber-Arp, Mark Tobey, and Victor Vasarely

Suggested Art Project	Correlative Art Appreciation
Printmaking: collograph, plastic meat-tray print, linoleum block, glue-line-relief print, monoprint	Albrecht Dürer, Leonard Baskin, William Blake, Mauricio Lasansky, Robert Colescott, William Hayter, Gabor Peterdi, Japanese ukiyo-e artists, Ando Hiroshige, Katsushika Hokusai, Rembrandt van Rijn, and Kitagawa Utamaro
Mask design and construction	African ritual masks; masks of Northern Pacific Indians; masks from Melanesia, Malaysia, Mexico, Indonesia; Japanese Noh play and Bugaku masks; Chinese opera, Greek drama, and Mardi Gras masks
Photographs	Ansel Adams, Tomie Arai, Margaret Bourke-White, Matthew Brady, David Hockney, Dorothea Lange, Sherry Levine, Yong Soon Min, Eadweard Muybridge, Gordon Parks, Adrian Piper, Cindy Sherman, Sandy Skoglund, and Edward Weston
Three-dimensional construction, earthworks, and use of found materials	Alice Aycock, Joseph Beuys, Lee Bontecou, Beverly Buchanan, Alexander Calder, Christo Bessie Harvey, David Hammons, Nancy Holt, Louise Nevelson, Judy Pfaff, Pablo Picasso, David Smith, and Robert Smithson
Abstract sculpture in plastic block, soapstone, firebrick, balsa wood	Jean Arp, Constantin Brancusi, Easter Island sculpture, Greek Cycladic figures, Judy Chicago, Nancy Graves, Barbara Hepworth, Henry Moore, Juan Bautista Moroles, Isamu Noguchi, Northern Pacific Indian totem poles, and Martin Puryear
Figurative sculpture	Magdalena Abakanowicz, John Ahearn, Fernando Botero, Doug Hyde, Iraqi Abu Temple sculptures, Luis Jimenez, Edward Kienholz, "King Mycerinus and Queen Chamernebty," Marisol Escobar, Michael Naranjo, Polykleitos, Alison Saar, George Segal, Rigoberto Torres, Manuel Neri, and "Winged Victory of Samothrace"
Collage and text	Luis Cruz Azaceta, Jean–Michel Basquiat, Georges Braque, Romare Bearden, Epoxy Art Group, Richard Hamilton, Edgar Heap-of-Birds, Jenny Holzer, Mary Kelly, Barbara Kruger, Henri Matisse, Catalina Parra, Howardena Pindell, Richard Prince, Robert Raushenberg, Kurt Schwitters, and Alexis Smith
Clay pots and containers	Korean Koryo period, ancient Greek vases and jars, Chinese Ming, Pueblo and pre-Columbia pottery, Japanese Jomon ceramics, Thai Sukothai period, Lydia Buzio, Peter Voulkos, and Shoji Hamada
Clay figure modeling	Clay figures of Greek Tanagra style; Japanese Haniwa period; Chinese Tang period; Hohokan pottery of Arizona; Mexican, Peruvian, and Guatemalan pre-Columbian ceramic sculpture

Students might sort art reproductions into chronological order or match those of similar cultures and describe similarities and differences among them. *Left:* Ashura, Buddhist deity, eighth century, dry lacquer, Kofukuji Temple, Nara, Japan. *Right:* The Calfbearer, ca. 560 B.C., Greek, stone.

FOR FURTHER READING

Clahassey, Patricia. 1986. "Modernism, Post Modernism, and Art Education." *Art Education* 39(2): 44–48.

Collins, Georgia, and Rene Sandell. 1984. *Women, Art, and Education.* Reston, VA: NAEA.

Corwin, Sylvia, and Ruth Perlin. 1995. "A Videodisc Resource for Interdisciplinary Learning: American Art from the National Gallery of Art." *Art Education* 48(3): 17–24.

Erickson, Mary. 1995. "A Sequence of Developing Art Historical Understandings: Merging Teaching, Service, Research, and Curriculum Development." *Art Education* 48(6): 23–24, 33–37.

Fitzpatrick, Virginia. 1992. *Art History: A Contextual Inquiry Course.* Reston, VA: NAEA.

Smith, Ralph A., ed. 1986. *Excellence in Art Education.* Reston, VA: NAEA.

WEB RESOURCES

For an excellent timeline of art history, along with clickable artist multimedia info, by the Baltimore Museum of Art:

http://www.brigantine.atlnet.org/GigapaletteGALLERT/websites/ARTiculationFinal/MainPages/Timeline.htm

For information on artists, search for their names on the Web, for example:

http://www.matisse-picasso.com.

For Cindy Sherman:

http://www.artcyclopedia.com/artists/sherman_cindy.html

For quotations by artists:

http://www.princetonol.com/groups/iad/lessons/middle/quotes.htm

For brief definitions of art terms:

http://www.artlex.com/

especially see "isms" and "postmodernism."

For a good beginning page to find artists' biographies:

http://www.biography.com/search/index.jsp

http://www.artcyclopedia.com/

For an ancient Egyptian lesson on canopic jars and other projects:

http://grove.ufl.edu/~rolandc/arted.html

For a compilation of art history material on the Internet useful for schools:

http://www.princetonol.com/groups/iad/lessons/middle/artnet.htm

For a history of art education by decades:

http://www.personal.psu.edu/faculty/m/a/mas53/timelint.html

For art games to teach art history:

http://www.princetonol.com/groups/iad/lessons/high/artgames.htm

For 700 women artists:

www.uwrf.edu/history/women.html

For a student-made website on art styles:

http://library.thinkquest.org/J001159/artstyle.htm

Chapter 22
Teaching Art Criticism and Aesthetics

*I*n the last two chapters, we have discussed art appreciation, a general topic, and art history, a specific topic. Now we will turn to two other ways of building students' artistic awareness: art criticism and aesthetics.

DISCUSSING ART CRITICISM

In art criticism, a major goal is the students' ability to point to evidence in the work to support their interpretations. During the primary grades, encourage the children to ask questions about visual phenomena, list special eye-catching items in the picture, and decide what they like. During the upper grades, have students discuss criteria for judgment (realism and accepted methods for representation) and determine categories of works. Have them hypothesize about how else a picture might have been made or what alternate messages it might have conveyed. Encourage them to bring out questions about social significance.

A highly condensed summary of the sequence of children's development from Grades 1 to 8 is:

Personal preference → Realism → Expressive aspects

While visits to art galleries and museums are ideal, it is usually necessary to bring the art to the students. If possible, use original art; if not, use colorful reproductions, color slides, and book illustrations.

The purpose of art criticism in schools is to develop students' appreciation and understanding of how visual culture reflects the larger culture. This purpose should not be confused with art criticism as it might occur in a college studio-art course, where the professor's objective is to judge and improve the students' artwork. Another helpful distinction for students to be aware of is the difference between portrayal criticism and persuasive criticism. Portrayal criticism helps the viewer to slow down and see what

the work includes. It suggests there is no one "right way" to see an artwork. In contrast, persuasive criticism (like some newspaper reviews) is judgmental and argues the worth of the work.

Three approaches to art criticism and aesthetics used in schools are art elements, themes, and cultures. An example of an art-element approach is exploring how color is used by various artists. An example of a theme approach is looking at artworks showing food-gathering from several times and places. An example of a cultural approach is studying the art of a particular culture or group, such as Inuit art. Much African, Asian, and Native-American art reflects different cultural values about making and responding to art, often nonacademic and unlike European tradition. You have an opportunity to redress the neglect that non-Western cultures have received. Your willingness to help students look at their own and each other's cultures is very important. Local artists and craftspeople can be invited to visit classes, demonstrate skills, and answer children's questions about what it is like to be an artist.

AN APPROACH TO ART CRITICISM

Students should search for answers in a scholarly way, through inquiry. Inquiry is a skill that will serve students throughout their lives, in many ways. In art inquiry, neither teacher nor student may know precise answers. But even if the teacher knows little about a work—who made it, its medium, or when or where it was made—learning can occur as long as an attitude of inquiry prevails. When students and teacher apply their minds as if solving a mystery, successful learning will occur. Any strategy will work so long as the student is motivated to persist long enough to get beneath the surface. Use the format that seems most compatible, following your inner directive. Let the students engage in activities that increase receptiveness,

Cirque, plate II, Jazz, 1947 (color stencil in gouache), Henri Matisse (1864–1954). National Gallery of Art, Washington DC. Gift of Mr. and Mrs. Andrew S. Keck.

Wheelchair-bound for the last 13 years of his life, the French artist Henri Matisse was unable to paint and was prepared for his death. Instead, he returned to making paper cutouts, a technique he had used decades earlier for stage decorations, and created some of the world's most life-affirming art work. What do you see in this picture? How did the artist arrange colors and shapes to make a beautiful design?

using, for example, initial impressions, fantasy role-playing, and copying poses to increase openness. (See psychomotor activities in Chapter 6.)

Art criticism usually occurs in an open, free-form manner. However, four questions can serve as beginning points for an open discussion.

- What is it?
- What does it mean?
- What is its value?
- What does it do?

Courtesy of Beverly Barksdale Mallon.

Courtesy of Frank Wachowiak and Mary E. Swanson.

Emulating the style of a famous artist is one way to teach an appreciation of that artist's achievement. Following a study of Matisse's *Swimmers,* fourth-grade students drew their figures on the white, nonsticky backside of self-adhesive letter scraps donated by a sign company. They then pulled off the paper backing and adhered the figures to their collages. Three periods.

In contrast to this relatively open approach, some teachers prefer to study an artwork's features in a more or less sequential way, like the following:

1. Identifying the content or subject matter of the art. *What do you see in this picture?*
2. Recognizing the technique or art medium. *What art materials did the artist use and how were they used?*

IN THE CLASSROOM

An "Observing" Game

Have one student facing the class describe an art reproduction that is turned away from the class so that the rest of the class cannot see it. As the student describes the work as thoroughly as possible, have the other students close their eyes and imagine what the art looks like, or even ask them to draw what they "see." Then, turn the artwork around toward the class. Students, who have often envisioned something completely different, will be amazed. A variation of this exercise is to use well-known artworks; when students in the class think they know which picture it is, they raise their hands.

Having studied Matisse's cutouts, students can use cutouts in collage to gain an awareness of the power of positive and negative shape. The abstractness of the collage medium makes it an excellent choice for an emotional theme.

3. Identifying the compositional or design factors in the art and recognizing their importance. *How did the artist tie the picture together?*
4. Recognizing the unique, individual style of the artist. *Why do we think this other picture might be by the same artist?*
5. Searching for the meaning of the art and thinking about the artist's intent. *What does the picture seem to be saying?*
6. Learning about the context. *What do you think might have been going on in the world at this time? How does that show up in this picture?*

Let's look at this sequence in more detail.

Identifying the Content or Subject Matter of the Art Often this approach comes first and sets the stage for understanding a work of art. What does the viewer see: a woman, child, dog, house, tree, vase of flowers? What event is being depicted: a wedding, riot, sports event, fair, family reunion, rite of passage? Enthusiastic student participation usually develops when the subject matter is real or recognizable. Ask your students to look beneath the surface to discover details. Try to complete a careful inventory of what is perceived before going on to interpretation.

While looking at a large art reproduction or projected slide, each student (either in the class as a whole, or half-class competing teams, or working in small groups) can take a turn naming something he or she sees in the artwork that no one else has brought up. In this exercise in perception and memory, the students should describe what they see as extensively as they can. The teacher can list on the chalkboard what students have seen.

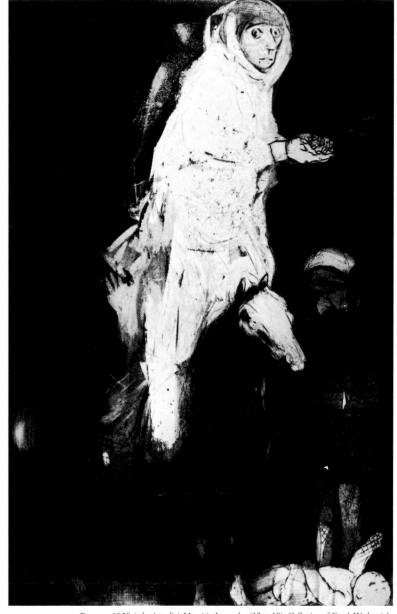

Espana, 1959 (color intaglio) Mauricio Lasansky (32 × 19). Collection of Frank Wachowiak.

A good way to begin thinking about a picture is to have students first describe what they see in it. Seated on a tiny white-faced horse is a large human figure, hands anxiously cupped together, eyes open very wide, and lips tightly drawn. It wears an unusual white costume. Also seen is an adjacent figure, probably a woman, in a skirt and with a scarf on her head, with head in hands and perhaps weeping. At their feet is a 1-year-old baby, with two upraised hands, lying on the ground.

Recognizing the Technique or Art Medium This approach to art criticism can give insight into how something is represented. For example, an outdoor watercolor implies an impression of nature made rapidly before the light changes; a large piece of public art suggests working with a committee of community representatives to arrive at something that resonates with the community's history or culture. Studio involvement by children with the media, techniques, and artist's materials helps them to appreciate the artist's solutions.

Identifying the Formalist Compositional or Design Features in the Art and Recognizing Their Importance This approach is one of the most enlightening. Detect the basic line structure, the main thrust, the avenues into the composition, and the dominant and subordinate themes. Find the rhythms, balances, and contrasts of line, shape, value, color, pattern, and texture, and pinpoint those that unify the picture. Developing these skills can make for a fascinating game of search and discovery.

Recognizing the Unique, Individual Style of the Artist When students, guided by a knowledgeable and imaginative teacher, achieve the critical and perceptual skills to identify an artist's individual style, they are on their way to a richer understanding and enjoyment of art's treasures. How inspiring that each of us is so unique that our uniqueness is evident in our art!

Searching for the Meaning of the Art and Thinking About the Artist's Intent This approach is at the heart of art criticism. A teacher can easily influence and/or convince the students with his or her own judgments and prejudices about an artwork's meaning. Yet if students merely parrot the teacher's views of art, they may not be able to relate the artwork to their own lives. Avoid telling the students what you see in the art and what you feel about it until they have had a chance to tell you what they see and feel. Children will spontaneously put forth their explanations of the artwork's meaning. While you may not agree with their analysis and judgment, do not force your opinions on them. The meaning that a student finds may not be the artist's intent, but that does not invalidate the student's interpretive process. Provoke curiosity by pointing up a problem or conflict. "If that is the interpretation, then why do you suppose that this other thing is shown in this seemingly conflicting way?" Using a leading question such as this forces the child to defend and rethink his or her theories.

As in the inductive method of science, let the students come up with hypotheses based upon the evidence they have assembled. Hypothesizing requires a high tolerance for ambiguity. It is rooted in curiosity and from this comes the search for meaning and inferences. It requires both the courage to think independently and the ability to think metaphorically and hypothetically. Interpretations are not so much right as more or less reasonable, informative, inclusive, and coherent. Older students can conjecture about the metaphoric meanings in objects and how these meanings add to the artwork's interpretation. Rather than staying strictly within the confines of description, analysis, and then interpretation, you can mix these steps in with interpretive analysis.

Good interpretations tell more about the artwork than about the viewer. Although we must use our feelings as guides, we must realize that the feelings depicted in the artwork are most likely different from our own. We must be receptive to our personal feelings, yet willing to set them aside to "hear" what the artwork is saying.

Allow the artists, craftspeople, and architects to speak for themselves through their art and their journals. For example, in a critique of the work of Vincent van Gogh, introduce the letters the artist wrote to his brother Theo. Help the students gain a deeper understanding of how van Gogh's painting related to his creative highs and his frustrating, disappointing lows. Artworks—not the artist's life situation—are the object of interpretation. However, such biographical information can provide insight into the work by revealing the sociocultural milieu in which the artwork developed. The general classroom teacher, who is charged with teaching interpretive writing, creative writing, and expressive writing, can have students write about artworks using metaphoric, expressive writing.

Learning About the Context This is an essential step in understanding an artwork. In examining the historical and social context of an artwork, students transfer learning from one discipline to another, from social studies to art. What was the artwork's function? What cultural concerns did it address? Was it made to signify status, territory, or kinship; to protect from natural disaster; to promote commerce, health, healing, or religion? What belief systems and economic forces were dominant in the world at that time? What was the social, religious, and economic nature of the artist's personal world? Students should learn that their perceptions and values, formed in their own culture, will likely differ from those held by people of other civilizations. The teacher can supply significant information, or, at this point, students might use materials either in an art-learning center, in the library, or—if older students—on the Web.

A new emphasis on cultural relevance and an openness to many different interpretations have come about in recent years, in part through developments in feminist art criticism and postmodern contemporary theories of art. This is in contrast to the past, when most art in the schools was presented in an apolitical manner. Conflict was minimized, and often historical-cultural value systems were ignored. Through today's art criticism, which emphasizes social-critical consciousness, students learn to deal rationally and fair-mindedly with conflicting points of view. They learn to support their opinions using facts, details, and information. Criticizing artworks requires the ability to identify problems, to examine and appreciate multiple perspectives, to take risks, and to develop the inner motivation to want to understand.

TWO PERSPECTIVES ON ART CRITICISM: FORMALISM AND CONTEXTUALISM

You may know or have sensed that there are two differing and often contradictory perspectives on art and art criticism: Should the study of art be primarily about *art,* or primarily about *society*? The first perspective leans more toward studio activities; the second focuses more on intellectual understanding and meaning. These perspectives are referred to as Formalism and Contextualism.

Formalists emphasize the elements and principles of art, the manipulation of materials, handsome well-crafted objects, and originality. Individual creativity leads to idiosyncratic works that people may have a hard time understanding. To Formalists, art *is* its form: how it looks, the materials it uses, and the skills used to make it. In short, a Formalist believes that art criticism should focus on the art itself.

Contextualists, on the other hand, believe that art is a social communication system. An artwork's meaning is determined in the context in which it is made. Its goal is not "art is nice," but rather "art is necessary for society." Contextualism fragments into a number of more extreme approaches to understanding art:

- *Instrumentalism* suggests that art is never for its own sake—that art should always bring to mind some external purpose, some thought or action beyond itself that is useful for improving society.

Courtesy of Mary Lazzari.

Formalist concerns about colors and shapes and textures make up this abstract design.

Left: *Petr Ginz (1928–1944), Moon Landscape, 1942–1944. Pencil on paper. Gift of Otto Ginz, Haifa. Collection of the Yad Vashem Art Museum, Jerusalem.*
Middle and right: *Courtesy of ICCA, Milner Library, Illinois State University.*

Children can address the contextual topics such as grief over a senseless death. **Left:** This 1944 drawing by fourteen-year-old Petr Ginz of a dangerous earth seen from the safe distance of the moon seems to express metaphorically the Jewish boy's yearning to leave the Terezin, Czechoslovakia, concentration camp where he was imprisoned. With thousands of other children from Terezin, Petr eventually died at Auschwitz. **Middle:** This contextual painting shows a youth enlisted into his nation's military forces and makes one think of the many challenges he faces. **Right:** The family's anguish over a death is communicated powerfully in this relief print.

- *Deconstructionism* often focuses on what the artwork suggests about the problematic social issues in a culture, such as its treatment of women and minority groups.
- *Reconstructivism* urges that the action suggested by an artwork should somehow change the existing social system.

Which approach is better in helping students understand art? As in many fields, bringing out both perspectives may allow your students a wider range of learning and appreciation. Neither a purely Formalist aesthetic approach with its emphasis on elements, principles, along with media exploration, nor a Contextualist approach with its emphasis on a socially relevant subject matter makes a complete, comprehensive art program. The two are not mutually exclusive concepts. Most art can be considered from both perspectives, although individual artworks may lend themselves more easily to one or the other, as do some artforms—for example, the design of Persian rugs vs. political posters. Fifty years ago, when abstract art was in its heyday, art in America emphasized Formalism. Today, in a society concerned with reshaping itself, the elements and principles of Formalism may seem less relevant when discussing many forms of contemporary Contextual art, such as conceptual art, feminist art, cooperative art, site art, and performance art.

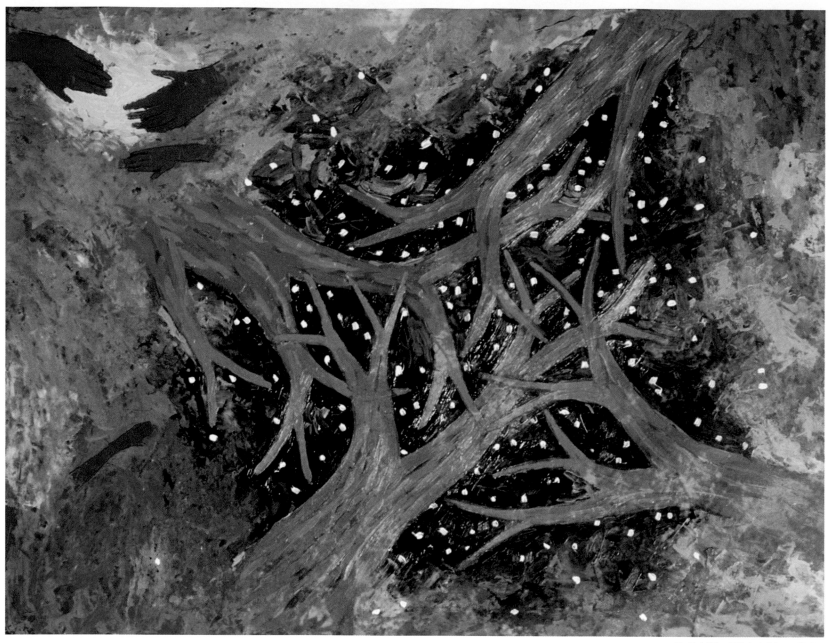

Untitled (36 × 24 inches). Private collection.

Wonder comes into one's mind contemplating the tornado-tossed trees against a starry night. Also, what could be the meaning of the red hands against a sun? This painting is by New York neo-Expressionist painter Louisa Chase.

DISCUSSING AESTHETICS: THE ROLE OF WONDER

In Discipline-Based Art Education, which forms the basis of this book, the four ways of learning about art are studio experience, art history, art criticism, and aesthetics. As teachers, we want our students to *think about* what makes objects and phenomena artistic; this is what constitutes aesthetics. Children love to ask "why" questions, which are central to aesthetics. The most important teaching strategy in leading discussions of aesthetics is to encourage students' questioning. Essential to success is the ability to admit there are things that we do not know. Most importantly, teachers must believe that students can gain something through being encouraged to question and to wonder about art ideas. Thomas Ewens (1990) said:

> Wonder is something which comes upon us, overwhelms us and suggests a kind of transcendence, out of the ordinary, the wonder-full, the extra-ordinary. It is a combination of the intellectual, the emotional, and the sensuous. It is the not-taken-for-granted. Our task is to protect the wonder of the young. The disciplines of thinking and artmaking grow out of and are nourished by this soil. Their roots are in wonder.

Teachers may want their students to be able to attain the following "wonder-full" goals, goals applicable both to aesthetics and to general education:

- Speculate
- See implications
- Handle abstract ideas
- Use language for clear thinking (about art)
- Raise questions and make statements (about aesthetics)
- Support their positions with reasons
- Listen to others' points of view, and ask questions about the other students' ideas

Furthermore, aesthetics is not just about knowing and thinking; it also is about feelings. Some objectives concerned with feelings, or affect, are that the students will be able to tolerate uncertainty, value questioning, be curious, and respect thoughtful disagreement.

Aesthetics in Ordinary Discourse Because aesthetics is so much a part of ordinary conversation, it can easily go unnoticed. Listen for questions and comments such as "Why is that weird thing supposed to be art?" and "Ugh, gross." Naturally occurring instances of art criticism need to be encouraged so that they can be transformed into significant discussions of aesthetics. On hearing students ask such questions and make such responses, we must learn to bite our tongues. We must not immediately answer, "Because the paint is so wonderfully thick, because it shows deep emotion, because it's in the Museum." Instead, ask questions back to the students. Let your interest in their comments guide the students to think more deeply.

Say to them, "What makes you say that?" "Does everyone agree?" Model for the students the use of strategies in good reasoning. Help them to learn how to think logically about their statements. Logical extension is one way: "If that is true, then how can [cave art] be explained?" Another way is through counterargument: "Is this always the case? Can anyone think of an instance when this isn't true?" The teacher's role is not to indoctrinate students with one "right" view or to inundate our students with information. This would defeat the purpose of aesthetic inquiry, its concern with contested issues. Our challenge is to promote critical thinking.

How to Start Discussions of Aesthetics Aesthetics and art criticism blend together, but a helpful distinction to keep in mind is that aesthetics focuses on the ideas behind the artwork and not on the artwork itself (which is the subject of art criticism). For starting aesthetic discussions and to use as reference, however, it is useful to have some art reproductions around the room or displayed over the chalkboard. Ask the students if any picture in particular has raised questions in their minds. The most obvious beginning is the open question, "What do you think about this picture?" Another good way to begin a discussion of aesthetics is by asking, "What's wrong with this picture?" because this presumes disputed ideas about right and wrong. Still another way of generating discussion is for students to select shocking or ugly art—anything out of the ordinary—and then to defend their selections. Have them examine boundary-breaking art, non-art, ugly art, anything that will skew normal expectations. Encourage students to defend their selections of whether a piece is artistic or not.

Topics and questions such as those in the following table can be brought up matter-of-factly when they arise as a part of an ongoing classroom discussion.

Topic	Aesthetic Question
Accident in design	Can a picture that looks like the artist just threw paint around be called good art?
Advertising art	Should art be used to make people want to buy things they do not really need?
Aesthetics	Are aesthetics frivolous and unmanly?
Anatomical accuracy	Is art better when figures depict muscles rather than sausage-looking arms? Are cave paintings with stick figures any good?
Architecture	Should design review boards and communities have the say-so in deciding whether a certain style of house or building can be built in a neighborhood, or should owners be allowed to do what they want? Can people go too far?

Topic	Aesthetic Question
Art's role in life	Is art work or play?
Artist's intention	If someone gets a different idea or meaning from your picture, does that mean that your art is not as good? Is it better if the person knows exactly what you wanted to say?
Artist's involvement	Can art be made by just calling up a factory and saying "make me a red metal cube 6 feet square"? Must the artist have hands-on involvement in making it?
Art critics	If experts say something is good or bad, must we accept this evaluation as our own?
Art institutions	Does putting something into a museum make it art? If an artwork is not in a museum, does that mean it is not art?
Art support by government	Should our government give money for art that some people think is bad?
Beauty	What is beautiful? What is not?
Clarity and metaphor	When you see an artwork and you cannot put into words exactly what the artist was saying, does that make it better or worse?
Commercial design	Can objects like bicycles, T-shirts, and fancy dress gowns be called art?
Design	Does our culture put too much emphasis on aesthetics, for instance, whether our clothes and hair and manner look cool?
Clothing design	Should people's choices in style of clothes be governed? Should kids in school have to obey dress codes and wear uniforms? Can people go too far in showing they have personal style?
Disabilities	If a person is color-blind and uses colors unrealistically, can the product still be called art—even though the person could not see it appropriately?
Economics	Are more expensive clothes and shoes more aesthetic? Because someone spends a lot of money for a piece of art, does that mean it is always good art? If no one spends any money for a piece of art, does that mean it is not art? How are economics and art related? Can richer people get "cooler stuff"?
Education	Are artists born or made? Does art that looks like little kids made it mean that it is not good art? Do people who go to school a long time usually make better art than people who do not go to school much?
Function	What good is art, after all? If art is used for bad purposes, is it still good art?

Topic	Aesthetic Question
Gender	Why aren't there more famous women artists? Why are women usually shown in art and movies as helpers and as just waiting around?
Government	Are certain things ugly and shouldn't be allowed, like having too many old cars around your house or leaving your garbage container out at the curb too many days?
Human art	Can monkeys make art?
Human endeavor	Why do people bother to make art when they could just relax and enjoy life instead of working so hard to make something that most people probably will not like much anyway?
Individual authorship	Is it really art if several people make it instead of just one person?
Judgment	Does an artwork mean whatever anyone says it means, or are there absolutely right and wrong answers?
Media	Should we trust our own aesthetic judgments for what is good, or should famous people and magazines and TV show us?
Mental and emotional functioning	Can people who have mental or emotional problems make good art even if it shows an upset world? Do people have to be sort of crazy to make art that has a special, weird quality?
Personal artistic style	Should each of us try to develop a personal style in our artwork, in our clothing, and how we talk and act?
Novelty	How important is novelty? If something is new and different, does that make it good? If it's copied, is it bad?
Quality and intent	Can you name some things that are bad art? What is the difference between things that are bad art and things that are not supposed to be art at all?
Realism	Can a piece of art still be called good art even if the objects in it are not drawn so that they look like they are in realistic three dimensions?
Realistic depiction of nature	Can a picture be good if the sky does not touch the ground?
Scale	Are buildings or pictures that are big usually better art than those that are little?
Source and object	Are real rainbows art? Are wasps' nests art?
Spontaneity	Are pictures that took a long time to make usually better than pictures that were done very fast?

Photo courtesy of Deborah Lackey.

Some questions in aesthetics can be "How important is originality to a work of art? Is it OK to copy somebody else's artwork? Is it valuable?"

Topic	Aesthetic Question
Technology	Can art made with machines be called art? If a camera or computer makes an artwork, can it be called art?
Text	Can art be just some words on a piece of paper, canvas, or a light–emitting screen? Why, or why not?
Time and effort	Can something that looks like someone just brought in a bunch of junk be called art?
Ugliness	Is art supposed to be only about beauty? Can it also be about ugliness?

Private collection.

Questions can be raised as to whether, in showing the figure, correct proportions and shading should be used to depict muscles. The direct expression of the African-American folk artist Mose Tolliver is shown here. His painting *Black Jesus* (20- × 12-inches) defies certain "expected" artistic conventions. Is realism always better? Is a balance between naiveté and realism desirable?

Remember that discussions of aesthetics can use students' everyday language—no special terminology is needed. It is the discussion itself that is central to the curriculum in an exemplary art classroom.

ART CRITICISM AND AESTHETICS AT HOME

Parents may be at a loss concerning what to do with their child's artwork when it is brought home. Some parents praise everything, while others feel compelled to criticize: "You're just like me—can't even draw a straight line!" A brief letter home to parents with the first artworks of the year can suggest ways for talking about those works. It can describe what will be taught in art history, art criticism, and aesthetics. This is a good way to connect the student's art production and art criticism abilities. Suggest ways to build confidence through displaying the works. Suggest ways that the child's art can serve as a vehicle for generating family dinner-table discussions and ways that the child's opinions about aesthetics issues can lead to the family's discussing such ideas. Let the parents know what your art-program goals are so that they can help to build their child's interest in art. Here is a sample letter:

Dear Parents and Guardians:

This letter is being sent home, along with one of your child's first art pieces done this year, to tell you something about our art program and to help you in talking with your child about the child's art learning.

This year we will be discussing what makes a good artwork. We will emphasize filling up the picture's space and capturing details. We will talk about whether looking real is the only thing that makes a picture good and how our friends and neighbors make art. In October, we will study mask making in many cultures. In January, we will study art history masterpieces, especially Egyptian art.

One way you can help to foster your child's interest is to talk with the child about his or her art. Just say "Tell me about your artwork." Also talk about artworks and sculptures you see together and interesting things you see in nature. I encourage you to post your child's art on the refrigerator door, refer to it from time to time, and help your child to talk about it when guests come. I also encourage you to visit museums with your child when possible, and to let your child participate in enrichment classes. Weekend art museum hours at the Quinlan Art Center (548–2314) are Saturdays, 9–3, and Sundays, 1–5, and it has Family Art Days on four Saturdays a year. The Recreation Department at Lyndon House Art Center (546–9968) has children's art classes on weekdays, 3:30–5.

Research shows that having a place for art materials at home and a quiet place in which to make art help children develop skills. Helping your child decorate his or her room with collections, artwork, and posters can also stimulate interest in art. If you have any artistic or cultural hobbies, I encourage you to involve your child (the inconvenience will prove to be time well spent!).

Photo courtesy of Frank Wachowiak.

Discussions of aesthetics might concern whether the medium that is used should look like itself or whether it should look like things. Can beauty in painting be created by using tools other than paint brushes? Is beauty always desired? What is beauty? If realism is not most important, what is? Here, James Herbert, a professor of painting at the University of Georgia, employs rubber-glove-encased hands to apply paint to his mural-sized canvas.

During the course of the year, we will be sending home about eight art projects, including a still life about nineteenth-century labor-saving devices, a group of figures in motion, a portrait of a classmate, a computer art design emphasizing quadrilateral symmetry, and a weaving related to mathematics. If you want to talk with me about your child's growth in art, or if you have access to human resources, art materials, or display facilities that could be used in our school art program, please call me between 2:00 and 4:00 or e-mail me (my contact information is below). I hope you'll be able to attend a PTO meeting (the last Wednesday of each month, 7:00 to 8:00 P.M.), where you will have the chance to see more of how our class's artwork contributes to their general education.

FOR FURTHER READING

Anderson, T., and S. McRorie. 1997. "A Role for Aesthetics in Centering the K–12 Art Curriculum." *Art Education* 50 (May): 6–13.

Anderson, Tom. 1988. "A Structure for Pedagogical Art Criticism." *Studies in Art Education* 30(1): 28–38.

Barrett, Terry. 1994. *Criticizing Art: Understanding the Contemporary.* Mountain View, CA: Mayfield Publishing Co.

Blandy, Doug, and Kristin Congdon (eds). 1991. *Pluralistic Approaches to Art Criticism.* Bowling Green, OH: Bowling Green University Press.

Clements, Robert D. 1979. "The Inductive Method of Teaching Visual Art Criticism." *Journal of Aesthetic Education* 13(3): 67–78.

Cromer, Jim. 1991. *History, Theory, and Practice of Art Criticism.* Reston, VA: NAEA.

DiBlasio, Margaret. 1987. "Reflections on the Theory of Discipline-Based Art Education." *Studies in Art Education* 28(4): 221–226.

Duncum, Paul. 2002. "Clarifying Visual Culture." *Art Education* 55(3): 6–11.

Eaton, Marcia. 1994. "Philosophical Aesthetics: A Way of Knowing and Its Limits." *Journal of Aesthetic Education* 28(3): 19–32.

Efland, A., P. Stuhr, and K. Freeman. 1996. *Postmodern Art Education; An Approach to Curriculum.* Reston, VA: NAEA.

Erickson, Mary. 1988. "Teaching Aesthetics K–12." In Steve Dobbs (ed.), *Research Readings for Discipline-Based Art Education.* Reston, VA: NAEA.

Feldman, Edmund. 1970. *Becoming Human through Art.* New York: Prentice Hall.

Freedman, Kerry. 1994. "Interpreting Gender and Visual Culture in Art Classrooms." *Studies in Art Education* 35(3): 157–170.

Freedman, Kerry. 2003. *Teaching Visual Culture.* Reston, VA: National Art Educational Association.

Funk, Farley, and Ron Neperud. 1988. *The Foundations of Aesthetics, Art, and Art Education.* Westport, CT: Greenwood.

Gardner, Howard, Ellen Winner, and M. Kirchner. 1975. "Children's Conceptions about the Arts." *Journal of Aesthetic Education* 9: 60–77.

Gates, Eugene. 1988. "The Female Voice." *Journal of Aesthetic Education* 22(4): 59–68.

Geahigan, George. 1983. "Art Criticism: An Analysis of the Concept." *Visual Arts Research* 9(1): 10–22.

Getty Center for Education in the Arts. 1986. *Beyond Creating: The Place for Art in America's Schools.* Los Angeles.

Getty Center for Education in the Arts. 1993. *Discipline-Based Art Education and Cultural Diversity.* Los Angeles.

Goldsmith, Lynn T., and David H. Feldman. 1988. "Aesthetic Judgment: Changes in People and Changes in Domains." *Journal of Aesthetic Education* 22(4): 83–93.

Goldstein, Ernest, Theodore Katz, Jo D. Kowalchuk, and Robert Saunders. 1986. *Understanding and Creating Art.* Dallas: Garrard.

Gude, Olivia. 2004. "Postmodern Principles: In Search of 21st Century Art Education." *Art Education* 57(1): 6–14.

Hamblen, Karen. 1984. "An Art Criticism Questioning Strategy within the Framework of Bloom's Taxonomy." *Studies in Art Education* 26(1): 41–50.

Hamblen, Karen, and Camille Galanes. 1991. "Instructional Options for Aesthetics: Exploring the Possibilities." *Art Education* 44: 12–25.

Hamblen, Karen. 1985. "Developing Aesthetic Literacy Through Contested Concepts." *Art Education* 38(5): 19–24.

Hamblen, Karen. 1986. "Exploring Contested Concepts for Aesthetic Literacy." *Journal of Aesthetic Education* 20(2): 67–76.

Hamblen, Karen. 1993. "The Emergence of Neo-DBAE." Paper presented at the American Educational Research Association Conference in Atlanta.

Haynes, Deborah. 1995. "Teaching Postmodernism." *Art Education* 48(5): 23–24, 45–50.

Henry, Carole. 1995. "Parallels between Student Responses to Works of Art and Existing Aesthetic Theory." *Studies in Art Education* 37(1): 47–54.

Hewett, G. C., and Jean C. Rush. "Finding Buried Treasures: Aesthetic Scanning with Children." *Art Education* 40(1): 41–43.

Holt, David. 1990. "Post Modernism vs. High Modernism: Relationship to D.B.A.E. and Its Critics." *Art Education* 43(2): 42–46.

Holt, David. 1995. "Postmodernism: Anomaly in Art-Critical Theory." *Journal of Aesthetic Education* 29(1): 85–94.

Kaelin, Eugene. 1990. "The Construction of a Syllabus for Aesthetics in Art Education." *Art Education* 43(2): 22–34.

Moore, Michael. 1995. "Towards a New Liberal Learning in Art." *Art Education* 48(6): 6–13.

Moore, Robert. 1995. *Aesthetics for Young People.* Reston, VA: National Art Education Association.

Parsons, M. J. 1987. *How We Understand Art: A Cognitive Development Account of Aesthetic Experience.* Cambridge, England: Cambridge University Press.

Parsons, Michael. 1994. "Can Children Do Aesthetics? A Developmental Account." *Journal of Aesthetic Education* 28(3): 33–46.

Prater, Michael. 2002. "Art Criticism: Modifying the Formalist Approach." *Art Education* 55(5): 12–17.

Russell, R. L. 1991. "Teaching Students to Inquire About Art Philosophically." *Studies in Art Education* 32(2): 94–104.

Schapiro, Meyer. 1953. "Style." In A. L. Kroeber (ed.), *Anthropology Today.* Chicago: University of Chicago Press, 81–113.

Tavin, Kevin M., and David Anderson. 2003. "Teaching Popular Visual Culture: Deconstructing Disney in the Elementary Classroom." *Art Education* 56(3): 21–33.

Vallance, Elizabeth. 1988. "Art Criticism as Subject Matter in Schools and Art Museums." *Journal of Aesthetic Education* 22(4): 69–82.

Zimmerman, Enid. 1990. "Issues Related to Teaching Art from a Feminist Point of View." *Visual Arts Research* 16(2): 1–9.

WEB RESOURCES

For questions related to one's art preference:

http://www.getty.edu/artsednet/resources/Viewpoints/three.html

For upper-elementary scope and sequence:

http://www.getty.edu/artsednet/resources/Scope/Developmental/level1.html

For a vocabulary helpful for art criticism:

http://www.artlex.com/

especially under "isms"

Part 6
Teaching Art Production

This sculpture, created in a casting center in southern Nigeria where the lost wax process of bronze casting was revived, was made in part to reinforce the idea of the power of the Benin Oba, or King—a power further amplified by the surrounding figures and their objects. Seen with the Oba are his two lieutenants (his secretary and his assistant with the spinal cone) and his children, and the maces, shields, clothing, and headdresses of authority. From around 1550 to 1650, the Kingdom of Benin was a major exporter of slaves and a feared military power. The beauty of the piece comes in part from its symmetry and repetition, as well as from its patterns of dots, zigzags, circles, and interlocked forms.

Cast bronze plaque, 1550–1650 A.D., Kingdom of Benin, Nigeria. The University Museum, University of Pennsylvania.
Photo Malcolm Varon, NYC © 1989, Malcolm Varon.

*M*ounting evidence, exemplified and corroborated by contemporary child-art creations such as those illustrated in this book, suggests that we have been underestimating children's capabilities. In many instances, we have not even begun to tap their true potential for "thinking" and "problem solving" through art media. The ensuing pages describe a host of art projects and techniques in both two and three dimensions that are recommended for a qualitative art program in elementary and middle schools.

These chapters should be most helpful to those classroom teachers who themselves may be untaught in the basic art disciplines of drawing, painting, printmaking, collage, and sculpture. The lessons described also will help art specialists who are searching for new dimensions and challenges in school art programming. Both the projects and their documentation resulted from many years of in-depth teaching by dedicated and knowledgeable instructors of both elementary- and middle-school art. This has entailed continuing motivational experimentation, media exploration, process and product evaluation, and research in qualitative art practices in schools around the world.

The art program should be planned at all levels for in-depth involvement and sequential growth. Although an in-depth method may not be as popular as a smorgasbord of quick, unrelated projects, in the long run it will produce greater gains as students come up with their own ideas and create art of the highest quality.

The following descriptions of art projects suggest topics and contexts for interdisciplinary learning, clarify complex art techniques, offer solutions for organizational and supply problems, and give evaluation criteria. These are not the only topics and methods, for as we all know, the best lessons, of course, are those that come from the teacher's heart and soul. Informed by the needs of the class, in combination with recommended art educational practices, your deep commitment results in the best lessons. However, the projects described in the following chapters have been found to be highly successful in situations typical of today's elementary and middle schools—in classrooms filled with eager, boisterous, fidgety, dreamy, energetic, inquisitive, and sometimes apathetic students.

Chapter 23

Drawing

*E*lementary-school children should draw every day. Drawing has been an important subject in American schools since 1870, when Massachusetts' first art superintendent, Walter Smith, led the state legislature to pass "An Act Relating to Free Instruction in Drawing; That the first section of Chapter 38 of the General Statutes be amended so as to include Drawing among the branches of learning which are by said section required to be taught in the public schools."

THREE KINDS OF DRAWING

A drawing curriculum should address not just one way of drawing but all three families of the world of visual art objects: depictions, patterns and designs, and maps and diagrams. This chapter will mainly address the first family, that is, realistic depictions that usually are thought of as "children's art"—the creation of drawings and paintings from nature and life.

Patterns and Design The second family—patterns and design—consists of creative play with abstract shapes and spacing. Because it doesn't try to represent figures or objects, this usually is thought of as design rather than drawing. But patterns and designs depicted in children's drawing and

Top row *by Samantha Libman,* second row *by Adam Levy,* third row *by Staci Gruen,* bottom left *by Jon Birnberg, and* bottom right *by Elizabeth Siegel. Courtesy of Baiba Kuntz.*

One design approach using shapes is this wonderful block printing lesson for seventh- and eighth-graders. Students plan their blocks with two opposite corners being B and D, and the other two opposite corners as A and C. The block can then repeatedly be printed side-by-side and turned to make different arrangements, as these two alternative printing arrangements of the designs show.

Courtesy of Gwenda Malnati.

A second kind of drawing (or design) is play with patterns. Here, primary student Dalton Tyler used a variety of colors and kinds of patterned lines. The teacher had talked about the patterning in Australian aboriginal art.

Courtesy of Saga Prefecture, Kyushu Island, Japan.

Encourage both ways of representation: what is conceived in the mind and how it appears. This beautifully detailed drawing of a tree was created by a second-grade youngster from Saga Prefecture, Japan.

painting contribute greatly to the beauty of the objects shown, be they clothing or floor tiles. Design receives more emphasis in later sections of this book, in discussions of architecture, mosaics, printmaking, clay, and sculpture. Designing patterns, however, also is important in making drawings and paintings. The doodles that one makes on a scratch pad while talking on the telephone represent this kind of play with shapes and spacing. A design approach using shapes, lines, and blocks was central in the Froebel kindergarten method, which influenced Frank Lloyd Wright's

IN THE CLASSROOM

Using Maps and Diagrams for Content Learning

Maps and diagrams can be part of a wide variety of content-area assignments. Ask students, for example, to map daily life events, diagram how a pumpkin grows or how our insides function, or map where the food we eat comes from. Ask children to make maps of their neighborhoods or show the cycle of evaporation and rain. Have them show how they get home from school, using international travel signs and symbols.

architecture so profoundly. It also was central in the teaching at a famous German design school, the Bauhaus. Because design is based on intuitive balance and measure, it lends itself well to correlational activities with mathematics, architecture, and engineering.

Maps and Diagrams Maps and diagrams—visual representations of what one knows rather than what one sees—comprise the third family in the world of visual objects. Conception, not perception, is the focus. Communicating an idea through a map or diagram is not governed by the constraints of realism, however; maps and diagrams are a means to promote visual literacy, ways to envision how something is or is to be built. During the Industrial Revolution, drawing was seen as an important way to represent and communicate technical understandings and inventions.

This type of "visual thinking" is embodied in such conceptual artworks as Alice Aycock's piece on cloud dispersion and Maria Merz's artwork based on Fibonacci series. Some other drawing activities that promote flexible visual thinking are drawing something from a nonhuman point of view, such as an ant's-eye or a bird's-eye view.

When preschool-age children draw their families, those drawings are like maps in that they draw what they know, not what they see. Similar visual representations of knowledge are found in works by folk artists as well as naive artists, who do not feel so constrained by demands for realism. Unfortunately, this kind of drawing is too often discouraged by some teachers who establish perceptual realism as a standard for artistic excellence. One example of a young child's "thought representation" that did not meet a teacher's criteria for perceptual realism occurred when the sculptor Henry Moore was in primary school. He felt crushed when his teacher criticized him for drawing feet pointing downward rather than realistically pointing sideways. The solution is not that teachers should be laissez-faire, but instead that they foster both ways of representation—perceptual and conceptual. This is especially important for teachers of young children. In a class, some children will draw what they know, others will draw what they see, and most will use a combination.

FIGURE DRAWING

Which skills and techniques in figure drawing should be introduced and developed in elementary- and middle-school art programs? Unfortunately, through lack of guidance, many students fail to meet their potential in drawing and painting the human figure. Instant art and gimmicky shortcuts, such as cutting and pasting photographs, keep students from developing the basic skills of creative figural expression.

If teachers want students to grow in their representation of the human figure, they must provide learning experiences and practice sessions for such growth. Direct the students' attention to details. Extend the child's frame of reference with statements such as, "Show us how your face looked when you were in the dentist's chair." Children want to be able to draw well. Students of all ages feel that the level of realistic representation is the most important criterion in determining the quality of each other's artworks.

Teachers can ensure a more intense awareness of the human figure and its characteristics by using posed models at every grade. The delineation of the figure in even the youngest child's drawings does not spring forth from a vacuum. It results from the varied encounters the learner has had in perceiving and conceptualizing the human figure, both in and out of school, through books, comics, television, and peers' art. Sadly, the drawings of most nonartistic and artistically untaught adults are no better than those of preadolescents: They draw a large head, ill-defined facial features, and a segmented body. Hands and feet often are not visible, and the picture shows an overall lack of organization. Given such results, too many students graduate from school with a sense of inferiority about how they draw. By offering instruction and guidance, however, teachers can help them to acquire or maintain confidence in their drawing ability.

Warming Up Try beginning with a warm-up session. Ask motivating, leading questions: What action is the model performing? What is the model wearing? What portion of the model do you see from your drawing station? How large is the model's head in comparison with her body? How big are his hands? Ask each student to place one hand over his or her own face to realize its size. Likewise, how large are the model's feet? They must be long enough and wide enough to keep the model balanced. At what point is the model's arm biggest—at the shoulders, elbows, or wrists? Where is the model's leg biggest—at the ankle, knee, or hips? At what places do the body, neck, leg, and arm bend? Are the feet pointing in different directions? How high can the arms reach above the model's head? How far can the torso of his body turn if his feet are planted in one position? How far down does the model's arm reach when she holds her arm at her side?

As the students draw, encourage them to look at the model constantly, carefully, and intently. Tell them to fill their eyes with the image. Caution them to avoid rushing through their drawing by scribbling or making hasty, random, meaningless lines. Remind them always to look first and then draw. Also, encourage them to make the figure large—to fill the page with it. In general, have children begin their drawing of a figure with the head at the top of the page. When children draw their classmates, be prepared for the occasional self-conscious titter or embarrassed laughter. Emphasize that we are all learning to see. Provide examples such as Jean Dubuffet's *art brut* drawings to show that realism is not the sole criterion of art. Be understanding when a student does not want to model for the class (perhaps because of embarrassment about appearance or clothing), because there always are other volunteers.

Head and Body Size In drawing figures, the size of the head generally determines the size of the figure. If students draw the figure's head too small, the body will not fill the page; however, if they draw the head too large, they will not be able to fit the whole body on the page. Children in the primary grades often draw a three-heads-high figure, like the *Peanuts* cartoon character Charlie Brown, and minimize the rest of the body to fit it on the page. Others will draw tiny heads and stretch the legs to reach the bottom of the page. In either case, the teacher should not discourage the results because the drawings capture the child's development at a moment of special charm.

Because many teachers believe they lack the expertise to guide children in drawing figures, they settle for what the students can accomplish on their own. Students need instruction, but the wrong kind of direction will not be helpful. Indeed, applying formulas such as stick or sausage figures and face proportions measured by rulers can create a stultifying dependence on stereotypes. The best instruction emphasizes heightened observation.

A middle-school life drawing class in action. Notice that tables were arranged to make a unified drawing area where the model can be viewed easily by all students. Paper size for sketching was 18 × 24 inches. Tools for drawing included sharpened dowel sticks and twigs dipped in India ink containers. If several drawings are planned, the model, as well as the position of the model, should be changed so that students are afforded a variety of views.

Courtesy of Mary Sayer Hammond.

A motorcycle was brought to the middle-school art room in order to draw it more true to life. After a careful line drawing, vibrant colors of oil pastel enhanced the composition.

Courtesy of Suzy McNiel.

How marvelously observed are the details: the eyelets, wristbands, folds in clothing, and cheekbones. The pattern changes in the falling socks. A first-grade child did this! Have high expectations and your students will rise to meet those expectations.

Contours and Contour Lines Adult artists pay careful attention to contours and how planes are implied. While you teach your class, you can point out these features to your students. As children learn to draw, they first use outlines that do not suggest form. These are followed by strong interior contour lines that overlap each other. Later, there is some implying of form through planes, and still later, children begin to join interior lines with outlines. In upper grades, teach contour-line drawing by discussing how the line of an interior edge becomes visible and then joins the exterior silhouette. As it rounds the form, it becomes hidden. Ask questions such as:

- Are the lines varied from thick to thin to create interesting linear movement and subtle space-in-depth?
- Is the line on opposite sides of a shape or object (body, tree, vase, fruit, and so on) drawn more heavily on one side and lighter on the other to create tension and space?
- Do the lines drawn complete a shape instead of floating in space?

In the upper grades, talk about planes—the plane of the front of the body, the plane of the head, or the plane of a box. Show how the plane is revealed by its edges. By using this approach, you will be pleased at how well some of your students can suggest planes in space.

Details Figure drawing, like all drawing from life, teaches students to observe at many levels. Those who are perceptually aware very quickly will notice and draw the rich embellishing details, such as belts, ribbons, shoelaces, buttons, necklaces, earrings, bracelets, wristwatches, pockets, collars, cuffs, wrinkles, zippers, pleats, eyeglasses, teeth braces, hair combs, and clothing patterns such as stripes, checks, florals, and plaids.

Drawing from Photos and Cartoons In addition to drawing live models, students may draw from photos or other artworks. Here the translating from three- to two-dimensions has already occurred. The positive effect of encouraging children to do such drawing manifested itself in the career of the Norwegian expressionist artist Edvard Munch. He and his brother grew up in a family that advocated drawing as an activity. As a child, he drew elflike characters and animals in a variety of settings, such as castles and street scenes. Combining sequential images and text, he transformed one character into another and depicted stories with complex plots filled with humor, delight, and pleasure. His childhood drawings presaged the narrative impulse later seen in his adult work.

Still another approach to figure drawing does not use a model but instead relies on the representational devices of comics and TV cartoons. Some young people's interest in drawing is triggered by comic-book-

Courtesy of David W. Hodge.

The contour-line technique is perhaps the most viable and successful drawing method for upper-elementary- and middle-school children. Urge students to draw slowly and deliberately with a soft-lead pencil. Urge them to look intently at the object they are drawing.

Courtesy of David W. Hodge.

Rich visual stimulation is extremely important for students to create quality artwork. Many teachers build an ever-changing still-life environment in their classrooms. Here, a young adolescent is attired in goggles, snowflake-patterned sweater, striped pants, and high boots while modeling against intriguing antique Americana artifacts.

Courtesy of David W. Hodge.

How exciting to draw a cowboy on a horse! Or a classmate holding a live animal pet!

IN THE CLASSROOM

Drawing from Life

Any number of subject areas lend themselves to learning through art. Students, especially in the upper grades, can later use their linear figure drawings in a painting, collage, print, or mural. The line drawings themselves, however, often have a validity, presence, and charm of their own. Social studies content might include using models in ethnic dress, interacting socially, or posing to reflect a current newspaper story—firefighters rescuing a child, perhaps. Science content might be taught through drawings of children brushing their teeth, working in a "lab" in a lab coat, or holding a pet. Sports provides wonderful opportunities for drawings that fill the space of the page—ballgames, swinging on a swing, cheerleading, biking, flying a kite. Pose a student in a colorful costume (clown, cowboy, dancer) or sports uniform on a table or a countertop so that everyone has a clear view. Or, pose the model in the center of a circle of sketching classmates, affording each child a different view. Challenge the students to use their imaginations. Let the action or stance of the model trigger a fantastic or legendary figure whom they can capture in line. Fill in the background with ideas from the imagination and remembered experiences. Assign different class members to take 5- or 10-minute turns posing in various sports actions. Urge the students to overlap the figures as they draw them. For an overlapping, multifigure composition, change both the action and the direction of the model in later poses. Encourage upper-elementary- and middle-school students to keep sketchbooks as a way to visually organize their perceptions of the world.

illustration techniques: scenes in a series, thought balloons, speed lines, star–and–lightning–bolt symbols of violence, and strongly contrasting effects of light on muscles.

Introducing New Techniques Introduce new drawing and sketching tools. Try free-flowing felt-tip markers, small watercolor brushes, Q-tips, eyedroppers, turkey feathers, twigs, and balsa woodsticks sharpened at one end as ink applicators, as well as charcoal and conté crayon. For action or gesture drawing that requires a looser, free approach, encourage students to hold the crayon, pen, pencil, charcoal, or chalk horizontally as they sketch, rather than in the tight, upright manner used in writing.

Pose the student model against a background sheet of cardboard, plywood, or Masonite approximately 4 × 8 feet—at minimum, slightly larger than the model. Use of a background will help the students to relate the

Bottom: *Courtesy of David W. Hodge.*

Top: In the center of the room, a standing girl and seated boy pose on a table. The table contains objects to break up space. **Bottom:** With stiff boards to back the drawing paper, peers draw each other in small groups.

size and dimensions. Try a 9 × 18-inch or a 12 × 24-inch sheet for a standing figure, or use a long, wide sheet for a group of figures. Challenge students to fill the page. If your room has sufficient space, have the students use 24 × 36-inch paper with wide felt-nib markers, giant chunk crayons, or big brushes.

Introduce a variety of papers: plain newsprint, cream or gray manila, recycled papers, assorted-color construction paper, computer-printout pages, and newspaper classified-ad pages. Newspapers may donate the ends of newspaper rolls, which are useful for large drawings. Inexpensive, lightweight drawing boards are excellent for field trips. Construct the boards using heavyweight chipboard, hardboard, or Masonite, cut to about 18 × 24 inches, with the edges protected with masking tape. During the drawing sessions, students can prop these boards against a table or desk, thus affording them a better working position from which to capture details.

PORTRAIT AND SELF-PORTRAIT DRAWINGS

The self-portrait or portrait of a classmate should be a part of every school art program curriculum. What more effective and immediate subjects are there for expressive drawings in all grades than the children themselves? Children of all ages like to draw the figure. While only a few 6-year-olds can draw reasonably correct proportions, the number increases to over half for 14-year-olds. A small number of 12-year-olds can draw true to appearance, as well.

If possible, discourage students from doing the typical portrait stereotype: the symmetrical frontal pose with arms hanging stiffly at the side. Instead, create contrasting directions of the arms and hands in unusual positions. Add interest and relevance with uniforms, costumes, a variety of headware, and assorted objects to hold. Encourage three-quarter or full-profile views. Have children pose sitting, kneeling, or standing, with arms akimbo or legs straddling a chair. Use your imagination—and let students use theirs—in finding interesting poses. Background adds immeasurably to the composition—a foliage arrangement, a multipaned window, a giant travel poster, a folding screen. Encourage students to add background elements that they remember or imagine, representing their interests or animals they love, for example.

Hasty, superficial observation usually results in stereotyped portraiture. Urge students to look intently at the model, whether it be their own image in a mirror or a classmate posing, and to pay close attention to the individual's unique characteristics. To encourage self-acceptance in self-portraiture, show portraits of famous women and men, and discuss their widely dissimilar, far-from-perfect features and the different shapes of their heads. Call attention to the hairline, and how the hair follows the contour of the head. No thoughtless scribbles for hair should be allowed!

posed figure to the boundaries of their paper. For additional interest, decorate the board with drapery, fishnet, or colorful posters.

Demonstrate new techniques and directions for drawing the figure: contour, gesture, scribble, and mass methods. Following Henri Matisse's example in his famous paper cutouts, have students cut the figure from construction paper without making a preliminary drawing. Vary the paper

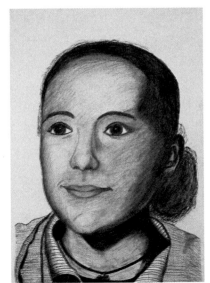

Courtesy of Baiba Kuntz.

These drawings of classmates by eighth-graders show virtuosic handling in (**Top left**) the hair and blouse by Jennifer Buntman, (**Top right**) the superb patterning of the shirt by Ashley Milne, and (**Bottom**) varied weights of blouse lines by Kasey Passen.

Top row and bottom left: *Courtesy of Baiba Kuntz;* bottom right: *Lawrence Stueck.*

Top left: Fifth-grader Alison Carey did her self-portrait in her winter coat holding her two cats and sitting on the front steps of her house. A classmate modeled for the legs. **Top right:** Fifth-grader Lauren Conway did her self-portrait with parakeet and brought in recalled imagery of her horse stable. **Bottom left:** Sixth-grader Mark Sward used his balcony for a background and caught every detail in the porch railing. **Bottom right:** This middle-schooler's portrait with carefully drawn collars shows the wide range of values possible with pencils.

Discuss the shape of the ears (tell them to feel their own ears) and their junction to the head. Discuss ways of delineating the nose, and show drawings by Pablo Picasso and Ben Shahn. Use a rich motivation of color slides or reproductions depicting different portraiture styles from a variety of times and cultures. Show how to draw the lips as two subtly differing forms and the eyelids' structure as complementary features to the eyes. Bring out the astonishing fact that no two faces—or even two sides of the same person's face—are alike.

In upper elementary and middle school, *blind contour drawing* is a good way for students to capture the spirit of the subject rather than to strive for absolute realism. In blind contour drawing, a student looks intently at the subject—but not at his or her paper—as the student draws. If students become concerned that their drawings do not look like the posed model, tell them that the aim of expressive portraiture is not to achieve a photographic likeness. Remind them that the same model drawn by various artists will look different in each rendition.

DRAWING THE LANDSCAPE OR CITYSCAPE

Although very young children in the primary grades enjoy drawing simple themes and single objects, such as a butterfly, a bird, a pet, themselves, a classmate, or a house, maturing students will respond to the challenge of complex composition: the still life, the landscape, and the cityscape. In the upper elementary grades and middle school, they are interested in outdoor sketching and the excitement of field trips. The busy and infinitely varied world beckons and unfolds at their doorsteps.

The most important and architecturally distinguished building in town makes a good subject, valuable for the study of drawing, architecture, and culture, as in this Colombian 13-year-old's inked artwork.

The teacher may need to locate sketching sites from a school window or nearby the school grounds.

IN THE COMMUNITY

Drawing What's There

Students are fascinated by what's outside their classroom. Think about potential sites for sketching trips that may also provide learning experiences in other disciplines. Consider, for example:

- A nearby building construction site (but be careful to get permission first and to establish safety rules)
- A colorful and crowded street of shops
- A boat marina
- The challenging perspective down an alleyway
- A cluster of farm buildings on a country road
- Your community's elaborate architecture
- The view from your classroom window

Courtesy of David W. Hodge.

The busy and varied world beckons to be recorded in art. Students enjoy sketching outdoors, especially on a beautiful day. A large-sized paper and a firm surface on which to draw are helpful.

These sites, as well as imagined cities of the future, can be the inspiration for sketches, compositions, paintings, prints, and collages. A variety of media can be used for field-trip sketching, including pencil, chalk (school chalk is recommended for sketches and preliminary drawings on colored construction paper backgrounds), charcoal, crayon, felt-nib or nylon-tip marker, conté crayon, and even a stick dipped in ink (depending on the maturity of the students).

Most children on a field trip draw with enthusiasm and confidence; however, some who are perplexed will besiege the teacher with questions: What should I draw first? Where should I start on the paper? Must I put everything in my picture? The complex view may overwhelm them, and the spatial and perspective problems often confuse them. Remind the students that they will be creating an entirely new aesthetic unity out of the vast conglomeration of visual stimuli. One recommendation for successful landscape and cityscape drawing is to use a light pencil or chalk sketch to establish the basic shapes and general outline. Values and details can be added later.

Another strategy—and one that is especially recommended for the complex view—is to have the students begin by drawing the shape in the center of the site (a doorway, window, telephone pole, tree) as completely as they can. Then have them proceed to draw the shape to the right and left of it, above and below it, and so on, until they fill their paper to the border. They will discover that incomplete shapes touching the paper's edge will create line avenues leading into their compositions. Encourage them to enrich their drawings with details, patterns, and textural effects.

Problems that students have defining distance in space often can be clarified by an understanding and use of the following guidelines. Objects or shapes in the foreground plane (those closer to the observer) usually are drawn larger, lower on the page, and in more detail. Objects farther away from the viewer (in the background plane) usually are drawn smaller, higher on the page, and with less observable detail (see in Chapter 2 the section about space). Effective space is created subtly by overlapping shapes and elements in the composition, such as a fence, tree, or telephone pole against a building.

Simple perspective principles based on employing the horizon line, vanishing points, and converging lines should be introduced when the students indicate a need for them. Some seventh- and eighth-grade students

Brush, ink, and watercolors on white drawing paper. Grade 9.

Viewed from the school window, this neighborhood scene uses free-form preliminary washes to tie the composition together. The overlapping trees create spatial depth, and the rooftops at all angles energize the composition. The houses and trees running off the paper's edge lead the viewer into the picture.

Courtesy of Frank Wachowiak.

Drawing landscapes or cityscapes directly at the site is recommended for upper-elementary- and middle-school children, but sometimes it can't be done. The center and bottom illustrations show what can be accomplished when youngsters draw from a sequence of projected color slides. First, slides of towers, steeples, and chimneys were drawn high on the page. Then, store-front facades and signs were projected for the middle plane. Finally, street furniture, lamps, telephone poles, hydrants, traffic lights and signs, parked cars, motorcycles, and trucks were projected to complete the foreground.

Courtesy of David W. Hodge.

Viewfinders help students to select the part of a scene to frame and draw. Just cut a little rectangle in a piece of oak tag.

will want to take up this challenge. Simple exercises in perspective may appeal to them, but remind them that mastery of perspective rules does not ensure that they will achieve compositional success.

Sketching Field Trips: Walking to the Site Sketching field trips should be undertaken only with adequate preparation by both the teacher and students. The teacher should scout out exciting subject matter beforehand. Avoid the barren view or monotonous vista that provides little opportunity for a varied breakup of compositional space. Note that permission to be away from school must be cleared with the principal's office and, when necessary, signed permission slips must be obtained from parents. Arrangements for using the school bus should be made well in advance.

Courtesy of David W. Hodge.

As near as the schoolyard, the child's knowledge of science, art, and nature comes together. Take advantage of the immediate environment—the school playground, the cafeteria kitchen, and the band room with its instruments.

A class discussion with slides and other visuals before the field trip should emphasize specific challenges. Tell the students to look for the architecturally significant character of the buildings, to see the value contrasts of windows in daylight, the foreground space allowed for steps and porches, and the receding of roads, sidewalks, and fences. Bring in aesthetic concepts. ("Will we see and depict nature as it is dominated and controlled by humans, or nature gaining control?")

On the day of the field trip, review rules of behavior and caution students to respect private property in the sketching vicinity. Directions for proceeding to and returning from the sketching site should be made clear, especially if it is within walking distance of the school. Keep the class in a line or group, bringing up stragglers when necessary. If roads are to be crossed, stop signs that the teacher or monitors can hold up to warn and halt traffic are recommended.

In most instances, supplies for drawing should be distributed to students before they leave the classroom. In some cases, however, the teacher may prefer to carry the drawing tools to the site and carry them back at the end of the field trip. If students walk to the site, they can be asked to carry their own drawing boards, however. When bus transportation is used, class monitors can bring the materials, drawing tools, sketchboards, extra paper, and thumbtacks to distribute at the site. Upon arrival at the sketching site, discourage students from sitting too closely together. Many a field trip can end up as a time-wasting social hour.

Remind students that they may use the artist's prerogatives of changing, adding, deleting, or simplifying what they see as they draw. Explain that the criterion is not necessarily photographic reality or rigidly measured perspective. Students may add more trees, fences, telephone poles, fire escapes, air vents, chimneys, or windows. They may change a roof line

Courtesy of Frank Wachowiak.

A motorcycle parked in the school lot will pique the imagination of students and will present many details for the students to draw.

or the cast of a shadow. They may delete a parked car or a trash dumpster. In the sky, they may add helicopters, birds, clouds, and fantasy creations. Each decision they make, however, should embody the dynamic rules of art: variety, unity, balance, emphasis, contrast, and repetition.

The most important responsibility of the teacher at the sketching site is to guide the students in a self-evaluation of their drawings, employing the perennial principles of composition and design. In the final analysis, if all the teachers have done is to bring the students to see something they have not really seen before, to notice something they have never noticed until that moment—a molding or cornice on a door or window frame, the shadow of a tree against a wall, the overlapping of shingles, the variety in tree bark, or the texture of a brick wall—then they have succeeded in enriching the lives of their students a thousandfold. In bringing a student to observe such details, the teacher may have started them on an exciting quest for shapes, patterns, textures, and color—an endless journey of visual discovery.

DRAWING THE STILL LIFE

Whether as inspiration for drawing, painting, print, or collage, the still-life arrangement fosters an appreciation of commonly observed, everyday objects. It encourages keen observation and sensitivity to shapes, contours, and overlapping. Beginning in the third grade, children can be guided to see the limitless design possibilities in still-life compositions. When acquiring objects for still lifes, scavenge at secondhand stores, flea markets, attics, basements, and garage sales. Avoid the trite, such as miniature figurines or bud vases. Especially seek objects for their ability to tap into individuals' thinking and personal experiences.

Large, bold objects that can be seen from a distance are better than smaller ones. Popular items are ballroom gowns, costumes borrowed from theater programs, athletic and military uniforms, as well as apparatus from army surplus stores. Objects from outdoor life and camping, as well as targets from archery ranges also will interest some students. Large art reproductions, posters from athletic wear stores and automobile dealerships, and unused billboard sheets make interesting backgrounds.

Top: *Courtesy of Frank Wachowiak.* Middle: *Courtesy of W. Robert Nix.* Bottom: *Courtesy of Joyce Vroon.*

Do you know someone who would be willing to lend your classes collectibles or antique objects? Perhaps the florist will donate flowers past their selling peak time.

Top: *Courtesy of Michael F. O'Brien*. Middle: *Courtesy of David W. Hodge*.

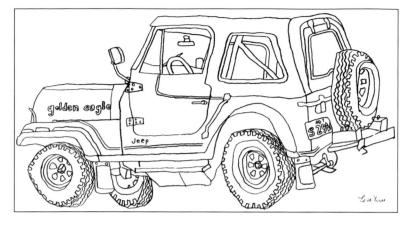

Still-life arrangements need not be limited to the usual floral arrangements; they are all around us. Consider the bicycles, Jeeps, campers, and minivans parked behind the school. Consider the open car trunk, took shed, cupboard, or closet. How about the piled-up desk, cluttered kitchen sink, box of playground equipment, or table set for dinner?

Arranging the Still Life The placement of the various objects is critical to the success of the still-life composition or design. Have the students participate in the arranging process. Make construction of the still life a motivating, adventurous part of the lesson. For example, arrange the objects on an antique table, old sewing machine, rocker, stepladder, window ledge, desk top, or table in the middle of the room so that as they draw, students can be seated in a circle around the still life. Employ a variety of heights and levels (use cardboard cartons and plastic or wooden crates or storage units as supports). Create space by placing some objects behind others. Work for an informal rather than a formal balance in the arrangement. Use assorted fabrics, colorful beach towels, flags, banners, fishnets, bedspreads, quilts, or tablecloths to unify the separate elements and create visual movement. Use large plants to break up otherwise empty spaces. In most cases, the more objects that are used in the still-life group, the more opportunities students will have for selection and rejection. Indeed, the more objects the students include in their compositions, the more likely they are to achieve design success.

Beginning the Still Life There are several ways to begin drawing a still life. Unless for class management reasons students must stay in assigned seats, encourage them to move around the still life and examine the objects. In this way, they can discover what to draw and from what vantage point, and they can make their own plans on how to go about doing the drawing. One successful strategy is to have students begin by drawing in the middle of their paper the central object in the still life, as seen from their individual point of view. They continue by drawing the objects next to it, left and right, above and below, until they have either filled the page or completed the still-life arrangement. Thus, the more varied and abundant the still life is, the more the students' compositions will fill the space. Some teachers suggest that students make a light, tentative sketch in pencil, charcoal, or chalk to indicate the general, overall arrangement. This preliminary drawing then is developed stage by stage, employing value (light and dark) and texture effects, pattern, shading, detail, and linear emphasis.

Another tactic when drawing a still life is to have students select items from a general collection of still-life material, choosing one object at

Dolls, fancy chairs, musical instruments, and lunch boxes make good still-life material. ***Bottom:*** Fourth-grader Elizabeth Thackston.

a time to sketch at their desks or tables. They will build their compositions gradually, employing the principles of variety in size and shape of objects, overlapping, repetition, avenues into the composition, and informal balance. Talk with the children about how shapes are described by their edges and how an object's interior lines and outlines join together.

DRAWING ANIMALS

Most children respond enthusiastically to drawing pets and other animals. Students in the upper-elementary grades and middle school often are especially interested in drawing horses. However, if the drawing of animals is to become a significant experience for the students, whenever possible have them observe live animals at zoos, aquariums, natural history museums, pet shops, or parks. Drawing at an animal shelter can also teach a socially valuable lesson about pet ownership. Pets brought to class can also provide a stimulating and immediate source of drawing inspiration.

Skill in drawing realistic animals develops slowly. Nearly all first-graders draw "just an animal"; by sixth grade, a third of students still do so. "Horselike" animals are drawn by 20 percent of second-graders and perhaps 50 percent of sixth-graders. Even by seventh grade, only 5 percent of students are able to make drawings that can be classified as "true to appearance."

Before an animal-drawing field trip, let the students look at celebrated animal drawings. Include Rembrandt van Rijn's lion and elephant; Rosa Bonheur's horses and those by Chinese Han- and Sung-period artists; Albrecht Dürer's hare, squirrel, and rhinoceros; and Andrew Wyeth's birds. Discuss the animals' special characteristics: the textural pattern of the rhino's skin, the repeated yet ever varied spots of the leopard, the rhythmic rings of the armadillo's protective shell, the beautiful op-art variations of the zebra's stripes, the gracefully curved horns of the antelope, and the wrinkled and leathery face of the orangutan.

Drawing of rabbits by a first-grade child, Japan.

Private collection.

African-American folk artist Nellie Mae Rowe's family plowed many hours with a mule. She brought this knowledge to her rich colored-pencil drawing. In the background, patterns of checkerboards and circular, floral, and scallop designs create a feast for the eyes.

Courtesy of Mary Lazzari.

These students are using plastic models of animals and dinosaurs as motivations for their painting.

Learning About Animals Through Art

Drawing is a particularly engaging way for children to learn about animals. You can, for example, discuss the animals' sociological and cultural significance, such as sacred tigers and cows, imperial dogs, and royal lions, symbolically representing the strength of the emperor. Encourage students to think of similarities between people and animals in resting, eating, running, bathing, grooming, and caring for their young. As the educator John Dewey wrote, "The roots of art and beauty are in the basic vital functions, the biological commonplaces man shares with birds and beasts" (Dewey, 1934).

To stimulate kinesthetic awareness, have students reenact the animal's poses and actions using their own bodies. Older students can be challenged to capture the animal's peculiar stance, the swinging rhythm of the chimpanzee, the arching stretch of the giraffe, or the sway of the elephant's trunk.

Careful observation and sensitive variation of line are required in drawing animals. As the students draw, remind them to fill the page. The larger the drawing, the more opportunities the child will have to define special details, patterns, and textures. Pencils, sticks cut to a point and dipped in ink, and felt-nib or nylon-tipped pens are good for small sketches. Charcoal, conté crayon, chalk, crayon, oil pastel, Q-tips, eyedroppers filled with ink, and large-size blunt or square-tipped ink markers can be used for large works.

Take time to draw a single animal developed in depth. Draw detailed studies of an animal's eye, ear, snout, or horns. Because textural nuances can be added later, when the students return to class, on-the-site drawings might be limited to capturing significant form, that is, it might be a sketch showing the animal's spirit rather than an attempt to make a completed, detailed study.

When sketching a live animal is not possible or practical, color slides, films, filmstrips, and opaque projections of illustrations can provide supplemental motivation. In the primary grades, the visual material might be discussed and then posted for reference on the bulletin board. Photos and slides fulfill a definite need, but they should serve as an inspirational and informational reference only and should not be traced or rigidly copied.

Remind the students to consider the entire composition. In too many instances, the animal is isolated in the middle of the paper, floating in space

Top and middle: *Ann Arbor Schools.* Bottom: *Courtesy of Ted Ramsay.*

The animal world has always interested child artists. ***Top:*** Rembrandt's use of wrinkle lines in the elephant's baggy skin indicate forms and can give children ideas for their drawings. ***Middle:*** This first-grader's elephant is large and fills the space. ***Bottom:*** A sixth-grader used oil pastel to draw the anteater at the natural history museum.

without a hint of complementary foreground or background atmosphere. Make the animal's form bump the paper's edges.

Encourage students to add compositional elements such as trees, shrubs, grasses, rocks, bushes, vines, hills, cliffs, clouds, and companion animals in the foreground or background. Follow the example of Henri Rousseau, who used his own houseplants as models to create his jungles. Use plants, dried foliage, roots, rocks, and twigs from the immediate school vicinity drawn giant size to become ledges, mountains, and jungle trees for the animals' imagined habitats. Or, for fantasy, add objects such as computers or bicycles, and imagined figures.

DRAWING MEDIA: MARKERS, CHALK, PENCIL, AND OTHER RESOURCES

Drawings can be strong and beautiful in just the drawn form, with no additional color added. Markers and bold, dark pencil drawings have produced many fine drawings in this book, such as those on pages 11, 142, 146, 177, and 179. However, in elementary-school art programs, markers often are used for pictures that are subsequently to be colored. Another popular way to draw pictures that are ultimately to be colored is first to use yellow chalk on white paper, white chalk on colored paper, or pencil. (Pastels and dark or black chalk are not popular since they can be messy for young children to use.)

Using white or light-colored chalk for the initial sketching allows mistakes to be ignored, and allows lines to be readily redrawn with no permanent effect showing in the finished artwork. Then bold marker lines are drawn over the lightly sketched chalk lines. Chalk's tentative quality makes it especially suited for drawing complex subjects, such as gardens.

Alternatively, on colored construction paper, rather than immediately covering the chalk lines with marker lines, students can follow a preliminary sketch in chalk in other ways with other subsequent media. For example, watercolor, oil pastels, or tempera paint are frequently used to fill in the big, empty areas between the light chalk lines, *but the white chalk line is left showing.* The basis for this idea in color theory is that colors often look cleanest and brightest when separated from one another by a neutral

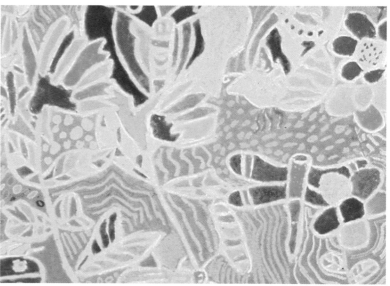

Top: *Courtesy of Beverly Barksdale Mallon.* Bottom: *Courtesy of Frank Wachowiak and Mary Sayer Hammond.*

Courtesy of Frank Wachowiak.

On colored construction paper, a white chalk drawing was gone over with black marker, then filled in with oil pastel. Such imagination! The teacher and the students discussed different ways to draw mouths, eyes, and noses. No two ways to depict a feature are alike.

Top: White Line Resist: (1) A pencil drawing is gone over with a heavy black marker; (2) these are then held up to a window and traced through another paper using a white crayon, followed by (3) crayoning, and (4) watercolor. Third-graders sang along with the CD, "I Can Fly." ***Bottom:*** Frank Wachowiak often used a different white line technique: After first being drawn on colored construction paper with chalk, the lines were then gone over with white oil pastel; then other colors of oil pastel were filled in. For his butterfly project, a collection of color photographs provided motivation. A host of patterns was used for the background: circles, dots, and wiggly, rippling lines.

or white or black line. This principle is shown in stained glass windows with their black lead lines between colors; since no colors touch, there is little problem of colors clashing.

A preliminary sketch in chalk also is used for "resist" techniques. For this technique, a gutter, or line, of plain paper on each side of the lightly sketched chalk line is left bare. This empty line or gutter should be from $\frac{1}{16}$ inch to $\frac{1}{4}$ inch in width. The subsequent oil pastel or tempera paint goes up to but does not touch the gutter. Thus, when a later overall application of black tempera or ink is used, the black paint or ink is absorbed by the blank paper but is resisted by the greasy oil pastel or the heavy tempera paint. (Subsequent sections explain these techniques in greater detail.)

Likewise, a chalk line can be traced over, through another sheet of paper, with a white crayon. This technique will give a white outline to forms when the painting is gone over with watercolors. Some teachers have the children first make a drawing with bold marker; then, with a sheet of white paper covering it, they use a white crayon to trace over the bold lines, which can be seen dimly through the covering paper, pressing hard as they trace. These white lines serve as barriers to the subsequent addition of watercolors. Their slightly ragged edge gives an organic quality to the artwork.

Drawing with Markers Much drawing in school today is done with markers. Whereas pencils leave a light line, markers leave a once-and-for-all dark line. Compared to pencils, markers are gaining increasing prominence, both because of their boldness, and because of their inexpensiveness. Compared to crayons, markers have a more bold and sure quality of line. One all-too-familiar disadvantage of markers, however, is that they will dry out if not tightly capped. A new product design, Capper®, addresses this problem by having all eight caps in one molded piece to help youngsters more readily keep track of the lids. (Also, Sanford's Colorific® markers have superior nondrying properties when inadvertently left uncapped.)

In the primary grades, teachers generally insist that children draw directly with the bold markers. The children's naive way of drawing has much charm, which the worrisomeness of pencil drawing first would only diminish.

In the upper grades, some teachers allow or encourage pencil drawing first, while other teachers strongly forbid it. Students, worried over making a mistake, much prefer to use pencil first. Teachers who eschew initial pencil drawings prior to using markers believe that the child's natural way of transcribing perceptions into marks has a distinct character that should be preserved. They believe that the belabored two-step process of first pencil and then marker obscures the drawing process's natural traces. These

Courtesy of Baiba Kuntz.

To preserve a freer quality to the drawing, no initial pencil drawing was allowed. Markers were used from the beginning for these carefully observed drawings of a bird still life.

Courtesy of ICCA, Milner Library, Illinois State University.

Markers were used in this elaborate drawing of an Indian art studio, filled with elaborate textures and patterns.

Teacher Susan Whipple. Courtesy of the USSEA art collection of Dr. Anne Gregory.

Keep Marker Strokes Parallel: When marker strokes are applied parallel and just slightly overlapping, an ordered appearance in a solid color is achieved. Siobhan McDermott's protective angel gains its beauty in part through its two pairs of complementary colors, red and green, and yellow-orange and blue-violet.

teachers are reluctant to give out a second sheet of paper (lest almost everyone ask for one) and, instead, tell their students, "No one messes up. The only way to mess up is to not make it your own way."

Drawings in which the pencil drawing is gone over with markers often have a "tighter" and less spontaneous quality. Paradoxically, teachers should encourage both careful observation but also a line quality "with life in it." "Look at Michelangelo's drawings; you will see lines that he did not feel were correct, yet he went on and drew them again where they should be. If he did not bother to fuss and erase, why should you?"

While marker drawing sometimes follows initial pencil drawing, another technique is that watercolors follow immediately after the pencil drawing is finished, with no intervening step of markers. Note, however, that if watercolor is to follow a marker drawing, then a waterproof marker, such as Sharpie®, must be used to prevent smearing.

Fifty years ago, the original markers were refillable, messy, and had a potent and harmful smell. Nowadays, many water-based markers, and even permanent markers, are odorless and nontoxic. Especially with permanent markers, look for the Art Products (AP) Nontoxic label. Fumes from a whole class of students using markers with a strong odor can be overpowering and cause headaches.

Any art supply catalog will present a vast array of alternatives to fit any budget: water-based, permanent, double-ended markers with one fine and one regular tip, brush pens, dual brush pens, markers with tips up to 2 inches wide, paint markers in 34 colors, Prismacolor® markers in 144 colors. While Pantone® makes three pointed markers in one pen, often the teacher wants just the normal fine point; that they are refillable cuts down on their expense. Markers can also be purchased at drugstores and discount stores. For writing on the markerboard (blackboard), use a low-odor, alcohol-based, dry-erase marker such as Sanford's Expo2®, as the odor from older types of dry-erase markers can be overwhelming.

Courtesy of Baiba Kuntz.

Scratchboard: Note how eighth-grader Joel Savitsky removed entire areas to create white areas; also note how an etching type of shading was done.

Generally, avoid the ultra-fine tips, as the lines do not show up well when the artworks are viewed from a distance. Also, the tips often dull quickly. Regular tips are preferable, although chisel-tips can substitute if used on a corner. Large areas of color can be beautifully and neatly applied when the chisel-tip markers are used in overlapping, perfectly parallel strokes.

Water-based markers are the least expensive by far. However, their relative slowness in drying can cause smearing if a protective shield of paper under the drawing hand is not used. Also there is the problem of smearing and bleeding if watercolor or tempera is subsequently used.

In middle schools, more unusual drawing methods such as scratchboard, silverpoint, conté crayon, and various ways of applying ink, such as by pen points, brushes, and even quill feathers, may find a place in the curriculum.

FOR FURTHER READING

"Symposium: On the Child's Pictorial World." 1994. *Journal of Aesthetic Education* 28(2): 51–70.

Abrahamson, Roy E. 1980. "The Teaching Approach of Henry Schaefer-Simmern." *Studies in Art Education* 22(1): 42–50.

Armstrong, Carmen. 1993. "Effect of Training in an Art Production Questioning Method on Teacher Questioning and Student Responses." *Studies in Art Education* 34(4): 209–221.

Auvril, Kenneth. 1990. *Perspective Drawing*. Mountain View, CA: Mayfield Publishing.

Colbert, Cynthia, and M. Taunton. 1987. "Problems of Representation: Preschool and Third-Grade Children's Observational Drawings of a Three-Dimensional Model." *Studies in Art Education* 29: 103–114.

Cole, Natalie R. 1940. *The Arts in the Classroom*. New York: John Day.

Edwards, Betty. 1979. *Drawing from the Right Side of the Brain*. Los Angeles: J. Tarcher.

Freeman, Nancy. 1980. *Strategies of Children's Drawings*. New York: Academic.

Golomb, Claire, and D. Farmer. 1983. "Children's Graphic Planning Strategies and Early Principles of Spatial Organization in Drawing." *Studies in Art Education* 24(2): 86–100.

Linderman, Marlene. 1990. *Art in the Elementary School: Drawing, Painting, and Creativity for the Classroom*. Dubuque, IA: Wm. C. Brown.

Lohan, Frank. 1986. *Wildlife Sketching: Pen, Pencil, Crayon and Charcoal Techniques*. New York: McGraw-Hill.

Lohan, Frank. 1993. *Drawing—The Drawing Handbook*. New York: McGraw Hill/Contemporary Books.

Nicolaides, Kimon. 1941. *The Natural Way to Draw*. Boston: Houghton-Mifflin.

Rottger, Ernst. 1970. *Creative Paper Design*. New York: Reinhold.

Schaefer-Simmern, Henry. 1948. *The Unfolding of Artistic Activity*. Berkeley: University of California Press.

Smith, Nancy, and C. Fucigna. 1988. "Drawing Systems in Children's Pictures: Contour and Form." *Visual Arts Research* 14(1): 66–76.

Strommen, Erik. 1988. "A Century of Children Drawing: The Evolution of Theory and Research Concerning the Drawings of Children." *Visual Arts Research* 14: 13–24.

Wilson, Brent, Al Hurwitz, and Marjorie Wilson. 1987. *Teaching Drawing from Art*. Worcester, MA: Davis Publications.

Wilson, Brent, and Marjorie Wilson. 1982. *Teaching Children to Draw*. Englewood Cliffs, NJ: Prentice-Hall.

Wilson, Brent, and Harlan Hoffa, eds. 1988. *History of Art Education: Proceedings from the Penn State Conference*. Reston, VA: NAEA.

Wolf, Dennie, and M. D. Perry. 1988. "From Endpoints to Repertoires: New Conclusions about Drawing Development." *Journal of Aesthetic Education* 29(3): 13–35.

Zurmuehlen, Marilyn. 1990. *Studio Art, Praxis, Symbol, Presence*. Reston, VA: NAEA.

WEB RESOURCES

For an art lesson on drawing the landscape:

http://www.smithsonianeducation.org/educators/lesson_plans/landscape_painting/index.html

For drawing a self-portrait:

http://www.arts.ufl.edu/art/rt_room/sparkers/self_portrait.html

For drawing a family portrait:

http://www.arts.ufl.edu/art/rt_room/sparkers/family/family.html

For ideas on teaching perspective:

http://www2.evansville.edu/studiochalkboard/draw.html

For drawing strategies:

http://www.goshen.edu/facultypubs/Bartel.html

For a lesson on drawing in one-point perspective:

http://www.olejarz.com/arted/perspective/index.html

For perspective by da Vinci and the Renaissance artists:

http://www.princetonol.com/groups/iad/lessons/middle/arted.htm#Perspective

Courtesy of ICCA, Milner Library, Illinois State University.

Crayon alone created the glowing rich colors in this 11-year-old Turkish student's illustration of four simultaneously shown scenes from the fable, "The Old Man, His Son, and Their Donkey." A handsome texture is achieved in the straw-colored area by scratching in a texture. Tunceli, Turkey.

CRAYON

At the turn of the twentieth century, crayons began to be manufactured for use in schools. Artists such as Henri de Toulouse-Lautrec, Georges Seurat, Henri Matisse, and Käthe Kollwitz used them. Today, they are available in over 64 colors. Resourceful teachers often combine crayon with other media to renew student interest in crayon's exciting potential. Some of these innovative techniques, which are described in the following pages, include crayon resist, crayon encaustic, crayon engraving, and multi-crayon engraving.

Chapter 24

Crayon and Oil Pastels

Courtesy of Shirley Lucas.

Crayon was richly used in this drawing of eight animals. The grassy terrain was outlined in a series of analogous colors.

Crayons' Solo Merits Unfortunately, the rich possibilities of the wax crayon, with its own singular merits as an expressive coloring agent, often are not fully investigated. Typical classroom projects in crayon usually are weak in color intensity, value contrast, and texture quality. In most instances, crayon is employed as a pallid, sketchy coloring agent instead of the glowing, vibrant, and excitingly expressive medium that it can and should be. If children are expected to grow in crayoning skills, the crayon's rich possibilities must be taught beginning from the first grade.

These crayon drawings of memories of a tree house began with questions, "How will you climb into it? Who will come into it?" A white chalk preliminary drawing was made on 18- × 24-inch colored construction paper to give a suffused overall tone.

Whenever possible, request that the students or school supply agent obtain the large 48- or 64-color crayon boxes, with their beautiful range of tints and shades and their wide selection of neutralized hues. To bring out the deepest, richest color, prompt the students to apply the crayon with heavy pressure. ("Who can make the color sing?" "Who can make it shout?" as opposed to "Who is making it mumble?") Have students use a lot of newspaper padding under the paper to be crayoned. Point out the effects of using contrasting colors and of juxtaposing dark next to light colors, neutral next to high-intensity colors. Challenge the students to create patterns of stripes, checks, plaids, diamonds, stars, spirals, and dots. Use paintings by artists such as Vuillard, Bonnard, Ida Kohlmyer, Mariam Shapiro, van Gogh, and Gauguin as exemplars of vibrant color. Show them Picasso's crayon drawings.

With Colored Paper The entire mood of crayon work changes when the crayon is applied to varicolored or varitextured surfaces. Work on backgrounds other than the commonly used cream manila or white drawing paper. Pleasing results come about when crayon is employed richly on pink, red, orange, purple, blue, green, and even black construction paper. Have the students allow some of the background to show between objects; the background paper color will unify their compositions. Color changes its appearance on different color papers: yellow changes to dull green on black construction paper; all of the warm colors are slightly neutralized when they are applied to green paper; and warm colors shimmer vibrantly when applied to red, pink, and orange surfaces.

Preliminary sketches for crayon pictures on colored paper may be made with school chalk or a light-colored crayon. Do not let students use a pencil, because they grow frustrated when they try to manipulate a blunt crayon to color in a pencil-sketch's tiny details. Encourage bold use of the crayon. Urge color repetition throughout the composition to achieve unity. Completed crayon pictures may be given a sheen by rubbing them with a facial tissue or a folded paper towel.

One vexing problem that the teacher of art faces is children who rush through their crayoning, who quickly color in a few shapes and then claim they are finished. Some suggestions for dealing with this are given in Chapters 3 and 4. As always, the most successful strategies involve a teacher's

Wax-crayon still lifes created by university students. College students should discover in their teacher-training classes crayon's luminous beauty. Then, they can help their students bring forth that same richness.

well-planned, resourceful motivation that taps the students' concerns. This leads to a richly detailed drawing, which sets the stage for the crayon's expressive coloring.

Crayon Resist For students of all ages, an exciting, creative art experience is the combination of vibrant, glowing wax crayon with translucent, flowing watercolors. For this technique, subjects that are rich in pattern and allover design, such as fish, birds, reptiles, insects, and butterflies, are recommended. Students genuinely are excited by the variety of insects in their environment, and the teacher can stimulate further scientific and aesthetic interest by having children collect specimens to share with classmates. Illustrated books, wildlife periodicals, color slides, and films will broaden the students' awareness of nature's adaptational variety. Studying the appearance of insects' bodies increases general knowledge of design. For example, help the students to see and draw the filigree pattern of insects' wings, the rhythmlike segments of a grasshopper's abdomen, the symmetrical balance of a ladybug's body, and the grace of a praying mantis's legs.

The pattern, details, and designs of the subject are of utmost importance in the crayon-resist technique, adding as they do to the sparkling effect of the finished painting. Whatever the theme, the more detail that is incorporated and the more overlapping of shapes that is achieved, the richer the design becomes. When the design is rich and complex, the negative areas evolve into varied shapes as well. Background embellishment—adding flowers, weeds, trees, vines, webs, and rock and cloud formations—will tie the composition together.

A successful crayon resist requires the following:

The crayon must be applied with very heavy pressure, so that it will resist the watercolor (or water-diluted tempera) in the final stage. A demonstration by the teacher of the results of light and heavy crayoning will make the point of how hard the students must press the crayon.

Put several layers of newspapers for padding under the paper facilitates heavy crayoning.

Leave some of the paper uncrayoned, such as between two solid shapes, two colors, and object and background color.

Negative space can be enriched with a pattern of radiating lines. These might include effects such as those formed around a pebble dropped in water together with dots, spirals, circles, hatching, and cross-hatching.

Encourage students to be imaginative in their choice of color. Reliance on natural or realistic colors should be minimized. Show the paintings of Raoul Dufy as examples of fantasy choices and use of washes. White crayon can be especially effective in this technique, providing a happy, magical surprise when the paint is applied. If a final black tempera wash is not planned, black crayon provides strong contrast.

Subjects for Crayon Drawing

In addition to the subject ideas mentioned earlier, the following themes are recommended for crayon-resist projects: a flower garden, fireworks display, the circus, the fair, umbrellas in the rain, a Halloween parade, falling autumn leaves, kites in the sky, in the swimming pool, underwater explorers, and jungle birds with plumage.

When the crayoning is completed and the student is given the teacher's go-ahead, either of two techniques of resist may be employed: the wet-paper process or the dry-paper process. In the dry-paper technique, students paint directly on their completed crayon work using watercolors or tempera. If tempera is being used, the teacher must first adjust the tempera's viscosity on a sample. Students may limit themselves to one color in painting the background or employ a variety of watercolors, as exemplified in the multileaf composition illustrated in this section. If the crayon has been applied heavily, paint can be applied directly over the crayoned area, producing an attractive texture.

In the wet-paper technique, the desks or tables first should be covered with newspapers. Because the paper is fragile when wet, students should put their already-drawn-upon paper on a solid surface such as a Masonite board and, at the sink, immerse both paper and board in water until soaked. Students then transport their pieces (still on the board) to the painting station and lift them off carefully. Next, students load their brushes with watercolor or diluted tempera and drop or float the paint onto the uncrayoned areas. They also may direct the paint-laden brush around the edges of the crayoned shapes and let the color flow freely. They may use one watercolor wash (blue or blue-green is a favorite) or a variety of hues. They must be careful, however, that several bright colors do not flow together to make a dull, neutralized color. The wet-resist method is especially suited for undersea, aviary, and sparkle and flying-insect themes.

Courtesy of Frank Wachowiak.

Steps in a crayon-resist painting: First class session, using white background paper, make a preliminary drawing with a light-colored crayon rather than a pencil. Second class, add the crayon patterns and background details; the children must apply the crayons with a strong pressure so the wax will resist the subsequent watercolor. Third class, watercolor with diluted transparent watercolors so the paint does not obliterate the crayon design.

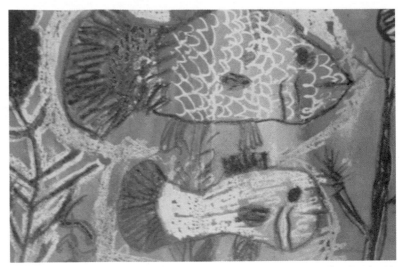

Courtesy of Frank Wachowiak.

Underwater themes are particularly good for crayon-resist paintings since most take on a watery feeling. Here, the child put a blue wash over most of the picture, but judiciously left space in the middle of the painting for a band of pink tempera wash.

To add to the picture's charm, leave some white areas of the paper unpainted. For a large class, the teacher might prepare in advance several containers of water-diluted tempera. A large table or counterspace near the sink can be designated as a painting area, and students can take turns applying the wash over their crayon composition while the rest of the class still is crayoning or otherwise engaged.

Crayon Engraving Crayon engraving, which sometimes is referred to as "crayon etching," is a fascinating technique. It involves the use of extra sturdy white drawing paper or manila file folders, wax crayons, black tempera paint, soap, brush, and engraving tools. It is a standard and popular school project, although its many possibilities seldom are carried to maximum expressiveness. If teachers allow students to be satisfied with quick, superficial scribble designs and later with random scratches, students will

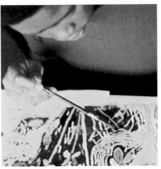

Top: *Courtesy of Donna Cummins.* Middle: *Courtesy of Frank Wachowiak and Mary Sayer Hammond.* Bottom: *Courtesy of Joyce Vroon.*

Crayon Resist: **Top and middle:** A heavy coat of crayon will resist the dark wash, which will bead up on the surface to create an enriching texture. **Bottom:** A second-grader paints with different areas of color around the crayoned forms, being careful the wash colors do not run together.

Crayon Engraving: Flowers and insects are expressed boldly through crayon engraving. In the foreground butterfly and in the huge, right-hand flower, the child's intuitive use of positive and negative pattern is brilliant. What youngsters depict so honestly and naively can be awe-inspiring.

never discover the new worlds of pattern and color overlay, or the rich enhancement that results when crayon engraving is combined with other media, such as oil pastel.

Technique

1. *The preliminary drawing.* The preliminary drawing for a crayon engraving should be made in pencil on a separate piece of newsprint or

manila paper that is the same size as the sturdy paper to be used for the final work. Because crayon engraving is a labor-intensive process, students with limited patience may prefer using paper of a small size such as 6 inch × 9 inch. Keeping sizes constant will prove to be beneficial for students retracing their drawings with dressmaker's white transfer paper.

2. *The solidly crayoned background.* The first step in a crayon engraving is to apply varied colors of crayon solidly to the sturdy paper's surface. The crayon should be applied evenly and with a strong pressure so that no part of the paper background shows. Coloring in two overlapping directions may help to ensure a rich coat of crayon, as will newspaper padding under the paper. The children may begin the crayoning phase by first making scribble designs in a light-colored crayon all over the paper and then filling in the resulting shapes solidly with a variety of bright colors. Alternatively, they may apply swatches or patches of color or have their crayoned areas coincide with their compositions. Avoid black and metallic crayons; use the most brilliant colors. After the crayoning has been completed, the surface crayon flecks should be brushed off with a cloth or paper towel. It is essential that students put their names on the backs of their crayoned sheets *before* the paint is applied.

3. *The black tempera overcoat.* The black tempera paint should be about the consistency of thin cream. Lest the black tempera paint not thoroughly cover the waxy crayon, make it adhere better by adding liquid soap or detergent to the black tempera. Approximately 1 tablespoon

Courtesy of Frank Wachowiak and Mary Sayer Hammond.

For crayon engraving, a heavy and thorough undercoat of crayon is needed. The children must press hard to lay down the necessary thick layer.

IN THE CLASSROOM

Science Topics
Crayon engraving uses a linear approach; therefore, materials that are rich in line, pattern, detail, and texture are ideal subject matter, and the natural sciences are a rich source. Some examples are animals such as the porcupine, anteater, armadillo, zebra, leopard, tiger, and rhino. Birds—especially those with exotic plumage—also are good subjects, as are reptiles such as turtles, iguanas, and horned toads and insects such as dragonflies, praying mantises, butterflies, grasshoppers, and beetles. Also of interest are crustaceans, such as crabs and crayfish; fish, shells, and coral of many species; and all varieties of plant life.

of liquid soap per pint of tempera is needed. Or, the tempera-filled brush can be rubbed over a bar of soap before it is applied to the crayoned surface. The teacher should make a test swatch and, when it is dry, determine its engravability. If the paint is too thick, it will chip off during the engraving.

4. *Transferring and engraving.* When the paint is thoroughly dry (overnight or longer), transfer the preliminary line drawing as follows:
   a. Coat the drawing's reverse side with white crayon or chalk, or use dressmaker's white transfer paper.
   b. Paper-clip the drawing (white crayon-surface down) to the black tempera–coated side of the sturdy paper, and, with a pencil or ballpoint pen, make the transfer.
   c. Engrave the lines through the tempera coating down to the crayon surface using a nail, scissors point, compass, or similar tool. (*Note:* Newspapers on the working surface are required, because the engraving phase can be messy.)
   d. Add textures, patterns, and details with nut picks, forks, and pieces of old combs.

5. *Bringing out areas.* High contrast can be achieved by using a plastic, picnic-type disposable knife to scrape away some solid-shape areas down to the crayon surface. A recommended tool, if the school budget permits, is the Sloyd or Hyde knife. This sturdy, short-bladed knife can engrave a fine line with its point or scrape away a large surface with its flat edge.

After completing the engraving, students may enrich their compositions by applying oil pastel colors back over some of the black tempera surfaces. Finally, the composition may be further enhanced by engraving details and texture through the newly oil-pasteled areas.

Facing page: In these three crayon engravings, students wisely preserved certain dark areas intact to contrast with the light-colored areas from which they scraped away the crayon. Approximately half of the areas are light and half of the areas are dark. The dark areas remain dark even after having been gone over with crayon.

Courtesy of Mary McCutheon.

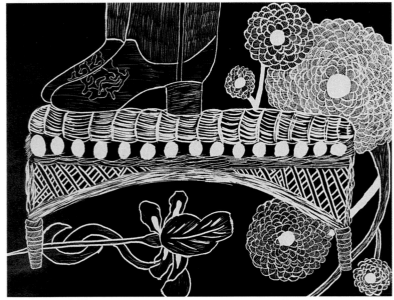

Eighth-grade. Courtesy of Baiba Kuntz.

Scratchboard is a related technique that might be considered a variation of crayon engraving and is superb for capturing textures. Notice the shades of gray achieved in the chrysanthemum heads' radiating scalloped patterns.

Crayon Encaustic: Note the floral fine-art reproductions that are displayed, the live anemone bouquet, the newspaper-covered table, and, for safety, the jars of melted crayon in a double-boiler-type pan-within-a-pan over a hot plate.

Crayon engraving is a challenging mixed-media technique. It opens up new avenues of discovery in line, color, contrast, pattern, and texture, especially for students at the upper-elementary level and above (see page 276).

Crayon Encaustic Crayon encaustic is a challenging painting medium to add to the upper-elementary- and middle-school art repertoire. Many museums contain ancient Egyptian Fayumic mummy portraits that still glow with the inner light of wax. The Greeks used encaustic on marble, and early Christians mixed little glass pieces, called *tesserae,* into it. The encaustic process is the kind of creative adventure that is reserved for those teachers who are brave in spirit, eager to try something new, and persevering enough to collect a year's supply of broken crayons. Some teachers make encaustic painting an annual late-spring event, which the students eagerly anticipate. One teacher times the activity with the blossoming of colorful anemones, which become the visual motivation for the project.

These charming paintings were created by employing the melted crayon or encaustic method. The size of the cardboard is approximately 8 × 12 inches. Color reproductions of flower paintings by artists such as Odilon Redon, Vincent van Gogh, Paul Cézanne, and Paul Gauguin were displayed and discussed during the project. A bouquet of freshly picked, multihued anemones provided the immediate visual motivation.

The steps are as follows: Remove paper wrappings from the crayons, break the crayons into small pieces, and put them in glass babyfood jars or similar containers (not made of plastic or paper) or metal muffin tins. Each jar or compartment should contain a different color. If a muffin tin is used, make sure that it fits into a deeper and slightly larger baking tin. This slightly larger cake tin containing water, making a double-boiler arrangement to heat the containers of wax, is required to prevent fires. Because of space limitations, the number of colors may need to be limited to the primary and secondary colors plus white, black, and a few tints.

The most functional working station for encaustic painting is a large, sturdy, newspaper-covered table. Place one end of the table against a wall near an electrical outlet. Place one or two electric hot plates in the middle of the table. Put the crayon-filled containers or muffin tins in a 2- or 3-inch-deep metal baking pan. Fill the pan two-thirds full of water, and place it on the hot plate. When the crayons have melted, reduce the heat and place one or more Q-tips or watercolor brushes into each crayon container. These brushes should be old and reserved for this encaustic project only. Keep the water at the temperature of the melted crayon to maintain a consistent flow of crayon.

White or colored cardboard approximately 9 × 12 or 12 × 12 inches is recommended for the painting surface. Scrap mat board, chipboard, gift-box covers, and grocery carton cardboard coated with latex are other possibilities.

A preliminary sketch for a crayon-encaustic painting is recommended, unless the theme is purely nonobjective, in the manner of Jackson Pollock, Helen Frankenthaler, and Hans Hoffman. Subject-matter possibilities include a flower bouquet, butterflies, an exotic bird in foliage, a fantastic fish among shells and seaweed, an imaginary monster, and a clown.

The teacher must supervise encaustic painting carefully. Never crowd the working station. The group must be limited to four to six students, depending on the size of the table. To prevent wax fires, the water must never be permitted to boil out of the pan. The electrical current may need to be turned off and on periodically so that the melted crayon does not cool off. Additional pieces of crayon will need to be placed in the containers. Remind students that brushes or crayon applicators should not be switched from container to container; students must wait their turn for a color. *Caution:* The crayon containers are filled with molten wax and must not be taken out of the heated pan during painting.

Crayon encaustic cannot be rushed; sometimes, the beauty of encaustic does not materialize until several layers of melted crayon have been applied. If layers are built up, the finished work will take on an exciting, thick impasto quality. When one color is applied over another, there is the possibility of further embellishment. This can be done by incising lines with a nail through the top coat to reveal the crayon color underneath. To solve the problem of an insufficient number of old crayons when a large area must be covered, powdered tempera can be mixed with melted paraffin. Crayon encaustic produces paintings with color richness and glow that are unsurpassed (see also page 280).

OIL PASTEL

The introduction of oil pastels in their rich and exciting array of hues has opened a whole new world of color exploration and expression in both elementary and middle schools. Oil pastels generally are within most schools' budget range. The only caution is that because of their oil content, they may stain clothing. The most attractive feature of oil pastels is the ease with which students can apply them to obtain shimmering, vivid, painterly color compositions. Thus, students can produce rich results without the pressure required for regular crayons. Oil pastels work especially well on deep-colored construction paper, in which the colored background serves as a unifying or complementary factor. Young students should be encouraged in their first efforts to apply the pastels boldly in solid-color areas, pressing hard to achieve a glowing surface, and to use color contrasts. Because the intensity of the pastel hues is affected by the paper color, students should note the effects of small color swatches on their paper's reverse side.

Courtesy of Frank Wachowiak and Mary Sayer Hammond.

Top: Oil pastel on black paper of birds in trees. **Bottom:** Astronauts in their spaceship, third-grade oil pastel.

Left: *Courtesy of Joyce Vroon.* Right: *Courtesy of Donna Cummins.*

Left: Oil pastel is much more widely used in schools than regular pastel, shown here in this fourth-grader's drawing of a pumpkin and corn on a crazy quilt. **Right:** This portrait was done in oil pastels on black paper based on van Gogh's post-Impressionistic technique of small directional strokes.

Recommendations for oil-pastel projects, especially when colored construction paper is used for the background, are as follows:

- Make the preliminary drawing or sketch with white or light school chalk or crayon. Chalk is excellent, because it is easily erased. (Use a paper towel or facial tissue if the students want to make changes.)
- Press for the richest effects. One suggestion for coloring in small or complex shapes is to apply the pastel in a line close to the chalk outline and then fill in the shape. Discourage haphazard, scribbled coloring.

Courtesy of Frank Wachowiak and Mary Sayer Hammond.

Oil-Pastel Resist: Steps: **Top:** Preliminary chalk drawing on colored construction paper. **Middle:** Oil pastel applied in solids and patterns up to but not covering the chalk lines. **Bottom:** Slightly water-diluted black tempera applied lightly with a soft-bristle brush.

Courtesy of Frank Wachowiak and Mary Sayer Hammond.

Oil-Pastel Resist: The resist color of wash goes into the lines left empty and creates a stained-glass effect and also adds texture on the plain areas.

- Remind students that colors have many tints and shades, which are especially important for capturing leaves and grassy fields with their nuances of light and shade.
- Black, white, and grey add to any color scheme.

Colors, both tints and shades, bright and dull, including the blacks and whites, should be repeated in different parts of the composition to create unity. This color repetition should employ differences of size, shape, and intensity. A hue that is repeated for unity should be differentiated in value so that the echo of the color is there without the monotony of pure repetition. Differentiation is especially important when the student is making a pattern such as bricks on a wall, tiles on a roof, or stones in a walk, where the repetition of the same color becomes static and lifeless unless sensitively varied. Remember that contrasting values are stronger than contrasting hues.

When it is desired that the colored paper background show through in a complementing way, apply the pastel impressionistically in strokes, lines, or dots. New colors can be created by applying pastel over pastel; however, a very light color cannot be totally darkened unless the light is first scraped off. A dark color can be lightened somewhat by the application of white, and colors can be dulled through application of their complements, such as red over green, orange over blue. To alter a color, first use soft pressure with varidirectional strokes, and then increase pressure.

Oil-Pastel Resist

Oil pastels alone can be beautifully employed as a final step in many techniques, such as tempera paintings, crayon engravings, and vegetable or found-object prints. However, they also can be used in the oil pastel–resist process with stunning results.

Teachers and students who are familiar with the crayon-resist technique will welcome oil pastel as another resist medium. It does not require the time or intense exertion on the part of the students that crayons demand.

The same steps as outlined for the crayon-resist technique should be followed:

- Make a preliminary drawing in chalk.
- Vary the width of the chalk line, and emphasize thicker lines.
- Apply the oil pastel heavily so that it will resist the final coat of black paint.
- Leave the chalk lines showing and uncovered.
- Use the brightest, most intense pastel hues.
- Avoid black.

Before applying paint, evaluate the final oil-pastel composition for a variation of repeated colors. Also, look for a variety of patterns: dots, circles, overlapping wiggly lines, radiating lines in circles or rays, ripple-in-a-stream lines, hatch and cross-hatch lines, stars, asterisks, diamonds, and spirals.

Before applying paint, also gently brush off the chalk lines. Place the composition on a newspaper-protected surface and apply a coat of black tempera paint. Applied with a soft brush, the paint must be of exactly the right consistency—not too thin, not too thick. Because paint formulas change, always do a test first (some tempera paints now contain an adhesive and cannot be used). If the paint covers the areas of oil pastel, it is too thick. The resisting oil in the oil pastels will dry out soon after it is applied to the paper, so do not wait too long to apply the black paint. Finally, oil pastel–resist compositions may be given a protective coat of gloss polymer medium to enhance their beauty.

FOR FURTHER READING

Harrison, Hazel. *Pastel School: A Practical Guide to Drawing with Pastels* (Reader's Digest Learn-As-You-Go Guide). Pleasantville, NY: Readers Digest Association.

Hughes, Jane. 1994. *Oil Pastels.* New York: Price Stern Sloan.

LaLiberte, Norman, and Alex Mogelon. 1967. *Painting with Crayons: History and Modern Techniques.* New York: Reinhold.

WEB RESOURCES

For lesson plans using crayons:

http://www.crayola.com/educators/lessons/index.cfm?mt=lessonplans

For a guide to website lessons on pastels:

http://www.wannalearn.com/Fine_Arts/Visual_Art/Painting/Pastels/

Courtesy of Beverly Barksdale Mallon.

What verve, what spontaneity is shown in this watercolor of daffodils! A free pencil sketch the previous period preceded primary student Annabelle Barbe's painting, which captures the very essence of springtime.

Chapter 25

Painting

PAINTING WITH WATERCOLORS

Although tempera is the most common and popular painting medium in elementary- and middle-school art programs, many teachers use transparent watercolors. These come in semimoist cakes or tiny tubes packaged in metal or plastic containers, and they are available in primary and secondary colors as well as black. Transparent watercolor painting demands special technical skills; mature painters devote countless hours to its mastery, employing a wide range of beautiful colors available in tube form and costly sable-hair brushes.

The watercolor painting on page 286 is by a Japanese elementary-school student. Children are provided with a spectrum of watercolors in tubes and painting palettes beginning in the first grade. Most of their watercolor paintings begin with a preliminary sketch in pencil or pen. In some cases, children moisten the paper before beginning the coloring. As these paintings reveal, many persevere to produce rich, space-filled compositions that exhibit transparent watercolors' characteristic spontaneity.

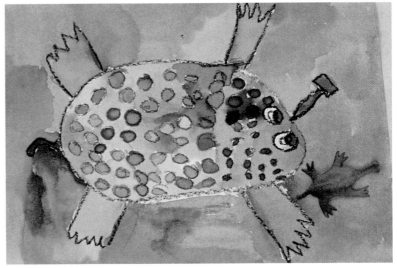

Courtesy of Melody Milbrandt.

To illustrate a story, a kindergartner painted this frog, made delightful by multihued bumps and the spectrum of colors on the body.

Teachers often employ the semimoist watercolors to teach about the color properties of hue, value, and intensity. Mixing primary colors will produce secondary colors, and mixing secondary colors will produce tertiary colors. Diluting a color with water in gradual stages can produce a color-value chart. Color can be neutralized by mixing with complementary hues, and creating watercolor washes on moist paper achieves dark-to-light sky and water effects.

The following recommendations constitute a "primer" for water-color projects:

White watercolor or construction paper is recommended.

Newspapers under paintings help to speed cleanup and also provide a practice surface.

Round, pointed, soft-bristle, camel-hair brushes are recommended. They should always be rinsed clean at the end of the period and stored either bristle-end-up or flat in a container.

Watercolor boxes containing the semimoist cakes of paint should be rinsed and wiped clean at the close of the period and then allowed to dry open.

Water containers should be changed when the water in them becomes muddy. Paper towels are handy for absorbing spills and blotting up excess paint on works in progress.

Preliminary sketches in pencil, felt-nib or nylon-tipped pen, or light watercolor applied with a small brush are recommended.

Areas that are to appear white or light in the final painting can be masked with masking tape before the paper is moistened or the painting begun. When the painting is completed and dry, the mask can be removed and a final touch-up made.

Watercolor washes of the same color in the same value applied over one another will darken the color. Students should begin a painting with light colors or values and build to darker colors for detail.

When painting is done on a wet surface, the paper may need to be remoistened by occasionally lightly sprinkling the surface with water.

Paintings appear vibrant and contrasting when moist but unfortunately lose their brilliance when dry. A second application of watercolor paint over a dried color may help.

While wet or moist, paintings should not be stored one on top of another. If no drying rack or counters are available, dry the paintings on the floor around the room's perimeter.

Some very successful watercolor projects are those in which watercolor is combined with colored crayons or oil pastels in a resist method (see the preceding chapter).

Top: *Courtesy of Joyce Vroon.*

Top: Watercolors color the marker drawings of toys and dolls. Notice the watercolor sets and the six-compartment plastic mixing trays for mixing colors. **Bottom:** "My Friend and Me," by a first-grade child in Japan, shows a hairy, toothy figure painted in complementary colors, yellow and purple.

Study art history exemplars: watercolors by Winslow Homer and John Singer Sargent, and brush paintings from China and Japan.

One aesthetic issue to be considered is the importance in art (and in life) of spontaneity, verve, and assuredness—a vibrant, fresh appearance versus a labored, fussy, muddled appearance.

PAINTING WITH TEMPERA

All children should have the opportunity to express their ideas with brush and paint. The best-quality tempera paints, whether in powder or liquid form, are rich in color and have excellent covering properties. Children who paint with tempera can apply color over color freely to achieve jewel-like effects or repaint areas with which they are not pleased.

Teachers are aware of the possibilities for colorful art expressions that tempera offers, yet they sometimes do not include it in their art programs because of its cost and the housekeeping chores involved. Tempera projects do require more preparation of materials, more careful storage, and more controlled cleanup procedures than watercolor or crayon projects; nonetheless, these factors should not prevent teachers from discovering how tempera painting can enrich children's art repertoire.

Even when classes are large and facilities limited, there are expeditious, time-saving methods for incorporating tempera into the art program. For example, cardboard soda-bottle containers and discarded glass-tumbler carryalls can be used as carrying cases. Likewise, discarded baby-food jars and half-pint milk cartons can serve as containers. To prevent the paint from drying out between sessions, the milk cartons can be resealed with spring clothespins.

Students can both perform a service and gain color knowledge by helping to prepare the tempera paint. They can mix various hues, tints, shades, and neutralized colors. For extra beauty in the paintings, consider restricting the color choices to, for example, only triadic colors, a narrow range of analogous colors, or all very light colors. For a class of 30 children, about 60 containers of varying colors should be prepared, as well as an additional six containers of white and four containers of black. Usually containers should only be partially filled to the length of the brush's bristles to keep paint from covering the brush's metal ferrule and the students' fingers.

Courtesy of Frank Wachowiak and Ted Ramsay.

Paint Large: Painting on large-paper surfaces (24- × 36-inch or larger) lets primary-grade children boldly express their ideas in paint. Cover the floor with newspapers, and let the children paint freely.

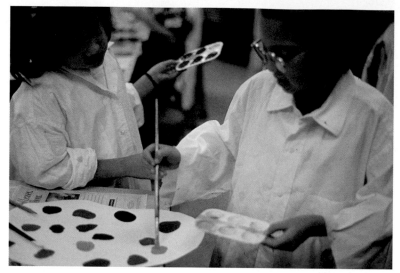

Wear Smocks: Old white shirts will protect students' clothing. Here, second-graders paint a large palette by mixing their new colors in little paint trays.

If class time is limited, the teacher may need to prepare the color assortment in advance. Those who object to this procedure because it does not give students the opportunity to learn about mixing colors should note that professional artists usually have a wealth of colors, tints, shades, and neutrals at their disposal to create paintings. Children deserve the same advantage. When the class is limited to a few basic colors because there is not enough time to mix a variety, the expressive output of the children suffers, and the joy in painting diminishes.

Place the individual containers of paint on a table or rolling cart that is accessible from all sides. It should be low enough so the various colors are visible. If possible, a separate brush should be available for every container. This procedure saves time, paint, and squabbles over brushes. The children take turns choosing and using a container of color, and when they finish with it, they return it (with its brush inside) to the supply station. Children should use only one color at a time—and use it thoroughly throughout

Visually appealing desserts might be donated by a caterer, for a lesson tied to Wayne Thibaud's dessert still-life paintings. Also note the tables arranged around the still life, and the egg boxes and trays for third-graders mixing the many tints and shades of tempera paint.

Left: *Courtesy of Zoey Timberlake-Walzer.* Middle: *Courtesy of Bess Durham.* Right: *Courtesy of Joyce Vroon.*

Left: If space and materials permit, paint very large, as this kindergartner did. **Middle:** The values in a portrait can be minimized to only four and a different color used for each value. **Right:** Tempera blocks are similar to watercolors in ease of use and cleanup, although the colors are more opaque.

the painting. Some teachers have used a timed swap of colors among their students. To achieve unity and balance in their paintings, encourage students to repeat colors around the picture. While primarily aesthetic, this injunction also has the practical advantage of minimizing traffic around the supply station.

Adequate time should be allotted for cleanup. Because brushes left standing for long periods of time in paint lose their elasticity, they should be taken out of the paint containers and squeezed so that paint remaining in the brush flows back into the container. The brushes should then be placed in a large basin of soapy water to soak overnight. The next morning, they can be rinsed in clear water and stored either bristle-end-up or flat in a box. Brushes with wood handles must be washed and stored to dry immediately lest the wooden handle be damaged. Unless the baby-food jars of paint can be covered, store the jars in an airtight cupboard or drawer, or put the containers on a tray and seal the tray in a giant plastic bag. To prevent the lips and edges of containers from sticking, they should occasionally be wiped clean or waxed.

Some teachers use plastic egg cartons or ice-cube trays as tempera paint containers. In this method, each student has a brush, and he or she washes the brush before using another color. To prevent drying of leftover paint seal the cartons or trays in plastic bags. To help prevent the unpleasant odor of aging tempera, a drop of wintergreen can be added to the big jars of tempera.

Semimoist cakes of opaque paint are now available in tubs or tins, and some teachers claim that these save time in cleanup and storage procedures. Others, however, say that paint in this form inhibits the free-flowing style that liquid tempera encourages in children. Indeed, during the primary grades, tempera painting is a hit. The very young child especially enjoys making bold, splashy designs in paint and needs only the materials and an invitation to start. Themes such as explosion in a paint factory, Fourth-of-July fireworks, butterflies in a flower garden, bunny rabbit's Easter party, a kite fight, and planets in outer space fire the imagination. Colored construction paper, including black, provides an excellent surface for tempera painting because the color of the paper can

Tempera painting on colored paper cut out and glued to a sponge-painted background paper: Using black paper, first-grader Tangenika Watson painted this elephant, inspired by the circus's arrival in town. Language arts teachers, look for the letter "E," for elephant, hidden in the animal's blanket.

unify the composition. Try adventurous choices such as wallpaper samples and newspaper classified pages.

The following strategies have proved to be helpful in tempera painting projects:

Encourage students to make preliminary sketches on their paper in chalk or with a brush and light-colored paint.

Minimize cleanup by using protective newspapers on paint supply stations and individual painting areas. Have moist towels available for accidental paint spills and use protective plastic on the carpet.

Develop preventive strategies for those likely to spill—for example, a minimal amount of paint in the containers, or special holders and containers.

Encourage children to wear protective clothing, such as an old shirt.

Remind students to wipe excess paint from their brushes back into the containers.

Lest the paint colors run together, children should avoid painting next to a painted area that still is wet.

When making a color change, urge students to wait until a color is completely dry before painting over it.

If brushes must be cleaned during the painting session, tell students to squeeze out the excess water thoroughly before using the brush to paint again. Otherwise, the paint in the individual containers will become water–diluted and less intense.

Fifth-grader Sarah Billington paints in the areas of her marker-drawn bird. She chose an assortment of colors in low values for a dramatic night effect.

Tempera-resist Painting: **Left:** A middle-schooler's bird painting shows a flowing division of shapes in analogous colors. **Middle:** In this painting of trees, the black resist line varies in width and creates interest. **Right:** In this painting of a dozen different flowers and a spider in its web, the bits of black that adhere to the solid-paint areas are preserved to add interest.

During upper elementary and middle school, students can explore other ways of painting. They can paint on moist, colored construction paper. They can use the dry-brush or pointillistic approach to achieve texture. They can explore mixed-media techniques, combining tempera and crayon, tempera and pastel, and tempera and India ink in a semibatik process.

Encourage older students to mix a greater variety of tints, shades, and neutralized hues to achieve a more individual and personal style. They can use discarded pie tins, TV-dinner trays, and plastic cafeteria trays for their palettes. They must be supervised and cautioned, however, to be economical and not to mix more paint than they need. For tints, they should add the hue a tiny bit at a time to the white paint rather than vice versa. Paint tins always should be rinsed out at the end of class.

Students cannot rush through a tempera painting project any more than they can hurry through any qualitative creative endeavor; therefore, sufficient time must be allotted for all phases of the undertaking. First comes the motivational time, then the preliminary sketching session. These are followed by the studio work, which involves choices of colors and then achievement of contrast, pattern, and detail. Throughout the studio activity, there should be evaluation of the work in its several stages. Finally, the completed paintings are exhibited and discussed. With so much to be gained from the experience, tempera painting should be included in every school art program!

TEMPERA RESIST

For middle-school students who have had many elementary-school experiences painting with tempera, try tempera resist. Tempera resist employs a thick liquid tempera underpainting followed by a final coating of India ink. It is a challenging technique replete with hidden surprises. Although highly recommended as an exciting project in painting, tempera resist presents some materials problems, the high cost of India ink among them.

The tempera paint that is employed should be a good quality liquid tempera. Powdered tempera is not recommended, although some teachers claim that powdered tempera works when it is mixed with a small amount of liquid glue. Whether liquid or powder, the paint must be of a thick, creamy consistency—not watery—and should be applied heavily. Watery paint will absorb the final ink coating rather than resist it. Bright, intense hues of tempera should be employed for the highest contrast of black ink against color. Avoid the use of dark blue, dark purple, and brown, which

will not show up. Subtle, lightly greyed hues, such as sienna, ochre, light umber, and light grey also are effective. White may be employed with discrimination but generally should be repeated, because a solitary white area often detracts from the rest of the composition. Recommended papers are construction paper in white or light colors and cardboard from store cartons.

Considerable time is needed for the various steps in the tempera resist process: the preliminary drawing, the tempera painting, the inking, the rinsing, and the optional coating with gloss polymer. The sketch or preliminary drawing should be made in chalk. Encourage students to vary the pressure of the chalk lines, making lines from thick to thin. The importance of this will be revealed in the second phase, when the ink is applied and soaks into the space left by the chalked lines. A relevant aesthetic consideration for this project is that the more the students break large shapes into small shapes, the more beautiful the finished result will be. As students paint with the tempera, urge them to paint up to, but not over, the chalked lines, leaving a gap from ⅟₁₆ to ³⁄₁₆ of an inch wide. The more varied in width the chalk lines and the spaces remaining between painted areas, the more successfully contrasting the composition will be. Remind students not to paint the shapes, areas, and details they want to be black in the completed painting.

Caution students that a tempera color painted over another dry tempera area will wash off in the final rinse; therefore, they must plan their color scheme in advance. Patterns painted into wet tempera areas can be effective, however. Encourage students to use exciting variety in their colors—for example, to employ varied kinds of green for grass and trees, or many values and intensities of blue for skies. After all of the areas to be colored are painted, the subsequent day's work must be stored to dry completely. For the India inking phase, cover a work surface with newspapers. With a tissue, wipe off the chalk remaining in the lines. Place the painting on the newspapers and paint it with the India ink in random, circular strokes. Totally cover the painting, and then again store it overnight to dry completely.

Because wet paintings tear easily, for the final rinsing phase put the painting onto a protective backing, such as a Masonite board or old

Top three: *Courtesy of Frank Wachowiak.* Bottom two: *Courtesy of David W. Hodge.*

Steps in creating a tempera–India ink resist (from top to bottom): **1:** A school-chalk preliminary drawing on white or light-colored construction paper is painted. **2:** With a quality brand of liquid-type tempera, paint up to the chalk outline, but do not cover the line, and allow it to dry completely. **3:** Undiluted India ink is applied generously over the tempera surface, allowed to dry thoroughly, and rinsed off at the sink. **4 and 5:** The before-and-after results of another picture.

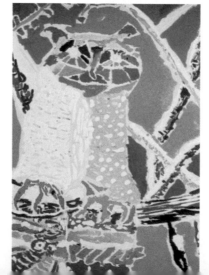

cafeteria tray. Place them into the sink and rinse with cold water, or take them outdoors and rinse them gently with a hose. Begin rinsing in the center of the work and move outward. Do not direct the water toward the same area for long, however, because too much paint will wash off or, even worse, the paper will disintegrate. A moist sponge or finger may bring out the color where the ink stubbornly sticks. After rinsing, very carefully lift the painting onto a counter or the floor and blot it with paper towels. When the tempera-resist painting is completely dry, give it a protective and enhancing coat of liquid wax or glossy polymer medium.

MURAL MAKING

Mural projects help students to acquire not only art knowledge but also another kind of knowledge—what it means to work with others to plan and carry out a project. Collaborative art builds self-esteem and diminishes alienation. Students learn positive methods for group interaction. Group involvement in projects of large scale and scope—for example, decorating the classroom for a celebration, or presenting a series of works on a central theme—builds memories.

Once a theme is selected, other questions follow: What medium or technique should be employed? How large should the mural be? Where can we work on it? Is there a nearby blank construction fence? Where will it be displayed when completed? How shall each student's contribution to the mural be decided?

Courtesy of Frank Wachowiak and Ted Ramsay.

The group mural "Fun at the Park" was painted by elementary-school children on a 10- × 200-foot plywood construction barrier. The fence was primed, a chalk preliminary sketch was done on it, and then its lines were painted with black enamel applied with ½- and 1-inch-wide utility brushes. Parents then donated leftover paints in a variety of colors to fill in the colors.

Courtesy of David W. Hodge.

Classroom tables are tipped on edge to make a solid surface against which kids in smocks paint their mural, "A circus comes to our city."

IN THE CLASSROOM

Constructivist Education in Action

With the teacher acting as facilitator, students can work as a group to generate ideas; children and teacher can be co-learners. Educational goals can be organized according to objectives, and strategies for assessing the project's effectiveness in addressing community concerns can be developed.

Some subjects have almost universal appeal to particular age groups, and certain themes are especially appropriate. For very young children, suggested topics are a butterfly dance, land of make-believe, fish in the sea, Noah's ark, and a flower garden. Intermediate- and elementary-school children favor the farm, birds in a tree, animals at the zoo or in the jungle, games on the playground, when dragons roamed the world, and fun at the beach.

Upper-elementary- and middle-school students react positively to astronauts in space, a kite-flying contest, aquanauts exploring the sea, rodeo, rock festival, block party, state fair, three-ring circus, winter carnival, world of the future, and where and how young people in our community play and relax.

The social studies curriculum can be brought in, and students and teacher can together identify issues relevant to the fabric of the community: conservation and pollution, affordable housing, changes in community businesses, vanishing open space, the relation of growth and quality of life. They can learn that their art can help bring these issues to community consciousness. And they will learn a lesson about the art of our postmodern era: that art is not an entity divorced from our lives and the community, but can be instead a vehicle for bringing about social change. (See Chapters 7 through 11 concerning integration with other subjects.)

Before the class begins a mural, the teacher who is interested in integrating art history and social studies with the project can ask, "Are there any murals in our community's public buildings, post offices, and schools? What was their original social, political, or educational intent?" Through discussion about the mural painter's intent, children can gain knowledge of the role of art in interpreting their community. The great Mexican muralists of the 1930s used art and design to show inequities in society. In our classes, we can represent real community concerns. If the mural is to be displayed out in the community, then the community is permitted to see its issues afresh through the eyes of its children.

A Collage Pin-Up Mural If, for example, a collage-type pin-up mural is agreed on, the following procedure is recommended: Urge students to make objects and figures both large and small. When all students have completed their individual contributions to the total mural, the teacher and students should devote at least one art session to composing the mural. Discuss the merits of the placement and design. Here, the teacher's tact and gentle persuasion play an important role. Bring to the children's attention that a mural in one sense is like a giant painting and requires the same compositional treatment. Urge students to strive for varied sizes of objects or figures, varied heights, and varied breakup of space in both foreground and background. Encourage overlapping of shapes, grouping of objects to achieve unity, and quiet areas to balance busy or detailed ones. Have students use larger shapes or figures at the bottom of the mural and smaller ones at the top to create an illusion of distance.

Children who complete their assigned segments early can enhance the compositions with space-filling elements, such as rainbows, clouds, and pets. They also might wish to add recreational and transportation equipment: balls, kites, cars, trucks, bicycles, motorcycles, frisbees, planes. Some can make street furniture—telephone poles, mailboxes, signs, fences, and

Courtesy of Frank Wachowiak and Mary Sayer Hammond.

A Cut-Out, Pin-Up Mural: Fourth-graders' oil pastel drawings of astronauts and spaceships were cut out and transformed into an exciting mural collage.

benches—and landscape elements—trees, bushes, and rocks. When the separate segments finally are arranged in a composition that is pictorially unified, they are stapled or glued in place. If the mural is attached to a separate piece of plywood or heavy carton cardboard, display it in the school's entrance foyer, hallway, or lunchroom for everyone to enjoy; exhibit it in a building out in the community; or exhibit it first in the school and then in the community.

For example, fun and fairness on the playground can be the theme for a collage (cut-and-paste) mural. Ask the following questions: What kinds of games or sports should be included? (List them on the markerboard or chalkboard.) How shall we decide which activity each student will portray? How many different areas of the playground will we include? What types of playground equipment will we show? Why shouldn't all children in the mural be the same size? Will they all be dressed alike? (Make a list on the chalkboard of the different kinds of clothing and uniforms the children in the mural might wear.) What patterns will we show on their clothes? (Wallpaper samples or fabric remnants may be used.) What else can we include? (Make a list on the markerboard or chalkboard: trees, fences, airplanes, signs, and so on.)

Scaling Up a Mural A different method, using measuring and mathematical scaling, teaches students how to scale up a mural. For example, for a figurative mural such as "Playing on the Playground," begin by making a tag board mannequin. Draw and cut from oak tag the parts of the bodies (a convenient conversion is one foot = five feet, which is about the size of a child), then arrange the parts into an action pose. The more exuberant and active the pose the better: upside down, doing handstands, etc. Then put a paper over the loose, arranged pieces and rub over it with a dark crayon. In order to scale up the drawing to mural size, measure and draw 1-inch squares on the small sketch—called a "cartoon" in mural-making terminology. If the cartoon sketch was on 9- × 12-inch paper, and the final size is to be three times as large, then students will need papers 27- × 36-inch ruled into 3-inch squares. A length of newsprint from a discarded newsroll will give this size. Write tiny corresponding numbers on each square of both papers to help in copying lines in the correct square.

To paint the mural, tape down the drop cloth and erect the scaffold. To transfer the figures (now on large paper) to the wall, either cut them out and trace around them or hold the paper up to a window and put colorful chalk on the back side where the lines are. Next, place the paper right side up on the wall and go over the lines, leaving a faint chalk line on the wall. Then go over the lines and paint the figures. To minimize student crowding at the mural, have students, working in small groups, paint throughout the day.

An upper-elementary student retouches the lines on the painted rhinoceros he contributed to a jungle-theme group mural. The school-chalk preliminary drawing was made on large, mattress-box cardboard sheets. Then, chalk lines were gone over with black tempera for unity of line throughout the mural. The children then painted up to, but did not cover, the black outlines. Finally, the murals were displayed in the children's ward in a local hospital.

Other mural techniques and media also can be used. For example, for freestyle, expressive murals that are painted directly on surfaces such as oaktag, cardboard, poster board, and hardboard, use tempera or latex acrylic paint. Use a preliminary outline in black paint to spark the composition and give it unity. Choose a design from among those submitted by individuals or small groups, or select several effective designs to be incorporated into one design. Then have small groups of students take turns painting.

FOR FURTHER READING

Hurwitz, Al. 1993. *Collaboration in Art Education.* Reston, VA: NAEA.

Morman, Jean. 1989. *One- Two- Three Murals: Simple Murals to Make Using Children's Open-Ended Art.* Everett, WA: Frank Schaeffer Publishers.

Smith, Nancy R. 1982. *Experience and Art: Teaching Children to Paint.* New York: Teachers College Press.

WEB RESOURCES

For a lesson plan for creating a mural:

http://www.haringkids.com/lessons/envs/live/htdocs/lesson119.htm

For some watercolor tips:

http://www.webindia123.com/craft/paint/water/watpaint.html

For first graders painting skies with motivation from van Gogh:

http://www.getty.edu/artsednet/resources/Sampler/b.html

For symbols in paintings by Edward Hicks and Jan van Eyvk:

http://www.getty.edu/artsednet/resources/Sampler/c-4.html#check

For a global mural project:

http://mural.dhs.org/

Top: *Courtesy of Melody Milbrandt.* Bottom: *Photo courtesy of Virginia S. Robinson.*

Top: Taking advantage of transmitted light for a stained-glass-window effect, fourth- and fifth-grade students stand atop the shelving to paint their jungle mural. **Bottom:** Hundreds of clay balls were flattened and stamped with designs. Some were stained. Then they were arranged by middle-school students into a mural of lasting beauty. See Virginia Smithwick Robinson and Robert Clements, "Mosaic Panels," *Arts & Activities,* May 1982.

Chapter 26

Paper Projects in Two Dimensions

COLLAGE

A popular form of visual expression in elementary and middle schools today is collage, with its related family of montage, decoupage, mosaic, collograph, and assemblage. Over 80 years ago, shocked dismay greeted the initial collages of Pablo Picasso, Georges Braque, Carlo Carra, and Kurt Schwitters, in which the artists dared to include cardboard and printed words. Today, their creations in paper, cardboard scraps, and paste (the word *collage* derives from the French *coller*, which means "to stick or to adhere") are priceless, and the collage technique has become standard in advertising art. The wellsprings from which contemporary artists such as Robert Rauschenberg and Alexis Smith now draw their materials are so bountiful that the technique is limitless in its possibilities.

Technical Suggestions The collage technique is especially suited for design using overlapping of shapes and colors, positive and negative shapes, value contrast, pattern, and texture. Students have the unique opportunity of rearranging the elements in their work until they achieve a satisfying composition. Approaches to collage range from simple cutting, tearing, and pasting of paper to complex sewing, shearing, and gluing of fabric, plastics, posters, plywood, cardboard, Day-Glo paper, wallpaper and rug samples, paint chips, colored tissue paper, and colored magazine pages. (The artist Jean Dubuffet even used coffee grounds and butterfly wings!)

A preliminary sketch is recommended when the subject matter is a landscape, figure composition, or still-life arrangement. For themes from the imagination, for fantasy, or for purely nonobjective designs, direct cutting, tearing, and pasting are acceptable. In either approach, however, permanent adherence of the separate parts should be postponed until both student and teacher critique the work's strengths and weaknesses. Some other suggestions for making collages are as follows:

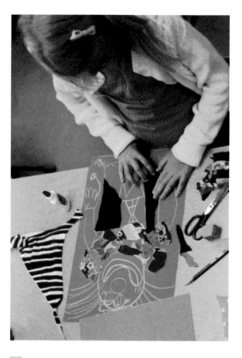

Courtesy of Frank Wachowiak.

Cloth Collage: A large drawing that fills the page is made with chalk on a piece of 12- × 18-inch colored paper. Then, to fill the areas, the child cuts and fits cloth scraps, yarn, buttons, rickrack, and colored-paper scraps to embellish the artwork.

Cut and arrange the large shapes or motifs first. If a colored background is used, allow some of the background to show to unify the composition.

Small details and patterns can be pasted onto the large shapes before they are glued to the background surface. Overlapping of shapes is a major feature of collage making.

Eye-catching materials, such as aluminum foil, synthetic silver and gold foils, shiny plastic, and cellophane, fascinate children, who tend to overuse them. Guide the students to use such materials only as points of emphasis. One way to force restraint is to give out only the tiniest piece of such potentially distracting material.

Repetition of a color, shape, value, pattern, or texture adds unity to a collage; however, instead of repeating the element, color, or shape exactly, vary it somehow. Recommend using an uneven repetition of elements; for example, repeat a certain shape or color three times rather than twice, five times rather than four.

Encourage the use of informal (asymmetrical) rather than formal (symmetrical) balance.

Avoid a lot of "sticky" problems by using discarded magazines as paste applying surfaces. When a clean pasting area is needed, turn to another page.

IN THE CLASSROOM

Collage Projects

Ambitious teachers may want to enlist both parents and children in making cloth banners from the students' paper designs. Army units in ancient Rome each had their own decorated standard. Cloth banners were first used in the Middle Ages during the Crusades, when each force had its own insignia. Artists such as Miriam Shapiro, Jim Dine, Henri Matisse, and Richard Lindner have had banners of their collage designs made. Social science topics might include world issues, international treaties, flags for nearby neighborhoods. Science topics: trees of the region, my pets, distinctive animals of each continent, endangered species.

Top: *Courtesy of Frank Wachowiak and Mary Sayer Hammond.* Middle: *Courtesy of Baiba Kuntz.* Bottom: *Courtesy of David W. Hodge.*

Top: Colored Construction Paper Scrap Collage: Primary-grade youngsters arranged colored paper scraps for their compositions. Supplemental details, patterns, and motifs were added with crayons, oil pastels, markers, paper punches, and brush and paint. **Middle:** Felt Collage: Following a preliminary drawing, sixth-grader Kate Roberts used colored felts for her fish collage. Notice how the overlapping layers and the split-complementary colors of blue-green versus red-orange and yellow-orange add richness to the design. **Bottom:** Cathy Hodge cuts scraps of paper and cloth to fit her drawing.

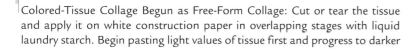

Colored-Tissue Collage Begun as Free-Form Collage: Cut or tear the tissue and apply it on white construction paper in overlapping stages with liquid laundry starch. Begin pasting light values of tissue first and progress to darker values. If a mistake occurs, paste a sheet of white paper over the area and start again. When dry, use black and colored felt-nib markers to outline recognizable shapes. Then finish with crayons and paint.

TISSUE-PAPER COLLAGE

On the first day of a tissue-paper-collage project, the teacher can surprise the class by unfolding a package of tissue papers of assorted colors. Students' excitement will grow as one color of tissue overlaps another on a white paper background or against the window. Students can tell the teacher which colors to overlap, and then they can invent a name for the resulting hue.

Non-Objective Design To encourage color awareness and exploration, a free-design, nonobjective, colored-tissue collage is recommended for children in the third grade and older. Using a 12- × 18-inch sheet of oak

This beautifully composed colored-tissue-paper collage is by a talented middle-school student. Photographs and color slides of matadors, toreadors, and "brave bulls" motivated the permanent marker drawing on white construction paper. Before applying the colored tissue, the student chose certain shapes—matador's trousers, jacket, etc.—for patterned embellishment with magazine picture patterns. The tissue was applied by first coating an area with liquid laundry starch and then placing the tissue over it, and then the area was re-coated with the starch, making sure that all edges were smoothly secured. Light-colored tissue was applied first, progressing to the darker colors. Caution was employed in the final stages so that dark-value tissue did not obliterate the important, form-defining ink lines.

tag, white drawing paper, or construction paper as a background surface, cut or tear different sizes and shapes of tissue. Adhere them to the background using undiluted liquid laundry starch as the adhesive, and overlap the various shapes. A ½-inch utility brush or a large watercolor brush makes an excellent starch applicator. Because it is difficult to change the value of a dark tissue by overlapping, begin with the lighter-colored tissues and proceed only gradually to darker values. Reserve the darker colors for the second phase of pasting.

First, apply a coating of starch to the area that is to be covered with tissue. Then, place the tissue carefully over the wet area and apply another coat of starch over it. If brushes pick up some of the color from the moistened tissue, rinse them. Be sure that all loose tissue edges are glued down well. Empty half-pint milk cartons are readily available starch containers. Because tissue is expensive and wrinkles and crumples very easily, storage boxes should be used to store the tissue, one box for each hue.

Finding Subject Matter Although the abstract composition has an aesthetic validity of its own, it can be augmented as follows: After students have filled their compositions to the borders of the paper, challenge them to look for hidden shapes. These might be suggestive of animals, birds, insects, fish, or fantasy creatures. Once a form emerges, students can glue on additional torn pieces or strips of tissue in deeper colors to represent appendages, which give the shape character and individuality. Avoid outlining the revealed figure so boldly that it is isolated from the rest of the composition. Employ a variety of dark-colored tissues for this step rather than a single hue. Black tissue can be used, but only in a most restrained way. Similarly, if students outline only one figure with a black felt-nib marker, that one figure will be isolated, but if all emerging figures are outlined in black, a unity will be achieved.

In addition to black markers, students can use crayons, colored markers, and tempera paint in white, gray, or black to delineate desired shapes, such as bark on a tree, scales on a fish, feathers on a bird, and veins in a wing or leaf. Wait until the tissue surface is dry, especially if using water-soluble markers.

Over a Bold Drawing The free-design approach using colored tissue described earlier is only one of many avenues for creating with such tissue. Another approach uses a preliminary bold drawing made with black or dark-colored crayons on light-colored, heavy paper. After the drawing is completed, the cut or torn tissue paper is applied; as in the previous method, begin with the lighter hues. Cut or tear the tissue sheet slightly larger than the drawn shapes. Drawn lines sometimes are obscured by dark tissue overlays, but when the tissue layer is dry, these lines can be redrawn for emphasis. Using lettering from printed publications in con-

Courtesy of David W. Hodge.

A drawing with permanent marker of a seated boy with bird and bicycle wheel was made on 18- × 24-inch white paper. Then, a tissue shape was cut or torn and an area selected for it. Next, laundry starch was applied to that area and the shape firmly pasted down. For added interest, tissue shapes do not follow the figure's form.

junction with colored tissue adds a new dimension to the tissue collage, and this is one way to incorporate text concerning social issues into the artwork—an important consideration in contemporary art expression.

MOSAICS

The multifaceted technique of mosaic art, with its colored pieces called *tesserae,* is a welcome, albeit challenging technique for children's art expression. It requires a generous time allotment, supplemental storage, and above all, students with both patience and persistence. Standard art materials (colored construction paper, paste, and scissors) are used. Creating mosaics, a pleasantly repetitive and creative project, calls for much small-muscle, tactile activity. It teaches that wholes are made of parts, which is an important concept in mathematics, science, and social studies.

In mosaic design, as with most two-dimensional art expression, first make a bold preliminary linear sketch the size of the anticipated mosaic's

IN THE CLASSROOM/IN THE COMMUNITY

Subjects for Mosaics

Motivation for the project might include visits to mosaics in the community. If available, show color films and slides of mosaic art, both past and present. This can include San Vitale in Rome, Gaudi's Cathedral in Barcelona, Simon Rodia's Watts Towers in Los Angeles, and the mosaic-paved avenues of Rio de Janeiro. Subject matter for paper mosaics that is manageable yet exciting includes birds, fish, and animals in their habitats; flower bouquets; butterflies in a garden; dragons; and clowns.

background. Make it from life and nature, from visits to museums, or from references to photographs and color slides. The preliminary sketches then are developed into a linear composition the size of the actual mosaic that is desired. The background surface may be colored construction paper, chip-board, or salvaged gift-box container.

Critical to the project's success is an adequate supply of tesserae. Cut narrow strips of colored construction paper, not necessarily the same width, and store them according to color in shoe boxes. Students then cut these strips as needed into individual tesserae. They need not cut all of the strips into perfect squares; some can be rectangular or triangular. Some adventurous teachers have used vinyl, tile scraps, linoleum, and even colored glass (with caution) instead of construction paper.

During a mosaic project, students should take turns selecting the desired color strips or tesserae from the supply-table boxes. Apply school paste or white glue to the background paper and press the tesserae firmly into the adhesive. Usually, it is best to begin on the outer edge of a shape and work inward toward the center. To achieve the mosaic effect, tesserae should not touch or overlap each other. The students should be reminded that in professional mosaic work, a grout is mortared between tesserae. Avoid a rigid, bricklaying technique—the minute, open spaces between tesserae should vary somewhat for best effect.

Courtesy of David W. Hodge.

Mosaics: Underwater themes are especially effective for mosaics, because of the variety of shapes, details, and patterns that are found in fish, shells, coral, and seaweed. These space-filled compositions are by upper-elementary students, who used a variety of sizes and shapes of the tesserae.

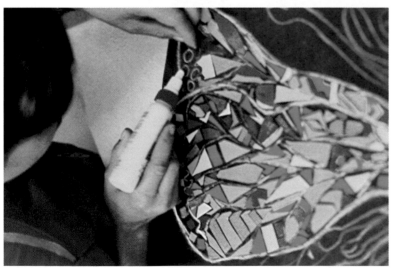

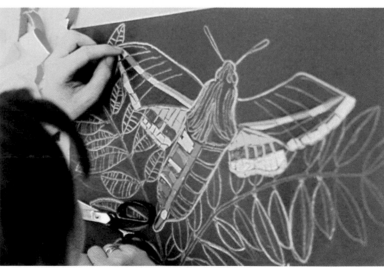

Courtesy of Frank Wachowiak and Mary Sayer Hammond.

A group mural in which each student's mosaic insect on black paper was cut out, with border preserved, and then mounted onto a large piece of brown cardboard.

Courtesy of Mary Lazzari.

These mosaics are of early maritime explorers of America.

Courtesy of Frank Wachowiak and Ted Ramsay.

The bird mosaic employed vinyl and linoleum tesserae glued to Masonite® board with tinted grout used as a filler.

Recommended background surfaces for paper mosaic projects include construction paper in assorted colors, railroad board, chip-board, oak tag, or discarded gift-box covers. Suggested adhesives include school paste, white glue, or glue sticks.

Students may create excitement with their mosaic compositions through a contrast of colors in specified areas. Contrast the wing of a bird against the body, the stamen against a flower petal, an insect against a leaf. One important strategy in achieving expressive mosaic quality is to employ several values of a color in the larger areas: for example, use two or three values of blue in the sky, and two or three values of green in the grass and leaves. Use several kinds of brown ochre, umber, and sienna colors for earth and tree trunks. The brightest, most intense colors may be reserved for sharp contrast or emphasis—on the beak or claws of a bird, the eyes of a tiger, the stamen of a lily, or the horns of a bull.

FOR FURTHER READING

Rottger, Ernst. 1970. *Creative Paper Design*. New York: Reinhold.

Roukes, Nicholas. 1993. *Sculpture in Paper*. New York: Sterling Publications, Inc.

Sheerin, Connie. 2001. *Backyard Mosaics*. New York: Sterling Publications, Inc. (Paper mosaic designs can be adapted to the outdoors.)

Zieger, Kathleen, and Nick Greco. 1996. *Paper Sculpture: A Step-by-Step Guide*. Cincinnati: F and W Publishers.

WEB RESOURCES

For a paper-folding project:

http://www.sgi.com/grafica/fold/page001.html

For using wallpaper sample books to make envelopes:

http://familycrafts.about.com/gi/dynamic/offsite.htm?site= http%3A%2F%2Fwww.kidsdomain.com%2Fcraft%2Fwpenv.html

For some origami projects:

http://familycrafts.about.com/od/origami/

For a lesson plan for creating a totempole:

http://artsedge.kennedy-center.org/content/2205/

Chapter 27
Printmaking

PRINTMAKING WITH FOUND OBJECTS

Colorful and successful prints can be made by very young children using found objects, such as wooden spools, bottle caps, mailing tubes, corks, sponges, and erasers. In addition, cord can be glued in a free design to the smooth metal top of a condiment container to produce a printing shape. Still another technique is to cut shapes from stiff sponge; then for a handle, use hot melt glue to glue a discarded film canister to it.

A science-correlated study of nature's symmetry can use assorted vegetables (okra, cabbage, mushrooms, peppers, carrots, artichokes) that are cut in half or in pieces, painted, and printed. The excitement quickens when students gain awareness of the hidden design in these natural forms. (However, in classes where children are poor and hungry, the use of food for painting is problematic.) The halved or quartered vegetables are painted on the cut side with colored tempera of a creamy consistency, or they are pressed on a tempera-coated, folded paper towel. Or water-soluble printing ink also can be used. Then, they are printed repeatedly on colored construction paper or tissue paper to form an allover or repeat design.

For best results, the vegetables must be fresh, crisp, and solid, and kept refrigerated between printmaking sessions. The most popular vegetable for this project is the potato. Cut in half, its flat, open surface is incised to create a relief. Children must be reminded to exercise caution when using sharp tools, however. Recommended tools include small scissors, fingernail files, nut picks, dental tools, and assorted nails. Melon-ball scoops are excellent for creating circular designs. In upper elementary and middle school, paring knives, Sloyd knives, or Hyde knives may be employed if they are used with extreme care. Students should strive for a simple, bold breakup of space in their cutout or incised designs. Suggest the use of cross-cuts, wedges as in a pie, assorted-size holes, and star, asterisk, cogwheel, sunburst, and spider's web effects.

Short words can be cut into large potatoes, but letters must be reversed to print correctly. Students should begin by making a preliminary drawing on paper of the shape of the cut potato to guide them in their cutting. Then hold the design to the windowpane and trace it onto the paper's back side; then apply colored chalk to the front side and trace the backwards design onto the potato surface. Cutting wedges out of the holding end can improve the student's grasp.

Construction paper in assorted colors is, perhaps, the most popular and serviceable surface for printing, although colored tissue, wallpaper, and fabrics have been used. Generous newspaper padding placed under the paper to be printed ensures a good impression. In addition, students should stand in order to exert firm pressure.

To develop a sense of how much ink or paint to use and the amount of pressure required, make a few practice applications of the vegetable stamp on scrap paper before beginning. In planning their printmaking, students might be encouraged to develop a repeat pattern in several places on their paper (this does not have to be a measured, mathematical repeat), thus allowing some prints to go off the page to create an allover effect. Discourage restamping without reinking. Also discourage rushing to finish, which results in sloppy printing. Often, however, the imperfection of a child's effort lends a fresh, spontaneous quality to the product. Encourage children's sharing of their stamps.

For a project correlated with writing, have the students use vegetable and found-object prints as covers for their creative-writing notebooks. The prints also can be used for pencil containers (glue the printed paper to a discarded box or can). In both cases, students can coat the surface with gloss polymer medium.

Vegetable and found-object prints, which are artistic even in their simplest form, also can be embellished for added richness. One or more

Courtesy of Frank Wachowiak and Mary Sayer Hammond.

Top right: A potato, with the pattern cut into it, is inked or painted before making the print. Do not insist on a measured, rigidly controlled design. Because caution must be exercised in cutting the designs, use nails, plastic knives, and melon scoops. **Top left:** Vegetable prints are enhanced by the application of oil pastels between the printed motifs, but allowing some of the background paper to show. **Middle left:** The light-blue pastel comple-

ments the yellow-orange paper color. **Bottom left:** The jagged edges of the oil-pasteled areas contrast to the potato's round form. **Bottom right:** Vegetable-print, allover repeat designs make excellent covers for notebooks, pencil holders (recycle a soup or coffee can), and household dispensers. To protect the surface and make it shine, apply a coat of gloss polymer medium.

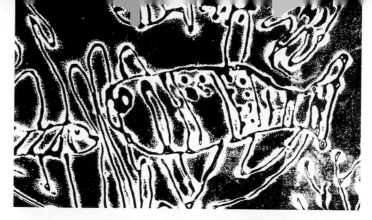

crayon or oil-pastel colors can be added in the negative spaces between the printed shapes. For unity, let some of the empty background show between the colored-in areas and the printed shapes.

GLUE-LINE RELIEF PRINTS

A printmaking process that is remarkably successful with students in all grades is the glue-line-on-cardboard print. It is a relatively simple technique, but it requires at least two class sessions. Time is needed both for the glue to dry overnight before printing and because students must take turns at the inking stations.

In addition to pencils, other required materials for making glue line-relief prints include the following:

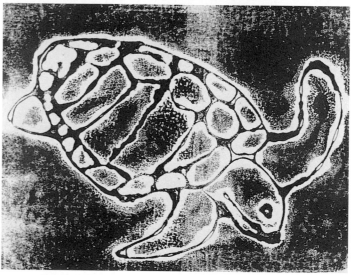

- Smooth-surfaced cardboard (discarded, glossy-surfaced gift-box covers are excellent) or tagboard to make the printing plate; recommended plate sizes are 9- × 9-inch, 9- × 12-inch, 12- × 12-inch, or 12- × 18-inch
- White glue in small plastic containers with a nozzle; even better, the new thick line variety
- Water-soluble printing ink (black is recommended)
- A soft-rubber brayer or roller for inking
- An inking surface, such as a discarded cafeteria tray or metal cookie sheet
- Protective newspapers
- Newsprint, tissue paper, or classified-ad pages on which to print

IN THE CLASSROOM

Subjects for Relief Prints

Appealing subject-matter choices for young children are butterflies, birds, fish, flowers, and animals. Students in upper elementary and middle school may choose more complex themes: historical legends, space and science explorations, still life, cityscape compositions, portraits, and figure studies.

Top: *Courtesy of Frank Wachowiak.* Middle: *Courtesy of Jackie Ellett.*
Bottom left and right: *Courtesy of David W. Hodge.*

Top: Glue-line technique produces beautiful flowing lines. **Middle:** The flowing glue-line technique adapts well to portraying the swimming of this determined sea turtle. **Bottom left:** A posed model drawn in glue line. The print was first printed in yellow and blue. **Bottom right:** Glue-line relief print by a sixth-grader based on a drawing from a posed model. Because of the pressure from the soft-rubber brayer, the printing ink covers much of the background as well as the glue lines.

Technical Suggestions A preliminary drawing definitely is recommended. Because intricate details will blend together in the glue line and get lost, make the initial drawing with chalk for boldness and simplicity. Fill the page. Limit the composition to one large motif (bird, insect, fish, animal) with its complementary foliage or seaweed rather than using several smaller motifs. With only one large figure, there will be room to clearly delineate details, such as eye, beak, whiskers, antenna, claw, feather, and fish scales. Evaluate the compositions with the student for space-filling design, shape variation, and pattern.

The cardboard printing plate with its linear composition now is ready for the glue application. Gently squeeze the container, trailing the glue over the drawn line. A linear variety is achieved naturally, because it is difficult to manage an even, steady flow of glue. Dots of glue will produce sunburst effects in the final printing. The glue must be allowed to dry thoroughly overnight before inking; when dry, the glue will be transparent and free of white ridges and welts.

See the section later in this chapter on printing for specific recommendations. The most successful prints are those that capture both the raised glue lines as well as the background inked areas. This will require pressure with palm and fingers into the smaller background areas. Uninked areas between glue lines and background provide the necessary light and dark contrast. For the demonstration, the teacher might use white tissue so that students can actually see the ink absorbing into the paper and detect areas requiring more pressure. Several prints can be made from the same plate. Trim borders, if necessary, and mount the print on colored construction paper for an exciting display. Or, students can combine their prints into a group arrangement.

COLLOGRAPHS

Students in intermediate and upper elementary as well as in middle school are interested in and challenged by more complex approaches to printmaking. Cardboard prints sometimes are referred to as *collographs* (a word combination of *collage* and *graph*), and collographs can be created with commonly available materials and nonhazardous tools. The final results, however, often are comparable to those of woodblocks and lino prints. An especially welcome advantage of this technique is the flexibility it allows in rearranging or deleting compositional elements before the final gluing.

The following tools and materials are required: a sheet of sturdy cardboard (such as the lid or bottom of a gift box), chip-board, discarded scraps of illustration board (tagboard is too thick and not recommended), glue, scissors, assorted-weight papers (smooth or textured), assorted-size

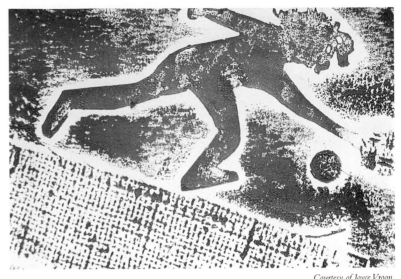

Courtesy of Joyce Vroon.

Collographs Made from Common Materials: In fourth-grader Graham Grubb's tennis collograph, burlap represents the net.

paper punches, a soft-rubber brayer, water-soluble printing ink in black or dark colors, newsprint, gloss polymer medium, a utility brush, and lots of protective newspapers.

The animal world is a favorite theme for collographs because it provides so many options for creating a strong, lively design. Especially important is using a variety of cutout shapes to fill the space. While helpful, an overall preliminary drawing is not required. Separate motifs or shapes may be drawn first before cutting. Large printing plates may create a management problem in crowded classrooms, however; therefore, a recommended plate size for students in the intermediate and upper-elementary grades is a sheet that is 9- × 9-inches, 9- × 12-inches, or 12- × 12-inches.

Students draw and cut out the individual shapes from construction paper, brown wrapping tape, and other assorted-weight papers. Then students create open patterns in some of these shapes, employing paper punches and utility knives, and arrange these elements on the background cardboard until they achieve a satisfactory composition. Some shapes may overlap for unity, spatial effects, and interest. Students can add a variety of found materials to create textural qualities, using gummed reinforcements, textured wallpaper samples, masking tape, fabric, string, yarn, confetti, liquid glue, and flat, found objects. If the relief is too high, however, such as from thick cord or buttons, the print will not be successful. When the students, with the teacher's guidance, achieve a satisfying, space-filling

Courtesy of Frank Wachowiak and Ted Ramsay.

Pattern in Large Collograph: "The Jungle," 18 × 36 inches. Group project by intermediate-elementary-grade children. Students used a paper punch to create patterns in the leopard and on the bushes. Pinking shears cut the palm

tree leaves. Additional cutout holes, as well as little squares and triangles of paper, were pasted down onto the cardboard plate. See especially the gorilla's exciting background at left. The plate was then printed.

design, they carefully glue down the pieces. Use a discarded magazine as a gluing surface, and turn to a clean page for each application. All edges must be glued securely.

The whole composition then is sealed with a coat of polymer medium to further prevent the separate pieces from coming loose during the printing and cleaning phases. Designate a separate table or counter that is protected by newspapers to be the sealing area. Allow the plates to dry overnight before inking. (See the section in this chapter on inking and printing.) Collograph plates do not need to be washed between printing sessions. Finished prints can be attractively mounted for display, and students may want to exchange prints. Also, the plate itself can be painted and mounted. In addition, it can be covered with heavy-duty aluminum foil and further embellished, as described later in this chapter in the section on aluminum-foil relief.

LINOLEUM PRINTS AND STYROFOAM® PRINTS

In the primary grades, Styrofoam® prints are recommended as a way to make relief prints. Everyone is familiar with this material in its common use as trays on which meats, vegetables, and fruits are sold in the supermarket. (Some store managers, if asked, will donate these trays.) If trays are to be used for printmaking, the raised rim must first be cut off. Alternately, large flat sheets of half-inch-thick, polystyrene foam, sold for insulation in 3- × 8-foot sheets (or ¼-inch thick, sold in rolls) at builder supply stores such as Home Depot, can be purchased and cut to the desired size.

The obvious advantage of foam over linoleum is that no cutting by the children is required. After the pencil sketch is transferred to the foam,

Courtesy of Frank Wachowiak and Ted Ramsay.

Steps in making a collograph print. ***Top left:*** Gluing down the paper-punched birds. Caution: If water-based printing ink is employed, the teacher must give the plate a protective, water-resistant coating prior to printing. ***Bottom left:***

Inking the collograph. ***Middle:*** A middle-school student peels back the print from the plate while checking that areas have been sufficiently inked and pressed. ***Right:*** The finished print with attractive tree shapes.

the design is incised by firmly going over it with a pencil or pen. Patterns of dots, circles, and squares can be made by using pencil points and hollow ¼" circular and square tubes.

A technically demanding form of relief printmaking recommended for students in the upper elementary and middle school is linoleum ("lino") block printing. A new product, flexible printing block, is gaining in usage over linoleum. Students are challenged by using diverse tools and by manipulating, if available, a heavy roller press. Because of these built-in attractions, teachers will have little trouble introducing lino prints into the art program.

The unmounted, grey, pliable "battleship" linoleum suggested for this project may be obtained from art-supply companies. Cut the linoleum plates large enough to give the students ample opportunity for a rich

composition. A minimum size of 9- × 9-inches, 9- × 12-inches, or 12- × 12-inches is recommended. A 4- × 9-inch size is good for cards as it conveniently fits into a standard-size business envelope. For middle-school students who want to make very large prints, luan plywood is suitable. The basic materials and tools needed include sets of lino-cutting gouges for the students to share, rubber brayers, inking surfaces of cookie tins or old cafeteria trays, and water-soluble printing ink.

A preliminary drawing on paper with black crayon, felt-nib pen, brush and ink, or white crayon on black paper is an important requisite for a successful lino-print project. It usually determines the final composition and establishes the dark and light pattern, variety of textural exploitation, points of emphasis, and lines of motion. Remind students that letters and numerals must be reversed in the sketch.

Linoleum prints with bold designs by fourth- and fifth-graders. The left picture of monkeys uses a series of monkeys—big, small, and smallest—to set up a rhythm. The right kangaroo picture has an interesting feature—a positive and negative cactus.

IN THE CLASSROOM

Subjects for Linoleum and Styrofoam® Prints

Effective subject-matter themes for lino and foam prints are those that promise a strong light- and dark-value composition, with a variety of shapes, pattern, and detail. Some possibilities are birds, jungle animals and their young, insects, fish, shells, old houses, legendary or mythological figures, portraits, and still-life arrangements composed of musical instruments, antiques, plants, household utensils, and sports equipment. A field trip to a natural history museum will provide a wealth of motivational material.

After preliminary drawings have been made and evaluated for design potential, the students may use them as a reference for their drawing on the lino plate. Or, the students may transfer the design to the lino plate with carbon paper or dressmaker's white transfer paper. If the lino surface is dark and no white transfer paper is available, first paint the lino block with white tempera paint. To reverse a sketch before transferring it to the block, hold it against the window, and trace lines on the back of the sheet. Another technique sometimes used is to transfer the design by placing the drawing pencil-side-down onto the block, taping it down securely, and rubbing over it with a metal spoon.

After the drawing has been made but before the cutting begins, check that there are enough sharpened gouges in various sizes for the entire class to use. Students should be introduced to the potential of the many gouges through a teacher demonstration emphasizing the correct way to hold and

Courtesy of Frank Wachowiak and Ted Ramsay.

This fifth-grader's linoleum print began with a sketching trip drawing animals at the natural history museum. Notice how the leftover linoleum lines in the sky were cut in an attractive movement to give a feeling of compositional unity. Note how some birds in the sky are black on white and others white on black.

manipulate the gouge. Never put a supporting hand in front of a cutting tool. To make lino cutting safer, a wooden bench hook can be anchored against the table edge to provide a supportive ridge to hold the block.

Each lino gouge makes its own particular cut, and although gouges are not as easily controlled as pencils or pens, they often produce lines that are more dynamic. The richest print effects are achieved by using a range of gouges, from veiners to scoops and shovels. Number 1 and 2 veiners or V-shaped gouges are suggested for making the initial outlines. Another approach is to use the scoop or shovel gouges, working from inside the shapes and thus minimizing tightly outlined compositions.

To prevent mistakes in cutting, students can mark an X on those areas to be gouged. Use directional gouge cuts to follow the object's contours, like ripples around a pebble tossed in a stream. Instruct students not to make their cuts too deep, however, because the low ridges that remain in the lino will produce an attractive texture. If students have difficulty cutting because the linoleum is too hard, heat it on a cookie tin over an electrical hot plate turned to a low setting. (See the following section for information on inking and printing.)

Wooden scraps, which often can be secured from building sites or lumber yards, are an alternative to linoleum for printmaking. Especially with small blocks, a bench hook is required for safety, however. Also, before inking, seal the wood's porous surface with diluted white glue.

PROOFING, INKING, AND PRINTING

This section applies to glue line, collograph, linoleum, Styrofoam,® and aluminum-foil relief prints. Proofs of the work-in-progress can be made (without inking) by placing paper over the design and, with the side of a black crayon or oil pastel, rubbing over the paper with a steady and even pressure. The resulting proof will reveal to the students how the print design is progressing. To avoid the need to give individual instructions, demonstrate the inking, printing, and wet-print storage procedures step-by-step one time for the entire class.

Inking and printing are very exciting, but without careful planning, this stage can develop into a chaotic bedlam. Designated inking and printing tables, covered with newspapers, should be positioned so that several students can stand and work comfortably. You will need to provide several inking surfaces and soft-rubber brayers that are 3 or more inches wide (do not use the gelatin type) as well as black water-soluble ink. At the inking station, squeeze out a brayer-width ribbon of ink onto the inking surface. With the brayer, roll out the ink until it is tacky—you will hear a snapping, hissing sound. Try to restrict the brayer's inking area to a limited size and away from the edges. Then

These woodblock prints of a bird and its hungry babies, cows at milking time, and three hens are by Japanese fourth- and fifth-graders. Proud of the Ukioye tradition, printmaking with woodblock-cutting tools is introduced in the third grade in Japanese schools. The whole space is filled. Note in the top design the skillfully cut pattern of positive and negative shapes in the leaves and branches.

Top: *Courtesy of Frank Wachowiak and Ted Ramsay.* Middle and bottom: *Courtesy of David W. Hodge.*

Woodblock Prints: The top and middle pictures are of endangered species: some hawks and baleen whales. **Top:** The hawk print, a seventh-grader found and created strong patterns in the tree branches and feathers, and the block was painted with colored tempera and printed in several stages to achieve the color overlays. **Middle:** This reduction print shows the endangered baleen whales. **Bottom:** A reduction print of a kangaroo.

apply the ink to the printing plate in both directions. Standing up to get more pressure, evenly ink every part of the plate, especially its edges and corners. Then, carefully and quickly, lift and carry the inked plate to the printing station.

Because water-soluble ink dries rapidly, make the print immediately. Use newsprint, brown wrapping paper, colored construction paper, colored tissue paper, wallpaper samples, fabric remnants, classified-ad pages, or

A woodblock print by Käthe Kollwitz (1867–1945) was the motivation for the three following self-portrait prints by upper-grade Japanese youngsters.

Courtesy of Frank Wachowiak.

Linoleum Blocks Printed over Colored-Tissue Collages: *Top:* Black printing ink was used over a lighter valued tissue underlay. *Bottom:* White printing ink over a dark tissue design. Which of these middle-school designs do you like better? Before pulling the print, be sure that the tissue is glued down firmly and smoothly and is thoroughly dry.

colored pages from magazines. Carefully place the slightly larger-sized sheet of paper over the inked surface, and pat it down with the palm of the hand. Beginning in the center, smooth out to the edges, being careful that the paper does not shift. Standing up, exert stronger pressure with a rubber brayer, heel of a hand, jar cover, spoon, or commercially available baren; go over the entire surface, especially borders and corners and between shapes. Wherever the print is to be darker, press harder. To check the impression, lift the paper partially off the block from various sides. If not satisfied, apply more pressure.

Courtesy of David W. Hodge.

On his linoleum plate, the boy is sure to cut away from his hands and body. He prints the plate over a well-sealed collage of colored-tissue scraps.

Courtesy of ICCA, Milner Library, Illinois State University.

Printmaking lends itself especially well to serious social topics. Since multiple copies can be made, its capability for dissemination and bringing about social change is enhanced. Here, a family grieves over the tragedy of a death.

Caution: Do not wait too long to carefully remove the newsprint from the plate. The water-soluble ink dries quickly, and it may cause the paper to stick to the plate. Therefore, pull the paper off the block carefully. So that all students may have a turn to print, limit the number of initial prints a student pulls. Remind the children that additional prints always can be made later.

ALUMINUM-FOIL RELIEFS

The aluminum-foil relief over collograph plate, collage, or glue line-relief plate is an exciting and novel technique to which students in upper elementary and middle school will respond enthusiastically. The process is not technically a printmaking process; rather, it is a subsequent process that follows the making of a glue-line or a collograph print.

Materials needed include heavy-duty aluminum foil, blunt-point pencils, soft-rubber brayer or inking roller, white glue (check for consistency—glue should not be watery), gold patina, masking tape, water-soluble printing ink (black or dark hue), and protective newspapers.

Attaching the Foil to the Plate If students have been pulling prints from a collograph or a glue-line plate, they can reink the plate and, while

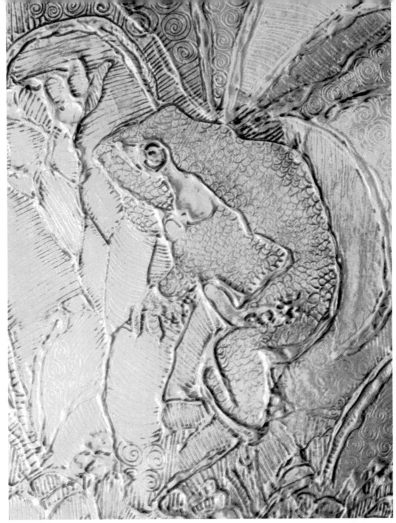

Courtesy of Frank Wachowiak and Mary Sayer Hammond.

Aluminum-Foil Relief Print: Its richness transcends the readily available materials from which it was made: household heavy-duty foil, cardboard, white glue, blunt pencils, and water-based printing ink. The glowing finished product becomes a family treasure for decades.

the ink still is sticky, cover it with a sheet of foil (shiny side up) that is cut slightly larger than the printing plate. Then, stretching the foil with the heel of a hand toward the edges of the plate, overlap the foil on the back of the plate. Secure the excess foil on the other side with masking tape. To keep the corners as flat as possible, carefully fold them.

However, if on an uninked collage, be sure the pieces of the collage are secured. With glue-line prints, be sure the glue-relief lines are thoroughly dry. Then give the plate a coat of white glue and, while wet, apply the foil.

Incising to Bring out the Design Next, using a blunt-pointed pencil, press into the foil along both edges of the glue lines and also along the edges of collage shapes to emphasize the relief. Avoid puncturing the foil. Teacher and student each should check to see that all of the relief edges have been sufficiently emphasized. To enrich the relief, indent the foil with the pencil point to create additional details, patterns, and textures. These can be leaves on a bush, veins in the leaves, grass, feathers on a bird, scales on a fish, bark on a tree, or ripples in a stream. Incorporate a variety of invented patterns, such as hatching and cross-hatching; dots, circles, and dots within circles; triangular and diamond shapes; wiggly, jigsaw, and radiating lines; asterisks; stars; and spirals. The more detail, pattern, and texture that are employed, the more effective the result.

Inking into the Crevices To ink the aluminum plate, apply water-soluble black printing ink to the surface with a soft-rubber brayer so that the whole plate is covered except for the deep pencil indentations. To be sure that ink gets into all the crevices, some teachers recommend applying ink with a dauber, made by rolling several paper towels into a tight cylinder and taping them together. See the previous section for directions on making the print.

Cleaning but Leaving in Crevices After making a print, make the foil relief from the plate itself. While the ink is still moist on the plate, use newspapers to remove the excess. Using a hand or a brayer, press one sheet at a time over the moist plate. When no impression is visible, take a folded flat (never bunched or crushed), moistened paper towel and wipe the plate gently to remove excess ink from all areas except the indented ones. When one side of the towel gets inky, unfold and fold it again to provide a clean surface. When the moist towel no longer shows an ink residue, use folded, dry paper towels to burnish the plate, being careful to allow ink to remain in the indented lines. This can be the completed foil relief, or you can enrich the raised surfaces of the plate by the slightest application of gold patina. Aluminum-foil reliefs can be attractively mounted and displayed, and they make excellent gifts.

FOR FURTHER READING

Daniels, Harvey, and Sylvie Turner. 1972. *Simple Printmaking with Young People.* New York: Van Nostrand Reinhold.

Toale, Bernard. 1992. *Basic Printmaking Techniques.* Worcester, MA: Davis Publishing.

WEB RESOURCES

For a glossary of printmaking terms:

  http://www.wellesley.edu/Art/ARTS212/html/Glossary.html

Courtesy of Frank Wachowiak and Mary Sayer Hammond. Student Cal Clements.

Aluminum-Foil Relief: The exciting adventure in bas relief and embossing has untold possibilities for exploration in the art program and affords an ideal medium for learning ways to create texture and pattern. Here, a frog looks this way and that, half-submerged in the pond and awaiting the next morsel.

For a seventh-grade linoleum-cut portrait lesson:

  http://www.taospaint.com/LessonSelfPortraitPrints.html

For a kindergarten gadget printing lesson on circles:

  http://www.princetonol.com/groups/iad/lessons/elem/elem38.html

For info on advanced printmaking technique:

  http://www.kamprint.com/printmak.htm#Printmakingrtmath.html

For printmaking ideas useful for middle school:

  http://www.princetonol.com/groups/iad/lessons/high/printmaking.htm

Chapter 28

Visual Technology: Computer Art, Photography, and Video

*I*n this chapter on visual technology, we will discuss photography, video, and computers. Yet even discussing computer art, photography, and video as separate subjects seems inaccurate. With digital cameras, scanners, photocopying, video capture, animation software, and downloading from the Web, the media interact with each other and assume new powerful hybrid forms.

Whereas much school curricula tend to be fragmented, by its very nature visual technology is multidisciplinary and intercultural. Cultural and personal meanings can be shared through highly interactive viewing modes, such as slide shows, videos, and projected movies and multimedia projects. Words and images can interpenetrate; students can develop scripts and images by chatting together on their home computers. Indeed, students interact with visual technology in a new way—one less focused on formalist concerns and more focused on expressivist concerns. And this linking, interconnectedness, and openness are also characteristics shared by both the Web and by postmodern art in general.

The electronic media encourage the constructivist view of education, as students redefine their personal knowledge bases and engage in active learning. While photos, videos, and multimedia presentations can be made of formalistic arrangements focusing on arrangements of the art elements, the new media lend themselves especially well to personally and socially relevant subject matter (see section on formalism and contextualism in Chapter 22). The students' lives, individuals' clothing styles, and their interactions with peers, for example, are powerful topics for personal statements. Likewise, the school itself, nearby food kitchens, child-care centers, and construction projects can present socially relevant subject matter.

Experiences with visual technology can be particularly useful in teaching social studies. Yet there is a caveat: with power comes responsibility. Especially with socially relevant photo and video projects, balance the obligation to use photographic documentation to critically highlight

Courtesy of Joyce Vroon.

Visual technology creates new ways of seeing and thinking about the nature of appearances. After studying David Hockney's photo collages, a sixth-grader made this photo collage of the remodeling going on in his home.

319

Keys and religious medals can be transformed into works of art. These photograms are of objects as simple as keys, religious medals, pins, and paper clips. They helped teach middle-school students the formalistic concepts of overall pattern and positive and negative shape.

society's problems with the obligation to build the school art program's good standing. Teach about individuals' rights to privacy and the need to get photo permissions from subjects. Before undertaking a potentially controversial documentation project, check first with relevant authorities, for in our very interdependent society many officials unfortunately view schools as agencies whose purpose is to reinforce the existing social order. Certainly, visual images can be a minefield, bringing with them value-

The voices and images of young people can affect public opinion on important issues: Alice Bowen's piece seems to protest the nearby factories' despoiling the air.

laden assumptions that are esteemed by social reconstructivist teachers, but may be eschewed by others.

COMPUTER ART

There are a number of advantages to including computer–art activities in the overall art program. Computers have become a central element in education; as a result, using computers in the art program can lend prestige to the program as a whole and help students gain valuable career skills. Another advantage is a practical one: Costly computer resources may be available on a scale far beyond that of traditional art-program budgets. In fact, computer equipment is available now in a growing number of elementary and middle schools, but teachers in the general classroom may not be trained or skilled in its use. In some cases, art teachers may find they have the equipment virtually to themselves. Or there may simply be more funds available for computer and software purchases than for more traditional supplies. Finally, early computer-art experiences can provide a bridge to skills and experiences that will spur students' interest in the "careers of tomorrow," many of which require high-level computer literacy.

IN THE CLASSROOM

Using Computers

Desktop-publishing programs are an exciting resource for creating school publications with top-quality design and graphics. Student artworks can be scanned onto the school's website. Computer graphics, banners, calendars, and announcements can serve not only as vehicles for teaching design, but they can help the school disseminate information. Computers also offer sophisticated ways to combine letter forms and words with graphic elements. Students can "publish," either electronically or in hard copy, their own stories set in type and with the pages graphically designed. In this way, computer art can perform a valuable educational role in integrating school art programs with writing programs.

Top left: *Courtesy of Pat Kerner.* Top right: *Courtesy of Carol Case.* Bottom: *Courtesy of Jackie Ellett.*

Top left: In an assignment about the Underground Railroad Secret Quilt code, quilt squares conveyed covert messages to other slaves; fourth-grader Cole Bryant's square tells how groups of runaways would come together and then split apart to confuse their pursuers. Note the blue background's spherized effects. **Top right:** Computerized blending is shown in the water lilies and a texturized paper effect used in the blue background of second-grader Erika Pshsniak's computer artwork of water lilies. **Middle:** The computer's cut, copy, and drag functions were used to create a marathon-race effect by multiplying the image this elementary student drew. **Bottom:** Triangular tessellation patterns filled with colored circular motifs by fourth-grader Mallory Brock.

The Computer as a Design Tool The computer, even more than most art media, focuses attention not so much on the product but on the process. Computers permit students to save progressive stages of a work and to create an infinite number of variations. Students are excited about the "trial-and-error" capability for "seriation," producing a series of images from a single image. They can test out colors, move shapes around, and recycle pictures quickly and easily while leaving the original intact. Morphing can show the interspaced steps between two images, for example, a person's head changes into the head of the school mascot. The

multiple levels of storing an original image and changing it or mixing others with it blurs individual authorship.

Using the computer as a design tool enables learners to "see" design operations that involve repeating and varying images:

cut	paste	duplicate	rotate
shrink	mirror	enlarge	texturize
fragment	blur	trace edges	twirl
make transparent	superimpose	magnify	ripple
distort	introduce bilateral symmetry	introduce four-way symmetry	pixelate

The computer allows students to manipulate scale—they can look at a work at normal size, then zoom in for close-up work. Pixel size can be manipulated as well, creating analogies to weaving and mosaics. Sophisticated visual effects can be achieved by using a range of special tools; for example, putting one image over another using different transparency functions, making forms grow according to predetermined patterns (fractalizing), or making forms appear as if they were in a reflecting orb (spherizing).

Several programs are available to support children's drawing and painting. One that has proved successful for many teachers is Kid Pix© (Broderbund Software), which not only helps students create visual art but also has capabilities for slide shows, QuickTime movies, and sound recording. Resulting pictures can be e-mailed to parents.

Implementing a Computer-Art Program A main barrier to implementing a computer-art program in the past has been the art teacher's ignorance and fear: fear that the equipment won't work appropriately, or that students will know more about the subject than the teacher does. Just push such fears aside: In constructivist classrooms, we are all learners together.

Another problem arises when there is not enough computer equipment to serve a whole class, so students cannot have individual time at the machine. Fortunately, research indicates that students can learn computer skills as effectively in small groups as they can individually. Computer art can be taught to small groups of children, and collaborative projects can be encouraged.

Balancing the needs of students working on computers with those of students who do not, for the moment, have access can be difficult, but good planning will help. One solution in such circumstances may be to have students do computer artwork only after they finish other assignments, or to have them come in either before or after class to use the com-

Courtesy of Pat Kerner.

In this Underground Railroad Secret Quilt, quilt squares conveyed hidden messages to other slaves: (from left to right, top to bottom) fourth-grader Blythe Coward wrote: "1. Winter is a good time to travel; 2. Boulders impede travel; 3. & 4. Spring and Fall are good times to travel; 5. Summer was a bad time to travel; 6. Rain and fishing were helpful; 7. Sand storms were difficult; 8. Night time was a good time to travel; 9. Canada was the slaves' destination." Note the variety in the background fill patterns.

puter. Another approach is to have traditional methods of drawing and painting included as a part of computer-generated projects. For example, storyboards illustrating story concepts need to be drawn. Sound effects need to be recorded. One group of students can begin a design on the computer and have a copy printed out for each student in the group. Then, those students can go to their desks to do the hand coloring, while other students, who have been generating design sketches by hand, render their work on the computer.

Still another way to deal with the shortage or absence of computers is to approach computer art as an activity in art criticism. Class discussion can focus on the computer-art imagery that students see daily—for example, in movies' special effects, in animated titles and images opening tele-

Courtesy of Alisa Hyde.

Students can display the computer artwork they make at home on a bulletin board in school. It is difficult to know if this boy wanted or did not want girls to come into his tree house.

vision programs, and in newspaper graphic layouts and special effects of lettering. Art criticism can deal with these mass communication images, both addressing their formal design elements and how they reinforce content. A bulletin board in the classroom can serve as a center of this collection and analysis.

To develop interest in computer art during elementary school, have students with computers at home bring their own computer designs to be mounted in an exhibit. Such an exhibit may spur school administrators to support a school computer-art program that would be available to all children. Those who have used computer-art programs at home then can use the school computers to teach those who have not had access to these machines. Also the teacher can arrange a virtual exhibition of student art on the school's website. Likewise, a teacher and her students in Japan can converse by e-mail with a class in Mississippi and view each other's artwork on the websites.

The ideal solution, of course, is that the teacher convinces the school administration that computers should be an integral part of the program—that using computers for art expression is just as essential for students' educational development as is using computers for programming, mathematical operations, and word processing.

ART AND ART HISTORY ON THE WEB

Art historical resources abound on the Web, readily accessible to students who want to use them to adapt their own reports and their own artworks and educational products. For example, for the Japanese artist Hokusai, there are 6000 images and 122,000 web page listings in the search engine Google. Searching Google for African art brings up 65,000 images—and six million web pages. Through computer art, teachers and students together can take on new, challenging roles as instructional designers, managers, and facilitators of art content.

Computer images from websites can also be jumping-off points toward generating other images. The main search engines such as Google, Yahoo, Excite, Altavista, Lycos, AskJeeves, and Snap are good starting places. Just type in "art history" or "art museums," or the names of individual artists, art movements ("Impressionism"), or time periods ("medieval art"). Although individual websites come and go—and many are simply commercial sites, selling products—these resources are nevertheless revolutionary in their range and ease of use. Just log on and go exploring!

PHOTOGRAPHY

Always a popular activity, taking pictures is now even more adaptable to art programs because of the prevalence of digital cameras. If your school is not able to supply cameras for students, some families may be willing to allow their child to use a home camera for a school project. With digital images, students need to learn not only the techniques of photography but also how to manage their pictures: how to digitally crop, adjust the lighting and color intensity, and how to share their photos via electronic scrapbooks, slide shows, and e-mail.

Although digital photography has become more and more widespread—and allows exciting possibilities with manipulating images—more traditional photographic techniques are also remarkably engaging for young students. For example, blueprint paper acquired from a local blueprint company or light-sensitive photographic paper obtainable from a photo store can be used by elementary-school children for beginning photographic experiences. Through this medium, they can create designs and learn concepts such as geometric, organic, sinusoidal, pierced, undulating, and lacy.

Before you begin, find a totally dark closet somewhere in the school building. Then, with your students, collect an array of opaque, translucent, and transparent objects of varying color values that have interesting shapes, patterns, and textures. Suitable items are fern leaves, grasses, confetti, flowers, ribbon, lace, torn-paper shapes, tissue, acetate, window screen, crumpled plastic wrap, shapes of figures and animals cut from paper, checkers, shoelaces, paper doilies, drawings on acetate or translucent tracing paper, and three-dimensional objects, such as coins and keys.

Children should first plan their designs. Next, they will arrange an assortment of these objects on a stiff sheet of clear acrylic plastic, acetate, or overhead transparency plastic. Properly supervised older students can use a piece of glass with its edges taped. Emphasize consideration of the negative shapes (the empty spaces). Also, urge students to think about repetition, unity, and variation. While the children are waiting for their turn in the darkroom, have them write a list of the objects they collected and the design concepts they embody; this will build the students' art vocabulary.

For the printing stage, have a student monitor govern when the darkroom door may be opened. Students take turns carrying their designs into the darkroom. In the dark—by feel or with a red safelight on—they position their designs on top of same-size pieces of blueprint paper. Then, the design of shapes (*on* the clear plastic *on* the blueprint paper) is taken outside and exposed to sunlight for about 15 minutes (or until the yellow paper turns white).

The print is then developed. Soak some cotton in a teaspoon of household ammonia and place the cotton in the bottom of a large jar with a fitted lid, such as a gallon mayonnaise jar from the school cafeteria. Roll

Courtesy of Brian Baugh.

Students combined many technologies, including photographic processes and re-photographing, as they made these self-portraits of themselves and their interests.

IN THE CLASSROOM

Photography and Content-Area Learning

To integrate art and language arts, have children make up a story using the slides, then put on a slide show complete with narration and sound effects and the children playing the roles. Digital cameras present opportunities for students to take photos at little cost, once the camera and computer are available. The children's photos then can serve as visual resources for art projects using other art media.

Use historic photos to help students understand social studies lessons: Matthew Hines's photos of child labor abuses in New England spinning mills, Edward S. Curtis's photos of Native Americans, and Matthew Brady's photos of the Civil War are some examples.

Photography and science can be integrated with a unit on the science of light, replicating the 1830s sun drawings of Henry Fox Talbot. Photos of scientific phenomena, close-up microscopic views, and macrocosmic views of outer space can be studied as works of art using the photographic vocabulary described earlier.

the print tightly enough to fit it into the jar, insert it, and recap the jar. The ammonia fumes will turn the paper blue in a few minutes.

If light-sensitive photo paper is available, the design transfer can be done in a darkroom, using a flashlight to expose the film, and then developed as you would a photograph. With either method, after the print is made, the designs may be left as they are, or students may use oil pastels and markers to add color. Another variation of this lesson, and one that is especially suitable following a contour line–drawing lesson, is to have the students go into the darkroom, and, using a tiny pocket penlight, draw the figure as they remember it on the light-sensitive photo paper. Picasso's drawings with this technique may be studied. Another variation is for students to draw on a sheet of translucent paper with a black marker and then make a reverse print in the darkroom; the results will be similar to the cliché verre process used by Corot.

Class discussion afterward should build art vocabulary through listing on the chalkboard or markerboard names for the shapes, patterns, and textures that the children have created with light. Discuss similarities between their works and those of Fox Talbot and Man Ray. Beginning in

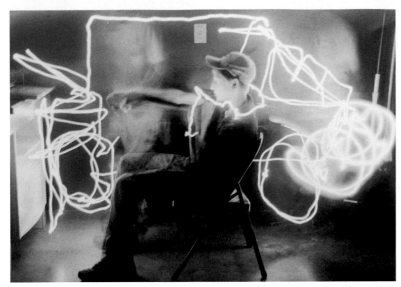

Middle-schoolers Daniel Kim and Dalton Tyler worked as a team to plan an image, "Driving a Car," captured on film by the shutter of the camera, on a tripod, being held open long enough to complete the drawing by a flashlight.

the fifth grade, students can use pinhole cameras to make their own photographs. Load the camera in a darkroom with slow-emulsion, plastic resin–coated paper. Have the children look around the school grounds and point the camera at what interests them—for example, a bicycle wheel, a friend's face, a tree silhouetted against the sky, patterns of bicycle shadows on the ground. Likewise, students might choose to document activities on the playground, an architecture field trip, the class garden, or vehicles used to travel to school. Tell students not to worry about composition or whether the subject moves. An impression is what is sought. Have the children develop the image inside the darkroom; a negative image can be contact-printed back for a positive. This lesson can be correlated with a study of such artists as Corot, Delacroix, Courbet, the Impressionists, and the futurists, who were fascinated by photography. Discuss what kind of day and light were captured. Was the light direct, soft, or diffuse? Look at the shadows and describe them.

Art criticism can be taught using a collection of photographic masterpieces. For example, clip photographs from an issue of *Life* magazine on the history of photography; with these photos, students can engage in some of the activities discussed in Chapter 22.

Left: Pinhole cameras were constructed by middle-school students. Then, students went into the schoolyard to capture light on the forms of sports cars, gravel, walkways, and buildings. **Right:** Pioneering video artist Nam June Paik uses hundreds of television monitors to create video walls of information. He wants them to humanize and demystify television technology, as does the figurative piece shown here that is constructed from TV sets.

Social studies is integrated with art in this project about slavery and freedom. "At night, follow the path of the Great Bear (the Big Dipper) to go North to freedom in Canada," fourth-grader Peter Bryant wrote and designed.

Courtesy of Joyce Vroon.

Up-close foreground to far distant background is shown in sixth-grader Mandy Freel's lake scene.

Teach children the vocabulary of photography. Terms and concepts about light include: light and shadow, direct light and reflected light, contrast, value, low contrast, high contrast, direction of light, high-key delicate lighting containing nothing darker than middle grey, low-key somber lighting containing nothing lighter than middle grey, sharp and diffuse shadows, point of view, low angle, distant shot, foreground, near ground, middle ground, and background. Terms about the technical process include: positive, negative, camera, shutter, lens, diaphragm, f-stop, focus, film speed (ISO), stop bath, and fixer. Historical terms include: daguerreotype, Talbot-type or Calotype, ambrotype, tintype, and cartes de visite (visiting cards with a photograph).

Digital cameras are becoming available in many middle schools; these are especially useful in creating web pages and electronic reports.

VIDEO

Video—the art medium of our time—is transforming the nature of art and of our lives. The famous video artist Nam June Paik said, "Information has to be recognized as an alternative energy source. Information changes our lifestyle" (1987). In many homes, information has become as basic—albeit less critical—to life as food and shelter. Video's power to capture the effect in human interactions, its accessibility, its spontaneity, and the ease with which it is disseminated are amazing. Videos can also be converted

Courtesy of Molly Chase and George Mitchell.

Probably only a young photographer could elicit the charming expressions of these children caring for children. Photography student Molly Chase captured a special moment of children at the neighborhood store. The photograph is structured by the geometry, repetition, and perspective in the mammoth Crisco® display.

into pictures and movies for multimedia presentations. Most homes now have videocassette recorders and DVD players; many families shoot their own home videos.

Some instructional objectives for a video art program include:

- Art production: Students will be able to use the video camera to apply spatial concepts involving close-ups and long shots and to manage the art elements of light and space. Students will learn the vocabulary of motion film and will identify instances of backlighting, soft focus, freeze frame, establishing zoom shots, slow disclosure shots, low-angle shots, long shots, and panning shots.

- Art criticism: Students will analyze techniques used in art-history videos as well as those made by famous artists, such as the installations of Nam June Paik and Laurie Anderson.
- Art history: Students will watch early videos and identify major technological advances.

To extend their learning, students can take videos home to view with their families and discuss how they achieved effects and used light, space, and action. Finally, videos of students creating in another art media can be used as a tool to help them critique their performance in achieving video-related art objectives.

Videos can also serve as documentation and evaluation of art learning. For example, art displays in elementary-school hallways can be video-taped as a way of documenting the quality of the work. This video can be shared with the students whose work is depicted as a way to give them feedback. It also can be shared with future classes when they embark on the same kind of project. A student can video his or her classmates making art, then take the videotape home and write a critique of the result. Students depicted in the video can take the tape home and watch it, then write a review of their art-making process, telling what they would like to do better or differently. Art concepts of light, space, movement, and time become vivid for students as they make, watch, and analyze video and film.

The community's important sights and events can be recorded through art using technology. Here, Alice Bowen's computer artwork shows the full moon's high tides at the lighthouse.

Courtesy of Melody Milbrandt.

A student gives a video-recorded demonstration in the classroom while another student does the recording.

IN THE CLASSROOM/IN THE COMMUNITY

Using Videos for Content-Area Learning

Video is a wonderful resource for teaching a variety of content. For social-studies projects, have students videotape interviews with senior citizens about their memories and experiences, with politicians about the way a town or county is governed, or with other people whose views might be of interest (with permission, of course!). For language arts lessons, have students write and then act out a story, and videotape the result. For science, take field trips to parks, zoos, or other nearby sites and videotape animal behavior, or native plant growth.

School-produced videos can also be shown at the local library as part of a humanities program. Gain valuable community support for your art-education program by documenting the historical contributions of community groups. Document your students' reactions to social and political events in the community, such as older siblings going off to serve in the military and the impact of their departure on younger siblings at home. Videos documenting community life can be shown at town festivals.

An elementary-school child videotapes a field trip speaker discussing his passion, raising horses.

Videos can also, of course, document events in the classroom, school, and community. Students who have received training in camera use can apply their skills by documenting school functions, game days, and seasonal festivities. The videos can then be played in the school halls or in classes to provide feedback to the participants. Art-club members can videotape the musical, dramatic, and dance performances of the other arts programs. In many middle schools, where art competes with orchestra, band, and chorus for enrollment, videos of the art program in action can be used as a way of recruiting students and building a program of quality. Teachers are amazed at the time and energy that children put into their involvement in video projects. This medium gives students a way to create their own reality.

FOR FURTHER READING

Duncum, Paul. 2003. "Visual Culture in the Classroom." *Art Education* 56(2): 25–32.

Eggenmeyer, Valerie. 2004. "Manipulation of the Family Photo Album: Esther Parada's Transplant: A Tale of Two Continents." *Art Education* 57(2): 19–24.

Freedman, Kerry. 1991. "Possibilities of Interactive Computer Graphics for Art Instruction: A Summary of Research." *Art Education* 44(3): 41–47.

Guhin, Paula. 1995. "Photograms, Compliments of the Sun." *Arts and Activities* 11(5): 28–29.

Johnson, M. "Orientations to Curriculum in Computer Art Education." *Art Education* (May 1997): 43–47.

Marshalek, Doug G. 2002. "Building Better Web-based Learning Environments; Thinking in '3's.'" *Art Education* 55(4): 13–18.

Marshalek, Doug G. 2004. "Four Learning Environments for Contemporary Art Education: Studio, Information, Planning, Electronic." *Art Education* 57(3): 33–41.

Matzer, Laura. 2003. "Drawing with Light: Focus on Four Photographic Processes." *Art Education* 56(5): 25–32.

Mitchell, Christina E., Amanda Martin-Hamon, and Elissa Anderson. 2002. "A Choice of Weapons: Photography of Gordon Parks." *Art Education* 55(2): 25–32.

Paik, Nam June, cited in Beverly J. Jones. "Toward Democratic Direction of Technology." In Blandy and Congdon, *Art in a Democracy.* New York: Teachers College Press, pp. 64–73.

Provenzo, E. F. 2002. *The Internet and the World Wide Web for Teachers* (2nd ed). Boston: Allyn and Bacon.

Sharff, Stefan. 1982. *The Elements of Cinema.* New York: Columbia University Press.

Smith-Shank, Deborah L. 2003. "Lewis Hine and His Photo Stories: Visual Culture and Social Reform." *Art Education* 56(2): 33–37.

Zakia, Richard. 1993. "Photography and Visual Perception." *Journal of Aesthetic Education* 27(4): 67–82.

WEB RESOURCES

Literally millions of websites are devoted to art and artists. Any random search will turn up a wealth of resources. Web addresses come and go, but here are some admirable sites that were available at the time this book was published.

- Find artists' biographies at www.biography.com, or at www.arthistory.net
- Learn about European historical artists at www.euroweb.hu/art or at www.ocaiw.com

Topics and Periods
African art:
http://viva.lib.virginia.edu/dic/exhibit/93.ray.aa/African.html

Native-American art: www.hanksville.org/NAresources and at www.powersource.com/powersource/gallery/default.html

Egyptian art: www.pharos.bu.edu/Egypt/Cairo

Art from India: www.lavanya-indology.com

Impressionistic art (the collection of Musee d'Orsay): www.meteora.ucsd.edu:80/~norman/paris/Musees/Orsay/Collections

Medieval art: www.georgetown.edu/labyrinth

American Museums

The Detroit Institute of Arts: www.dia.org

The Metropolitan Museum of Art in New York City: www.metmuseum.org

The National Gallery in Washington, DC: www.nga.gov

The Museum of Modern Art in New York City: www.moma.org

The Smithsonian Institutions: www.si.edu

Information about museums both on and off the Web can be found at: www.archive.comlab.ox.ac.uk/archive/other/museums.html

Museums Abroad

Museums in Paris (including the Louvre): www.paris.org.:80/Musees The Louvre Museum is also at: www.atlcom.net/~psmith/Louvre

The Uffizi Gallery in Florence, Italy: www.televisual.it/uffizi

General

Art history websites and bibliographies: www.ilpi.com/artsource/general.html

An art history research center: http://art-history.concordia.ca/AHRC.index.htm

Artists' quotes and links: www.art.net

Curriculum Resources

For an excellent guide to electronic art ed resources, such as developing a class website:

http://www.princetonol.com/groups/iad/lessons/middle/arted.htm# Technology

For Craig Roland's research on website:

http://grove.ufl/edu/~rolandc/webdesign.html

For a lesson plan for computer-art tessellations:

http://syrylynrainbowdragon.tripod.com/tes.html

For a lesson plan for colorizing a photo on the computer:

http://syrylynrainbowdragon.tripod.com/tiles.html

http://syrylynrainbowdragon.tripod.com/colorize/html

For making an electronic collage:

http://www.nga.gov/kids/zone/collagemachine.html

For lesson plans for Sandy Skoglund's photos:

http://www.getty.edu/artsednet/resources/Skoglund/index/html

For making movies in iPhoto and iMovie:

http://ali.apple.com/ali_sites/ali/exhibits/1000879

For Dorothea Lange's photos about Depression migrant worker photos:

http://www.getty.edu/art/exhibitions/lange/index.html

For information on how to get your students' school artwork online:

http://www.princetonol.com/groups/iad/artroom/artroom.html

For Zoetrope and other pre-video and video activities for students:

http://cmp1.ucr.edu/exhibitions/education/vidkids/lessons.html

For a site where children can experience computer drawing of a portrait:

http://www.nga.gov/kids/zone/pixelface.htm

Chapter 29
Three-Dimensional Design: Additive and Subtractive Sculpture

Courtesy of Frank Wachowiak and Ted Ramsay.

In box sculpture, allow the shape of the box itself to trigger the student's imagination. Square and rectangular boxes are much easier for young children to assemble.

$\mathcal{M}$any challenging sculptural techniques, both additive and subtractive, await those upper-elementary- and middle-school students and their teachers who are willing to make a serious, time-consuming commitment to a painstaking yet adventurous task. Too often, sculpture in the elementary school has been presented as a therapeutic activity, with minor emphasis on its expressive potential. If sufficient time cannot be allotted for students to become thoroughly involved in the sculptural process, postpone it until the middle-school years, when more time is budgeted for art and the students' perseverance and constructive skills are more developed. If the elementary-school teacher of art understands the sculptural media and can motivate the students to carry projects through to culmination, however, the sculpture experience can be one of the most fulfilling in the upper-elementary grades art program.

The major consideration often is not so much of student motivation as of material resources, preliminary planning, special techniques, cleanup, and storage. A class of 25 or more students working on additive or subtractive sculpture poses several organizational problems. Teachers must decide beforehand whether they want the entire class to use the same medium or whether they will allow students to work with materials of their choosing. Skilled instructors may be able to control a large class in which some students are working on toothpick or balsa-wood construction, some on plaster block carving, and some on wire or metal sculpture. The resulting products, however, must show evidence of the students' growth in sculptural design. If, as often is the case, the teacher becomes merely the dispenser of various materials and tools and has little time to evaluate work in progress with the students, it is much wiser to limit the offering and have the entire class use only one sculptural medium. In such instances, the teacher can organize the materials, tools, and storage space more effectively. A rich motivational plan and evaluation plan can be developed over the several days necessary for the project.

This chapter will first discuss box sculpture and constructions in space, then masks, and, finally, subtractive sculpture in plaster.

BOX SCULPTURE AND CONSTRUCTIONS IN SPACE

Older and more mature children often need a change of pace. New challenges, materials, and techniques can spark a growing interest in art. Using cardboard boxes, mailing tubes, and assorted found objects gives upper-elementary- and middle-school students a rare opportunity to express their individual ideas in a unique, three-dimensional form. They find value in recycling discarded materials at the same time they struggle with a complex construction problem. They come to appreciate in a creative way the adage "the whole is greater than the sum of its parts."

An exciting new world of additive sculpture has opened up with the burgeoning exploitation of found materials. These include applicator sticks, drinking straws, thin dowels, assorted toothpicks, reeds, discarded game parts (for example, Tinkertoy pieces), pick-up sticks, scrap lumber, and plastic packing materials. The resulting constructions have many labels: stabiles, mobiles, space modulators, combine art, scrap sculpture, or assemblage. Constructions definitely will add an adventurous dimension to art programs and hold the interest of today's students.

In many instances, students will be eager to create nonobjective, abstract, and geometrically oriented constructions, allowing the materials to dictate the form. This is particularly true when straws, applicator sticks, toothpicks, and reeds are the building elements. The design grows stick by stick, straw by straw, dowel by dowel. Unless the construction itself is stable, an auxiliary support or separate base of wood, plywood, or Masonite is essential. Determine the placement of supports that are required, then drill or hammer holes into the base at these points. Begin the structure by securely inserting and gluing the initial supports into these holes.

A host of materials can embellish stick or straw constructions. Experiment, for example, with bottle corks, thread spools, beads, cord, Ping-Pong balls, small rubber balls, pegboard pegs, construction paper, mailing tubes, colored cardboard, cardboard spools from tape dispensers,

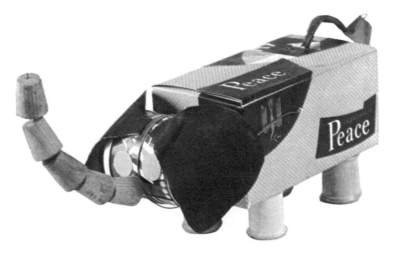

Top: *Courtesy of Frank Wachowiak.* Bottom: *Courtesy of Frank Wachowiak and Ted Ramsay.*

Top: After the boxes have been taped together, the sculpture is allowed to dry and become sturdy. Then, the sculpture can be painted. **Middle:** Cardboard boxes can be joined to make a large sculpture dinosaur capable of holding two persons. **Bottom:** As with this elephant, it is not always necessary to paint box sculpture. Some boxes already have colorful printed designs.

miniature cardboard boxes, plastic pieces, wood or plastic buttons, and 35mm film canisters. Outdoors, the teacher can give completed constructions a coat of black or white spray paint, which contributes to a striking unifying visual impact.

Additive sculpture also can be made using more challenging materials and techniques. Wire can be combined with found metal pieces. Toothpick and applicator-stick constructions can be dipped into melted crayon, wet plaster, or liquid metal. Corrugated cardboard can be cut into various shapes that are then slotted, joined, and glued together to form a stabile. Cardboard mailing tubes can be cut into multisized cylinders and rings, then assembled into animals, insects, and figures. Exacto knives, Sloyd knives, or utility knives are necessary to cut cardboard boxes, but they must be used only under a teacher's strict supervision. A coping saw or a small vibrating-table jigsaw is useful for cutting heavy cardboard, chipboard, Masonite, and heavyweight cardboard tubes.

At least 2 to 4 weeks before the project begins, students should start collecting discarded cardboard boxes. A letter to their parents listing materials that are needed will help to build a necessary store of discards, scraps, and remnants. This early, personal involvement on the part of the students builds interest in the expressive adventure ahead. Store the accumulated boxes and objects until needed in a giant cardboard carton, or have students store their personal collections in a grocery sack labeled with their name.

Useful fastening materials (either for temporary or permanent attaching) include straight pins, masking tape, paper clips, string, double-faced tape, rubber bands, gummed tape, white liquid glue, school paste, scissors, paper punch, nails, and wire.

One way to start the project is to invite students to select three or four different-size boxes and a set of cardboard mailing tubes (for small constructions, use toilet-tissue tubes), then juxtapose these in various configurations until an idea is triggered. Another approach is to have a theme in mind and select boxes to form this preconception. After students decide on a basic shape for their creations, making sketches will help them to plan. The excitement builds as students see the creation grow. Sometimes, an unusual box turns up that is just right for the head of a monster and triggers the design for the rest of the construction. Often, a box can be

Top: *Courtesy of Frank Wachowiak.* Middle and bottom: *Courtesy of Frank Wachowiak and Ted Ramsay.*

Top: Recycled materials can be made into wonderful sculptures, as in this grasshopper of wood strips. **Middle:** A cruise ship ingeniously employs box sculptural forms. **Bottom:** This construction of reeds and construction paper by a sixth-grader shows a good use of restraint, using only triangles to unify the design.

Left: *Courtesy of Barbara Thomas.* Right: *Courtesy of Beverly Barksdale Mallon.*

Left: With the use of a piece of ¾-inch Styrofoam® insulation for a base, the structure grows with shish-kebab skewers, Popsicle sticks, and golf tees. **Right:** A two-foot-high giraffe was made over a foundation of wire, sticks, and newspaper, held together with brown paper tape. To strengthen it, it was then covered with newspaper strips soaked in wallpaper paste, prior to being painted.

partially opened and hinged to become the mouth and jaws of a voracious, mythical lion or dragon. What began as a dream car might easily emerge in the final stages as a space station.

The most challenging part is fastening the separate boxes together and securing the appendages. The recommended method includes first gluing and then tying, pinning, paper-clipping, and/or taping the boxes together until the glue dries overnight. Finding an adhesive with ideal properties can be problematic, however, because many adhesives have some, but not all, of the desired properties. For example, white glue (such as Elmer's glue) is safe, available in most schools, and reasonably effective, although its tackiness and drying time are not ideal. A new product, Elmer's Tacky Glue, has more tackiness and therefore is superior for box and wood-scrap sculptures. Glues such as airplane glue and Duco Cement should *not* be used in classrooms because these glues contain the harmful solvents xylene or toluene. A teacher might use a hot-melt glue gun for difficult attachments. (See safety section in Appendix A.)

IN THE CLASSROOM

Three-Dimensional Design

Plan out ahead of time three locations: for the found objects, for the supply of fastening devices and materials, and for the constructions in progress.

Some suggested box-sculpture topics that can pique students' imaginations are: astronauts, spaceships, space stations, robots, creatures from another planet, engines, planes, toys, rockets, homes, vehicles and computers of the future, fantastic designs for playground equipment, masks, nonobjective space modulators, and imaginative animals, bugs, birds, and fish.

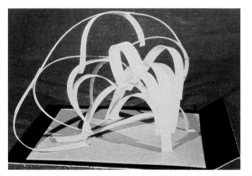

Left: *Milwaukee, WI.* Right: *Three-Fold Manifestation II (steel painted white, 32 feet high). Alice Aycock. Storm King Art Center, Mountainville, NY. Gift of the artist. Photo: Jerry L. Thompson.*

Left: A sixth-grade student created this space modulator with construction paper strips and school paste. **Right:** Perhaps such a project will inspire one of your students to become a sculptor and to create pieces, not 30 inches high, but rather 30 feet high. In any event, because of the school experience that you provide, all students will be able to appreciate more intensely the rhythm, repetition, and construction in such works as Alice Aycock's 1987 sculpture.

Working on a stiff base, such as a 1-foot-square piece of cardboard or Masonite, gives increased stability to the piece-in-progress and facilitates its rotating so that all sides can be studied. In constructing standing figures, students must decide how to make the figure stand upright. If necessary, a stabilizing third leg or support can be created. A tail can be added, or the

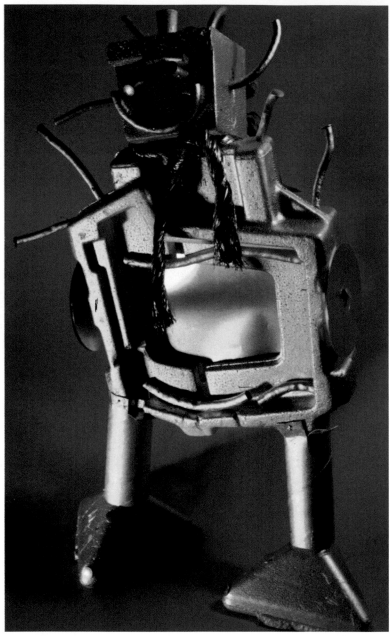

Courtesy of Ted Ramsay.

A sixth-grade student combined plastic discards to produce this imaginatively constructed robot. Only the teacher, not the students, should use spray paint, and, even then, spray outdoors.

figure can hold gear, such as a spear or banner standard, that touches the ground. Heightened interest, decoration, and texture can be added by using egg cartons, corrugated and embossed cardboard, paper drinking straws, plastic packing noodles, clothespins, toothpicks, paste sticks, dowels, corks, pipe cleaners, reeds, beads, Tinkertoy pieces, Ping-Pong balls, and game parts.

Sometimes, the containers themselves with their printed designs and logos are so exciting that painting them would only mask their bold design qualities. Rather than painting boxes that already contain graphics or lettering, another possibility is to camouflage them with colored paper, comic-book and magazine pages, tissue paper, wallpaper samples, cloth, or gift-wrapping papers. If the sculpture is to be painted, the features that give it individuality must be emphasized, especially the eyes, mouth, nose, ears, and horns. If the boxes' glossy surfaces resist water-based paint, make it adhere by adding soap to the paint. Spray paints are not considered safe for student use, and any spray painting must be done by the teacher outdoors. Silver, copper, or gold paints may be employed for a robot, knight in armor, or astronaut. Clearly, there are endless possibilities in box and found-object sculpture. The teacher and students who are resourceful, persistent, and patient enough to try this project have a real art adventure awaiting them.

MASKS

Always a popular undertaking, maskmaking in the elementary and middle schools has, unfortunately, been one in which design considerations are too often secondary. Too often, basic compositional factors have been minimized and raw colors are applied in a random, slapdash, form-negating manner. On occasion, very young children can create colorful, expressively naive masks when richly motivated. Because of the cultural and symbolic connotations of maskmaking and the often complex techniques required for implementation, however, maskmaking is best postponed until students reach upper elementary and middle school.

Decoration is used to heighten the mask's visual appeal. Taking a cue from maskmakers of the past, students should use lines or shapes to reinforce and emphasize the dominant features. They should create pattern and texture on the face, delineate hair and beard, and emphasize eyes by using highly contrasting colors and values. Color must be used with restraint, however, lest it jeopardize the mask's impact or appeal. Color must be integrated with the features—not superficially applied—and it must complement rather than detract. Subtle, limited color harmonies should be encouraged, and primary colors should be used with discretion (generally only to provide a necessary contrast).

This second-grader loved making his dramatic mask headdress of blue waves and four patterned water snakes. From tagboard, the upper part becomes the headdress, and the bottom 6 inches of the paper are cut in partway to form a headband and mask.

Students discuss their papier-mâché masks along with actual masks borrowed from the nearby museum's school outreach program.

IN THE CLASSROOM

Studying Culture Through Masks

Multicultural education certainly will include the study of masks. Rather than tying maskmaking to overworked Halloween motifs, the activity is on a firmer academic base when integrated with a social-studies cultural unit: In Africa, likenesses of departed chiefs are used in memorial services. Native Americans use masks in rain-making and agricultural ceremonies. Judges in New Guinea wear masks to heighten their authority. The masks worn by medieval mummers might signify one of the seven deadly sins, biblical characters, or forces of nature. In China, Burma, and Ceylon, masks were worn to prevent illness and cure diseases. Thieves wear them to conceal their identity. Police officers, firefighters, hospital personnel, and football players wear masks for personal protection.

The most inspired and evocative masks of past centuries and cultures almost always have been based on an abstract, stylized concept rather than on natural appearance. To emphasize certain features, maskmakers often abstracted the face, whether human or animal, into combinations of ovals, squares, and circles. A study of masks such as those by tribal Africans and Native Americans reveals recurring aspects. Whereas facial features that capture the mood or spirit usually are exaggerated, they seldom are distorted to the extent that they appear to be something so alien and trite as star-shaped eyes. The most expressive masks are imbued with the essence and vitality of a particular mood or emotion: astonishment, serenity, power, anger, dignity, joy, fury, frenzy, benevolence, or wonder. Another recurring characteristic is continuity of facial forms and features, as exemplified by the linear flow of the nose structure into the eyebrow contour.

Papier-mâché over a clay foundation still is the most popular and effectively controlled technique, allowing for highly individualized interpretations and detailed facial modeling. Also recommended is papier-mâché or plaster-impregnated gauze applied over a mixing or salad bowl, small dishpan, balloon, or beach ball. As the pasted form develops, it can be embellished with additional pieces of plastic foam, bent cardboard, and found objects to create nose, eyes, mouth, and ear shapes. String, yarn, raffia, and plastic packing material may be used for hair, beard, and other textures. These details are covered with a final layer of gauze or glue-moistened paper toweling. When dry, the mask can be painted.

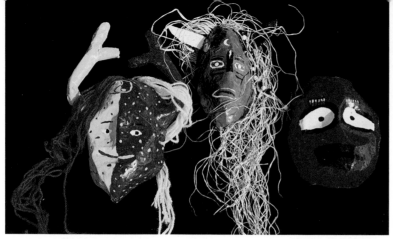

Courtesy of Nancy Eliot.

Middle-school students made these papier-mâché masks and decorated them imaginatively with straw and fiber hair, one mask with a half-yellow, half-red face with antlers and another dark mask with white and black horns.

Courtesy of Leonard Piha.

The papier-mâché process, useful for masks, can also be used to make many forms, here, for example, pots.

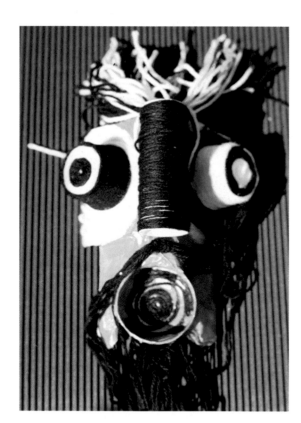

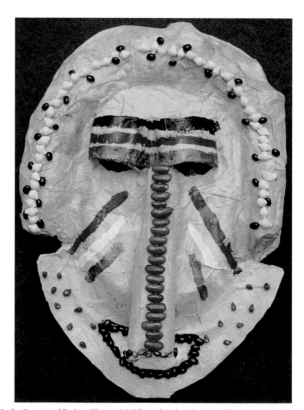

Left: *Courtesy of Barbara Thomas.* Middle and right: *Courtesy of Frank Wachowiak.*

Varied approaches to maskmaking. **Left:** Boxes, spools, paper cups, and yarn create a face of conical forms. **Middle:** Construction paper is bent into a canoelike shape and raffia added. Feathers could also be incorporated.

Right: Beth Pearson used red, white, and black beans to create repeated patterns and lines. Basic mask forms also may be achieved by applying newspaper strips with wheat paste or liquid starch over a balloon or mixing bowl.

Kindergarten children created their own Halloween costumes by recycling paper garment bags. If such bags are not available, fasten together with glue or masking tape two large-size grocery bags, one with the bottom cut off.

Courtesy of Frank Wachowiak.

Posing on the jungle gym with their scary outstretched clawlike hands, first-graders loved making these giant colored-construction-paper masks.

Courtesy of Frank Wachowiak and Ted Ramsay.

Colored-Construction-Paper Masks: A three-dimensional effect in the masks was achieved by cutting short slits into the borders of the sheets of paper and then overlapping the resulting tabs and stapling them together. Masks make highly decorative artifacts to brighten up the classroom.

Another popular maskmaking technique is the paper- or cardboard-construction process. This generally requires intricate cutting and scoring of the paper to achieve an effective, three-dimensional quality. It has many possibilities, however, and because of the availability of materials and tools, it can be pursued in the ordinary classroom. Unlike papier-mâché projects that involve a lengthy cleanup period and abundant storage space, paper-sculpture masks are simpler to manage and store. For children in the primary grades, creation of a paper-plate, paper-sack, or plastic meat-tray mask is the most practical and successful technique, because it does not involve a complex, three-dimensional process.

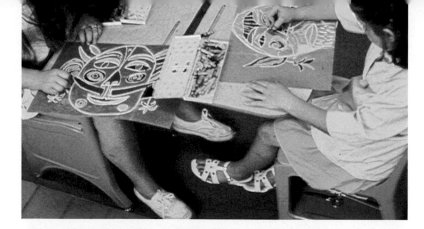

Studying Culture Through Totem Poles

A study of early Pacific Coast Native-American life provides rich motivation for several art projects, including the group construction of a totem pole; however, the culture of the Northwest Native Americans must be genuinely examined. Cross-cultural comparisons can be made about the role of art in their culture and their beliefs about nature, death, religion, and the roles of men, women, and children. For the Native-American carvers, art is empty when it omits the spiritual dimension of life. As was the custom of the totem carvers, encourage students to identify with some other living entity or with an animal or bird school symbol.

TOTEM POLES

Use a sheet of colored construction paper 12 × 18 inches as the background for each totem mask. With the paper placed horizontally on the desk and the 18-inch border at the bottom, students draw with chalk the outline of their mask in the center of the paper. The top and bottom of their mask should touch the edge of the paper. The larger they draw it, the better, but they should leave some of the paper plain at each side to wrap around the pole. When the drawing is complete, the mask may be painted with tempera paint or colored with crayon or oil pastels. Students should be encouraged:

- to exploit unusual color combinations in their masks, including the use of black and white;
- to repeat colors for unity;
- to create contrast by juxtaposing light and dark colors;
- and to emphasize important parts of their masks through a selection of vivid, dominant colors.

After the mask is colored, make parts of it three-dimensional by cutting slits with scissors around an ear or nose and either folding these pieces outward from the main mask or bending them back. A backing sheet of a contrasting color, 12 × 18 inches, may be added when assembling the several masks into the totem form. Students also may add supplementary shapes of multicolored construction paper for teeth, fangs, horns, ears, earrings, and eyebrows.

There are several ways to construct totem poles from the separate masks. One way is to obtain an empty gallon food tin from the school cafeteria for a base foundation, and fill it with sand or clay. Then, wrap a 24 × 36-inch sheet of tagboard around the can, and secure it with masking tape, creating a 36-inch-tall cylinder. Build another cylinder above the

Courtesy of Frank Wachowiak.

Masks created for a totem-pole project. Colored construction paper, 12 × 18 inches, and oil pastels were used. Noses, teeth, ears, and cheeks were made by cutting slits in the mask. These portions then were bent out and stapled to create three-dimensional forms. Completed masks were secured to discarded food tins from the school cafeteria.

first, if desired. Secure it again with tape, and with the tagboard cylinder as a steady foundation, fasten the masks around it with glue, masking tape, or staple-gun tacker. Another type of pole can be made from a cardboard cylinder from a carpet showroom, likewise embedded for stability in a heavy base.

Once the basic totem pole is sturdily constructed, embellish it with supplemental wings, feet, and arms made of cardboard. Display the completed totem poles at a cultural celebration or in the school foyer as a way of sharing the multicultural learning experience with the school at large.

Top left: *Courtesy of Frank Wachowiak.* Bottom left: *Courtesy of Barrow Elementary School.* Top and bottom right: *Courtesy of Alice Ballard Munn and Diane Barrett.*

Totems usually are made in conjunction with a study of Native-American culture. **Top left:** Cylindrical forms were made by stacking a column of school cafeteria cans and taping them together. **Bottom left:** A tree was used for the vertical column, and masks by upper-elementary-school children were attached to the column. **Top right:** In a second-grade class, each child selected an animal thought to have special powers and made a Northwest Native-American totem dedicated to it. **Bottom right:** Northwest Haida women's hats were made and the women's stories told.

SUBTRACTIVE SCULPTURE IN PLASTER

For school use, ideal materials must be safe, economical, relatively easy to carve, and allow quick cleanup. Recommended and readily obtainable materials for subtractive sculpture include plaster-of-paris, leather-hard clay, balsa wood, porous firebrick, and large bars of soap. Sand core is a metal-casting by-product and consists of sand held together with binders, may be available free from a local metal foundry.

Plaster usually is the material chosen for subtractive sculpture in school programs because it is cheap and easy to get. Plaster should be mixed with additives such as white sand or fine-grain zonolite to give it a texture and make it easier to carve. Approximately one-part additive to

Courtesy of Frank Wachowiak and Ted Ramsay.

Subtractive sculptures. **Top left:** Sandcore, a by-product from metal casting, and porous firebrick can be carved. Notice how cleverly this child has solved the problem of thin legs breaking off by keeping a central band intact between the legs. **Top right and bottom left and right:** Teachers usually add vermiculite to plaster of paris so it can be carved more easily. The vermiculite also gives a rough texture. Observe in this bear, mountain goat, and rhinoceros how these sixth-graders have solved the problem of delicate parts breaking off by using volumetric compact forms.

one-part dry plaster will produce a fairly porous and workable carving block. A half-gallon or quart-size milk or juice carton made of waxed cardboard makes a sturdy, leak-proof mold.

Students begin by making preliminary front-, side-, and back-view sketches for their sculptures on paper cut to the size of their plaster block. (Clever students with foresight can design and tape inside their cartons curved cardboard dams to cut down on the amount of carving.) While the class is sketching, the teacher can help two or three students at a time to make their plaster molds. All necessary materials and tools should be on a newspaper-protected table or counter and near a water source (if possible). Have ready the molding plaster, vermiculite or sand, scoops or cups, milk cartons opened wide at the top, water, small-size rubber or plastic dishpan, wood stock or paddle, dry tempera colors (if desired), and lots of newspapers to line the nearby wastebaskets and both cover (and recover) the

Plaster formed in a milk carton was carved by sixth-graders into a bouquet of purple tulips and into a black-and-white abstract sculpture.

IN THE CLASSROOM

Studying Culture Through Sculpture

Subtractive sculpture (carving) has appealed to artists of all cultures throughout history. Wood probably has been the most popular medium for sculptors, but exquisite creations have been carved in a host of materials, including jade, ivory, bone, marble, soapstone, and alabaster. Many of these art materials are, of course, unsuitable for the usual art class. They may be banned (such as ivory), too costly (such as jade), or too dangerous (such as soapstone, which may contain asbestos).

Subjects that students can handle successfully include fish, nesting birds, animals (especially those in repose, to prevent thin legs from breaking off), and portrait heads. Organic or nonobjective free forms can be developed from motifs based on rocks, shells, nuts, pods, and other natural or biomorphic forms.

counter and floor around the plaster-mixing area. Plaster cleanup is messy: limit foot traffic in the area.

Fill a milk carton three-fourths full with water, and pour the water into the dishpan. Sift plaster into the water slowly, using a hand, cup, or scoop. When islands of plaster appear above the water, add zonolite or sand. Stir the mix gently yet swiftly by hand, squeezing out the lumps until thoroughly mixed. The mixture will thicken very quickly; be ready to pour it immediately into the milk carton. After pouring it into the carton, tap the carton on the table to remove trapped bubbles, or stir it quickly with a stick or paddle.

Caution: Never pour plaster down the sink, or even rinse plaster-coated tools there. Instead, scrape excess plaster left in the dishpan, on hands, and on tools into the plastic-bag-lined wastebasket. Then, rinse hands and tools in another plastic-bag-lined pail of water, but do not pour this rinsing water down the sink either. Let the plaster settle out overnight.

Allow the plaster mold or block to dry overnight. If color is desired in the plaster block, mix tempera powder into the dry plaster before it is combined with water. Neutral colors such as umber, ochre, sienna, and earth-green are recommended.

Students may transfer preliminary pencil sketches to the block using carbon paper, or, using their sketches as a reference, they may draw directly on the block with a pencil or ink marker. The sculpture should make fullest use of the block. Remind students that no amount of texture, detail, or pattern will redeem the work if the basic form is weak. Caution

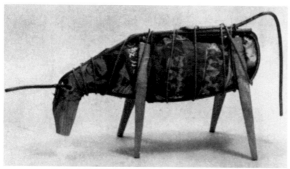

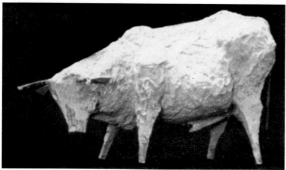

Often, plaster is used both additively and subtractively on the same sculpture. Shown here is a sturdy interior form called an armature, which is then covered with plaster. For larger projects, bend and weld reinforcing bars together. Then fill out the form with thinner wire, mesh, string, wood, and paper. Finally, add plaster and carve away the excess.

them not to choose a subject that is too intricate and complex or that might be expressed more easily in wood, wire, metal, or clay.

The recommended tools for the carving process are a Sloyd or Hyde knife with a 2-inch blade, a utility knife (a knife with a metal handle encasing a replaceable blade), or a small plaster rasp. Students should cut, file, rasp, or chisel away the excess plaster to delineate the dominant profile or outline view. Next, they may refer to their top, front, and rear sketches and carve away to define those contours. They should proceed cautiously as they remove the plaster, turning the block around to define all forms consistently. As they carve, encourage them to think about how each part flows freely and naturally into the next.

Tables and floors in the working areas should be covered with newspapers or plastic dropcloths to expedite cleanup. Cleanup also may be minimized by having the students hold the plaster block inside a large, shallow cardboard box as they carve. In fair weather, minimize mess by having the class carve outdoors, working on drop cloths away from high-public-visibility areas such as building entrances.

When sculpting animals, heads, or human figures, keep the base part strong and undefined during most of the carving process. This way, the piece does not become top-heavy, topple over, and break. Help the students to evaluate their in-process sculpture: to be aware of large masses contrasting with small forms; to capture the characteristic stance or action; to emphasize a feature, such as the beak or claws of a bird; and to enrich the surface of their creation through texture and pattern. Delicate appendages such as hands, ears, horns, tusks, beaks, tails, and other jutting forms should be kept undefined until the basic shape is well established. During the final stages, carve textural and decorative details with nails, discarded dental tools, or nut picks.

Seal the sculpture with dilute white glue and let dry overnight prior to staining, glazing, waxing, or metalizing. A paint stain in subtle shades can be applied freely and allowed to penetrate into the incised areas. After letting the stain set briefly, judiciously wipe the raised areas to bring out highlights. A complementary sculpture base of driftwood, stained blocks of wood, a flat rock, or sections of tree trunks with the bark left intact can help to give the carving distinction.

Courtesy of Claire Clements.

Excitement lights the eyes of first-grader Cal Clements as he assembles wood scraps into a found object sculpture.

FOR FURTHER READING

Golomb, Claire. 1974. *Young Children's Sculpture and Drawing: A Study in Representational Development.* Cambridge, MA: Harvard University Press.

LaLiberte, Norman. 1966. *Masks, Face Coverings, and Headgear.* New York: Reinhold.

Lommel, Andreas. 1981. *Masks: Their Meanings and Function.* London: Ferndale.

Rottger, Ernst. 1961. *Surfaces in Creative Design.* London: Batsford.

Rottger, Ernst. 1969. *Creative Wood Design.* New York: Reinhold.

WEB RESOURCES

For a lesson on the cultural significance of masks:

  http://edsitement.neh.gov/view_lesson_plan.asp?ID=310

For subtractive sculpture, specifically the granite sculptures of Jesus Moles:

  http://www.getty.edu/artsednet/resources/Moroles/index.html

For lesson plans on animal sculptures:

  http://www.getty.edu/artsednet/resources/Look/Animals/index.html

For a lesson plan on public art:

  http://www.getty.edu/artsednet/resources/Aeia/teach-lp.html

For a site on how students create landscape sculptures:

  http://www.getty.edu/artsednet/resources/Aeia/studio-lp.html

For a relief sculpture lesson plan:

  http://artsedge.kennedy-center.org/content/2206/

For sculpting a famous character in literature:

  http://artsedge.kennedy-center.org/content/2210/

For creating a monumental animal sculpture:

  http://artsedge.kennedy-center.org/content/2201/

Chapter 30
Architecture

*A*rchitecture has been called the mother of the arts, because it contains all other visual art forms. Architectural education conducted in elementary school can introduce future citizens not only to the delights of studying architecture but also to the importance of wise community design decisions. Unfortunately, architecture has not been a well-established component in the crowded elementary-school art curriculum. Nevertheless, teachers with an interest in architecture should bring their passion about the field to their students through an architecture learning experience.

Courtesy of Joyce Vroon.

In this sixth-grade marker drawing of a Victorian house, the structure is clearly delineated, and decorative moldings, columns, and stonework are shown. Even the shutters, lamps, and cat in the window are included.

Courtesy of Lawrence Stueck.

Children can gain awareness of architectural form and construction by helping to build a playscape.

Courtesy of Joyce Vroon.

A series of house facades drawn on accordian-folded tagboard comprise Josephine Allen's street-front scene.

Architecture is an art form that is readily comprehended and is essential to the visual essence of our communities. Architecture lends itself readily to integration with environmental education, history, and social studies. For example, the architecture of Monticello illustrates Thomas Jefferson's rejection of English colonialism and his commitment to the rationalistic ideals of French enlightenment thought. (However, the slave quarters behind his home show other social realities.)

Design sources can be photographs, slides, or drawings of the actual buildings. Small boxes, such as hand-appliance, cereal, shoe, and drugstore gift boxes, can be used for the basic structure. These can be covered with construction paper, or they can be painted. Signs and architectural features can be cut from paper, decorated, and attached. Temporarily arrange the buildings onto a large piece of cardboard, such as from a major appliance. Then, the streets and grounds can be sketched in, the background painted, and models of vehicles, street signs, and street furniture, such as benches and stop signs, added. The project might be given a public display, and publicity, at the meeting of a community development group, such as at the Chamber of Commerce or downtown development authority.

Models of local architecture can be constructed not only in cardboard; clay is especially appropriate. Then, these can be attached with

Students can go on a sketching tour of their community's most illustrious buildings and list their architectural features. They can construct models of their town's most architecturally interesting buildings. This activity can also integrate ideas of engineering structure and math with art. Some instructional objectives include the following:

- Students will create a model of an existing building incorporating the design qualities of repetition, pattern, and texture.
- Students will discuss the reasons particular buildings have certain architectural character. An objective might be that they will be able to identify examples of neo-Classical, Victorian, and Prairie-style. Intermediate-grade students will be able to find examples to show that the design of buildings changes over time.
- Students will arrange their model buildings to showcase their community's architecture.

construction adhesive to plywood to make a mural for long-term educational display and appreciation. Three-dimensional clay models of historic buildings may become prize community possessions. Pen-and-ink drawings of buildings can be assembled for a community calendar, or a cloth quilt based on historic community buildings can be made for public display.

Sketching fantasy houses is another architecture lesson. Correlate this to a study of historic styles, such as Victorian, Renaissance Revival, and flamboyant contemporary buildings by Frank Gehry; list the devices each style used. Sketches of one's dream house might include exotic architectural features, such as moats, drawbridges, and crenelated towers.

Students of a more practical mindset may want to design something for actual use, such as a design for the interior of their bedroom or a corner of a garden. Students enjoy expressing their personalities through the choice of artwork, interior design, furniture arrangements, color schemes, plants, and bushes. A scrapbook of components can be put together from department-store newspaper advertising sections, home and garden design magazines, and postcards and photocopies of historical exemplars, and the collection can be used by students as the basis for a colorful overall design plan. A follow-up activity is to have students take before-and-after photos of places where aspects of their designs were actually implemented.

Young primary-level children can enrich their architectural imaginings about castles and fortresses through use of a sandbox. Using their

Courtesy of Baiba Kuntz.

Top: *Courtesy of Baiba Kuntz.* Bottom: *Courtesy of Joyce Vroon.*

Top: Fifth-grade student Lisa Molinaro's sketch of an imaginary house shows arched second-story windows in groups of two and four. **Bottom:** Good clay-working tools are essential for the careful work that is entailed in making a clay house bas-relief. **Above right:** Lisa's finished house showing the series of arched windows, a bay window, and an arched front door, along with landscaping.

Ceramic low-fire underglaze colors and clear glass glaze enhance the finished quality of the clay house bas-relief by sixth-grader Whitney Brown.

The architecture of Antonio Gaudi and other fantastic architecture can be shown to children to motivate their imaginative structures, such as these sea castles by young Japanese schoolchildren. In most instances, constructions like these are assigned as group table projects.

bodies, they can enact architectural forms, such as arches, tunnels, and tiny spaces, and imagine what it feels like to be a building. With string or rope, several students in a group can make geometric shapes. Students can experience the architectural element of "forms in space" by developing design criteria and temporarily rearranging the classroom chairs and tables. Primary-grade children can learn the idea that engineers and designers figure out how to make things that people need.

On a walk around the school, have students sketch the architectural elements they see—for example, triangular pediments, quoins at corners, columns, arches, fan windows, foyers, and courtyards. In art criticism and art history, teams of students can critique their classroom, school, and community buildings: How do the parts work together? What messages about society are conveyed by the forms? How do you feel about the different spatial arrangements in our school building? How does it show its functions? How would you characterize it, as heavy, serene, or lively? Does the size suggest power or influence? If we could redo it, how would we change it? Students can critique the design of their school as to whether the building's materials and forms connote what occurs inside or say something else.

A local architect can be invited to share building plans with a class, and students can do sketches for the visitor to critique. During a follow-up group discussion, students can share their reasons for preferring modern or traditional styles, classical or romantic designs.

Middle-school students can study the role of an architectural designer: part engineer, architect, drafter, sculptor, graphic designer, and salesperson. They can learn that design uses a team approach; that ergonomics is how the human interacts with the object, and that form often follows function. Students can play the role of an architectural historian detective and figure out "How did the community come to be this way? What economic forces at the time spurred this construction boom?"

Courtesy of Fay Brassie.

A drawing of a local historic home by a middle-school student is an excellent way to foster architectural awareness.

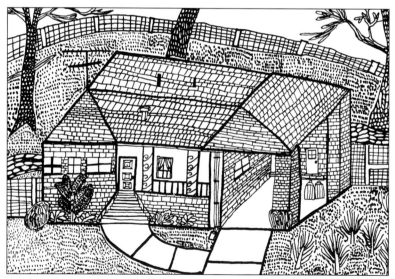

Courtesy of Frank Wachowiak and Mary Sayer Hammond.

Challenge children to become aware of their environment. Encourage them to become "noticers." For 2 hours, third-grader David Nix, using a felt-nib pen, drew his home from memory.

Courtesy of the National Building Museum, photo by Jack Boucher, HABS.

It was determined that it would be in the nation's best interests to set aside a building dedicated to the study of architecture. The National Building Museum, Washington, DC, was established by Congress in 1980 to encourage the nation's aesthetic sensitivity to architecture. It is in the National Pension Building, built in 1881 in the Italian Renaissance style. Its Great Hall, shown here, is considered to be one of America's most architecturally thrilling interior spaces. Outstanding architectural education materials for schoolchildren are available there.

BUILDING CITIZENS

Informed citizens should be able to interpret architectural plans before buildings are actually constructed. As one way to develop such a skill, students can analyze and critique plans that were used for existing structures or areas, such as their school or a nearby recreation center, park, neighborhood, or subdivision. They can judge whether design strengths and shortcomings found in the built structures were foreshadowed in the plans.

Nelson Goodman believed that a building is a work of art only insofar as it signifies, means, refers, or symbolizes in some way. Students can discuss the "meanings" of buildings—the messages that buildings send out. Some other aesthetic issues might be addressed by asking such questions as: How does the visual complexity of patterns affect the "interest quotient" of a building? Can a building have too much regularity? Do size and cost determine the quality of a building?

Students can debate what qualities should be considered when ranking buildings ("What is more important, complexity or orderliness?"), and then do a class poll to determine whether preference relates to personality. Because architecture is so public an art form and so open to community response, aesthetics and art criticism activities in which learners learn to look critically at their own environment are especially valuable.

FOR FURTHER READING

Donougho, Martin. 1987. "The Language of Architecture." *Journal of Aesthetic Education* 22(3).

Marshall, Alison, Anne Taylor & George Vlastos. 1991. *Architecture and Children; Teachers Guide.* New York: School Zone Institute.

Taylor, Anne. 1988. *Architecture and Children.* New York: Horizon Communications Publishing.

WEB RESOURCES

For architecture lesson plans for Grades 1 through 6:
  http://www.getty.edu/artsednet/resources/Sampler/b.html

For lesson plans on architecture of the Getty Museum:
  http://www.getty.edu/artsednet/resources/Arch/welcome.html

For a site on how to draw your house:
  http://www.arts.ufl.edu/art/rt_room/sparkers/house/house.html

For a lesson plan on expressive function in architecture:
  http://artsedge.kennedycenter.org/content/2004/

Chapter 31

Crafts

The term *crafts* covers a very broad area. Some materials and techniques that it almost always includes are works in cloth and fiber, as well as jewelry and metalwork. Examples of these are shown in this chapter. Also, note that other crafts are mentioned elsewhere in this book; for example, cloth banners and quilts are described in the section on collage. The aluminum-foil relief process (described in the section on printmaking) is a variation of repoussé metalwork. Also usually considered as crafts are ceramics and sculpture. Sculpture is discussed in Chapter 29, and ceramics is covered in Chapter 32.

Although the initial designing may take only a short time or be done even as the project is made, most crafts require considerable labor-intensive handwork during the execution phase. This results from the repetitive, cumulative nature of many craft activities and handicrafts, such as spool weaving, beadwork, shag pillows, and metalwork. Teachers often decry students' avoiding activities requiring focused, long-term attention and their seeking seemingly instantaneous rewards. Crafts can play a role in building a student's attention span. The lesson that is learned from attending to criteria over a considerable period of time to produce something of significance is valuable—and one that crafts can teach. This attending to goals and applying principles over a period of time is at the heart of the qualitative method espoused in this book. Also central to the qualitative method is the student's receiving expert guidance and evaluation, which point out the student's accomplishments as well as areas in which he or she could profit by additional effort. Craft activities can help to promote the habits of careful craftsmanship and the taste for and love of things that are well executed.

The relationship between the craftsperson's effort and the response of the material that he or she works with is central to the African concept of "Mana," which means being sensitive to the spirit within the object one is making. For example, the Hausa people urge those making their subtractive embroidered robes to have "an ear for what the cloth wants to

Courtesy of Frank Wachowiak and Mary Sayer Hammond.

Metal repoussé can begin with preliminary drawings on paper taped to a sheet of copper or aluminum of a limited size such as 6- × 9-inches or 9- × 12-inches. Using a blunt pencil, transfer the design through the paper to the metal. Then work directly on the metal, adding details. To show off the embossing further, apply black shoe polish and then wipe it off.

Left: *Courtesy of David W. Hodge.* Right: *Courtesy of Claire Clements.*

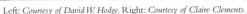

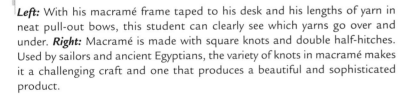
Left: With his macramé frame taped to his desk and his lengths of yarn in neat pull-out bows, this student can clearly see which yarns go over and under. **Right:** Macramé is made with square knots and double half-hitches. Used by sailors and ancient Egyptians, the variety of knots in macramé makes it a challenging craft and one that produces a beautiful and sophisticated product.

say." To Africans, shaping material with one's hands involves both a giving out and a taking in; it entails sensing the reciprocating spiritual force between the hand of the maker and the material being made.

Because crafts often require a special love and special skill, as well as specialized tools, it is desirable that a teacher with real interest in the activity conduct it. Let the activity be that teacher's forte—something for students to look forward to as they proceed through the years; let it be a quality, in-depth experience driven by the motivation from within the teacher's heart.

Techniques must be taught. The teacher must create the vessel in which self-expression can occur. The initial work almost always requires specific directions made quite clear. Consider Friedrich Froebel's instructional pattern: from structured activities to semi-structured and on to free activity. This conceptual model for craft technical instruction offers a way

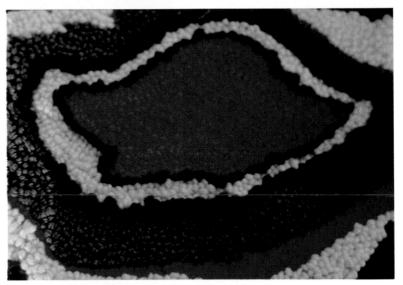

Top left: *Courtesy of David W. Hodge.* Top right and bottom: *Courtesy of Claire Clements.*

Hooking is done with a crochet hook through a mesh or burlap. **Top left:** a hanging of an eagle. **Top right:** a bee and an abstract pillow cover. **Bottom:** Rug hooking is also an excellent group project.

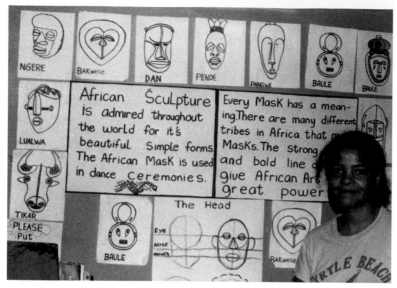

This teacher has drawn African mask characteristics' charts from (clockwise from top left) the Ngere, Bakwele, Dan, Pende, Pangwe, Baule, Balle, Tikar, and Lualwa cultures.

Metalwork repoussé, done with heavy gold embossing foil, can be related to the study of African masks.

to bring in both the structured beginning as well as the later, imaginative opportunity.

While the structured beginning is important, so is the last phase—the individually creative and personally meaningful ending. ("Does anyone have an idea how they can make it in their own unique way?") Always work to personalize and give added meaning to the project. ("Who will you give it to?" "What colors do you associate with that person, maybe the yellow and red of a campfire you sat around together?") Urge students to come up with their own meanings for their designs. Help them to learn to think symbolically as a way of giving depth to personal experiences and developing abstract thinking skills.

A class of students totally involved in a craft activity is a joy to behold; eyes, brains, and hands are in synchronicity with each other, producing an aesthetic experience. Crafts also are excellent for students who come to school early or have idle time around lunch or recess. Some crafts can even be done while riding the bus to and from school. Some students with special needs may find crafts to be an especially satisfying avenue for achievement, perhaps because of the calming, repetitive activity.

There may be certain special-needs students who will require additional help in the psychomotor operations that crafts require. Team up these students ahead of time with those who can perform the operations easily. Using peer teaching can prevent students' frustration as well as afford the other child an opportunity to teach. Also, peer teaching can

Yarn pictures can be stitched by children. The effect is best when the children take the time to solidly fill in areas with color. **Left:** Notice the variety in the directions of the stitching of this red-headed figure. **Right:** The columns of pink stitching seem akin to the folds on the face of a heavy-set person.

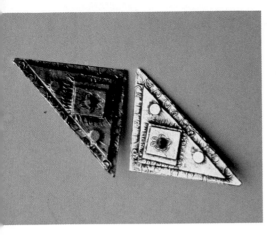

"Silver" Jewelry: *Left:* Earrings can be made by building up layers of thin cardboard and using an aluminum foil repoussé process. *Middle:* Bracelets can also be made: glue cutout shapes, cut and punched from thin cardboard, onto a strip of oak tag, then glue that strip into a circular bracelet shape, wrap it with aluminum foil, and engrave it with a pencil. *Right:* Metal repoussé book covers for handmade books.

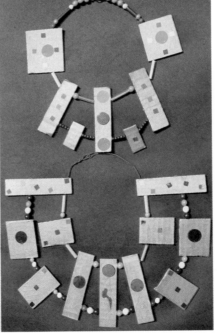

Left: Children love to make porcelain medallions using their initials, and hang them from their own macraméd necklaces. *Middle:* Third-graders made these Egyptian-style necklaces from rectangular shapes of cardboard, gummed stick-ons, beads, and telephone wire. *Right:* Attractive pins and earrings can be made by gluing together several layers of colored papers and cardboard, and then sanding the edges to reveal a series of colored parallel lines surrounding the shape.

spare the teacher the personal frustration of, for example, being asked to tie knots for 30 students in a brief time. For gifted students, have craft examples by more mature artists available to motivate and extend the gifted students' efforts and abilities.

IN THE CLASSROOM/IN THE COMMUNITY

Integrating Crafts with Content-Area Learning

Crafts can readily be integrated with other academic areas. Develop a social-studies unit on how famous individuals have related to the craft form. For example, Paul Revere and his silversmithing might be tied to a repoussé lesson on aluminum-foil relief. In social studies, examine how the economy and governmental policies interfaced with the craft—for example, nontraceable purchases of indigenous Southeast ceramic jugs during Prohibition. For history, point out how a craft technique has been used in other cultures and for other purposes, perhaps for utilitarian, secular, and governmental articles of apparel and display. Reading can be brought in through stories about people practicing the craft—for example, *Silas Marner* and weaving. Mathematics can be integrated through studying the units of measurement required, such as lengths of yarn required for fiber crafts. Finally, bring in economics by discussing how entire cultures flourished through trade in certain crafts, such as East Asian silks during the sixteenth and seventeenth centuries.

Involve the community's craft practitioners with your instructional unit. Through a display in the school of community craftspeoples' work, give students a vision of the craft form carried out at a more elaborate and mature level. Conversely, have the students' productions exhibited in the adult members' venues, such as at a fibercrafts guild meeting or a community art fair. Seek the involvement of industries in the community. For example, a carpet mill might donate yarn for shag rugs, or a store's drapery department might donate discontinued sample books to use for making banners.

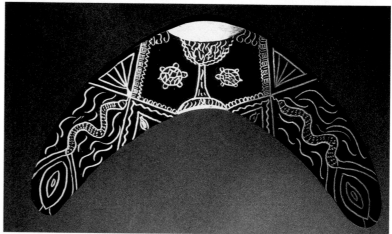

Top: *Courtesy of Howie Oakes.* Middle: *Courtesy of Dahria McClelland.*
Bottom: *Courtesy of Athens Academy.*

Use people in your community for crafts resources. **Top:** Gary Carroll, a computer salesman, shows his hobby, the western Ukranian art of the Hutzel people called pysanki—eggs, either hard boiled or blown out, are decorated with colors and symbols. **Middle:** Australian symbols of Aboriginal peoples are applied to boomerangs. **Bottom:** Mexican Huichol Indians made nearikas—yarn art pictures—by pressing bits of scrap yarn into softened wax. Here, third-graders used white glue instead of beeswax, and pasted small scraps of yarn to a hard backing to make a jungle mural.

WEAVING

Weaving is the interlacing and crossing of threads to form cloth. The warp threads run lengthwise and form the skeleton of the fabric. Putting the warp threads on the loom is called *warping the loom*. The weft threads run at right angles and bind the warp threads together. The weaver alternates threads, lifting alternate ones up and going underneath the others. To simplify the task, there are varieties of heddles—devices for lifting alternating rows of threads. Other variations of weaving include plaiting or braiding as well as looping, which includes knitting and crocheting.

One way to introduce weaving to kindergartners is to have several students stand in a row, side by side, in front of the room. Then, have a volunteer take the end of a long piece of rope and go in front of the first student, behind the second, and so on. When the volunteer reaches the end of the row, he or she then comes back to the beginning in the same fashion. This is a good way to refresh the children's concepts of "in front of," "behind," "over," and "under" as they relate to weaving. Early weaving

Above left: *Courtesy of David W. Hodge.* Top: *Courtesy of Deborah Lackey.*
Middle: *Courtesy of Jo Nan Tanner.* Bottom: *Courtesy of Barbara Thomas.*

Above left: A primary-grade girl weaves on a cardboard loom. Notice how her black marker drawing on the cardboard beneath guides her as she fills in the areas with her weaving. ***Top:*** Weaving equipment can be simple or elaborate. In this well-equipped art classroom, a boy works on his woven hanging. He uses a floor loom that alternates his warp threads up and down to facilitate his weaving through of the weft threads. ***Middle:*** Cardboard Box Looms: The two long sides of a sturdy shoe box are cut diagonally and the upper material is removed, along with the one short end. The top and bottom cardboard edges are measured at one-half-inch intervals and cut one-half-inch deep. The warp threads are put on, and then the horizontal weaving of the colorful weft begins. ***Bottom:*** Kids can weave on the floor.

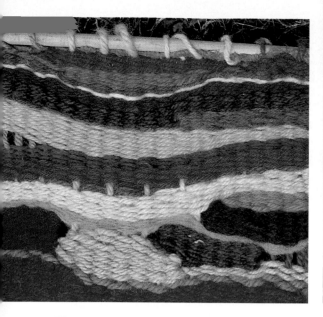

Left: The primary-grade child who made this weaving showed an intuitive mastery of color and undulating shapes. **Middle:** The God's Eye technique can be used to make bowls. **Right:** The thin black warp threads are woven partially together in discrete areas with heavy yarn and sticks.

activities usually include paper weaving, in which the warp is cut on a folded piece of paper (but not so far as to cut through the edge). Pre-cut lengths of rug yarn and regular yarn, along with lengths of natural fibers such as weeds, often are woven through these papers, along with strips cut from colorful photos and foils.

Weaving's rhythm of over and under also can be taught through the ever-popular *Ojo de Dios* (Eye of God). Crossed sticks, or tongue depressors, are used for the warp structure of decorative weavings made in Central American countries and hung above doorways to protect and bring good luck.

A really easy and convenient loom is made from plastic soda straws. They can be used full length or cut in half for little hands. Four or six is about the limit that one can hold between thumb and forefinger. A little half-inch slit is made in the top of each straw, the lengths of warp yarn are sucked through the straw, and the top is firmly taped in the slit. Then, holding the pack in one's left hand, the over-and-under wrapping proceeds, always adding the new row on the top. Eventually the weaving fills up the straws, causing the weaving to be pushed off onto the loose warp threads. Varicolored yarn can be used, or just tie on a different yarn when a change in color or texture is desired.

Cardboard purse looms are a good early weaving activity. The top and bottom of a stiff piece of cardboard are slit a half-inch deep at half-

inch intervals and the warp thread is wrapped around the cardboard. For a cylindrical variation rather than a rectangular shape, weaving can be done on an oatmeal box. A cardboard-box loom can be easily made from a sturdy shoe box or other sturdy cardboard box cut diagonally on its two long sides and the upper material removed along with the one short end. First, the top and bottom cardboard edges are measured off in half-inch intervals, cut a half-inch deep, and the warp threads put in place. The horizontal weaving of the colorful weft then begins. The advantage of this diagonally cut box is that a large, open area beneath the weaving is provided for manipulating the over-and-under threading. Simple wood-strip looms also can be made. Just drive finishing nails at half-inch intervals slanted outward on the top and bottom boards, and then string or "warp" the loom. Alternately, old picture frames or unused stretcher strips can be used.

Finger weaving (really knitting) using a skein of varicolored yarn is a pleasant introductory activity guaranteed to keep any active child occupied. Wrap yarn over and under around the four fingers of one's left hand (assuming one is right-handed) and then back again, then use the fingers of the right hand to pick up the bottom layers and cast them over the top. Proceed to wrap the fingers with another course of yarn, over and under, and then cast what is now the new lower course once again over the top. Eventually, a long knitted rope will fall off the back of the hand. A similar

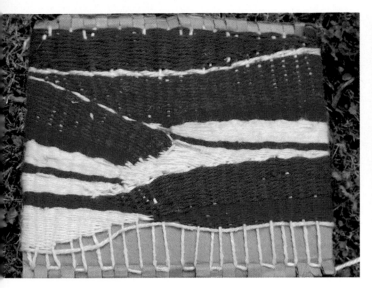

Courtesy of Claire Clements.

Left and middle: Purses on and off the cardboard loom. **Right:** A great gift, which can be used in the home, is this woven placemat.

Left: *Courtesy of Claire Clements.* Right: *Courtesy of David W. Hodge.*

Left: These bags seem to be just the right size for these proud first-grade boys to use to hold their valuables. **Right:** Students can weave on stretcher strip frames, such as those used for canvas paintings.

knitting activity uses an empty spool and fine metal wire. On a large, empty spool from the sewing box, five tiny headless brads are pounded around the hole. Fine metal wire is then woven around them and cast off, with a pointed object such as a large nail, down the hole in the middle of the spool. The cords that are formed can then be used to make jewelry.

From time to time, embroidered jackets and jeans become a fad that sweeps a school. Students may use embroidery as a way to celebrate and comment upon one's own culture. This interest can afford a good opening for the teacher to develop a unit on embroidery and to bring out its design constraints and opportunities for expressing in fresh ways the values of the young people. Exploring ways to decorate wearing apparel can also bring in related fibercraft methods, such as batik, appliqué, and molas. One strong feature of appliqué and related techniques is that it is appropriate for all ages and costs practically nothing.

STARCH-RESIST BATIK

Batik originated in ancient Egypt and is very popular in modern India and Java. For cloth batik, first wash the cloth to remove sizing. The process can be as easy as making a simple paste of flour and cold water. Slightly over one cup of flour is gradually added to one cup of water, and this mixture is brushed on or squeezed through a plastic condiment bottle and/or

Top left: *Courtesy of Claire Clements.* Others: *Courtesy of Joyce Vroon.*

Batiks: **Top left:** This batik in a radiating design was dyed in successive yellow, red, and brown dyes. Before each successive dyeing, a larger area of the cloth was masked out and the cloth crinkled to make the network of fine lines. For natural dyeing, boiled onion skins will give a gold color, and sumac berries will give an orange-brown. **Middle:** Colorful wax batiks hang outside on the line to dry. **Bottom:** Designing requires a knowledge of geometric pattern, here, how geometric shapes repeat to create patterns in these fourth-graders' batik bandanas. **Right:** Children use rubber gloves and tongs to assure that dye reaches all areas of the cloth.

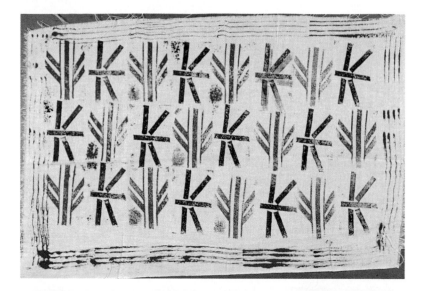

Top: *Courtesy of Jackie Ellett*. Middle and bottom: *Courtesy of Pat Kerner, Aurum Studio.*

Adinkira is a patterned fabric made by the Ashantis from the African Ivory Coast. It is made by stamping designs on the cloth's surface with a photo-like calabash dipped in dye. Also printings are done with lines made with a wooden comb. For this adinkira rubber-stamp design, a fourth-grader used strips of rubber innertube glued to blocks of wood and printed in rows and columns. Adinkira and batik make attractive pillows.

spread with a fork or stick. Dry overnight, and then, rather than dipping, brush or sponge on the dye color.

For a higher-quality recipe, follow the "adire eleko" starch-resist paste cloth pattern design technique of the Yoruba people of Nigeria. They used cassava tubers, and the cloth was subsequently dyed with indigo (which grows in the southern United States). The starch paste first was tinted with rust to make it easier to see and then applied with a chicken feather. Then a paste is made of ¾-cup pearl tapioca and an equal amount of water, cooked in a double-boiler pot until smooth. In a ½-cup of cold water, dissolve 6 tablespoons of gluten flour and cornstarch, and blend into the tapioca mixture in ½-cup portions. Cook uncovered in a double boiler until thickened, add ½ teaspoon of alum, and refrigerate. For best results in using the paste, spread the starch on thickly with a tongue depressor, and scratch lines in it before it dries. After the starch is thoroughly dry, dye the cloth, and then remove the starch by peeling, scraping, or soaking. The Yoruba women used indigo and avocado leaves, which they chopped and boiled for their blue and rust colors of dye. In our elementary schools, starch resist avoids the hazards of hot wax.

IN THE CLASSROOM

Integrating Fibercrafts

Fibercrafts are particularly appropriate to integrate with the study of other cultures, because a culture's clothing and other fiber articles may be quite distinctive. For example, the Crow Indians of the American Plains had distinctive parfleches (leather storage bags adorned with geometric designs). Likewise, the Inca people of South America's west coast are famous for their patterned tapestry weaving and feather work. Finally, the artistic designs used in Panamanian appliqués and the molas of the Cuna Indians convey to us something of the values and unique traditions of their civilizations.

Courtesy of Joyce Vroon.

The intricate beauty of a batik design of plant leaves is seen in this fifth-grader's project done on tableau paper.

FOR FURTHER READING

LaLiberte, Norman, and Shirley McIlhany. 1966. *Banners and Hangings: Design and Construction.* New York: Reinhold.
Markowitz, Sally. 1994. "The Distinction between Art and Craft." *Journal of Aesthetic Education* 28(1): 55–70.

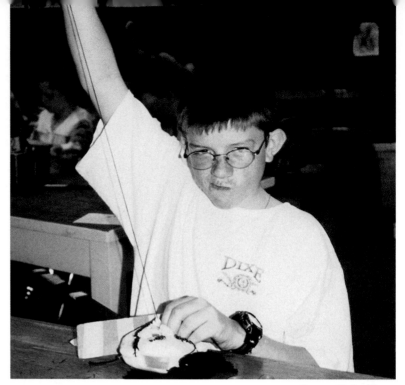

Courtesy of Barbara Thomas.

Boys, as well as girls, find both pleasure and challenge in doing stitchery projects.

Mattil, Edward, and Betty Marzan. 1981. *Meaning in Children's Art: Projects for Teachers.* New York: Prentice-Hall.
Winfrey, Anita. 1995. "Adinkra Prints." *Arts and Activities* 118(3): 24.

WEB RESOURCES

For how to make craft projects, for example, jewelry:
   http://familycrafts.about.com/cs/jewelrymaking/a/082399.htm?terms=making+jewelry

For an overview of crafts by type:
   http://familycrafts.about.com/od/craftprojectsbytype/

For how to make an Indian batik:
   http://www.webindia123.com/craft/paint/batik/batik.html

For stencil painting on fabric:
   http://www.webindia123.com/craft/paint/fabric/fabpaint.html

For quilting with children:
   http://www.thecraftstudio.com/qwc/

Courtesy of Sharon Burns-Knutson.

Fifth-grader Phyllis Helwig's weaving shows a judicious use of greys that make the red, white, and black stand out.

Courtesy of Sharon Burns-Knutson.

Sixth-grader T. J. Meyerholtz made his weaving after studying bold geometric Native-American designs. Among the Hopi Indians, it is the men who weave; among the Navajo, it is women.

Chapter 32

Clay Modeling

$\mathcal{A}$ll children, both in elementary and middle school, should have the opportunity to create and express their ideas in clay. Clay is a hands-on wonder—sensuous, malleable, unpredictable, and on occasion, messy. Some students respond to clay more enthusiastically than others, but all children benefit from the unique challenges provided by this gift from Mother Earth.

CLAY IN THE PRIMARY GRADES

Young children work with clay in several ways. Most add clay pieces to the basic form. A few will pat clay into a pancake and draw into it, and a very few will pull out features from a ball or lump of clay. The teacher's main responsibility in the early stage is to provide the children with an adequate supply of workable clay. Check the plasticity of the clay at least a day or two before the project takes place. Clay should be as soft as possible without being sticky. If the clay is too sticky or wet, put it on cloth- or canvas-covered boards, layers of newspaper, an absorbent surface such as Celotex®, or a plaster bat to dry.

If the opposite problem occurs, that is, if the clay is too dry to easily work with one's hands, flatten it to a 1½-inch thickness, poke holes in it, and fill the holes with water. Let it set, and then pour off the excess water. If clay is rock hard, have children break it into small chunks with a hammer and a screwdriver as wedge; put the clay pieces in a bucket and cover them with water. When the clay becomes soupy, pour it onto a plaster bat so that the excess water may be absorbed.

If powdered clay is used, mix it several days (or months or even years) ahead, as its plasticity improves with age. Indeed, the older it is, the better. For brave teachers only (with excellent housekeeping skills), an experience students remember forever is using their bare feet to mix powdered clay with water.

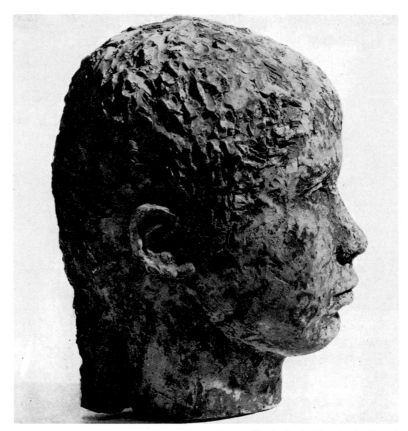

Courtesy of London Sunday Mirror, London, England.

Terra-cotta clay sculpture by a middle-school adolescent, London, England. Notice how the textural quality of the clay has been retained to give the work a spontaneous naturalness.

Courtesy of David W. Hodge.

Note the heavy armatures used as these youths model life-sized heads. When leather hardens, the clay form will be removed from the armature and hollowed out to less than 1-inch thickness prior to being fired.

If clay is stored in plastic bags, double bag it in case of a tear in one of the bags. The bag itself can be first dipped in water to add moisture. Keep clay in a lidded airtight pail. To create a moist climate in the airtight pail, damp sponges or similar materials can also be put in.

A ball of clay the size of a baseball is recommended for each child, along with extra clay to be used for additions. Use newspapers or plastic sheeting to protect desks or tabletops.

A period of experimentation with the clay should precede every project. Before students can express a particular idea, they first need to acquire the feel of the clay. During these orientation sessions, call the students' attention to the desired plasticity. Discuss keeping excess clay moist by rolling the pieces and crumbs into a single ball (with less evaporative surface), and explain the mechanics of cleanup.

Emphasize how touch experiences help to give shape to objects. One way of introducing students to the exciting tactile potential of clay is to play the clay-in-a-paper-sack game. A student puts a ball of clay about the size of an orange into a sturdy paper sack and, without looking, manipulates it until it has an interesting form. Encourage the children to think with their hands—to stretch, squeeze, and poke the clay. They must not peek inside the sack at any time during the process, however. When the exercise is complete, display the finished pieces. Ask the students if anyone sees a real form hidden in the clay creations—an animal, a bird, a fish? How did playing the game help the students learn about clay?

IN THE CLASSROOM

Animals and Science

Animals and their young are a stimulating topic for most children, and classifying animals or their continental habitats can integrate science knowledge through art. Four-legged mammals are especially suitable because the child can model sturdy legs to make the figure stand. Use animals to help children learn about a variety of topics:

- Farm animals (horses, cows, pigs) to learn about food cycles or economics
- Wild animals (hippos, elephants, or rhinos) to learn about Africa or about endangered species or bears to learn about North American wilderness
- Marine animals (whales, dolphins, starfish) to learn about classification

Group projects, such as creating a three-ring circus, a zoo, a farm, or a jungle, are very popular with young children as well. Standing human figures can be difficult, however, and children must be guided to provide additional supports or to model thick, sturdy legs and bases to hold the figure erect.

Primary-school children especially love clay's plastic changeability as they poke, squeeze, pound, stretch, and roll it. They may describe a sequence of action with one figure, such as a clown or an acrobat, manipulating it to create various postures—standing on its head, bending backward and forward, and falling down. The clay manipulating and modeling seems to fulfill a therapeutic and a storytelling need.

Some students will pat and pound their clay into a flat, cookie shape. More-advanced students will hold the clay ball in their hands to model their animal's body in three dimensions. They will pull out or add legs, tails, trunks, horns, beaks, and wings. Because figures made in pieces often come apart during drying and firing, many teachers strongly advocate that students be taught to pull out appendages from the body rather than to add them on. Encourage students who insist on adding the appendages to make holes in the body with a stick or fingers and then insert the appendages into those holes to strengthen the joint. Older students can learn to score and join clay with slip (a paste made of clay and water). To prevent the sagging of a form, use temporary clay or cardboard supports, such as a "fifth leg" under the animal's body, until the clay is leather-hard. Always emphasize the importance of a sturdy basic form.

Facing page: Top: Three stages in the additive construction of a clay hippopotamus are illustrated. First, a basic body with legs and tail added. Second, a tongue depressor can be used to create the open mouth. Third, addition of characteristic details: ears, eyes, teeth. **Bottom:** The directness of clay manipulation holds a universal fascination for children. The delightful clay figure illustrated at right possesses a mobility that only the clay medium captures so well. Youngsters can first take a variety of poses themselves and feel the kinesthetic awareness in their own bodies before making a figure in clay perform similar action-packed feats. Children might strut, twist, dance, juggle, bend, and even stand on their heads.

Courtesy of David W. Hodge.

Left: This sturdily constructed clay elephant was made by pulling out forms. Then the elephant was decorated with pattern and texture. Youngsters can employ objects such as tubes, pencil erasers, bottle caps, bark, wire mesh, and pinecones to add imaginative texture and pattern to their clay creations. **Right:** This young artist contemplates the clay elephant she has formed.

Left: This elephant's head, necks, ears, and front legs were pulled out from the clay rather than being added onto; encourage children to hold the clay in their hands when modeling small sculptural pieces, especially in the beginning stages. This promotes sturdiness. Michelangelo said that a good sculpture should be capable of being rolled down a hill without parts breaking off. **Right:** The kangaroo's large tail provides support to the burden of the adolescent contentedly sitting in its pouch. The theme of an animal and its young is a surefire hit—one with which all children can identify.

Although many children in the primary grades are not concerned with detailing, some will enjoy experimenting with textures and pattern on their creations. A collection of found objects (which should be washed at the close of the project) such as plastic forks, popsicle sticks, bottle caps, nails, screws, toothbrushes, dowels, and wire mesh will spark their interest and entice them to experiment.

Young children often pound their clay into cookie shapes. Here, two projects suitable for students at this stage are shown. One is a bas-relief face to which features have been added. For the decorated mirror frame project, the teacher breaks up a mirror into little pieces and traces around them on paper. These paper shapes are then cut out and given to the children, who form a donut-shaped or squarish frame suitable to cover the mirror scrap. These pieces then are glazed, and the teacher tapes in the mirror scrap. Prior to firing, remember to put in a hole, by which the piece can be hung.

CLAY ALTERNATIVES

Children enjoy making small figures not only of clay but also from a variety of other moldable, plastic materials. Teachers also appreciate not having to be concerned with firing a kiln. These alternatives to clay are especially useful if real clay cannot be obtained. Homemade mixtures contain varying proportions of material, binder, and water. Here are few "formulas" for such mixtures:

- Everyone is familiar with mixing flour and water in equal parts to make modeling mixtures for relief maps. A firmer mixture can be used to model objects.
- Also easy to make is salt ceramic, made from 1 cup of salt, ½ cup of cornstarch, and ¾ cup of water.
- Another popular mixture, often used for seasonal ornaments, is baker's clay, for which 4 cups of flour, 1 cup of salt, and 1½ cups of water are mixed, shaped, and then baked at 350 degrees for 1 hour until hard.

The white animal at top is made of WetSet Clay®. The in-process figure at bottom is made by Sculpey®. As Sculpey® is somewhat expensive, give the children tiny squares of the various colors. Eighth-graders worked for weeks in Baiba Kuntz's class on their Sculpey® figures.

For Careers Day at the elementary school, a potter demonstrated throwing pots on a wheel.

- For a sawdust–wheat paste mixture, use 2 parts sawdust, 1 part flour or wheat paste, and hot water. (Optionally, ½ part of plaster can be added.) This is good for tennis-ball-size puppet heads and will withstand a lot of bumping. For the puppet's neck, roll a cylinder of oaktag paper around one's index finger, tape the edges of the tube together, and, for sturdiness, tear or cut and flare out the tube's top edge to facilitate embedding it into the mixture. Then pack more mixture around the tube to make the head.

Supply budget permitting, water-set clay, such as Wet-Set Clay®, is suitable for young children and requires no firing. It will not harden in air, so students can work on their forms for a period of days. Unbelievably, it hardens when placed in water for at least 3 hours. Since it is relatively heavy, it is also good for sculpture bases for sculptures of all kinds, and it can be painted with acrylic paints.

Somewhat more expensive are the commercially made polymer clays, such as Sculpey® and Fimo®, which come premixed in 30 colors. Because of the cost, these clays may be more suitable for upper grades, where permanence is a greater concern. Polymer clays stay permanently pliable at room temperature. Using clays in the numerous colors solves the problem of painting in fine details. With polymer clays, each part is completed in full detail at the time it is modeled (for example, beginning with the head baked in an ordinary oven at 275° to preserve it), and then the next part is added. Since it does not shrink at all as it dries, these figures can be built over sticks and wires for stability. Polymer clays can also be used for jewelry projects and made into millefiori.

CLAY IN THE UPPER GRADES

Older students are more successful in mastering the complexities of advanced clay modeling, but they may ask for help with specific problems. For example, figures and appendages may sag or come apart, and students may need assistance with balance and proportion, or with the intricate delineation of eyes, mouth, nose, and ears.

Emphasize structural elements that can give the piece character. Talk about the sway of the body, stance of the legs, swing of the tail, tilt of the head, action of the jaws, flow of the mane, or flare of the wings. An imaginatively expressive creature also may combine the characteristics of several different animals. In upper elementary and middle school, a preliminary drawing of figures to be modeled in clay often helps students to clarify their ideas. The polymer clays mentioned above are excellent for fine detail work.

Courtesy of David W. Hodge.

The handsome branch pots made by seventh-graders started as basic coil, slab, and pinch-pot forms. Through the addition of complementary clay and feet and the elegant decoration of surface forms, they emerged as distinctive, one-of-a-kind ceramic containers. After staining, if the stains appear to be too intense, earth can be rubbed into the surface to subdue the effect. Further embellishment can be achieved by inscribing designs through stained surfaces, and liquid wax gives a subtle sheen as well as a protective surface.

IN THE CLASSROOM

Clay and Dinosaurs

Clay and dinosaurs go well together, for dinosaurs' ponderous mass, protective armor, and wrinkled scaly skin evoke the quality of the ancient earth itself. And clay dinosaurs can integrate the study of prehistory and geology. Children's creatures can be placed into the Mesozoic period's Triassic, Jurassic, and Cretaceous eras and the continental plates, cut from cardboard and covered with their dinosaurs, can break up before their very eyes! Toy three-dimensional models can provide children with ideas for their own animals.

Extra clay may be needed, especially for reinforcing junctures. To prevent cracking and exploding when the clay is dried and fired, avoid using armatures, such as sticks, inside the structure. To develop the form three-dimensionally, the sculpture should be viewed from all sides. Use a 12- or 16-inch-square Masonite sheet or a turntable as a working base to facilitate rotation.

Whether on a clay pot, figure, animal, or tile, there are almost no limits to clay-relief pattern and textural ornamentation. To make scaly, armorlike dinosaur hide, students might roll out balls, coils, and ribbons of clay, then apply them to the body of the creature. Slip can be used as an adhesive to secure the pellets and coils of clay to the main surface. Discarded broken saw blades and combs can be used for linear effects. Squeezing moist clay through window screen produces masses of clay strings for manes or tails.

CONSTRUCTION TECHNIQUES

Hand-Building In overcrowded middle-school classes, the beleaguered art teacher would find it difficult, if not impossible, to instruct everyone in the sophisticated, highly technical, and time-consuming craft of throwing pottery on a wheel. Do not frustrate a majority of students by demanding skills that college ceramics majors work long hours to attain. Instead, concentrate on teaching hand-building techniques that all students can master.

Students must be guided to avoid trite bud vases and ashtrays. Show films and photos of contemporary ceramic and hand-building techniques. Introduce students to the exciting work of contemporary potters, such as Mary Engel, Andy Nassisse, and Shoji Hamada, and to the beautiful, functional clay vessels of the pre-Columbian craftspeople of Mexico, Guatemala, Colombia, and Peru. Encourage students to collect an assortment of stones, shells, seedpods, nuts, and driftwood to trigger ideas.

The basic form must be the first critical concern. No amount of additional embellishment or decoration can redeem a piece that is weak in formal concept or structure. Critiques of clay work-in-progress should be standard procedure during every studio session, and students should share their discoveries with their classmates.

Variety in the basic sculptural form should also be emphasized, however. Because students are accustomed to symmetrically styled ceramics, the teacher must guide them to see the beauty of asymmetry. Variety can be achieved through contrasting the forms of the appendages, handles, lids, spouts, necks, and feet.

Unity also is vital to the total impact of the clay structure. There should be a natural flow from one plane or contour to another. Appendages should grow naturally from the basic body structure and be in

Right: *Courtesy of Baiba Kuntz.*

Hand-building in clay holds students' interest. **Left:** A boy studying ancient cultures constructs a model of a cliff dweller's home. **Right:** This tall pot is constructed from coils, which are then smoothed together for strength. Rows of bold balls and loops give contrast.

scale with it; they should complement, not detract from, the whole. The same is true of decorations: designs should go with the form, not compete with it or ignore it.

Clay-Slab Construction Slabs of approximately 12- × 18- × ½-inch should be prepared in advance. Moist clay, a rolling pin, a burlap- or linen-covered board, guiding strips of wood ½-inch thick, and plastic covering to keep slabs moist during storage also are needed. Additional slabs can be made as the project progresses. Impress fired clay-relief stamps and found objects into the moist slab to enrich the surface before beginning construction of the container. Divide the large slab into the number of slabs that will be needed for the sides and bottom (and sometimes top) of the container. The junctures where two slabs are to be joined should be scored (roughened) and covered with water or slip before attaching the slabs. When slabs are joined, use a wooden paddle to secure them and form the container's shape. Two or more clay-slab constructions in different sizes may be joined to make a larger, more complex structure.

Pinch-Pot Sculpture For pinch-pot sculpture, approximately 5 pounds of moist clay per student is recommended. First, a large portion of the clay is shaped into a large ball and cut in half. Then, each half is formed into a

pinch-pot shape, keeping the walls fairly thick and each pot similar in size. Students then join together the two pinch pots (scoring and moistening the junctures) and pinch the seams tightly to form a hollow ball. Holding the hollow ball of clay in one hand, the student paddles it until the pinched seams disappear. To create a decorative surface effect, use a piece of wood, approximately 1 × 2 × 15 inches and wrapped at one end generously with cord. Students must rotate the clay ball as they paddle so that the entire ball will be paddled evenly. This action packs the clay and seals in enough air to support the walls. During paddling, students can change the shape of the ball to resemble a pod, nut, or gourd. Although a cord-wrapped paddle produces an attractive texture, additional decoration may be done by using stamped, incised, and bas-relief motifs.

For unusual effects, students may apply clay pellets, straight and undulating clay ribbons or snakes, and clay coils to the surface. Be sure the surface clay is sufficiently moist for the adhesion of any additions. If not,

Courtesy of Frank Wachowiak.

An ancient ceramic Haniwa horse from the pre-Jomon period, Japan. Hollow clay cylinders form the animal's basic shape. Clay coils were flattened and added for the reins and saddle.

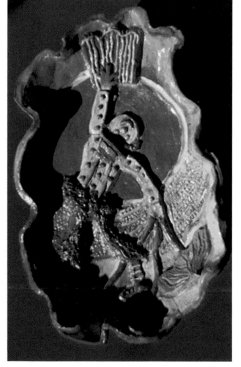

Left and right: *Courtesy of David W. Hodge.* Middle: *Courtesy of Nancy Eliott.*

Left: A pinch-pot mug adorned with a hairy texture from a garlic press. **Middle:** Face mugs allow a study of caricature and create memorable objects. Students have adorned their face mug characters with mustaches, beards, and a monocle. **Right:** Ceramic glazes add beauty to this ceramic slab dish. The piece's undulating sides make it unique. Many glazed pieces of children's art stay in families for decades as heirlooms.

moisten it, or use slip. Feet, handles, bases, legs, animal necks, and heads may be added, but to preserve strength, the sealed ball should not be opened until the whole container is complete. Once opened, spouts and vase necks may be added. Many exciting forms result when students combine two or more pinch-pot balls of various sizes and shapes into one unified structure.

DRYING, FIRING, GLAZING, AND STAINING

If a kiln is available, clay sculptures should be allowed to dry evenly and slowly in a cabinet or under a sheet of plastic before firing. If the finished object is to be kept and fired, and the "body" is larger than your fist, hollow out the bottom before it is leather-hard so the walls won't be much thicker than 3/4 inch. Another way of allowing air to escape during firing is to poke pin holes in the leather-hard piece. Trapped air can cause an explosion, and one exploding piece can destroy a kilnful of other pieces! Other preliminary precautions are proper wedging of the clay to remove air bubbles, and adding grog to increase the clay's strength. Of course, the kiln should be off-limits to curious children and prying hands. The kiln should ventilate to the outdoors.

It is relatively easy to fire greenware. Raw-clay pieces may be stacked closely inside of or on top of one another, rest against one another in the kiln, and even rest against the kiln's sides (taking care they do not touch the heating elements). Engobe-decorated pieces, in which a clay slip is applied before the first firing and scratched through for graffito designs, can be fired in a similar manner; however, do not let the clay get too dry before applying slip decoration, lest peeling and cracking occur during firing.

Keep the kiln lid cracked open for an hour or more with the temperature on Low. A precaution to avoid a kilnful of exploded pieces is to fire almost a whole day at lowest temperature. The slower the raising of the initial heating, the better. (Pieces even 2 inches thick can survive firing if the heat is raised very slowly over a period of days.) Then fire several hours at medium, and a few hours or more at high. In cooling the kiln, do not rush; leave it untouched at least overnight to cool with the lid closed. Resist the urge to look inside. In the morning, prop up the kiln lid an inch with a tiny block for a few hours, then more later before finally opening it all the way.

Glaze firing requires more care. Kiln glazing of bisque-fired clay pieces (those that already have been fired once) is a way for ambitious

Courtesy of Mary Lazzari.

Ceramics can play a role in a multidisciplinary approach correlating art with science and social studies. ***Left:*** Intermediate-elementary children studying ocean life made clay fish. Fish shapes were cut out of clay slabs and attached to the ocean-floor bases. Pieces then were bisque-fired and painted with acrylic paint. The two fish on the left are kissing; the top left fish dines on another fish. ***Right:*** The role of monsters in medieval culture and cathedrals' use of grotesque gargoyle waterspouts was studied; then second-graders made these clay monster plaques, painted with simulated-stone spatter paint.

teachers to bring the ceramic process to a rich culmination. Children create beautiful pieces, which frequently become family treasures. (Because old glazes found at the back of a supply closet may contain dangerous elements, such as lead and arsenic, use only glazes certified as being safe, especially for food containers.) The glazed pieces must be stacked carefully so that no piece touches another or the wall of the firing chamber. Because molten glaze will adhere the piece to the kiln's floor, a protective kiln wash is useful. The bottom and lower ¼- to ½-inch of the piece should be wiped free of glaze, and/or supports such as stilts or pins should be used. Weeks of firing may be necessary, especially if many students have created large clay structures. The large student populations of elementary schools, limited budgets, and limited kiln size frequently make it impractical to glaze large pieces.

An alternate way to beautify fired clay is to rub neutral colors of pigment, moist dirt, or soil of another shade into the incised areas. Before the dirt or applied stain dries, the raised surfaces may be partially wiped with a moist rag to create contrasting effects. In most cases in which staining or coloring (try gluing on torn pieces of colored tissue paper) is applied to bisque-fired clay, adding a final coat of liquid wax or clear gloss polymer is advised.

CLAY PLASTER RELIEFS

Students in upper elementary and middle school often are self-critical concerning their drawing ability and need the satisfaction and challenge of creating in an art medium more dependent on design skills. Creating plaster reliefs, which involves manipulative skills with special tools, materials, and surprise effects, is one such challenging adventure. (Other art projects in this general category are metal repoussé, ceramics, papier-mâché, stitchery, weaving, and mobiles.)

For a plaster-relief project, you will need moist clay, plaster, a plastic or rubber dishpan, and a container for the clay mold (shoe box, cigar box, or half-gallon or gallon waxed-cardboard milk carton). Also needed are an assortment of found objects (spools, nails, wire, cogwheels, lath, screws, keys, clothespins, buckles, rope, bolts, cord, reed, dowel sticks, bottle caps, jar lids, coins, printer's letters, combs, plastic forks and spoons, and natural objects, such as twigs, pinecones, acorns, nuts, seashells, and bark). To finish the piece, you will need a plaster-sealing medium, such as white glue or polymer medium, a 1- or 2-inch utility brush, and stains.

The first step is to reinforce the box sides with masking or strapping tape. Use the lid under the box to reinforce the bottom, and line the

Courtesy of David W. Hodge.

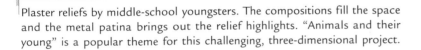
Plaster reliefs by middle-school youngsters. The compositions fill the space and the metal patina brings out the relief highlights. "Animals and their young" is a popular theme for this challenging, three-dimensional project.

Suggest that students limit the stains to neutral colors at first to achieve unity. Be sure to apply one or two coats of white glue to the plaster relief before staining it. Allow the stain to flow into the incised lines.

inside of the box with wax paper. Milk cartons requiring no protective lining can be cut in half lengthwise and the open end resealed. If the separate reliefs are to be assembled later into one large group mural design, uniformity of sizes may be desirable. A free-form relief shape can be made by using a sheet of tempered Masonite as the working surface and building a clay wall around the slab of clay.

There are two methods for making the basic slab of clay. The simplest is to roll out the clay into a slab approximately ½- to 1-inch thick, cut the slab to the size of the box, and place the slab in the bottom of the box, ready for the next stage of the process. In the second method, the clay is placed pellet by pellet into the box until the bottom is filled with a clay layer ½- to 1-inch thick. If a very flat surface is desired, the clay may be stamped down with the end of a 2- to 4-inch woodblock.

Before students begin their relief designs, incisions, and textural impressions in the clay slab, they should practice on a sample slab. Demonstrate that impressions made in the clay will be reversed in the plaster cast. Designs that are pressed or incised in the clay will bulge out in the plaster version. Show students examples of relief sculpture throughout art history. For example, the Greek Parthenon frieze, coin designs, and sculptures by the modern artist Marino Marini can be used in discussions about the beauty of high and low relief. Letters and numbers must be imprinted backward in the clay to read correctly in the final product. Once the teacher makes these basic principles clear, students are free to be expressive and innovative.

Courtesy of Julie Daniell Phlegar.

This plaster bas-relief pond scene by a sixth-grader teems with life: frogs, a toad, and flowers.

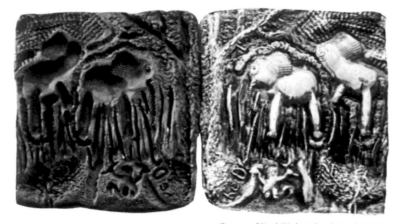

Courtesy of Frank Wachowiak and David W. Hodge.

A clay negative mold and its completed plaster relief. Letters and numerals must be impressed backward into the clay mold to read correctly in the final relief; shapes pressed into the clay bulge out in the plaster version. A seashell was used to make the elephant's ears. Other effective imprinting objects include beads and discarded costume jewelry, plastic forks and spoons, crumpled heavy-duty aluminum foil, heavy cord, reed, and wire.

There are several ways to model in the slab. A very free and natural approach involves the use of hands and fingers. Commercial ceramic tools also may be employed. Coils, pellets, and ribbons of clay cut from a thin slab may be applied with water or slip.

With younger children, it might be wise to limit designs to those that can be achieved by pressing into the clay, because it is more difficult to dig lines out of the clay. (In addition, the digging approach often produces sharp, hazardous edges in the final plaster cast.) For straight lines, use applicator sticks, popsicle sticks, or the edge of a thick piece of cardboard. For curved lines, use bent reed, cord, or the edges of round containers.

When the impressed and incised designs are completed, mark your initials on the top of the box's edge. Then pour liquid plaster-of-paris over the clay to a ½- to 1-inch thickness. (Plaster-mixing procedures are described in Chapter 29 in the section on subtractive sculpture.) Before the plaster sets, insert wire one-third of the way from the top and, twisted at the ends, for a hanger. The hardening capabilities of plaster vary widely; semihard pieces are easily broken, and the teacher should allow time for

Subjects for Plaster Reliefs

Many subjects can be illustrated appealingly through plaster reliefs. Recommended themes to fit in with science, social studies, or math lessons include: birds with plumage, fish, insects (especially butterflies), animals in their habitat, flowers, theater or clown faces, heraldic devices, personal insignia or monograms, symmetrical designs, and abstract, imaginative, nonobjective designs. By combining individual efforts into one large "mural" composition, a project of significant scope can be achieved.

the plaster to harden. Hardening takes at least 1 to 2 hours; plaster should be allowed to set overnight.

If your class does a sand-plaster project at a beach, care must be taken to form the mold far enough up the beach so that the plaster will not be affected by dampness at the water's edge. If there is too much moisture in the sand, the plaster will not harden. If you are at a saltwater beach, use fresh water, because salt can weaken the plaster's strength. Sand will not hold nearly as much detail as clay, so the outer edges of sand-plaster reliefs usually form the shape of the object. Sand-plaster reliefs often require coat hangers, wire, or sticks added quickly after the plaster is poured for added strength.

When the plaster is quite hard, the student pries open the cardboard container and separates the plaster from the clay. If the separation is done carefully, most of the moist clay in the mold can be salvaged for a future project. (*Note:* If the clay contains bits of plaster, do not reuse it for a clay project that is to be fired; the plaster may cause the clay to explode.)

To prepare the plaster relief for staining, students should file or sandpaper away the excess edges and any sharp, abrasive points. The relief then should be washed with water, using a discarded toothbrush or nail to clean away the clay from narrow recesses. Before staining, give it a generous coat of slightly water-diluted white glue, and allow it to dry thoroughly. Then apply stain, and wipe the raised areas to bring out highlights.

Plaster reliefs are a good project for upper elementary and middle school teachers and students. The project's appeal comes from its being not totally dependent on drawing skill, from its sophisticated, finished

Courtesy of Bess Durham.

Plaster plaques based on Impressionist painters' river scenes.

appearance, and from the unusual inverse bas relief three-dimensional carving experience.

CONCLUDING STATEMENT

Wherever art programs of quality and promise exist, there is an enthusiastic, resourceful, knowledgeable, imaginative, and gifted teacher, unselfishly dedicated and enthusiastically involved. We hope that this teacher is you, helping students to open their eyes and hearts to the design, color, form, rhythm, texture, and pattern in the world about them. Students learn a new language, a language with which to give form to and make meaning from their personal experience, and learn to share something of this with others. The teacher knows that art has the capacity to transform and reorganize our conceptions of the world, the capacity to make ordinary experiences extraordinary. In this happy, charged environment of children's searching, discovering, and creating, art reveals its unique, spirit-enhancing, and rejuvenating power. Our hope is that you have partaken of and, in the future, will partake increasingly in this emphasis on art—art as an adventure; a flowering; a celebration; and a discipline with its own singular demands, unique core of learning, and incomparable rewards.

FOR FURTHER READING

Brown, Eleese V. 1984. "Developmental Characteristics of Clay Figure Modeling by Children: 1970–1981." *Studies in Art Education* 26(1): 56–60.

Douglas, Nancy, and Julia B. Schwartz. 1967. "Increasing Awareness of Art Ideas of Young Children through Guided Experiences with Ceramics." *Studies in Art Education* 8(2): 2–9.

Golomb, Claire, and Maureen McCormick. 1995. "Sculpture: The Development of Three-Dimensional Representation in Clay." *Visual Arts Research* 21(1): 35–50.

Rottger, Ernst. 1963. *Creative Clay Design.* New York: Reinhold.

WEB RESOURCES

For a clay tile lesson plan:

http://www.princetonol.com/groups/iad/lessons/elem/elem32.html

For monsters on architecture:

http://aardvarkelectric.com/gargoyle/

For an example of an effigy clay container lesson:

http://www.princetonol.com/groups/iad/lessons/elem/linda-effigy.html

Safety Concerns, Art Materials, Modeling Formulas, and Recycling Materials

SAFETY CONCERNS: TOXIC MATERIALS AND INHALANTS

Toxic art materials are particularly harmful to children. Their nervous systems, internal organs, and reproductive systems are more at risk because their cells are still dividing. In 1990, Congress passed a law requiring that all toxic art materials have labels warning of their toxicity. However, many toxic materials still do not have such labels. Also, old materials purchased before the law went into effect may still be on the shelves, and these materials should be discarded. School shelves may hold pigments containing lead (lead white or flake white), cadmium, mercury, chromates, manganese, and cobalt. All of these are toxic. The main risk is ingestion while working through eating and nail biting.

One in six U.S. children—3.5 million youths—have harmful levels of lead in their blood. Elevated blood lead is linked to learning disabilities, lower IQs, and dropout rates. Toxic ceramic glaze chemicals may be especially dangerous if used on ceramics that are then used for food or drink. Wheat paste contains toxic preservatives, yet it is used in over half of the schools. The use of all toxic materials should be banned in elementary schools.

Other health hazards include:

- Carbon monoxide, sulphur dioxide, and nitrogen oxide from unvented kilns. School kilns should be vented to the outdoors through a canopy hood. Dusts from carving can cause lung irritation, so work outside or use fans that do not pull the contaminated air past one's face.
- Turpentine and other solvents. Over a 3-hour period, one-fourth to one-half of a small cup of turpentine can evaporate. Inhaling high concentrations of fumes from turpentine or mineral spirits can cause narcosis, dizziness, nausea, fatigue, and respiratory irritation. Drinking 6 ounces of turpentine is fatal. Nowadays some elementary schools ban oil paints because turpentine might be used in the cleanup. (Odorless mineral spirits are less hazardous.) Prolonged exposure to all solvents containing aromatic hydrocarbons can cause skin allergies. Ingestion of benzene, toluene, and xylene can be fatal. Teachers are urged to use gloss polymer medium, rather than varnish, when a sealant or a high sheen is desired. At this time, alternatives to mineral spirits, akin to baby oil and vegetable oils, are being developed.
- Adhesives. Building supply adhesives and household cements, such as model cement and Duco cement, contain hydrocarbons, which are harmful when inhaled.
- Markers. Permanent felt-tip markers contain aromatic hydrocarbons, can be very toxic, and should never be used in elementary classrooms.

Aerosol spray paint contains chemical compounds that can be extremely harmful when inhaled by students who use this "legal drug" for a cheap, brief, and intense high. The student first sprays paint into a plastic bag. Then the student blows the bag up the rest of the way and puts the narrow opening to the mouth and inhales. Some students spray paint into a soda can and then innocently appear to be drinking. Some children paint their nails with typewriter correction fluid repeatedly throughout the day.

Inhalants are particularly prevalent in the eighth, ninth, and tenth grades. Paradoxically, as drug use declines nationally, inhalant use is increasing. Telltale signs are loss of interest in appearance, food, and family activities. Spaced-out behavior, lack of coordination, sores on the nose and mouth, frequent coughing, dried spray paint on clothes, and empty aerosol cans, from hair spray to Scotchguard© to Reddi Whip©, may be indications of inhalant use. Long-term effects of sniffing are mood swings, depression, hallucinations, memory loss, and impaired judgment. Brain, kidney, and liver damage, damage to the central nervous system, and heart failure may also result.

MATERIALS AND SUPPLIES

The following art materials and tools are frequently found in elementary and middle schools today, furnished by either the school or the students. Teachers should learn to use the supplies creatively, know available sources, order them in economy lots and sizes, and store them properly.

Expendable Materials

Pencils	School paste
Wax crayons	Clay
Craypas	Manila paper
Colored chalk	Newsprint
School chalk	Construction paper
Fingerpaint	White drawing paper
Tempera paint	Oaktag (tagboard)
Watercolors	Fingerpaint paper

Nonexpendable Supplies and Equipment

Art slides and slide projector	Paper cutter
Art reproductions	Overhead projector and projection screen
Scissors	Rulers, compasses
Watercolor brushes	Hammer, saw, stapler
Easel brushes	

Generous-Budget Supplies and Equipment

Video player, TV, art videos, and VCR	Computers
Felt-nib or nylon-tip pens	Art gum erasers
Printing inks (water, oil-base)	White liquid glue
India ink	Felt-nib watercolor markers
Brayers (rubber rollers for printmaking)	Linoleum and tools for block cutting
Clay kiln	Clay glazes
Poster board (for mats)	Tissue paper (assorted colors)
Gloss polymer medium	

PRACTICAL SUGGESTIONS FOR ALL ART CLASSROOMS

Keep all tools and materials in order. Store them in cigar boxes, shoe boxes, freezer containers, coffee or vegetable-shortening tins, commercially available tote trays. Label the containers. Paint tool handles with a bold identifying color.

- Keep all tools clean. Do not let metal tools get rusty. Wipe them dry if they get wet, and oil them if they are to be stored. Do not use scissors for clay or plaster projects. Never pour plaster in any form down a sink drain.
- Drill holes in the top of a hollow Masonite® box to use as a container for scissors.
- Mount motivational resource photographs on oaktag (tagboard). Store them in labeled accordion folders or flat drawers, or put them in plastic looseleaf protectors and keep them in notebook binders.
- Wash brushes clean (use detergent if necessary) and store them with bristle ends up in a jar or tall coffee can. Be sure students rinse and clean watercolor tins. Leave them open and stack them to dry overnight. Order semimoist cakes of watercolor in bulk to refill empty tins.
- Store scrap construction and tissue paper flat in drawers or discarded blanket cartons to prevent the paper from being crushed.
- When placing orders for tempera paint, always order more white paint, because a great deal is used to mix tints of colors. You can also order crayons or oil pastels in colors in bulk.
- Hardboard in 4- × 8-foot pieces in ¼-inch thickness is excellent for drawing boards and working surfaces on desks or tables. For drawing boards, have the lumber dealer cut the hardboard into either 18- × 24-inch or 12- × 18-inch rectangles, depending on which size works best in your situation. For longer wear, mask the edges of the boards with tape.
- Yarn purchased on skeins should be rewound on balls or spools for ready use. A closed cardboard carton with holes punched in it for the yarn to pass through may be used as a dispenser.
- Keep school paste in jars until ready to use; then dispense it on small squares of cardboard. When finished, scrape off the unused paste back into the jar at the close of class; moisten it slightly with a few drops of water and cap tightly.
- When crayons break and do not fit easily into the original carton, store them in discarded coffee tins, or freezer containers.
- Powder tempera is much easier to store than the liquid kind, but liquid tempera has definite advantages. It is always ready to use if sealed properly, and it usually has a smoother texture. The most vexing

Courtesy of David Harvell.

Left: Organized materials not only make things go better but also teach children that order facilitates learning. Matched boxes of supplies have been attractively covered in wallpaper and labeled. The colored paper dispenser facilitates putting up bulletin-board displays. **Right:** Open bins make collecting, sorting, and distributing tools and supplies easy. Bins hold fine and broad markers, crayons, bottles of white glue, and palettes.

problem in tempera projects is what to do with the liquid tempera remaining in multicompartment muffin tins, plastic egg cartons, or ice-cube trays. It can't be poured back into the original containers. That is why paint should be doled out a little at a time, with refills as needed. To minimize spills, the teacher should, if possible, be in charge of paint distribution. Before closing covers on tempera jars, check the plasticity of the paint. If the paint is too dry, add a little water to ensure moistness and then cap the jar tightly. To prevent liquid tempera lids from becoming stuck tight, wipe the jar rim before closing, or put a little petroleum jelly on the rim. To prevent liquid tempera from becoming sour, add a few drops of wintergreen or oil of cloves to each container.

FORMULAS FOR MODELING MIXTURES

As many, many materials can be used for modeling and thus substituting is quite feasible, it is helpful to consider the three basic elements in modeling mixtures.

1. A material to give bulk and substance to the material; this may be something like sawdust, or clay, or plaster, or gardener's Vermiculite®, or flour.
2. The glue or binder. It may be white glue such as Elmer's Glue-All®, or carpenter's glue, or wallpaper wheat paste. (*Caution:* Wallpaper wheat paste nowadays often has poison added to it to discourage rodents.) Flour (or plaster) acts both as a binder and a source of bulk or substance.
3. A liquid to make the material plastic so it can be modeled. This is almost always water in sufficient quantity to create a plastic substance.

Of course, a fourth element is most important—willpower, and the desire to form, create, or re-create. Students love to make re-creations of things familiar to them, such as dogs, birds, and human figures and motivation is rarely a problem. Occasionally, students, often very young children, may be tactile resistant to slimy or mucky materials, but this can be minimized by the material's being just the perfect consistency of plasticity, not too mucky, not too hard or too stiff.

Sawdust and glue (or wheatpaste) is a tough material useful for puppet heads and small models which get bumped together. Acquire fine sawdust from a building supply store, lumberyard, or parent's woodshop and dampen it. Add white glue such as Elmer's® or wallpaper wheat paste.

A Playdough®-like mixture can be made of 4 cups flour, 2 cups salt, and about 2 cups of water. A variation of the formula calls for 2 or 3 cups flour, 1 cup salt, a spoon of salad oil to alleviate stickiness, and just enough water to cook until it releases from the sides of the pan, cool and knead to a consistency that won't stick to hands. It will take two or three days to dry.

For a salt and cornstarch dough, heat 1 part water and 3 parts salt, slowly add 1 part cornstarch, stir well and knead. Coloring the dough is optional, as is adding oil of peppermint and cream of tarter, which help the mixture to keep for several months. After being modeled, the mixture can just be let set to dry, or alternately it can be baked 1 hour on low heat for additional hardness. This is called Baker's clay, and is often used for seasonal ornaments. For ornaments, give each child a golf-ball-sized piece.

RECYCLING MATERIALS

Recycled materials not only enrich artworks, their use conveys a valuable lesson about conservation of the earth's limited resources. In America's productive and wasteful society, there are vast resources that teachers of art can tap for nontraditional art materials. Using imagination and skill, discarded items, empty containers, scraps, and remnants ordinarily thought

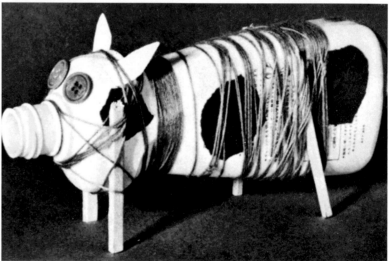

Courtesy of Frank Wachowiak and Ted Ramsay.

Recycling material conveys an important ecological lesson. Wood scraps, usually burned or discarded, can become imaginative animal sculptures. Care must be taken when cutting into plastic, and it is best to reserve this for the upper grades. Rather than discarding materials, recycling can serve a higher purpose, to build the minds and imaginations of tomorrow's creative, adaptive, inventive leaders.

Even the root of a tree can become a work of art. Here a piece by famous folk artist Ralph Griffin.

Private collection.

of as worthless can be recycled into artworks. But students should not regard the use of interesting materials as an end in itself. The artwork must transcend the materials to be a whole that is truly more than the sum of its parts.

Interesting sizes of cut-off paper can be secured for free from printing companies, and newsroll ends often are donated by newspapers. Other paper sources are computer printouts from institutions and businesses, cardboard boxes from appliance stores, and unused printed billboard papers from outdoor advertising companies. Virtually every company that produces objects has some discarded materials that may be useful in sculptures, collage, weavings, etc. The company might even underwrite an exhibition crediting their contribution. Most teachers of art are not shy about requesting materials for such a societally worthy cause as children's art expression. A note to parents requesting items such as the following can be sent home accompanying a completed artwork, with an explanation of the project's objectives and future plans:

Acorns
Baby-food jars
Balls (rubber, polystyrene, Ping-Pong)
Bark (tree)
Beads
Blades (saw, broken)
Blinds (matchstick, plastic)
Blotters
Bolts and nuts
Bones
Bottle caps
Bottles
Boxes
Bracelets
Buckles
Burlap remnants
Buttons
Cardboard
Carpet samples
Cartons
Cellophane
Celotex
Checkers
Clock parts
Cloth scraps
Clothespins
Coat hangers
Confetti
Cord

Corks
Cotton
Dowels
Driftwood
Earrings
Fabric remnants
Feathers
Felt
Foam rubber (scraps)
Foil (aluminum)
Greeting cards
Gourds
Leather remnants
Linoleum scraps
Magazines
Marbles
Masonite scraps
Meat trays (plastic foam)
Mirrors
Nails
Necklaces
Newspapers
Nuts
Paper bags
Paper cups and plates
Paper tubes (toilet tissue, mailing)
Paper towels
Paper (shelf, gift wrap, crepe, tissue, plain, colored)

Pebbles
Pie plates
Pinecones
Pins
Pipe cleaners
Polish (shoe)
Q-tips
Reed
Ribbon
Rope
Rubber (innertube)
Rubber bands
Sand
Sandpaper
Sawdust
Screening
Screws
Seashells
Shades (window)
Spools
Sticks (applicator)
Straws
String
Tile (acoustic, vinyl)
Tongue depressors
Toothpicks
TV dinner trays
Wallpaper samples
Wood scraps
Yarn remnants

Courtesy of Frank Wachowiak and Ted Ramsay.

In view of today's widespread ecological concerns about our planet's diminishing resources, sculptures from recycled materials take on added significance. Some soldering skills were necessary for this metal construction by a middle-school student. It is another example of the adage "The whole is greater than the sum of its parts."

SPECIAL MATERIALS AND TOOLS

The following items are exciting resources but will not always be available:

- Hardboard—For drawing or sketching board, as protective coverage for desks or worktables, and for mural projects.

- Brayer (rubber roller)—For inking plate in printmaking. Get the sturdy, soft, black rubber kind for longer wear (not the gelatin type).
- Celluclay—Commercially available dry mixture for use in papier-mâché-type projects.
- Dextrin (powdered)—Add to dry or moist clay (5 to 10 percent) to harden completed work without firing.
- Drywall joint cement—For creating relief effects on a two-dimensional surface; can be painted when dry.
- Firebrick (porous, insulation type)—For upper-elementary-grade and middle-school three-dimensional and relief-carving projects.
- Grog—Aggregate for plaster molds, clay conditioner.
- Masonite (tempered)—For clay modeling boards, inking surface in printmaking projects, and rinsing board in tempera or crayon resists; also practical as a portable sketching board.
- Pariscraft—Plaster-impregnated gauze in varied widths for additive sculpture projects.
- Plaster of paris (molding plaster)—For plaster sculpture and reliefs.
- Polystyrene—For printmaking plates, collage and craft projects, and printmaking stamps.
- Posterboard (railroad board)—For multicrayon engraving project; available in several colors.
- Sloyd knife (Hyde knife is similar)—All-purpose utility knife with a semisharp blade; excellent for carving in plaster and for delineating details and pattern in crayon-engraving projects.
- Dressmaker's transfer paper—A white carbon paper useful in crayon engraving projects.
- X-acto knife—Craft knife with sharp interchangeable blades for paper and cardboard sculpture. (*Caution:* To be used by the teacher only.)

FOR FURTHER READING

Consortium of National Arts Education Associations. 1998. *Opportunities and Learning; Standards for Arts Education.* Reston, VA: NAEA.

Goodwin, MacArthur. 1993. *Design Standards for School Art Facilities.* Reston, VA: NAEA.

McCann, Michael. 1985. *Health Hazards Manual for Artists.* New York: Nick Lyons Books.

McCann, Michael. 1991. "Oil Painting Hazards in Classrooms." *Art Hazards News* 14:2.

National Art Education Association. 1986. *Safety in the Artroom.* Reston, VA: NAEA.

Qualley, Charles A. 1986. *Safety in the Artroom.* Worcester, MA: Davis.

Rossol, Monona. 1990. *The Artist's Complete Health and Safety Guide.* New York: Allworth.

Addresses of Professional Associations, Art Materials Suppliers, and Audiovisual Sources

$\mathcal{A}$lthough these lists are by no means complete, they can serve as starting points to obtain further information.

PROFESSIONAL ART EDUCATION ASSOCIATIONS

National Art Education Association, 1916 Association Drive, Reston, VA 22091–1590. 703–860–8000. (www.naea-reston.org)

The Association also has interest groups. Some of them are:

The Women's Caucus (email: elizabeth.sacca@concordia.ca), The Electronic Media Interest Group (http://www.cedarnet.org/emig), and The Social Theory Caucus, which has as its goal for art education to go beyond a formalist, modernist, studio orientation. (email: ghowenstein@artic.edu or dfehr@ttu.edu).

Also, each state has a state art education association. Contact your state department of education for information.

International Society for Education through Art, c/o Prof. Kit Grauer, University of British Columbia, Dept. of Art Education, Vancouver, B.C. V6T 1Z5 Canada.

United States Society for Education through Art (USSEA), c/o Dr. Mary Stokrocki, School of Art, Arizona State University, Tempe, AZ 85287 or Dr. Mary Alice Arnold, 252–328–6475. (arnoldm@mail.ecu.edu)

ART AND CRAFT MATERIALS SUPPLIERS

A few addresses of representative arts and crafts suppliers.

American Ceramic Supply 817–535–2651, Fax: 817–536–7120.

Dick Blick Art Materials, P.O. Box 1267, Galesburg, IL 61402-1267. (www.dickblick.com)

Nasco Arts and Crafts, 901 Janesville Ave., P.O. Box 901, Fort Atkinson, WI 53538–0901 1–800–558–9595. (www.nascofa.com)

Pyramid Art Supply, 923 Hickory Lane, Mansfield, OH 44901–8104. 800–637–0955. Fax: 419–589–1786.

Sax Arts and Crafts, P.O. Box 51710, New Berlin, WI 53151. 800–558–6696. (www.saxarts.com)

Triarco Arts and Crafts, 14650 28th Ave. No, Plymouth, MN 55447. 800–558–6696. (www.etriarco.com)

Utrecht Art Supply. 800–223–9132. (www.utrechtart.com)

Searching for "art supplies" in phone book yellow pages, or on the computer at Mapquest.com, will also help you locate art supply stores in your area. For common supplies, you might also check big-box merchandisers, such as Target, as well as regional educational service agencies' ordering systems.

SOURCES FOR AUDIOVISUALS: REPRODUCTIONS, SLIDES, VIDEODISCS

The National Gallery of Art, Constitution Avenue and 6th Street, N.W., Washington, D.C. 20001, offers a program of semipermanent loan of their video and slide resources, called the Extended Loan Program. Materials, 36-slide sets and 22 videos, are lent for a year with an automatic renewal; the only provision is that the borrower is asked to file a semiannual report of use. (email: www.nga.gov)

"The Art Education Video Series," color videos on the several areas of DBAE, are available from Getty Trust Publications, P.O. Box 2112, Santa Monica, CA 90407.

A CD-ROM for the Macintosh computer, entitled "Your Own Art Teacher," is available from Art Instruction Software, 38 Balsam Dr., Medford, NY. 212–596–2610.

A CD-ROM for children to use to make their own tesselations, "MECC TesselMania," is available from Macromedia, 1–800–685–MECC, ext. 529.

The Shorewood Art Program for Elementary Education has art by many cultures and topics for each grade: Grades 1–2, seasons; 3–4, early transportation; Grades 5–6, how do I feel. Twelve reproductions are in each of 16 sets. Shorewood Reproductions, Inc., 475 Tenth Avenue, New York, NY 10018, or at (www.dickblick.com)

American Library Color Slide Co., 222 West 23rd Street, New York, NY 10011. 800–633–3307. (www.artslides.com)

BFA Educational Media, 11559 Santa Monica Boulevard, Los Angeles, CA 90025. (www.phoenixlearninggroup.com)

Crystal Productions, Box 2159, Glenview, IL 60025. 1–800–255–8629, fax: 1–800–657–8149. (www.crystalproductions.com)

Films for the Humanities and Sciences, P.O. Box 2053, Princeton, NJ 08543–2053. 1–800–257–5126. (www.films.com)

Media for the Arts, P.O. Box 1011, Newport, RI 02840. (www.artmfa@art_history.com)

The Roland Collection of films and videos on art. 22-D Hollywood Ave., Ho-H-Kus, NJ 07423. 1–800–59–ROLAND. (www.roland_collection.com)

Universal Color Slide, 8450 South Tamiami Trail, Sarasota, FL 34238. 800–326–1367. (www.universalslide.com)

WEB RESOURCES

For definitions of 3600 art and visual culture terms:

  http://www.artlex.com

To locate a reproduction of specific artwork, type the artist's name and the artwork's name into the web search engine, such as Google, to locate many sources for the reproduction.

Glossary

Abstract. In art, objects or figures that are depicted in a simplified or stylized way (in which nonessential aspects are discarded) yet remain recognizable. Similar to nonrepresentational.

Aesthetic. Dealing with art theory or issues of appreciation in art; the beautiful as related or contrasted to the good, the true, or the useful.

Aesthetics. How people think, write, and discuss issues in art, such as what makes artworks beautiful or good or artistic (sometimes contrasted to art criticism, the qualities in one specific artwork).

Analogous colors. Closely related colors; neighbors on the color wheel.

Appliqué. Decorative design made by cutting pieces of one fabric and applying them by gluing or stitching to the surface of another fabric.

Armature. Framework (of wood, wire, and so on) employed to support constructions of clay, papier-mâché, or plaster.

Assemblage. A sculptural form using found materials, often being three-dimensional.

Balance. A principle in art. May be formal or informal, symmetrical or asymmetrical.

Balsa. A strong, lightweight wood used for model building and stabiles.

Baren. A device made of cardboard and bamboo leaf that is used as a hand press in taking a print (of Japanese derivation).

Bas relief. In sculpture, when the objects or figures remain attached to the background plane or project only slightly from it.

Bat. A plaster block used to hasten drying of moist clay.

Batik. A method of designing on fabric by sealing with melted wax those areas not to be dyed.

Bench hook. A wood device secured to a desk or table to stabilize the linoleum block during the gouging process.

Bisque. Clay in its fired or baked state (unglazed).

Brayer. A rubber roller used for inking in printmaking processes.

Burnish. To make smooth or glossy by a rubbing or polishing action.

Calligraphy. The art of fine writing often done with a brush or pen.

Ceramic. A word used to describe clay constructions and products thereof.

Charcoal. A drawing stick or pencil made from charred wood.

Chipboard. Sturdy cardboard, usually gray, of varying thicknesses, used for collage, collograph, sketching boards, and in construction projects.

Classical. The art of ancient Greece or Rome, or more broadly, any art based on a regular, clear, rational structure, emphasizing proportion and balance.

Clay. A natural, moist earth substance used in making bricks, tile, pottery, and ceramic sculpture.

Collage. A composition or design made by arranging and gluing materials to a background surface.

Collograph. A print made from a collage. Relief plate created with an assortment of pasted or glued items such as pieces of paper, cardboard, cord, string, and other found objects.

Color. An element of art. Also referred to as *hue*.

Color, analogous. Closely related color; neighbors on the color wheel: green, blue-green, yellow-green, for example.

Color, monochromatic. All of the tints and shades of a single color plus its neutralized possibilities.

Colors, complementary. Colors found opposite one another on the color wheel: red and green, for example.

Colors, primary. Red, yellow, blue; three basic hues.

Colors, secondary. Green, orange, violet; achieved by mixing primary colors.

Construction paper. A strong, absorbent, semitextured paper available in a wealth of colors and used for paintings in tempera, drawings in crayon, and oil pastel, printmaking, collage, and paper sculpture. A staple item in the school art program.

Content. In a work of art, the meaning or message in or conveyed by the artwork.

Contextualism. A way of thinking about art that emphasizes art as a social communication system, with its meaning largely determined by the societal context in which it is made (as contrasted to formalism).

Contour drawing. A line drawing delineating the outer and inner contours of a posed model, still life, landscape, or other selected subject matter.

Deconstructivism. A contextualist term in art criticism about what the artwork suggests about some problematic social issue in a culture such as its treatment of women or minority groups.

Domination. A principle in art. Opposite term is "subordination." These principles complement each other.

Easel. A wood or metal frame to support an artist's canvas during painting. A simple version is found in many kindergartens for use in tempera painting.

Embossing. Creating a raised or relief design on metal or leather by tooling or indenting the surface.

Emphasis. A principle in art. Important elements in a composition are emphasized.

Encaustic. A painting process employing hot beeswax mixed with color pigment. Sometimes used to describe melted-crayon creations.

Engobe. Clay slip, colored or white, used to decorate greenware before firing.

Engraving. A process of incising or scratching into a hard surface to produce a printed image, as in copper engraving or crayon engraving.

Expressive. Artwork that seems to spring directly and honestly from the artist's feelings.

Fibonacci series. A numerical number sequence wherein the sum of the two preceding numbers equals the next number: 1, 1, 2, 3, 5, 8, 13, 21, 34, 55, ...

Findings. Metal clasps, hooks, loops, and so on used in jewelry making.

Firing. In ceramics, the baking of clay in a kiln or an outdoor banked fire; also see Raku.

Form. The physical characteristics of an object.

Formalism. A way of thinking about how artworks especially use art's elements and principles and media (as contrasted to contextualism, i.e., what the art means in society).

Found objects. Discards, remnants, samples, leftovers, and throwaways that are exploited in collages, junk sculpture, assemblages, and as stamps in printmaking projects.

Frieze. A decorated, horizontal band in paint or in relief along the upper part of a building or a room.

Glaze. A transparent or semitransparent coating of a color stain over a plain surface or another color used in oil painting, plaster sculpture, or ceramicware.

Gradient. A gradual shift from distinct to blended together, as in a textural gradient, or from one color to another, as in a color gradient (or graduated color blending).

Greenware. Unfired clay in leather-hard stage, firm but not completely dry.

Ground. The background or empty space between objects in a two-dimensional artwork.

Grout. A crevice filler such as the conditioned plaster sealed between clay, glass, or vinyl tesserae in a mosaic.

Gum eraser. A soft eraser used in drawing. Available in cube or rectangle form.

Harmony. A combination of objects or design motifs that pleases an individual, contrasted to a clashing or unharmonious arrangement.

Hue. Another name for *color.*

Impasto. In painting, heavy thick paint applied like butter to a surface.

India ink. A waterproof ink made from lampblack. Used for drawing, designing, and in tempera resists.

Instrumentalism. A term related to contextualism, advocating that art is never for its own sake, but it should rather bring to mind some external purpose, useful for improving society.

Intensity. The level of richness or saturation or, conversely, dullness or subtlety of a color.

Intermediate colors. A color between a primary hue (red, blue, or yellow) and a secondary hue (orange, green, violet); for example, blue-green is between blue and green.

Kiln. An oven used for drying, firing, and glazing clay creations.

Kneaded eraser. A gray eraser made of unvulcanized rubber that must be stretched and kneaded to be effective. Used most often in charcoal drawing.

Line. An element in art. The basic skeletal foundation of a design or composition.

Loom. The supporting framework for the crisscrossing threads and yarn in weaving.

Macramé. Lacework made by tying, knotting, and weaving cord in a pattern.

Manila paper. A general-purpose drawing or coloring paper, usually cream color.

Masonite. A pressed board made of wood fibers. Used for clay-modeling boards, inking surfaces in printmaking, and rinsing boards in tempera and crayon resists.

Mat board. A heavy poster board, available in many colors and textures, used for mounting or matting artwork.

Mobile. A free-moving hanging sculptural construction in space; Alexander Calder's innovation to the art world.

Monoprint. One-of-a-kind print, usually made by incising or marking on an inked glass plate and taking an impression.

Mosaic. A design or composition made by arranging and gluing tesserae or geometric pieces of material next to one another, but not touching, on a background surface.

Motif. A recurring pattern (or figure, symbol, or artistic device) in an artwork.

Mural. A monumental artwork on the inside or outside walls of a building. Executed in paint, mosaic, metal repoussé, or a combination of materials.

Negative space or shape. A background shape as seen in relationship to the foreground objects.

Newsprint. Newspaper stock used for sketches, preliminary drawings, and prints.

Oil pastel. A popular coloring medium consisting of a combination of chalk and oil; available in a host of exciting colors.

Papier-mâché. Name given to paper crafts that use newspaper moistened with wallpaper paste or laundry starch. Also called *paper pulp constructions.*

Patina. Originally the color produced by corrosion on metal—the antique sheen of old age—now artificially obtained through use of patinalike wax pastes.

Pattern. Design made by repeating a motif or symbol (all-over pattern).

Perspective. The creation of a three-dimensional space illusion on a two-dimensional surface by means of vanishing points, converging lines, and diminishing sizes of objects.

Plaster. A white, powdery substance that, when mixed with water, forms a quick-setting molding or casting material (sometimes referred to as *plaster of paris*).

Positive-negative. Positive shapes in a composition are the solid objects—the people, trees, animals, buildings. Negative shapes are the unoccupied empty spaces between positive shapes. Atmosphere, sky, and earth considered negative space are sometimes designated as "foreground" and "background" space.

Prime. In painting, to put down a first coat of paint, usually white, to seal the surface and onto which the actual painting is done.

Radiation. Lines, shapes, or colors emanating from a central core. Sun rays, fan leaf, ripples around a pebble thrown into a stream.

Raku. A ceramic firing process using a primitive kiln and producing smoky and iridescent effects.

Reconstructivism. A contextualist position which urges that the actions implied in an artwork should somehow help to change the existing social system.

Representational. Resembling in appearance the known likenesses of objects in nature.

Relief. A projection from a surface. Low relief as in a coin is called bas relief.

Repetition (rhythm). A principle of art. Repetition of lines, shapes, colors, and values in a composition creates unity.

Repoussé. A design in metal art in which tooling and hammering are employed to achieve relief effects.

Resist. An art technique wherein a material such as wax or starch is used to mask out areas that are to remain temporarily of a different color or value.

Rhythm. The way that repeating, varying, and spacing elements create the equivalent of notes and pulses in music.

Schema. A repeating visual scheme, often using geometrical shapes, for drawing objects and figures.

Scoring (clay). To make rough indentations in clay with a nail or similar tool as a step in cementing two pieces of clay together. Also used to describe the guiding indentation in paper-sculpture curved-line folding.

Selvage. The edge of a fabric where the weft returns to weave its way to the opposite edge.

Shade. Refers to the darker values of a color or hue. Maroon is a shade of red; navy blue is a shade of blue.

Shape. A two-dimensional area defined by lines, colors, or values.

Sketch. Usually a preliminary drawing made with pencil, pen, crayon, charcoal, brush, pastel, or similar tool.

Slip. Clay diluted with water to a creamy consistency. Used as a binder to join two pieces of clay in ceramic construction.

Space. In art, the area and/or air occupied by, activated by, or implied to be in an artwork.

Stabile. A sculptural construction in space resting on the ground, akin to a mobile, which hangs.

Still life. An arrangement of objects, usually on a table, as a subject for drawing, painting, collage, and so on.

Stipple. A pattern of closely spaced dots or small marks used in drawing and printmaking that may suggest modeling.

Storyboard. A series of drawings or sketches to visualize the movement of a movie or video, done before the actual shooting.

Subordination. A principle of art in which parts of the composition are subordinated so that others may dominate and be emphasized.

Tactile. Pertaining to the sense of touch, such as the use of textured materials and surfaces, often for an aesthetic purpose.

Tagboard. Sometimes referred to as *oaktag*. A glossy-surfaced, pliable cardboard used in collage, collographs, glue-line prints, and paper constructions.

Tempera paint. An opaque, water-soluble paint available in liquid or powder form. Also referred to as *showcard* or *poster paint*.

Tessera. A small segment of paper, cardboard, vinyl, ceramic, and so on (usually in geometric shape, such as a square or rectangle) that is fitted and glued to a background surface to produce a mosaic (plural: *tesserae*).

Texture. The actual or visual feel of a surface—bark on a tree, fur on an animal, sand on a beach.

Tint. The lighter values of a color or hue. Pink is a tint of red.

Unity. A principle of art. When everything in a composition falls into place through use of fundamental principles of art, unity is achieved.

Value. In color terminology, the lightness or darkness of a hue.

Warp. The thread or yarn that supports the weft in weaving.

Watercolors. Water-soluble colors, generally transparent or semitransparent. Can be employed thickly to become opaque. Available in semimoist cakes or tubes.

Wedging. A method of preparing moist clay by kneading and squeezing to expel the air pockets and make it more plastic.

Weft. The thread that goes across the warp from side to side in weaving; also refers to the yarn used as weft.

Photo Credits

Index

*I*n this index, topics and related illustrations usually appear on the same page or within a range of pages. For this type of situation, page numbers are given in regular type. When an illustration on a particular topic appears elsewhere in the text, and not on the same page with its related text topic, the page number is given in italic type. When several listings are given for a topic, the main listing is underlined.

	Pre-1000 B.C. (Paleolithic, Neolithic, Sumerian, Minoan, Mycenaean)	900 B.C. to 400 B.C. (Golden Age of Greece)	400 B.C. to 400 A.D. (Roman, Hellenistic)	5th century to 12th century (Byzantine Romanesque, Medieval)	13th and 14th centuries (Gothic)	15th century (Late Gothic, Renaissance)	16th century (High Renaissance)
Painting and Sculpture	African rock paintings, cave paintings at Lascaux and Altamira, Cycladic sculptures, Egyptian wall paintings, the Sphinx, Tutankamen's tomb	"Apollo Belvedere," "Discus Thrower," Greek red- and black-figured vases, "Kouros," Phidias, Polycleitus, Praxiteles	"Laocoon," "Venus De Milo," "Victory of Samothrace," Egyptian encaustics, Emperor Qin's terra cotta army at Xian, Gandhara Buddhist sculptures, Nok fired clay, Roman busts, Roman sarcophagi, wall paintings from Teotihuacan, Mexico, and Herculaneum, Greece	Bayeux tapestries, Byzantine mosaics, "Chacmool," Olmec giant head	Asian giant Buddha sculptures, Chinese silk paintings, Cimabue, Easter Island figures, Giotto, Kamakura figures	Boticelli, Della Robbia, Donatello, Fra Angelico, Fra Lippo Lippi, Ghiberti, introduction of perspective, Leonardo da Vinci, Mantegna, Piero Della Francesca, pre-Columbian art of South and Central America (Mayan, Aztec, and Incan), Van Eyck, Verrochio	African bronze heads, Bosch, Bramante, Breughel, Cellini, Donatello, Dürer, El Greco, Holbein, Michelangelo, Moghul miniatures, Raphael, Tintoretto, Titian, Vasari, Veronese
Architecture	Great Pyramids of Mycerinus, Stonehenge, Sumerian ziggurats	Acropolis and Parthenon, Doric, Ionic, and Corinthian temples	Arch of Constantine, Coliseum, Great Stupa, Great Wall of China, Machu Pichu, Nazca lines, Pantheon, Trajan's Column	Ajanta caves, Angkor Watt, Carolingian churches, Great Mosque, Hagia Sophia, Ise Shrine, Ravenna basilica, Uxmal and Chichen Itza pyramids	Amiens, Cathedral of Chartres, Chola India temples, Doges Palace, Exeter Cathedral, the Alhambra	Brunelleschi	St. Peter's Cathedral, Suleyman Mosque
Politics, Literature, Religion	Babylonian clay tablets, Hatshepsut, King Darius of Persia, scrolls, papyrus, Shang Dynasty *TOYS: chess and checkers, backgammon, marbles, kites*	Alexander the Great, Aristotle, Herodotus, Homer, Lao Tze, Pericles, Plato, Sophocles, Zhou Dynasty	Cleopatra and Caesar, Constantine, Roman Empire's peak, Rosetta stone	*Beowulf, Book of Kells,* Charlemagne, Eleanor of Aquitaine, illuminated manuscripts, *Lindesfarne Gospel,* Norman Invasion, Tang Dynasty	African gold trade, Boccaccio, Crusades, Genghis Khan, Magna Carta, Marco Polo, Petrarch, Song Dynasty	Discovery of America, Erasmus, Gutenberg Bible, Joan of Arc, end of Hundred Years War, Machiavelli, Medicis, Ming Dynasty, Persian manuscripts	Akbar, Cervantes, Donne, Luther and the Reformation, Queen Amina, Queen Elizabeth of England, Shakespeare
Science, Math, Technology	Bronze, brass, numbering, sundial, wheel, writing	Abacus, gunpowder, musical notation, Platonic solids, Pythagoras	Astronomical calculator, calendar, compass, Euclid, paper and quill pen (China)	Concept of "zero" (Mayans and Arabs), gunpowder, movable type, paper (Europe), woodblock printing	Arabic numerals, chocolate (Aztecs), public clocks, rockets & fireworks	Age of Exploration, oil paint, printing press	Copernicus, etchings, Magellan circles the globe, Mercator, microscope

Please note that this timeline is intended to be representative, not comprehensive.